Private Sector Entrepreneursh

INNOVATION, SCALE, AND SUSTAINABILITY

Poor access to care in low- and middle-income countries due to high costs, geographic barriers, and a shortage of trained medical staff has motivated many organizations to rethink their model of health service delivery. Many of these new models are being developed by private sector actors, including non-profits, such as non-governmental organizations, and for-profits, such as social enterprises. By partnering extensively with public sector organizations, these non-state actors have enormous potential to scale innovation in global health. Understanding how these leading organizations operate and target hard-to-reach groups may yield key insights to sustainably improve health care for all.

Private Sector Entrepreneurship in Global Health includes writings by management, medicine, and social science experts who have studied trends in private sector health care innovations over the last ten years. It provides a wide range of examples from many regions and health areas and outlines tools to assess the performance of innovative private sector health programs in low- and middle-income countries. The studies reported in this volume explore new marketing and finance models, digital health innovations, and unique organizational processes emerging from the private sector to serve those most in need. Drawing on the analysis of over one thousand organizations engaged in health market innovations, this volume is a valuable resource for researchers and students in management, global health, medicine, development studies, health economics, and anthropology, as well as program managers, social impact investors, funders, and policymakers interested in understanding approaches emerging from the private sector in health care.

KATHRYN MOSSMAN is a research coordinator at Women's College Hospital and manager of the Toronto Health Organization Performance Evaluation (T-HOPE) team at the University of Toronto.

ANITA M. MCGAHAN is a professor and the Rotman Chair in Management at the Rotman School of Management at the University of Toronto.

WILL MITCHELL is the Anthony S. Fell Chair in New Technologies and Commercialization at the Rotman School of Management at the University of Toronto.

ONIL BHATTACHARYYA is a family physician and the Frigon-Blau Chair in Family Medicine Research at Women's College Hospital in Toronto. He is also an associate professor in the Department of Family and Community Medicine and the Institute of Health Policy, Management and Evaluation at the University of Toronto.

Private Sector Entrepreneurship in Global Health

INNOVATION, SCALE, AND SUSTAINABILITY

EDITED BY

Kathryn Mossman, Anita M. McGahan,
Will Mitchell, and Onil Bhattacharyya

UNIVERSITY OF TORONTO PRESS
Toronto Buffalo London

© University of Toronto Press 2019
Rotman-UTP Publishing
Toronto Buffalo London
utorontopress.com

ISBN 978-1-4875-0273-7 (cloth)   ISBN 978-1-4875-2213-1 (paper)

Library and Archives Canada Cataloguing in Publication

Title: Private sector entrepreneurship in global health: innovation, scale, and sustainability / edited by Kathryn Mossman, Anita M. McGahan, Will Mitchell, and Onil Bhattacharyya.

Names: Mossman, Kathryn, editor. | McGahan, Anita M. (Anita Marie), editor. | Mitchell, Will (William Gordon), editor. | Bhattacharyya, Onil, editor.

Description: Includes bibliographical references and index.
Identifiers: Canadiana 20190086149 | ISBN 9781487522131 (paper) | ISBN 9781487502737 (cloth)

Subjects: LCSH: Medical care – Developing countries – Case studies. | LCSH: Health services accessibility – Developing countries – Case studies. | LCSH: Medical policy – Developing countries – Case studies. | LCSH: Social entrepreneurship – Developing countries – Case studies. | LCGFT: Case studies.

Classification: LCC RA441.5 .P75 2019 | DDC 362.109172/4—dc23

University of Toronto Press acknowledges the financial assistance to its publishing program of the Canada Council for the Arts and the Ontario Arts Council, an agency of the Government of Ontario.

Canada Council   Conseil des Arts
for the Arts   du Canada

ONTARIO ARTS COUNCIL
CONSEIL DES ARTS DE L'ONTARIO
an Ontario government agency
un organisme du gouvernement de l'Ontario

Funded by the   Financé par le
Government   gouvernement
of Canada   du Canada

Canada

For our students and those around the world who have bet their careers (and lives) to create healthy communities

Contents

Tables and Figures

Tables

Figures

Acknowledgments

The editors sincerely thank all of the authors who contributed to this edited volume, without whom this book would not have been possible. A special thank you to members of the Toronto Health Organization Performance Evaluation (T-HOPE) team who, over the last ten years, have inspired us and provided their insights to further the field of global health innovation. This includes Ameya Bopardikar, Jieun Cha, Tiana Corovic, Earl D'Almeida, Pavanpreet Gill, John Ginther, Daniela Graziano, Leigh Hayden, David Leung, John A. MacDonald, Himanshu Parikh, Kerry Patterson, Leigh Pharand, Ilan Shahin, Raman Sohal, Jason Sukhram, Diane Wu, Winnie Yau, Christopher Yao, and others. We'd also like to thank our research partners, including the Global Impact Investing Network (GIIN), Innovations in Healthcare at Duke University, and the Reverse Innovation Working Group.

We sincerely appreciate the support of Jennifer DiDomenico at University of Toronto Press in guiding us through the publishing process. We also would like to express our gratitude to Tiana Corovic for her help and assistance in assembling this manuscript.

Our heartfelt thanks to our families and colleagues for their ongoing support, patience, and encouragement.

We are fortunate to have received support for our research efforts on health innovation from different funding organizations. This includes the Social Sciences and Humanities Research Council (SSHRC), Results for Development (R4D), the International Centre for Social Franchising (ICSF), the Rapid Routes to Scale group, and the Commonwealth Fund. We should note, however, that the authors are responsible for the content of their chapters, and no statement in this book should be construed as an official position of the funders, who had no role in the study design, data collection, analysis, or decision to publish these works.

Introduction

Low- and middle-income countries (LMICs) face daunting health care challenges. Patients in these countries experience not only a high incidence of infectious disease such as malaria and tuberculosis, but also must manage the rise of chronic conditions such as diabetes, cardiovascular disease, and respiratory disease (Nugent 2008). Organizations in these countries strive to address these complex health problems by engaging in novel approaches to counteract these trends. Because of resource constraints on public-sector health systems, most LMICs have many private sector providers (both formal and informal), whose performance must be better assessed to understand both their potential and limitations. This includes examining the ability of private sector organizations to help achieve universal health coverage (Lagomarsino et al. 2012) (Nishtar 2010). This book focuses on the subset of innovative private sector organizations that have developed promising new models to improve care for poor communities and examines their performance, scale, and sustainability.

This volume compiles and synthesizes a series of articles and reports produced over the last decade by the Toronto Health Organization Performance Evaluation (T-HOPE) team based at the University of Toronto. T-HOPE is an interdisciplinary research team composed of a diverse group of health, management, and social science experts studying global health innovations. The T-HOPE team includes a family physician and health services researcher, Onil Bhattacharyya; two professors of strategy and management, Anita McGahan and William Mitchell; and an anthropologist, Kathryn Mossman; as well as a team of research associates, MBA students, and medical students. This volume is divided into four broad sections, including an exploration of emerging models of health innovation, relevant health performance measures, innovations that target vertical health areas, and innovations specific to horizontal and integrated approaches in LMICs. This analysis highlights our efforts to identify successful innovations to improve health care quality and access, measure performance of private health care organizations, and define key strategies for scale up and sustainability of impactful health initiatives.

Private Sector Organizations in Global Health

The private sector in this context refers to non-state organizations that include for-profit and not-for profit entities (Hanson & Berman 1998), such as private clinics and hospitals, non-governmental organizations (NGOs), social enterprises, and private companies. "Innovation" refers to the execution of new ideas, or ideas perceived as new by the target population, to create value and drive change in health care (Kastelle & Steen 2011, Weberg 2009). While the term "global health" has been used in a variety of ways, our use of the term refers to the study of health and health care with the priority of improving health for all (Koplan et al. 2009). While much of our research focuses on LMIC contexts, we also explore the connections and opportunities for learning between LMICs and HICs.

Innovation among private sector organizations in global health takes many forms. We found a subset of private sector organizations in global health that were early adopters of mobile devices, information technology, and social media. As described in Section A, we identify innovation in business models such as franchising, microfinance, and vouchers. Traditional management approaches including training, marketing, and financing are also applied in novel ways. The use of new delivery and management models to deliver high-quality medical care to disadvantaged groups is promising.

Overall, many private sector organizations innovating in global health are understudied and poorly understood outside the local context. The range of private sector organizations in health care is extensive: traditional healers, midwives, street dentists, multinational corporations, small entrepreneurial companies, local pharmaceutical companies, private hospitals, specialty clinics, non-governmental organizations that seek to provide care to the public, humanitarian aid agencies, privately practicing physicians, IT companies, and a range of others. Despite the range of engaged organizations, few studies address the activities of a broad cross section of private sector organizations engaged in health care. There is limited evidence on which private health sector approaches work best under various circumstances in low-income countries (Mills, Brugha, Hanson, & McPake 2002). Indeed, it is essential that we develop a better understanding of the effectiveness, scale, and scope of the private health sector in LMICs, given that evaluation of such initiatives is lacking (Hanson et al. 2008).

While a large literature has developed on the measurement of affordability, accessibility, and impact in global health, these criteria are difficult to implement in practice in resource-limited settings. We know of no organization that organizes itself around these criteria. To address this problem, the Center for Health Market Innovations (CHMI), an initiative of the Results for Development Institute (R4D), developed a database in an effort to track the performance of a large number of health market innovations in developing countries. We formed a partnership with CHMI to analyse this data, and have relied on the CHMI database as a starting point for evaluating organizations on criteria that are both relevant and theoretically robust. We found that the gap between theory and practice was greater than in almost any other area of study that we have encountered, especially given the wide variety of organizational models and services provided. Indeed, because organizations adopt different strategies, assessing their contributions requires a more complex assessment than simply focusing on access, cost, and quality. Measuring impact effectively requires both management and health care criteria, which we built into our framework assessment tool, described in Section B. Having developed this tool, we then sought to develop insights from the application of these criteria and explore the emerging models and their evidence in both vertical health areas – either disease or demographic groups – in Section C, and horizontal health areas like primary care in Section D. Our assessments focused particularly on smaller organizations rather than large multinational corporations.

Most health care in LMICs is delivered by a mixed health care system, where service delivery and financing of care is predominantly provided by private actors alongside publicly funded government health provisions (Nishtar 2007; Nishtar 2010). These private actors are a common source of health services and essential to addressing certain health conditions in many low-income countries (World Bank 2008). However, some have voiced concerns about their ability to serve the poorest, the quality of the care they provide, and the often limited regulation of their activities (Basu, Andrews, Kishore, Panjabi, & Stuckler 2012; Bennett 1992; Patouillard, Goodman, Hanson, & Mills 2007; Brugha & Zwi 1998; Mills et al. 2002). These are significant concerns and they raise important questions about the limits of this sector. However, we have found that some private sector organizations are particularly adept at tailoring approaches to particular contexts and enabling specialized care. For example, some have found that while private sector health care in LMICs is not necessarily more medically effective, accountable, or efficient than the public sector, it may be superior in the areas of patient experience and timeliness of care (Basu et al. 2012), and have better availability of medications and equipment (Basu et al. 2012). Some private sector programs have also been shown to provide very high-quality care to LMIC patients, such as Narayana Hrudayalaya Hospital in India. Its high-volume, low-cost model for heart surgery has resulted in average mortality rate of 1.4 per cent within 30 days of coronary artery bypass graft surgery, a lower rate than the 1.9 per cent average reported in the US in 2008 (Anand 2009; Center for Health Market Innovations 2017). Private sector programs may also have useful strategies for managing staff, which could provide lessons for the public sector, given that attracting and retaining health workers, such as nurses and doctors, is a major challenge in some LMICs due to poor management, lack of recognition or promotion, inadequate training, and problems with remuneration (Kober & Van Damme 2006; Chimwaza et al. 2014). Thus, we have found that there are opportunities for the public and private sector to learn from each other and, in fact, private sector organizations may complement public sector approaches. For example, through public-private partnerships, Karuna Trust, a charitable trust in India, manages state-owned primary care centres in remote and rural areas that were performing poorly. It has improved both patient satisfaction and health outcomes at a lower cost, and reaches more than one million people through 68 primary care centres in seven Indian states (Karuna Trust 2017). In addition, the public sectors in some LMICs have invested in and supported innovation through collaborations with the private sector. This includes the Rwandan Ministry of Health's support of scaling up RapidSMS with a variety of private sector partners. This open-source mobile SMS platform helps community health workers monitor pregnant women and babies, saving hundreds of thousands of lives (Ngabo et al. 2012; World Health Organization 2013). While these examples are not necessarily common, they provide learning opportunities and show potential for further collaboration and partnership.

The significant role of the private sector in LMICs has been broadly acknowledged, and some have encouraged greater engagement with private sector organizations to help fill gaps in the move towards universal health care through greater regulation, coordination, integration, and transparency of their activities (Mills et al. 2002; Bennett 1992; Bennett, Bloom, Knezovich, & Peters 2014; World Health Organization Maximizing Positive Synergies Collaborative Group et al. 2009; Hanson et al. 2008; Lagomarsino, Nachuk, & Singh Kundra 2009; Kim, Farmer, & Porter 2013). However, one of the challenges faced by the private sector, particularly for non-profit organizations, is how to operate strategically and sustainably in contexts where financial resources are limited and variable (Yang, Farmer, & McGahan 2010; Gruen et al. 2008; Gilson, Sen, Mohammed & Mujinja 1994). While there are a number of exceptional organizations operating at impressive scale and serving many millions of people, such as Aravind Eye Care System in India (32 million outpatients and 4 million surgeries since its inception) (Center for Health Market Innovations 2017a) and Building Resources Across Communities (BRAC) in Bangladesh (currently reaching more than 92 million people) (Center for Health Market Innovations 2017b), in our ten years of study, we have found that many struggle with scale and sustainability, and have thus far not achieved their ambitious objectives for growth. This highlights the necessity of organizations having more than an innovative idea, but also a strategy for achieving long-term viability and scale up. Strategic management knowledge and skills can help to facilitate these goals, and we have found that the application of management theories can provide important insights on the processes of scaling and of achieving sustainability in this field (Cooley & Kohl 2006; Porter & Siggelkow 2008; Porter & Derry 2012; Kumar & Puranam 2011a; Kumar & Puranam 2011b; Bryson 2011).

Structure of the Book

This book offers both a background and a synthesis of these ideas and highlights the findings of our T-HOPE team over the last ten years. It includes four sections. Section A focuses on exploring the types of innovations that are emerging in resource-constrained settings, including application of new technologies, marketing strategies, financial models, and operational designs. It also considers how these private sector organizations sustain themselves in these markets and lessons that might apply to HICs. Section B considers how these innovative models are measuring their impact and provides performance measurement frameworks that are feasible and credible. Section C focuses on innovative approaches that have emerged in specific health areas, including malaria, tuberculosis, diabetes, and mental health, and considers the evidence available on these new models, and identifies areas for further research. Finally, Section D explores innovation in the areas of maternal, newborn, and child health (MNCH) and primary care, while also examining factors shaping successful scale up and integration of these models. Each section includes an introduction that describes the key themes, frameworks, and recommendations of the section chapters.

Finally, the T-HOPE team took on its name because of our deeply held optimism about the potential for private sector organizations to improve human health – and especially the health of the poor – sustainably and at scale. In the book's conclusion, we point to the implications for both practical and academic action to advance the health of those most in need.

REFERENCES

Anand, G. 2009. "The Henry Ford of Heart Surgery." *The Wall Street Journal*. http://online.wsj.com/article/SB125875892887958111.html.

Basu, S., Andrews, J., Kishore, S., Panjabi, R., & Stuckler, D. 2012. "Comparative Performance of Private and Public Healthcare Systems in Low and Middle-Income Countries: A Systematic Review." *PLoS Medicine* 9(6): e1001244. https://doi.org/10.1371/journal.pmed.1001244.

Bennett, S. 1992. "Promoting the Private Sector: A Review of Developing Country Trends." *Health Policy and Planning* 7(2): 97–110. https://doi.org/10.1093/heapol/7.2.97.

Bennett, S., Bloom, G., Knezovich, J., & Peters, D.H. 2014. "The Future of Health Markets." *Globalization and Health* 10(1): 51. https://doi.org/10.1186/1744-8603-10-51.

Brugha, R., & Zwi, A. 1998. "Improving the Quality of Private Sector Delivery of Public Health Services: Challenges and Strategies." *Health Policy and Planning* 13(2): 107–20. https://doi.org/10.1093/heapol/13.2.107.

Bryson, J.M. 2011. *Strategic Planning for Public and Nonprofit Organizations: A Guide to Strengthening and Sustaining Organizational Achievement*. San Francisco: Jossey-Bass.

Center for Health Market Innovations. 2017a. "Aravind Eye Care System (AECS)." Accessed 13 March 2017. http://healthmarketinnovations.org/program/aravind-eye-care-system-aecs.

Center for Health Market Innovations. 2017b. "BRAC." Accessed 13 March 2017. http://healthmarketinnovations.org/program/brac.

Center for Health Market Innovations (CHMI). 2017. "Narayana Hrudayalaya." Accessed 12 January 2018. http://healthmarketinnovations.org/.

Chimwaza, W., Chipeta, E., Ngwira, A., Kamwendo, F., Taulo, F., Bradley, S., & McAuliffe, E. 2014. "What Makes Staff Consider Leaving the Health Service in Malawi?" *Human Resources for Health* 12(1): 17. https://doi.org/10.1186/1478-4491-12-17.

Cooley, L., & Kohl, R. 2006. *Scaling Up – From Vision to Large-Scale Change: A Management Framework for Practitioners*. Washington, DC: Management Systems International.

Gilson, L., Sen, P. D., Mohammed, S., & Mujinja, P. 1994. "The Potential of Health Sector Non-governmental Organizations: Policy Options." *Health Policy and Planning* 9(1): 14–24. https://doi.org/10.1093/heapol/9.1.14.

Gruen, R.L., Elliott, J.H., Nolan, M.L., Lawton, P.D., Parkhill, A., McLaren, C.J., & Lavis, J.N. 2008. "Sustainability Science: An Integrated Approach for Health-Program Planning." *The Lancet* 372(9649): 1579–89. https://doi.org/10.1016/S0140-6736(08)61659-1.

Hanson, K., & Berman, P. 1998. "Private Health Care Provision in Developing
    Countries: A Preliminary Analysis of Levels and Composition." *Health Policy
    and Planning* 13(3): 195–211. https://doi.org/10.1093/heapol/13.3.195

Hanson, K., Gilson, L., Goodman, C., Mills, A., Smith, R., Feachem, R., ... Kinlaw,
    H. 2008. "Is Private Health Care the Answer to the Health Problems of the World's
    Poor?" *PLoS Med* 5(11): e233. https://doi.org/10.1371/journal.pmed.0050233.

Karuna Trust. 2017. "Welcome to Karuna Trust." http://www.karunatrust.com/.

Kastelle, T., & Steen, J. 2011. "Ideas Are Not Innovations." *Prometheus* 29(2):
    199–205. https://doi.org/10.1080/08109028.2011.608554.

Kim, J.Y., Farmer, P., & Porter, M.E. 2013. "Redefining Global Health-Care Delivery."
    The Lancet 382(9897): 1060–9. https://doi.org/10.1016/S0140-6736(13)61047-8.

Kober, K., & Van Damme, W. 2006. "Public Sector Nurses in Swaziland: Can the
    Downturn Be Reversed?" *Human Resources for Health* 4(1): 13. https://doi.org/
    10.1186/1478-4491-4-13.

Koplan, J.P., Bond, T.C., Merson, M.H., Reddy, K.S., Rodriguez, M.H.,
    Sewankambo, N.K., ... Consortium of Universities for Global Health Executive
    Board. 2009. "Towards a Common Definition of Global Health." *The Lancet*
    373(9679): 1993–5. https://doi.org/10.1016/S0140-6736(09)60332-9.

Kumar, N., & Puranam, P. 2011a. "Have You Restructured for Global Success?"
    Harvard Business Review 89(October): 123–8.

Kumar, N., & Puranam, P. 2011b. *India Inside: The Emerging Innovation Challenge to
    the West.* Boston: Harvard Business School Publishing.

Lagomarsino, G., Garabrant, A., Adyas, A., Muga, R., Otoo, N., McEuen, M., &
    Healthcare, for T.L.I.G. for U. 2012. "Moving towards Universal Health Coverage:
    Health Insurance Reforms in Nine Developing Countries in Africa and Asia."
    The Lancet 380(9845): 933–43. https://doi.org/10.1016/S0140-6736(12)61147-7.

Lagomarsino, G., Nachuk, S., & Singh Kundra, S. 2009. *Public Stewardship of
    Private Providers in Mixed Health Systems.* Washington, DC: The Rockefeller
    Foundation.

Mills, A., Brugha, R., Hanson, K., & McPake, B. 2002. "What Can Be Done about
    the Private Health Sector in Low-Income Countries?" *Bulletin of the World Health
    Organization* 80(4): 325–30.

Ngabo, F., Nguimfack, J., Nwaigwe, F., Mugeni, C., Muhoza, D., Wilson, D.R., ...
    Binagwaho, A. 2012. "Designing and Implementing an Innovative SMS-Based
    Alert system (RapidSMS-MCH) to Monitor Pregnancy and Reduce Maternal
    and Child Deaths in Rwanda." *The Pan African Medical Journal* 13: 31. https://
    doi:10.11604/pamj.2012.13.31.1864.

Nishtar, S. 2007. "Politics of Health Systems: WHO's New Frontier." *The Lancet*
    370(9591): 935–6. https://doi.org/10.1016/S0140-6736(07)61442-1.

Nishtar, S. 2010. "The Mixed Health Systems Syndrome." *Bulletin of the World
    Health Organization* 88(1): 74–5. https://doi.org/10.2471/BLT.09.067868.

Nugent, R. 2008. "Chronic Diseases in Developing Countries." *Annals of the New York Academy of Sciences* 1136(1): 70–9. https://doi.org/10.1196/annals.1425.027.

Patouillard, E., Goodman, C.A., Hanson, K.G., & Mills, A.J. 2007. "Can Working with the Private For-Profit Sector Improve Utilization of Quality Health Services by the Poor? A Systematic Review of the Literature." *International Journal for Equity in Health* 6: 17. https://doi.org/10.1186/1475-9276-6-17.

Porter, M., & Siggelkow, N. 2008. "Contextuality within Activity Systems and Sustainability of Competitive Advantage." *Academy of Management Perspectives* 22(2): 34–56. https://doi.org/10.5465/AMP.2008.32739758.

Porter, T., & Derry, R. 2012. "Sustainability and Business in a Complex World." *Business and Society Review* 117(1): 33–53. https://doi.org/10.1111/j.1467-8594.2012.00398.x.

Weberg, D. 2009. "Innovation in Healthcare: A Concept Analysis." *Nursing Administration Quarterly* 33(3): 227–37. https://doi.org/10.1097/NAQ.0b013e3181accaf5.

World Bank. 2008. *The Business of Health in Africa: Partnering with the Private Sector to Improve People's Lives.* Washington, DC: World Bank.

World Health Organization. 2013. *Assisting Community Health Workers in Rwanda: MOH's RapidSMS and mUbuzima.* Geneva: World Health Organization.

World Health Organization Maximizing Positive Synergies Collaborative Group, Samb, B., Evans, T., Dybul, M., Atun, R., Moatti, J.-P., ... Etienne, C. 2009. "An Assessment of Interactions between Global Health Initiatives and Country Health Systems." *The Lancet* 373(9681): 2137–69. https://doi.org/10.1016/S0140-6736(09)60919-3.

Yang, A., Farmer, P.E., & McGahan, A.M. 2010. "'Sustainability' in Global Health." *Global Public Health* 5(2): 129–35. https://doi.org/10.1080/17441690903418977.

SECTION A

Private Sector Health Care Innovation in Low- and Middle-Income Countries

Private sector health care organizations in low- and middle-income countries (LMICs), both for-profit and non-profit, play important roles in providing health services to the poor. These organizations are developing new models involving innovations in marketing, finance, information and communication technologies (ICTs), operations, and organizational design. In doing so, they are helping to achieve gains in health access, quality, and efficiency. These activities provide learning opportunities not only for LMIC contexts, but also for high-income countries (HICs). The core finding of this section is that private sector organizations are important sources of innovative models, which could complement public health provision in serving the poor in resource-constrained settings.

Chapter 1 ("Innovative Health Service Delivery Models in Low- and Middle-Income Countries – What Can We Learn from the Private Sector?") describes 10 private sector health care organizations that have generated innovations in marketing, finance, and operations in LMICs, such as India and Thailand.

Chapter 2 ("Global Health Innovation: Exploring Program Practices and Strategies") highlights the activities of 80 programs in the Center for Health Market Innovations (CHMI) database. They fit into three sets of strategies to improve efficiency, availability, and quality.

Chapter 3 ("The Future of Health Care Access") describes ways in which private sector health care organizations are using ICT to empower and educate both patients and providers of health care services. These innovations help address shortages of health care providers and other health care services in LMICs.

Chapter 4 ("For-Profit Health Care Providers at the Bottom of the Pyramid") compares the activities of for-profit and non-profit health care providers by assessing the ways in which 175 private sector programs in the CHMI database incorporate ICT into their services.

Chapter 5 ("Criteria to Assess Potential Reverse Innovations") describes a methodology to identify opportunities for HICs to learn from innovations in LMICs. The chapter outlines a two-step process to identify promising innovations, first by evaluating program success in LMICs and then evaluating a program's potential to succeed in HICs.

The ideas and examples in this section provide exploratory insights that scholars, program managers, investors, and other stakeholders can build upon. The information is mostly descriptive, while providing details on the operating, marketing, and financial innovations of a range of leading organizations, noting that all of them incorporate strategies from each of these areas. It also provides a nomenclature of activities and highlights clusters of mutually reinforcing strategies. It unpacks the range of uses of ICT to educate and empower both patients and providers, which helps frame how these technologies can improve access. The CHMI database allows for quantitative comparisons of for-profit and non-profit firms operating in LMICs. They use ICT in similar ways, but for-profit firms are more likely to operate in middle-income countries, more dense or urban regions, and areas with a wider range of income groups. They are also more likely to provide general primary care. Lastly, one of the benefits of studying innovations from LMICs is the potential for identifying promising approaches that could improve access or reduce cost in HICs. We worked with a diverse group of experts to develop criteria to identify successful strategies from LMIC and then assess their applicability to a HIC. There are only a few examples of successful replication from low- to high-income settings currently, but the increasing number of innovations emerging from LMICs suggests that this will be a promising source of innovations in the future.

1 Innovative Health Service Delivery Models in Low- and Middle-Income Countries – What Can We Learn from the Private Sector?

ONIL BHATTACHARYYA, SARA KHOR, ANITA MCGAHAN, DAVID DUNNE, ABDALLAH S. DAAR, AND PETER A. SINGER

Introduction

There is a need for improved health services for the 2.6 billion people living on less than US$2 a day (The World Bank 2008). The poor experience considerable barriers to health care such as limited purchasing power and health insurance, low health literacy, and residence in slums or remote rural areas, which are frequently underserved (Rangan, Quelch, Herrero, & Barton 2006). These barriers must be considered in the way services are marketed, financed, and delivered to this group to ensure that quality care is made available and affordable to the poor.

In part due to gaps in public health services, the private provision of health care has grown (Private Sector Participation in Health 2004). The presence of private health providers in low- and middle-income countries (LMIC) is significant. Recent estimates suggest that poor people seek care in the private sector for 35–95 per cent of cases of childhood diarrhoeal and respiratory illnesses across a wide range of countries (Bustreo, Harding, & Axelsson 2003). Private provision of care is not without its critics. The main concerns about private health care delivery are the underprovision of public goods in free markets, lack of access to care for the indigent, and the potential for providers to induce demand for unnecessary services to generate profit (Bennett, McPake, & Mills 1997). However, since public health services are not always available or in some cases perceived to be of poor quality, private health care delivery has been widely used in LMIC. It is therefore worthwhile to understand the private sector's potential contribution to health systems.

One area where the private sector may contribute is as a source of "disruptive innovators" – organizations that develop simpler and cheaper services that enable the participation of new sets of consumers previously excluded from conventional markets (Hwang & Christensen 2008). Providers in the private sector may operate on a for-profit or a not-for-profit basis (Bhattacharyya, McGahan, Dunne, Singer, & Daar 2009), but there is a growing number of social enterprises that aim to develop models of pattern-breaking social change that can scale up easily, which can include novel financial strategies (Nicholls 2005). These social entrepreneurs attempt to improve the affordability, availability, or quality of care for the poor. While this topic is of growing interest, the range of existing strategies used by the private sector has not been fully described. Recent reviews have either focused on specific strategies to engage the private sector (concluding, on the whole, that there is no rigorous evidence of benefit) or described a few organizations, focusing on commercial viability and not analysing a series of cases highlighting the range of mechanisms for improving care for the poor, as we do here (Jossey-Bass 2007; Karamchandani, Kubzansky, & Frandano 2009; Patouillard, Goodman, Hanson, & Mills 2007).

Our goal is to describe a series of high-profile social enterprises, describe the areas of innovations in their health service delivery models, and explore the potential of these models to create more inclusive and effective health services in resource-limited settings.

Methods

Selection of Case Studies

We searched MEDLINE for peer-reviewed articles, searched the grey literature including websites, and contacted experts on the health systems of LMIC to identify private sector organizations considered to be exemplars of business model innovation in health service delivery for the poor. We adopted Weberg's (2009) definition of innovation in health care, which emphasizes the impact of the innovation on the market or population: "Innovation is something new, or perceived new by the population experiencing the innovation, that has the potential to drive change and redefine health care's economic and/or social potential" (Weberg 2009). The "newness" in an innovation can be achieved by "recombining old ideas in a new way, creating a new process or product, using a process from another industry in one that has not used that process, or reordering an organization in a new and different way" (Weberg 2009). Business models consist of four components: i) a product or service; ii) managers that bring together a set of resources required to deliver the product or service; iii) processes where employees and resources work together to repeatedly generate the product or service; and iv) a profit formula to ensure that the costs of the resources and processes are covered (Hwang & Christensen 2008). Health service delivery models are business models adopted in the provision of health services. We focused on organizations that employed innovative health service delivery models to bring about positive social impact, that is to improve affordability, accessibility, and/ or quality of health services for the poor, particularly those that had expanded beyond pilots, and had detailed descriptions of their strategies.

From an initial sample of forty-six, only six had sufficient information on their activities and impact in the peer-reviewed and grey literature for initial inclusion in this study. We attempted to contact the other forty organizations, and we received ten replies. Structured, open-ended surveys were sent to these ten organizations and staff members were interviewed where possible to complement available information (Bhattacharyya et al. 2009). After reviewing the compiled information on their business models, we used purposive selection to eliminate organizations with very similar business strategies from the same geographical regions and/or disease areas in order to maximize variation and to highlight a wide range of activities. We further excluded those who did not provide health services directly. This left ten organizations: six from the original search and four from the surveys. Table 1.1 lists the selected organizations and describes their scope of services, social impact, and sources of funding. Case studies for each of these organizations were developed based on a content analysis of information from sources such as peer-reviewed literature, technical reports, external evaluations, websites, news articles, and interview results. The quality of the data for each organization was variable, as shown in table 1.1. Most of the evidence comes from self-reported reviews on websites and published reports. Only half of the organizations have third-party evaluations on their performance and social impact was often inferred from the available information. For example, information on availability was based on descriptions of the volume and reach of services (e.g. within poor areas), data on affordability was based on pricing strategies, while information on quality (either technical quality or patient experience) was based on comparisons with existing services or use of strategies for quality improvement such as training, monitoring and evaluating.

Analysis of Case Studies

Innovations can be characterized within the steps of a health care delivery value chain, as described in Michael Porter and Elizabeth Teisberg's "Redefining Health Care" (Porter & Teisberg 2006). A value chain describes each step in

Table 1.1 Innovative private sector organizations benefiting the poor

Organization (Country/Year Started) Scope of Services	Overall Performance	Social Impact			↑ Improved ↔ No Change ? Unknown	Quality of Evidence	Sources of Funding
		Availability	Affordability	Quality of Care			
Aravind Eye Care System (India/1976) *Eye care services:* Manufacture of intraocular lenses; cataract surgery; vision screening	Largest and most productive eye care facility in the world; 2.5 million have received outpatient eye care and >300,000 have undergone eye surgeries from April 2009 to March 2010	↑ Increased availability of services to rural areas through outreach camps, internet kiosks, and vision centres	↑ Cost of cataract surgery reduced to $25; 70% of patients receive care subsidized or free	↑ High quality of services, with lower infection rate than UK		Self-reported evaluations; externally reviewed publications	Local entrepreneur
Dentista Do Bem (Brazil/2002) *Dental care for youths:* Free treatment provided by existing practitioners	Reached >12,000 children in 27 states in Brazil in 2009; model is being replicated in 6 Latin American countries	↔ Existing practitioners provide free services	↑ Services provided by existing providers for free to poor youth	↔ Use of existing providers; provide systematic follow-up and feedback to ensure quality of care and motivate dentists		Self-reported questionnaire and review; foundation website	Local entrepreneur supported by partnerships with dentists and fundraising

Organization	Network/Scale	Reach	Serving the poor	Quality	Evaluation	Funding
Greenstar Social Marketing Pakistan (Pakistan/1991) *Reproductive and child health*: Education; intervention, monitoring, and evaluation	Second-largest family-planning provider after the government in Pakistan with a franchise network of over 7,500 active providers	↑ Outreach workers reach over 2.5 million people every year	↑ Serves higher proportion of poor clients than the government and provides over 26% of all modern contraceptives at affordable prices	↑ Continuous training and monitoring result in higher quality services than existing private facilities	Self-reported review and questionnaire; third-party evaluation	Initially funded by international NGO with support from various government and private foundations and user fees
Jaipur Foot (India/1968) *Lower limb prosthetic*: Manufacture and fitting	Distributed >200,000 artificial limbs in India and >13,000 in 18 other countries	↑ Distribution through clinics and outreach camps, 24 hours a day	↑ Reduced cost of a prosthetic leg and fitting to $35; prosthetics are distributed to clients for free	↑ Prosthetics are designed to meet the daily needs of the poor; focuses on customer orientation and quality service delivery	Self-reported statistics; third-party evaluation	Local entrepreneur supported by local government and donations
K-MET (Kenya/1995) *Maternal and child care*: Trains existing providers on reproductive health; family planning; safe abortion care	Network of 204 health providers and community-based workers	↑ Provides care for rural communities where government services are unavailable	↑ Serves clients slightly poorer than community average; services benefit all income quintiles	↑ Gives loans to clinics and provides training to improve facilities and ensure safety and high quality of care	Externally reviewed publications; third-party evaluation	Local NGO with support from donations and international grants

(Continued)

Table 1.1 Continued

Organization (Country/Year Started) Scope of Services	Overall Performance	Social Impact Availability	Affordability	↑ Improved ↔ No Change ? Unknown Quality of Care	Quality of Evidence	Sources of Funding
Narayana Hrudayalaya Heart Hospital (NH) (India/2001) *Coronary artery disease:* Heart surgeries and cardiac care	The 800-bed hospital performs high quality surgeries with eight times more volume than average Indian hospitals	↑ High-volume hospital; 54 telemedicine centres, outreach camps, and buses reach out to the rural poor	↑ High-volume strategy allowed NH to reduce cost of cardiac surgery to Rs 65,000 from Rs 150,000 (average Indian private hospital); 18% of patients receive care subsidized and 1% free	↑ Ensures high quality and efficient services by training surgeons and nurses, and using top-quality equipment; higher overall success rate in coronary artery bypass surgery than the US average	Self-reported review; externally reviewed publications; third-party evaluations	Local entrepreneur with the help of capital funding from family members and Asia Heart Foundation plus user fees
Population and Community Development Association (PDA)	Contributed to the decrease of Thailand's population growth rate from 3.3% in the 1970s to	↑ Nationwide public education campaigns; outreach and mobile clinics reach 10 million	↑ Most services are free; owns innovative commercial ventures to fund	? Quality of care unclear; aims to improve safety of services (e.g. reinforced safe abortion	Self-reported review; Gates Awards press release; published reports	Local entrepreneur with support through donations and revenue from

(Thailand/1974) *Family planning and HIV/AIDS care:* Education; contraceptive/ vasectomy/ pregnancy termination services	0.6% in 2005; helped establish national HIV/ AIDS prevention program in Thailand, which reduced potential new infections by 90%; model adopted by the governments of many countries	Thais in 18,000 villages and poor urban communities; provide blood tests, family planning, and pregnancy termination services for the poor where services were previously unavailable	community health and development projects	practices, etc.) and provides health education to the public		their own commercial ventures ranging from restaurants to industrial health services
PSI's Top Reseau/100% Jeune/Centre Dushishoze (Madagascar, Cameroon, Rwanda/1999)	Increased contraceptive use among young men from 29% to 53%, among young women from 20 to 39%	↑ Broad reach through multimedia campaigns and outreach	↑ Provide services at a subsidized rate (Madagascar) and cheaper than other health clinics (Cameroon)	↑ Continuous evaluation to ensure high-quality and effective youth programs	Externally reviewed publications; third-party evaluations	International NGO supported by grants and user fees

(Continued)

Table 1.1 Concluded

Organization (Country/Year Started) Scope of Services	Overall Performance	Social Impact		↑ Improved ↔ No Change ? Unknown	Quality of Evidence	Sources of Funding
		Availability	Affordability	Quality of Care		
Sexual/ reproductive health: Peer counselling; education; contraceptive services; multimedia promotion	increased number of people getting HIV test in Rwanda and reproductive services in Madagascar;					
Vision Spring (India/2001) *Vision correction:* Screening; provides glasses, adjustments	"Business in a bag" strategy allows 1,200 Vision Entrepreneurs to distribute >100,000 pairs of glasses in 13 countries	↑ Entrepreneurs distributed glasses in poor communities and rural areas; door-to-door service with easy screening and testing methods	↑ Glasses are $4 a pair instead of $40–60 at optical shops	↑ Quality of glasses are in general lower than those from expensive optical retailers, but higher than competitors within their price range	External case studies; externally reviewed publications	Foreign entrepreneurs supported by venture philanthropy, philanthropic investors and user fees

| Ziqitza 1298 (India/2005) *Ambulance services:* Transportation and emergency care; public education | 70 ambulances in Mumbai and Kerala have served more than 60,000 patients | ↑The first single emergency number for ambulance service in Mumbai; 24-hour ambulances with GPS tracking | ↑Cross-subsidization made services more affordable to the poor | ↑90% of ambulances in urban India did not have adequate equipment and trained paramedics; Ziqitza's ambulances provide trained paramedics, life support equipment and continuous evaluation to ensure safety and quality of services | Self-reported review; funders' review | Local entrepreneurs supported by venture philanthropy and user fees |

a process that adds value to a product or service before it is delivered to the ultimate customer, in this case, a patient. Health care is divided into medical processes (monitoring and preventing disease, diagnosis, intervention, rehabilitation, and ongoing management) and business processes, which support medical care. The value chain served as a starting point for our analysis of the cases, extracting different elements of the business processes, and adding financial functions that were not included in Porter's original model. We abstracted information on these processes, focusing on those that were described as innovative. We scanned the description of these innovative processes for themes, and after multiple iterations, the categories were restructured to more clearly highlight new strategies used by these organizations to improve care for the poor.

Results

The ten case studies were analysed using constant comparison of emerging themes, and we found that these organizations had business-process innovations in the following functions: marketing, financing, and operating. Figure 1.1 shows areas of innovation in business processes in the organizations reviewed. Interestingly, all of the organizations innovated across all three categories, with particular strategies described below.

Marketing Activities

The marketing strategies used by many of these organizations included both the promotion of services to the poor and design of these services to meet the needs of this group.

SOCIAL MARKETING
Social marketing refers to the application of marketing techniques to achieve behavioural changes. It is not a new concept, but Population Services International (PSI) in Africa and the Population and Community Development Association (PDA) in Thailand have both applied this strategy in innovative ways. PDA uses Thai humour to address taboo subjects such as contraception and HIV awareness and has achieved unprecedented success in garnering positive public attention (Population and Community Development Association). Their social marketing initiatives include "Condom Nights" and "Miss Anti-AIDS Beauty Pageants" in the red-light districts of Bangkok. PDA has also established training and peer education programs that focus on behaviour change in the country's schools, prisons, sex industry, and the public in general. Their condom-distribution network penetrates one-third of Thailand.

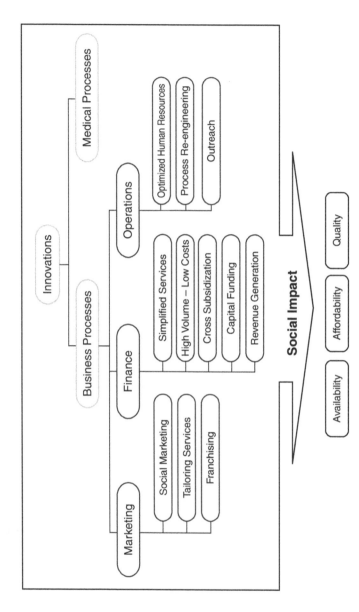

Figure 1.1 Business model innovations in health service delivery

Their family-planning effort contributed to the decrease in the population growth rate in Thailand from 3.3 per cent in the 1970s to 0.6 per cent in 2005. The organization developed a national AIDS education program in partnership with the government, contributing to Thailand's 90 per cent reduction in new HIV infections in 2004. PSI, meanwhile, operates three social marketing programs that offer educational programs on reproductive health for urban youth in Africa. The programs address the taboo subject of safe sexual behaviour through means that target the youth, such as magazines, television spots, call-in radio shows, and radio drama (Porter & Teisberg 2006). A survey found that 90 per cent of the youth had read the monthly magazine at least once and 70 per cent had viewed the television spots, with corresponding increased rates of contraceptive use and HIV testing, demonstrating the potential of these educational social marketing programs (Plautz & Meekers 2007).

TAILORING SERVICES TO THE POOR

Another marketing tool employed was tailoring the design of products and services to the needs of the poor. The Bhagwan Mahaveer Viklang Sahayata Samiti (BMVSS) is an Indian organization that has developed the Jaipur Foot, an artificial lower limb prosthetic intended to meet the needs of amputees living in developing nations, where squatting, sitting cross-legged, and walking barefoot is common to the poor but largely impossible with typical prosthetic limbs (Macke, Misra, & Sharma 2003). In addition to providing a novel product, the BMVSS clinics have adapted their services to the poor, allowing patients to check in at any time of day or night. Furthermore, they provide patients with free room and board if they have to spend the night and provide their families with free meals at the clinic. Since fittings can be completed in one session (as opposed to several), time away from work and number of visits are kept to a minimum, which is very important to patients with limited means and mobility. This specific tailoring of products and services make them more accessible and attractive to the poor.

FRANCHISING

Franchising has been used to facilitate rapid expansion and the sustainable distribution of products and services of a specified quality in reproductive health. Greenstar Social Marketing Pakistan is one of the first health franchisers, and has grown to provide over 26 per cent of all contraceptives in Pakistan. It targets low-income nonusers of contraceptives through a total market approach, which has different price points for each segment of the population (Clemminck & Kadakia 2008). The organization operates a franchise network of over 7,500 private independent health care providers, most of which are located in low-income urban and peri-urban areas in Pakistan. Greenstar signs franchising agreements with providers for distribution of products or social services, and keeps regular contact with the aim of ensuring adequate quality. It provides medical training, supply of goods, public education, technical support, quality control, and program evaluation to its franchisees. Greenstar has invested in developing a strong brand associated with high quality care and reliable information.

Financial Strategies

Most organizations in this study were funded by local entrepreneurs who wanted to make an impact on society, while two of the organizations initially received funds from international NGOs and have later grown to be more independent (see table 1.1). Many received support from partnerships, government funding, grants, and donations, and some recovered part of their costs from user fees. Our analysis of these cases revealed that while some organizations innovated to generate funds for sustainability, many organizations redesigned cost structures in ways that allowed products and services to be more affordable to the poor. Dramatic reductions in cost were reported to have been achieved by rigorous expense management, capital funding, and revenue-generating programs.

LOWER OPERATING COSTS THROUGH SIMPLIFIED MEDICAL SERVICE

Operating costs were lowered by simplifying the medical services provided and using less than fully qualified providers. For example, VisionSpring's financial strategies include a "business in a bag," which involves training rural community members to become Vision Entrepreneurs (VEs) who can provide vision screening, identify far-sightedness, and provide glasses for vision correction. VEs are provided a kit with items intended to help launch a business, including multiple styles, colours, and powers of reading glasses; screening equipment; and marketing materials (Clemminck & Kadakia 2008). Vision-Spring helps replenish supplies of reading glasses and provides additional support as required. This "business in a bag" strategy is intended to enable motivated workers to gain access to an entrepreneurial opportunity without the barriers of high set-up and operating costs.

HIGH VOLUME AND LOW UNIT COSTS

The Narayana Hrudayalaya Heart Hospital (NH) in India, the largest provider of paediatric heart surgeries in the world, has reduced the unit cost of cardiac surgeries through volume (they do eight times more surgeries per day than the Indian average), which maximizes the use of infrastructure (Khanna,

Rangan, & Manocaran 2005; Narayana Hrudayalaya Hospitals). The hospital rents machines for blood tests and pays only for reagents, which satisfies suppliers given the high volumes. NH reduces cost by relying on digital X-rays rather than expensive films and by reducing inventory and processing times using comprehensive hospital management software. The quality of care has not been compromised by the high volume. In fact, NH uses high volume to improve the quality of care by allowing individual doctors to specialize in one or two types of cardiac surgeries. Their success rates are high (1.4 per cent mortality rate within thirty days of coronary artery bypass graft surgery v. 1.9 per cent in the US) (Anand 2009). NH's average cost of open heart surgery is about US$2,000, for which NH charges $2,400 as compared to $5,500 in the average Indian private hospital (Rangan 1993). A third of the patients actually do not pay out of pocket. The founder of NH partnered with the state of Karnataka to start the farmer's insurance plan, which costs $3 a year per person and reimburses the hospital $1,200 for each surgery. The hospital makes up the difference by charging more from the 40 per cent of patients who do not have a plan and the 30 per cent who opt for private/semi-private rooms (Anand 2009). NH's high volume and tiered fee strategies allow them to provide affordable quality heart surgery to the poor. The next section will address tiered-fee strategies in more detail.

CROSS-SUBSIDIZATION

Some organizations have achieved financial sustainability through a cross-subsidization strategy, where they exploit the greater willingness and ability to pay among the wealthier patients to cross-subsidize expensive services for lower-income patients. They have developed efficient ways of assessing financial need and implementing cross subsidy. Aravind Eye Care System, the largest eye care provider in the world, attracts wealthier patients who pay market rates, and then provides the same services for the poorer 70 per cent of their patients at a highly subsidized rate or for free (Aravind Eye Care System; Rangan 1993; Shah & Murty 2004). They establish differential pricing by the patients' choice of amenities and the type of lens to be inserted in the eye, not by the quality of treatment the patient gets. All patients – regardless of ability to pay – receive the same medical care, but paying patients can choose soft lenses and sleep in private rooms, while nonpaying patients are given the basic hard lens and sleep in open dormitories on mats. This approach, called quality targeting, is an efficient way of assessing financial need, because those who can afford private rooms and soft lenses are much more likely to choose them. Another example is 1298 Ziqitza Health Care Limited, which provides private ambulance services using a tiered-fee system (Ziqitza Healthcare). Patients call the ambulance service and are charged according to the hospital they have arranged to be transported to – those going to private hospitals are charged above cost, those going to free government hospitals pay a nominal fee, and trauma patients do not pay. In this strategy, a patient's ability to pay is gauged from the choice of hospital, and again patients have an incentive to accurately represent their ability to pay because it impacts the quality of hospital care they receive subsequently. Approximately 20 per cent of patients carried by the ambulance service over the last three years were subsidized, allowing Ziqitza to be financially sustainable.

In addition to formal tiered payment systems described above, an informal system of cross-subsidy can be created by encouraging providers to provide subsidized services to poor people. Dentista Do Bem is a large network of private, for-profit dentists in Brazil who have agreed to see a few poor patients every day for free (Fábio Bibancos de Rosa: Turma do Bem). This is a form of charity that has a limited impact on the earnings of for-profit providers, with paying customers indirectly "subsidizing" the cost of caring for poor patients within a given practice. Children are screened in schools and recruited to join the program until age eighteen. Though each dentist only sees a few free patients a day, the large number of participating dentists made it possible to see more than 12,000 children in 2009 (Bhattacharyya et al. 2009; Fábio Bibancos de Rosa: Turma do Bem). Providers derive some satisfaction and recognition for providing this service and the network is an efficient organizational structure to leverage existing human resources to reach poor people across all twenty-seven Brazilian states, and in six Latin American countries (Dentista do Bem, a project in Sao Paulo city).

CAPITAL FUNDING

Capital funding for franchisees or service providers to start up or improve the quality of their health programs is a key feature of the Kisumu Medical and Educational Trust (KMET), a franchise that gives training in reproductive health to private providers in Kenya (Montagu, Prata, Campbell, Walsh, & Orero 2005). KMET improves the availability of funds to private franchisees through revolving loan programs (microfinance). This allows community-based providers to expand services and improve the quality of the reproductive health services offered. KMET has expanded to 125 franchisees since start-up in 1995.

GENERATING REVENUE

Thailand's PDA developed sixteen for-profit companies that are affiliated with the organization and are mandated to put funds towards the NGO to facilitate expansion and supplement operating costs. One of PDA's many innovative commercial ventures is the "Cabbages and Condoms" restaurants, located in different parts of the country, where condom-themed food and drink help bring money into the organization (Cabbages and Condoms). This unique setup allows the companies to independently generate revenue while using novel social franchising mechanisms to spread information about safe-sex practices.

Operating Activities

These health care organizations appear able to modify operating strategies to increase the availability of services in remote areas and make judicious use of human resources in a context of widespread shortage of skilled labour.

OPTIMIZING HUMAN RESOURCES

While this strategy is not unique, these organizations have expanded the use of lay health workers into new areas. They help laypersons acquire skills that were previously exclusive to trained professionals: distribution of oral contraceptives (PDA) or eye exams and business operations (VisionSpring). By shifting tasks to trained laypersons, these organizations have reduced operating costs, increased availability of staff, and empowered the local community. Aravind Eye Care System trains high school graduates from rural areas into paramedical staff like patient flow managers, providers of simple diagnostic procedures, and even optical technicians (Rangan 1993). Another approach for leveraging human resources is increasing the quality of care provided by established health care workers. KMET trains existing health workers in safe abortion procedures and provides manual vacuum aspiration kits for safe abortions. Education, resources, and a professional network are designed to further enhance the quality of maternal and child care given by this group (Montagu et al. 2005).

PROCESS AND PRODUCT RE-ENGINEERING

In addition to distributing ready-made eyeglasses for the far-sighted, Vision-Spring is working together with the d.o.b foundation to offer new adjustable lens (U-specs) for the near-sighted population, and especially for children (Gudlavelleti, Allagh & Gudlavalleti 2014). The innovative design of U-specs comprises two adjustable lenses that can be shifted to adjust the refractive strength of the glasses. This makes mass production easier, reduces costs, and offers an alternative to the traditional customized construction of eyeglasses.

Aravind Eye Care System improved efficiency by re-engineering their operating rooms to allow surgeons to work on two tables in alternation by shifting from one case to another. While one surgery is in progress, a team of four nurses and paramedical staff prepare the next patient. This innovation allows Aravind to perform a cataract surgery in ten minutes – one third of the industry standard of thirty minutes. Despite the shared space for patients, their infection rates are 4 per 10,000 cases, which is better than the published rate in the UK of 6 per 10,000 (Shah & Murty 2004). Aravind also tracks surgical outcomes by surgeon and provides support to those who are below average, which contributes to improvements in quality of care.

INCREASING OUTREACH

Aravind Eye Care System and Narayana Hrudayalaya Heart Hospital provide health camps to reach patients in rural areas. NH provides camps that focus on cardiac diagnosis with transportation to the hospital for patients who require it. In addition to health camps, Aravind has also set up internet kiosks in remote villages run by community members, who take pictures of patients' eyes using a webcam and send the images to a doctor from Aravind along with a completed online questionnaire about the patients' symptoms (Bhattacharyya et al. 2009). The doctor is able to access the images instantaneously, and chat with the patient online in real time to assess whether the patient requires consultation at the hospital. These kiosks reduce both the time and expense incurred by an unnecessary hospital visit.

Discussion

This study characterized ten high-profile private sector innovators that have improved health services for the poor, reviewed their strategies, and found several trends across the organizations.

Complete Marketing, Finance, and Operations Solutions

Analysis of each organization's strategy showed that they innovated across marketing, finance, and operations. Exemplary practices include patient experience–focused strategies such as tailoring designs and services to meet the needs of the poor and cross-subsidization, efficiency strategies such as specialization and high-volume, low-cost approaches, and operational approaches to increase availability of services, such as outreach and telemedicine. All of the organizations that we studied had at least one unique innovation in each of the key business processes. There appears to be no single effective approach to improve health delivery. This may serve as a caution to organizations looking for "silver bullets" to improve care for the poor. The World Bank's recent review also showed that there are no blueprint planning approaches for improving the performance of health organizations (Peters, El-Saharty, Sladat, Janovsky, & Vujicic 2009). In fact, each exemplar in our study has developed a novel and comprehensive approach, simultaneously addressing the fact that poor people are often unaware of services, have limited funds, and live in hard-to-reach areas. This finding is similar to that of Karamchandani et al.'s stating that social service organizations that have scaled up successfully in emerging markets provide "end to end solutions" (Karamchandani et al. 2009).

Narrow Clinical Focus

All of the organizations in our study had a narrow disease focus built around a few medical processes with multiple innovations, allowing them to market their services on a large scale, reduce costs, and streamline operations to target poor patients effectively. While this may be an artefact of our search strategy, we found that none of the organizations identified here provided broad-based comprehensive health services. This finding could be related to the fact that it is easier to manage and experiment within well-defined health care delivery systems with a narrow focus. The predictability of the health problems and treatment strategies make it easier to simplify processes, delegate tasks to lower trained personnel and measure quality, all of which can reduce costs while increasing reach and quality. Though vertical approaches have limitations, they may lead to innovations whose benefits could be captured by replication or by linking them to broad-based health services, as in the case of PDA's collaboration with the Thai government on HIV control. The partial integration of PDA's program into health system functions contributed to a nationwide reduction of the HIV infection rate. In fact, studies show that seldom are interventions wholly unintegrated (purely vertical) or fully integrated into health system functions, and the heterogeneity in the extent of integration is influenced by intervention complexity, health system characteristics and contextual factors (Atun, de Jongh, Secci, Ohiri, & Adeyi 2010). Since the organizations chosen for our study vary by disease area, geographical, economic, and political environment, there is no doubt that the intent and extent of integration of these targeted health interventions into the health system, if any, will also vary.

Disruptive Innovations

Some of the organizations we studied have developed "disruptive" services and products designed to enable the participation of poor consumers who were previously excluded. For example, Jaipur Foot developed an artificial foot that is affordable, easy to fit, and has functions better suited to the needs of the poor. VisionSpring provides ready-made reading glasses on the spot to customers, using a kit that has very simple eye screening equipment and procedures, such as threading a needle. These customer-oriented products and services are "disruptive" in the sense that they fill gaps in the conventional markets, but have not yet displaced previous approaches. Both Jaipur Foot and VisionSpring have effectively increased accessibility to medical services to the poor through their simple and affordable designs. The vertical approaches described above could also be described as incorporating a value-added process business model, which allows for the refinements in quality while reducing cost through simplification and delegation of certain processes to less skilled providers (Christensen, Grossman, & Hwang 2009). For the most part, they do not pursue a low-cost, low-quality service strategy. Most organizations adapt services to the needs of their clients, and some reduce the "frills" but aim to provide high-quality clinical care.

Business Process Innovation

The core innovations of most organizations we reviewed are in business rather than medical processes, demonstrating that it is possible to have large-scale impact by implementing existing care processes using innovative marketing, finance, and operating strategies. For example, PDA's national success relies strongly on its innovative marketing campaigns for family planning and HIV prevention in Thailand. Ziqitza's ambulance services use standard protocols, but achieve financial sustainability and affordability through its novel approach to cross-subsidy. Given the wide range of affordable and effective medical interventions, which are currently underused (Jamieson et al. 2006), it seems that many of the problems in global health require improvements in management rather than new interventions. Some of the strategies described here have been successfully reproduced by the Thai government in the case of PDA, and by other hospitals using the consulting services of Aravind Eye Care System (Rangan 1993). This suggests that the private sector may be a viable source of innovative management practices.

One of the main concerns with heath care delivery from exemplars of private sector innovation is the issue of quality. In our study, quality of care was rarely compared to existing services, and improvements in quality were only measured for a few organizations. Some organizations focus on affordability like Dentista Do Bem, which presumably did not improve availability or quality of care since they leverage existing providers. PDA did not provide any evidence on quality of their family planning or HIV educational programs, but the national scale up of their strategy coincided with a significant decrease in population growth rate in Thailand, which indirectly suggests some social impact. The only organizations that had more rigorous evaluations of quality of services were Aravind Eye Care System, PSI, Greenstar, and NH. The quality of care for the rest was inferred through changes in structure, like built-in quality improvement mechanisms, training, monitoring, and evaluation. Despite having chosen among the best-documented organizations, there is a lack of rigorous evidence for many measures of impact. Future work should focus on improving data collection for impact assessment, encouraging third-party appraisal, and possibly reinforcing evaluations by changing funding requirements where relevant.

Due to the nature of our search strategy, we are only able to capture organizations that are relatively well documented and high profile, and some worthy innovators who are less successful at marketing their story might have fallen under the radar. Another limitation to this study is establishing what is truly innovative. For this study, we relied on reputation and a review of organizations for which data was available rather than a systematic review of all existing organizations to ensure that there was no overlap. However, high-profile innovative organizations that have scaled up their operations are likely to be copied, in which case they may not be the only ones using a given strategy at this time. For example, Aravind Eye Care System contributed to the development of the Lumbini Eye Institute, which operates on a similar model and now provides 25 per cent of all sight-restoring surgeries in Nepal. More in-depth studies are required to assess associations between a given strategy and social impact. The organizations identified here should not be seen as representative of the private sector in general; rather, they were selected as exemplars of what this sector might contribute. They may in fact be islands of excellence in a sea of mediocrity, though it was beyond the scope of this study to determine if this was the case.

This is the first study to characterize and compare a wide range of activities among the best-documented health care organizations into a coherent framework. Unlike previous studies, this study focused on health care, included all countries in the initial search (as opposed to only India or Africa), and looked for patterns across a series of cases sampled for maximum variability. This study is not an attempt to build a complete database of innovative private sector providers (like the Center for Health Market Innovations), but rather an attempt to lay the groundwork for larger studies to determine the association between a given strategy and improved outcomes. With increasing investment in social enterprises from groups like Acumen Fund and the Global Impact Investing Network, more attention to rigorously measure the impact of these organizations would be beneficial. An independent group like the International

Initiative for Impact Evaluation could develop appropriate metrics and provide a platform to independently and reliably assess the impact of organizations that receive funds from impact investors or government, especially around quality of care. Researchers could work with these investors to evaluate social impact and develop reliable measures that are appropriate to organizations that are scaling up quickly, since many evaluation designs provide results too slowly to assess effective growth.

Conclusion

The poor in low- and middle-income countries have limited access to quality health services for a variety of reasons. A subset of private health organizations have emerged, often called social enterprises, which have developed innovative techniques to improve care for the poor. In this review, ten high-profile health service organizations were studied, and were found to innovate across the areas of marketing, finance, and operation. Rather than providing a wide range of services, these organizations had a narrow clinical focus, which may have facilitated experimentation with delivery processes. This review of many of the best-known innovators in health services for the poor found relatively little rigorous information on quality of care. Linking future investments to robust measures of social impact would help identify effective approaches and unleash the potential of innovative delivery models to transform health services for the poor.

REFERENCES

Anand, G. 2009. "The Henry Ford of Heart Surgery." *The Wall Street Journal*. http://online.wsj.com/article/SB125875892887958111.html.
Aravind Eye Care System. 2015. "About Us." https://www.aravind.org/default/aboutuscontent/genesis.
Atun, R., de Jongh, T., Secci, F., Ohiri, K., & Adeyi, O. 2010. "A Systematic Review of the Evidence on Integration of Targeted Health Interventions into Health Systems." *Health Policy and Planning* 25(1): 1–14. https://doi.org/10.1093/heapol/czp053.
Bennett, S., McPake, B., & Mills, A. 1997. *Private Health Providers in Developing Countries. Serving the Public Interest London*. United Kingdom: Zed Books.
Bhattacharyya, O., McGahan, A., Dunne, D., Singer, P.A., & Daar, A. 2008. "Innovative Health Service Delivery Models for Low and Middle Income Countries – What Can We Learn from the Private Sector?" https://www.r4d.org/resources/innovative-health-service-delivery-models-low-middle-income-countries.

Bustreo, F., Harding, A., & Axelsson, H. 2003. "Can Developing Countries Achieve Adequate Improvements in Child Health Outcomes without Engaging the Private Sector?" *Bulletin of the World Health Organization* 81(12): 886–95.

Cabbages and Condoms. http://www.cabbagesandcondoms.net/.

Christensen, C.M., Grossman, J., & Hwang, J. 2009. *The Innovator's Prescription: A Disruptive Solution for Health Care.* New York: McGraw-Hill.

Clemminck, N., & Kadakia, S. 2007. *What Works: Scojo India Foundation.* Washington, DC: World Resources Institute.

Dentista do Bem, a project in Sao Paulo city. http://www.turmadobem.org.br/br/index .php?pagina=conheca_nossa_turma&sub=projetos&id=dentista_do_bem.

Fábio Bibancos de Rosa: Turma do Bem. https://www.schwabfound.org/awardees/ fabio-bibancos.

Gudlavalleti, V.S., Allagh, K.P., & Gudlavalleti, A.S. 2014. "Self-adjustable Glasses in the Developing World." *Clinical Opthalmology* 8: 405–13. https://doi.org/10.2147/ OPTH.S46057.

Hwang, J., & Christensen, C.M. 2008. "Disruptive Innovation in Health Care Delivery: A Framework for Business Model Innovation." *Health Affairs* 27(5): 1329–35. https://doi.org/10.1377/hlthaff.27.5.1329.

Jamieson, D., Breman, J., Measham, A., Alleyne, G., Claeson, M., Evans, D., Jha, P., Mills, A., Musgrove, P. 2006. *Disease Control Priorities in Developing Countries.* Washington DC: World Bank and Oxford Press.

Jossey-Bass. 2007. *The Business of Health in Africa: Partnering with the Private Sector to Improve People's Lives.* International Finance Corporation. Washington, DC: World Bank.

Karamchandani, A., Kubzansky, M., & Frandano, P. 2009. *Emerging Markets, Emerging Models: Market-Based Solutions to the Challenges of Global Poverty.* Cambridge, MA: Monitor Group.

Khanna, T., Rangan, V.K., & Manocaran, M. 2005. *Narayana Hrudayalaya Heart Hospital: Cardiac Care for the Poor.* Boston: Harvard Business Publishing.

Macke, S., Misra, R., & Sharma, A. 2003. "Jaipur Foot: Challenging Convention." Michigan Business School case.

Montagu, D., Prata, N., Campbell, M.M., Walsh, J., & Orero, S. 2005. "Kenya: Reaching the Poor through the Private Sector A Network Model for Expanding Access to Reproductive Health Services." HNP Discussion Paper.

Narayana Hrudayalaya Hospitals. http://www.narayanahospitals.com/.

Nicholls, A. 2005. *Social Entrepreneurship: New Models of Sustainable Social Change.* New York: Oxford University Press.

Patouillard, E., Goodman, C.A., Hanson, K.G., & Mills, A.J. 2007. "Can Working with the Private For-Profit Sector Improve Utilization of Quality Health Services by the Poor? A Systematic Review of the Literature." *International Journal for Equity in Health* 6(1): 17. https://doi.org/10.1186/1475-9276-6-17.

Peters, D.H., El-Saharty, S., Sladat, B., Janovsky, K., & Vujicic, M. (2009). *Improving Health Service Delivery in Developing Countries: From Evidence to Action.* Washington, DC: The World Bank.

Plautz, A., & Meekers, D. 2007. "Evaluation of the Reach and Impact of the 100% Jeune Youth Social Marketing Program in Cameroon: Findings from Three Cross-sectional Surveys." *Reproductive Health*: 4(1). https://doi.org/10.1186/1742 -4755-4-1.

Population and Community Development Association. http://www.pda.or.th.

Porter, M.E., & Teisberg, E.O. 2006. *Redefining Health Care Creating Value-Based Competition on Results.* Boston, MA: Harvard Business School Press.

Private Sector Participation in Health. 2004. http://www.eldis.org/document/A18908.

Rangan, V.K. 1993. "The Aravind Eye Hospital, Madurai, India, in Service for Sight." Harvard Business School Case Study.

Rangan, V.K., Quelch, J.A., Herrero, G., & Barton, B. 2006. *Business Solutions for the Global Poor: Creating Social and Economic Value.* San Francisco, California: Jossey-Bass.

Shah, J., & Murty, L.S. 2004. "Compassionate, High Quality Health Care at Low Cost: The Aravind Model." IIMB Management Review, 16.

Weberg, D. (2009). "Innovation in Healthcare: A Concept Analysis." *Nursing Administration Quarterly* 33(3): 227–37. https://doi.org/10.1097/NAQ .0b013e3181accaf5.

The World Bank. 2008. "Poverty Data: A Supplement to World Development Indicators 2008." http://siteresources.worldbank.org/DATASTATISTICS/Resources/ WDI08supplement1216.pdf.

Ziqitza Healthcare. https://www.zhl.org.in/.

2 Global Health Innovation: Exploring Program Practices and Strategies

ONIL BHATTACHARYYA, ANITA MCGAHAN,
WILL MITCHELL, KATHRYN MOSSMAN, RAMAN SOHAL,
JOHN GINTHER, JOHN A. MACDONALD,
HIMANSHU PARIKH, AND ILAN SHAHIN

Introduction

Health programs in low- and middle-income countries (LMICs) are engaging in a variety of innovative practices as part of their strategies to better meet the health needs of poor populations. In order to understand "what works" in this emerging field of global health, there first needs to be a robust understanding of the innovative practices and strategies pursued by LMIC health programs. In this chapter, we explore the innovative practices of a purposive sample of 80 diverse, data-rich programs from the Center for Health Market Innovations (CHMI) database and we consider how these practices are employed to provide accessible and affordable care for LMIC populations. This involved reviewing the categorization of innovative program practices described in the literature and developing a comprehensive list. The 80 programs were then explored and coded for innovative practices. This allowed us to analyse trends involving the innovative practices carried out in different regions and health areas, and consider how they address particular barriers to health care. We also explored how some innovative practices are clustered together by groups of programs pursuing similar strategies in different geographic and disease contexts. By examining programs' innovative practices, we can better understand their strategies and how they employ innovative practices in mutually reinforcing ways to achieve their goals.

Background

Innovation, Strategy, and Operational Effectiveness

The poor face a number of barriers to accessing health care, including low health literacy, residence in remote rural areas or slums, and limited purchasing power and access to health insurance (Rangan et al. 2007 as cited in

Bhattacharyya et al. 2010). In order to ensure that quality care is affordable and accessible to the poor, services must be financed, marketed, and delivered in a way that considers these substantial barriers. Social enterprises in LMICs are attempting to address issues of health care accessibility and quality through innovation. Innovation is defined as something new, or perceived as new, by a population that has the potential to redefine the economic and/or social context of health care and drive change (Weberg 2009). As Weberg (2009, 231) notes, innovation "can be accomplished by recombining old ideas in a new way, creating a new process or product, using a process from another industry in one that has not used that process, or reordering an organization in a new and different way." Health care innovation must be compatible with existing organizational values or change those values before it can occur, and it must create competitive advantage, whether that involves better health or better outcomes (Weberg 2009).

Innovative practices are important for an organization's competitive strategy, since they can involve new ways of creating value for clients. Kaplan and Norton (2001) describe strategy as the sustainable and unique way an organization creates value, adding that formulating and implementing strategy should be considered a participative and continual process. According to Porter (1996, 65), "Strategic competition can be thought of as the process of perceiving new positions that woo customers from established positions or draw new customers into the market." Competitive strategy is the broad formula of how a business competes, its goals, and the policies it carries out to achieve those goals (Porter 1998). Porter (1996, 62) cautions that strategic positioning should not be confused with operational effectiveness, which he defines as "performing similar activities *better* than rivals perform them." While operational effectiveness is necessary for superior profitability, few companies can compete successfully on the basis of operational effectiveness in the long term due to the rapid diffusion of best practices (Porter 1996). As well, in letting operational effectiveness replace strategy, companies can be drawn towards imitation, homogeneity, and zero-sum competition (Porter 1996, 64). As a result, organizations must focus on developing competitive strategies that differentiate them from their rivals and help them meet their organizational goals.

Strategies can consist of a number of innovative practices that are combined by organizations to differentiate themselves from their competitors, contribute towards their competitive advantage, create value, and achieve organizational goals. Innovation can be an integral part of strategy, given that innovative organizations are able to succeed by defining new business models and finding new ways of either creating or enhancing value for clients, fundamentally shifting the competitive dynamics within a sector (Ojha et al. 2011). In the

LMIC health care sector, this often occurs through engaging in multiple innovations to better meet the needs of poor populations.

Business Process Innovations in Health Care

In order to improve the availability, affordability, and quality of health care for the poor, social enterprises in LMICs are developing innovative health service delivery models (Bhattacharyya et al. 2010). Here we define health service delivery models as business models that have been adopted in the provision of health services (Bhattacharyya et al. 2010). Hwang and Christensen (2008) suggest that in health care, greater business-model innovation is needed given that disruptive technologies alone have failed to result in higher quality, greater accessibility, and lower costs. Furthermore, organizations aiming to use market-based approaches to attract low-income customers require business models that are suited to the extreme circumstances and conditions of low-income markets (Kubzansky et al. 2011). With these issues in mind, Bhattacharyya et al. (2010) have identified three types of business-process innovations social enterprises that provide health care for the poor engage in: marketing, financing, and operating. Innovations in marketing promote services to the poor and design these services to meet the needs of poor populations, while innovations in finance generate funds for sustainability and redesign cost structures through capital funding and rigorous expense management (Bhattacharyya et al. 2010). Innovations in operation increase the availability of services to the poor in remote areas, and modify human resources practices to adapt to a context of limited skilled labour (Bhattacharyya et al. 2010). In a review of 10 high-profile private sector innovators, Bhattacharyya et al. (2010) found that all of these social enterprises engage in multiple innovations across marketing, finance, and operations, developing approaches that simultaneously address the issues poor people face: limited funds, low awareness of services, and geographic remoteness. For real breakthroughs involving sustainable and disruptive innovations, organizations must incorporate innovative practices across multiple aspects of their organizations (Ojha et al. 2011). Since innovative organizations engage in a variety of innovative practices to achieve their goals, it appears that there is no single effective approach to improving health care delivery (Bhattacharyya et al. 2010, 8). Porter (1996, 68) also argues that there is no one ideal position or strategy for an organization, since a single set of activities cannot meet all needs, produce all varieties, and access all clients. Innovative practices can be incorporated as part of unique organizational strategies, and different programs may engage in a variety of similar innovative practices. Such elements can be tracked and studied across programs for trends and comparisons.

Methods

To develop a comprehensive list of innovative practices, we began by examining the 11 business process innovations pursued by LMIC social enterprises in the health care field as presented by Bhattacharyya et al. (2010). We also explored Monitor Group's 17 business models used by social enterprises to provide products and services to the poor in areas such as health care, energy, agriculture, and financial services (Kubzansky et al. 2011). We then considered how the models described by Monitor Group mapped onto those described by Bhattacharyya et al. (2010), incorporating them where appropriate. For example, we found that one of Monitor Group's business models, "no frills" (a pared-down service for ultra-low prices that generates profits through high volume, high asset utilization, and service specialization), could be mapped onto Bhattacharyya et al.'s (2010) "high volume, low unit cost" innovation category, which includes programs like Narayana Hrudayalaya that have reduced the unit cost of services through serving a high volume of patients and maximizing the use of infrastructure. We then reviewed the 25 health market innovations developed by CHMI (2012), where we found considerable overlap, and incorporated these innovations into our list of innovative practices.

Our team members reviewed the list of innovative practices and applied them to a sample of 80 well-documented programs,[1] revising definitions and categories as needed. We then coded the 80 programs and further revised the list of innovative practices. Using this iterative approach, we developed a list of 29 innovative practices pursued by the eighty programs.[2] After coding, we conducted the analysis, first by measuring the frequency of innovative practices across programs, and then by exploring the frequency of innovative practices by geographic region and health area. We examined clusters of innovative practices in order to understand how some of these practices are used in combination as part of unique program strategies to address health barriers.

Results

Overall Frequency of Innovative Practices

In the analysis of the 29 innovative practices engaged in by our sample of 80 programs, we found the practices reported most frequently include mHealth (43 per cent of programs), health outreach (39 per cent of programs), provider training (38 per cent of programs), and health awareness/education (26 per cent of programs) (figure 2.1).

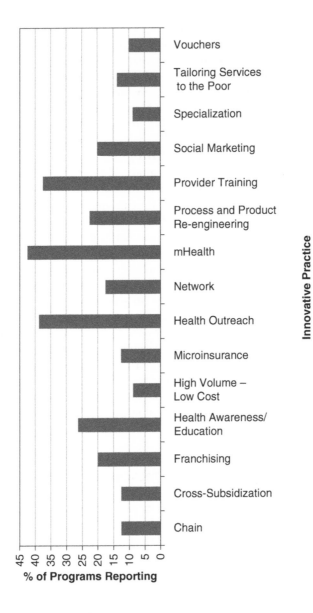

Figure 2.1 Most reported innovative practices by 80 well-documented programs

Among the bottom 14 reported innovative practices, the least reported practices include mobile money, pay for performance, and government health insurance, tied at 1 per cent of programs, followed by monitoring standards, integrated delivery systems, and policy development, each engaged in by 3 per cent of programs (figure 2.2).

Innovative Practices by Geographic Region

The eighty programs studied carry out their operations in 41[3] countries in eight different regions in Africa, Asia, and Latin America.[4] These regions include Southern Africa, Western Africa, Central Africa, Eastern Africa, Southern Asia, Eastern Asia, Southeastern Asia, and Latin America. Five of these regions will now be explored more in-depth with regard to the innovative practices engaged in by programs in these areas.[5,6]

SOUTHERN ASIA

Half of the 80 programs operate in four countries in Southern Asia, including 28 that operate in India, the country with the largest number of programs in this sample. Other Southern Asian countries with programs in this 80-program sub-set include Bangladesh, with seven; Pakistan, with five; and Nepal, with two.[7]

For programs operating in the Southern Asia region, the most frequent innovative practices are mHealth (50 per cent), health outreach (48 per cent), and provider training (40 per cent).[8] According to the WHO (2011, 6) mHealth refers to " medical and public health practice supported by mobile devices, such as mobile phones, patient monitoring devices, personal digital assistants (PDAs), and other wireless devices." The frequency of these innovative practices suggests that programs in Southern Asia are particularly interested in accessing populations in difficult-to-reach areas and capitalizing on mobile technologies, along with ensuring access to skilled practitioners. India has the fastest growing market for wireless technologies in the world (Prahalad 2006), and the growing availability of mobile phones among the world's poorest populations suggests that mHealth offers huge potential for health care, including collecting health care information, encouraging healthy behaviours, and providing mobile diagnostic tests (Howitt et al. 2012). For example, in India, Operation ASHA's health workers visit community members in their homes, using mobile phones to collect information on patients with tuberculosis, receiving SMS notifications if a patient has missed a treatment. These health workers are community members who are trained on tuberculosis treatment, including recognizing symptoms, types of medication and dosing, and other critical health issues at the program's main office in New Delhi (CHMI 2012).

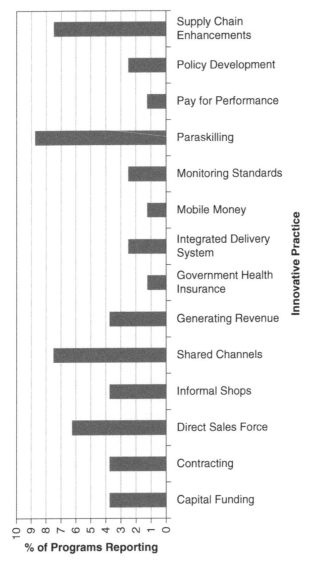

Figure 2.2 Least reported innovative practices by 80 well-documented programs

By practicing health outreach, providing health training to community members, and using mobile technologies, Operation ASHA is able to bring tuberculosis treatments to the doorsteps of 3.5 million disadvantaged slum-dwellers (CHMI 2012).

SOUTHEASTERN ASIA

Eight of the 80 programs have operations in six countries in Southeastern Asia. This includes two each in Indonesia and Vietnam, and one each in Cambodia, Thailand, the Philippines, and Burma (Myanmar).[9]

The most frequently described practices in Southeastern Asia include health awareness/education (50 per cent), social marketing (38 per cent), mHealth (38 per cent), and provider training (38 per cent).[10] This suggests that programs in this region are focusing on changing health behaviours through health education/awareness and social marketing, which is "the use of marketing to design and implement programs to promote socially beneficial behavior change" (Grier & Bryant 2005). These programs also try to ensure that health practitioners have sufficient training to provide effective services. In a majority of Southeast Asian countries, maternal mortality and morbidity is high, sexually transmitted infections are widespread, and HIV infections continue to rise in the general population (Scortino 2005). BlueStar Pilipinas is an example of a program that aims to counter these issues by incorporating social marketing, health awareness, and provider training. It operates as a family-planning social franchise in the Philippines, and provides training to licenced midwives. It also engages in a variety of social marketing and health awareness activities, including organizing mothers' parties to discuss pregnancy services and family planning, community bingo with reproductive health terms like "IUD" printed on the bingo cards, and motorcade parades with advertisements for the brand name and services (CHMI 2012). Overall, only 10 of the 29 identified innovative activities are practiced by programs in this region, although the sample size (eight) is small.

EASTERN AFRICA

Within our sample of 80 programs, there are 22 programs operating in nine West African countries. Twelve programs operate in Kenya, four in Tanzania, three in Uganda, two in Zambia, and one each in Rwanda, Mozambique, Madagascar, Malawi, and Zimbabwe.[11]

The top reported innovative practices for programs in Eastern Africa include provider training (45 per cent), mHealth (32 per cent), and franchising (27 per cent).[12] Franchising involves a contractual agreement between providers to provide services under the franchise brand and receive membership benefits, such as access to medications, training, advertising, and business loans (Prata et al. 2005, 276–7). The high frequency of provider training by these programs suggests that training laypersons to work in health care and enhancing provider skills through training may be important activities to deal with shortages in skilled labour in this region. Indeed, the WHO (2006) notes that there is an estimated shortage of over 800,000 doctors, nurses, and midwives in Sub-Saharan Africa, and an increase of almost 140 per cent is needed to correct this deficit. In addition, franchising activities appear to be an important practice in Eastern Africa. Health franchising is an attractive innovation in Africa given its utility in integrating private providers into public health programs and increasing service availability (Prata et al. 2005). For example, Living Goods is a franchise of community health promoters operating in Uganda who provide health education and sell essential health products door-to-door at affordable prices. The franchise system provides training, the use of the brand, health supplies, and capital loans (CHMI 2012). For the programs operating in Eastern Africa, 11 of the 29 identified innovative practices were not pursued.

WESTERN AFRICA

There are five programs in the 80 extracted programs that operate in Western Africa. Four programs operate in Nigeria, and one each operates in Gambia, Ghana, and Mali.[13]

Like those in Eastern Africa, the most frequently reported innovative practices of Western African programs are provider training (60 per cent) and mHealth (40 per cent). However, other frequently reported practices are microinsurance (40 per cent), health awareness (40 per cent), and health outreach (40 per cent). Microinsurance involves providing insurance to low-income populations, a group that is most exposed to financial risks, yet frequently the least protected against the consequences of adverse events (Roth et al. 2007). The pursuit of these activities suggests that programs in this region pursue strategies to encourage greater financial and geographic access to health care.[14] In Roth et al.'s (2007, ii) survey of microinsurance in the world's 100 poorest countries, they found that "microinsurance for the world's poor is growing fast, with most of its recent growth coming from the private sector." There is a significant presence of health microinsurance in poor countries, particularly those in West and Central Africa (Roth et al. 2007). In Nigeria, for example, the Hygeia Community Health Plan is offered by the private, not-for-profit organization, Hygeia Nigeria Limited, which works in partnership with the Dutch Health Insurance Fund. This plan aims to provide access to quality health care services for low-income communities, and covers basic and specialist medical services including hospitalization, antenatal care and deliveries, minor and intermediate surgeries, and HIV/AIDS management (CHMI 2012). Only 13 of the 29 identified innovative practices were being used by the five programs operating in this region.

LATIN AMERICA

There are nine programs in Latin America represented by those in the 80-program sample. This includes three operating in Mexico, Bolivia, and Brazil, two each in Paraguay and Peru, and one each in El Salvador, Guatemala, Nicaragua, Argentina, Chile, Colombia, Ecuador, and Venezuela.[15]

In this region, health outreach (56 per cent) is the most frequently pursued innovative practice. Health outreach involves physically connecting practitioners and patients through methods such as health camps and mobile clinics. The other most frequent practices are service delivery chain (33 per cent), cross-subsidization (33 per cent), social marketing (33 per cent), health awareness/education (33 per cent), franchising (33 per cent), process and product re-engineering (33 per cent), and provider training (33 per cent).[16] The highly dense urban markets and highly dispersed rural markets of poor populations represent an opportunity to innovate distribution methods; therefore, it is critical to design low-cost methods to access the poor and reach these consumers (Prahalad 2006). Marie Stopes Bolivia, a program operated by Marie Stopes International, is considered one of the most important providers of reproductive and sexual health services in Bolivia. It provides health services such as contraceptives and family planning counselling to 100,000 clients in six medical centres located in Bolivia's major cities. For those with difficulty accessing these clinics, it also operates five mobile units that visit rural and remote semi-urban areas in over 100 municipalities, serving an additional 12,000 clients through these activities (CHMI 2012). Only 12 of 29 identified innovative activities are practiced by programs in this region.

Innovative Practices by Health Areas

The 80 programs provide care in 14 health areas. The most frequently reported health area is general primary care, practised by 36 per cent of programs, followed by family planning and reproductive health, practised by 29 per cent of programs, and maternal and child health,[17] by 22.5 per cent of programs. Rehabilitative care (1 per cent), chronic diseases (3 per cent), and dentistry (3 per cent) are the lowest reported health areas of those reported in this 80-program sample (figure 2.3).

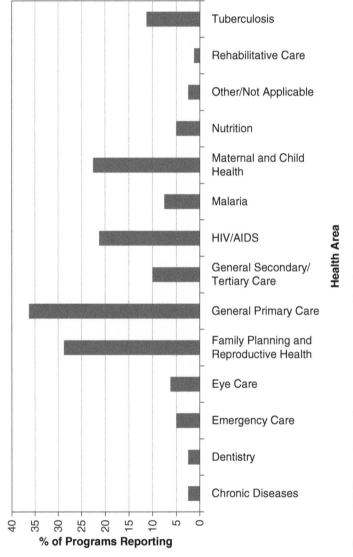

Figure 2.3 Percentage of programs engaged by health area

GENERAL PRIMARY CARE

The most frequently pursued innovative practice for general primary care programs is mHealth, practiced by 55 per cent of programs. This is followed by health outreach (34 per cent), provider training (28 per cent), health awareness/ education (28 per cent), microinsurance (24 per cent), service delivery network (24 per cent), and process or product re-engineering (24 per cent) (figure 2.4). Since primary care provides a range of services that the general population needs, these programs focus on making care widely available, which includes providing access to trained health practitioners and employing mobile technologies to efficiently connect with patients. CARE Hospitals is an example of a primary care program employing a number of these innovative practices. CARE is one of the fastest growing hospital chains in India, providing general primary care as well as tertiary health care services through its primary health clinics and hospitals. It also trains community members to become Village Health Champions (VHCs) who collect data, refer patients, and provide basic care and health education within communities, using point-of-care diagnostics and robust technology platforms to provide VHCs with access to health information, health care personnel, and guidance on medical evaluation through pre-developed algorithms (Kumar 2011). By combining mHealth, health outreach, provider training, and process re-engineering, CARE Hospitals provide accessible and cost-effective general primary care to poor populations in India.

FAMILY PLANNING AND REPRODUCTIVE HEALTH

Programs practising family planning and reproductive health engage in 20 different innovative practices, the most frequent of which are franchising (57 per cent), provider training (48 per cent), social marketing (43 per cent), and health awareness/education (43 per cent) (figure 2.5). Family planning and reproductive health programs have a wide customer base, and connecting dispersed providers through franchising is a way to increase geographic access. Programs in this area also need to overcome stigma related to seeking advice on and engaging in safe reproductive health practices. To counter this, countries like Zambia are implementing HIV/AID prevention programs, and most use social marketing and health education through mass media and interpersonal communication campaigns to encourage contraceptive use and safer sexual behaviour (Van Rossem & Meekers 2007). Population and Community Development Association (PDA) in Thailand, for example, operates family-planning clinics in Thailand, in addition to engaging in social marketing campaigns that aim to change sexual behaviour norms, particularly those of people involved in the sex industry and young people, as well as the general public. They put on events like "Condom Nights," "Miss Anti-AIDS Beauty

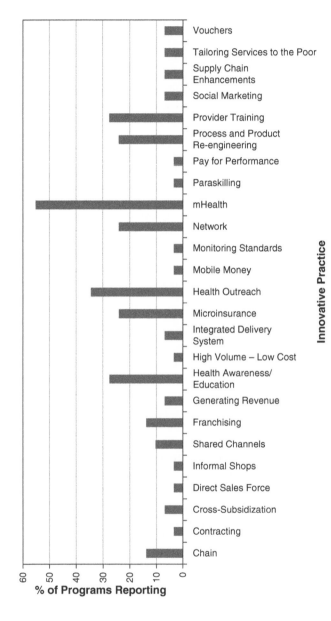

Figure 2.4 Percentage of innovative practices in general primary care

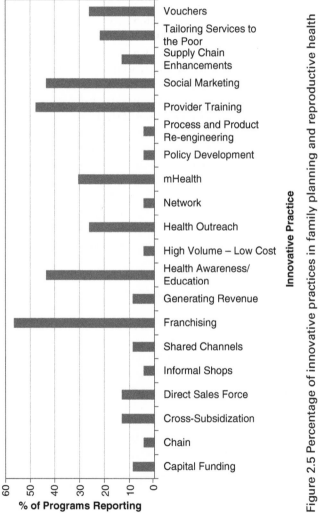

Figure 2.5 Percentage of innovative practices in family planning and reproductive health

Pageants," and vasectomy festivals, using the media coverage to reach populations that may not otherwise be reached (Melnick 2007).

MATERNAL AND CHILD HEALTH

In maternal and child health programs, we found that health awareness/education (44 per cent), health outreach (39 per cent), provider training (33 per cent), mHealth (28 per cent), and franchising (28 per cent) are the most frequently reported innovative practices (figure 2.6). Women often have difficulty accessing health services during pregnancy and labour, and 60 million women – more than half of the world's mothers – give birth without a skilled attendant every year (Lawn et al. 2006). As a result, many of the programs in this area engage in health outreach as a means of providing care to those in remote and difficult-to-reach areas, as well as providing necessary training to birth attendants. They also provide health awareness and education on child and maternal health to encourage healthy behaviours for these often underserved and marginalized populations. One Heart World-Wide is a program operating in Mexico, China, and Nepal that trains community members, health care providers, and outreach workers in obstetrics and neonatal care, and operates in remote communities to assist local women and infants who may not have been able to access care due to limited personal resources, sociocultural barriers, or remote living conditions (One Heart World-Wide 2012). This program provides culturally sensitive training and raises awareness with the goal of increasing the number of births attended by a skilled birth attendant, ultimately aiming to save the lives of women and children in need (CHMI 2012).

Notable Innovative Practice Clusters

In our analysis of the innovative practices carried out by CHMI programs, we found a number of interesting groupings pursued by a variety of programs in different contexts and health areas. Many programs (67.5 per cent) engage in at least three innovative practices. Often, these practices are combined in mutually reinforcing ways to address the particular health barriers these programs aim to overcome, including poverty, lack of awareness, difficult-to-reach locations, and low population density. Sustainable and disruptive innovations involve incorporating innovative practices across multiple aspects of an organization (Ojha et al. 2011). Monitor's Ten Types of Innovation Framework describes ten different ways organizations innovate (Ojha et al. 2011). This includes innovations in finance (the business model and networking), process (enabling process and core process), offering (product performance, product system, and

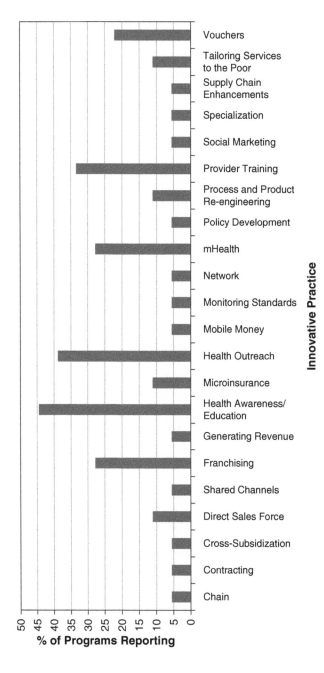

Figure 2.6 Percentage of innovative practices in maternal and child health

service), and delivery (channel, brand, and customer experience) (Ojha et al. 2011). In this section, we consider how programs engage in three notable clusters of innovative practices, and how these align with Monitor's Ten Types of Innovation Framework. We define a cluster as three or more organizations using the same combination of three or more practices, and highlight how they have been combined to provide affordable and accessible health care to the poor.

CLUSTER ONE: SOCIAL MARKETING, VOUCHERS, AND SOCIAL FRANCHISING

This cluster of innovative practices includes social marketing, vouchers, and social franchising, a combination of activities practiced by Greenstar Social Marketing Pakistan (GSMP), DKT Mozambique, and Top Reseau. Social marketing involves the systematic application of marketing techniques to achieve behavioural change for a social good. Vouchers are certificates distributed to a targeted population for free or subsidized health goods and/or services. Social franchising adopts principles of franchising to programs and initiatives that aim to generate social change (McBride & Ahmed 2001), grouping existing providers under a franchised brand (Montagu 2002). The franchisees must comply with a set of requirements, including the provision of certain socially beneficial services, meeting quality and pricing standards, and payment of fixed or profit-share franchisee fees. Providers in a franchise network are able to take advantage of several incentives, including training, branding and brand advertising, subsidized or proprietary supplies and equipment, ongoing support services, and access to other professionals in the same field (Social Franchising for Health 2016). This cluster of practices involves finance and delivery innovations described by Ojha et al. (2011), such as networking, brand, and channel innovations. We'll now further explore the models of GSMP and DKT Mozambique.

Greenstar Social Marketing Pakistan (GSMP). Pakistan has a high birth rate, and significant financial barriers to accessing reproductive health services, social taboos, and women's limited autonomy in decision-making hinder access to family-planning methods (Hardee & Leahy 2008). The GSMP program aims to overcome these barriers by using vouchers to target poor women and social marketing to counter taboos. It delivers affordable and integrated family planning and reproductive health services, as well as maternal and child health and tuberculosis care to low-income clients nationwide. GSMP began its effort by using social marketing to increase the use of contraceptives in Pakistan. However, it realized that social marketing is better suited for delivering reproductive health products when product information can be disseminated through educational material and advertising campaigns, and when a client does not need a service provider for guidance or to administer a method (McBride &

Ahmed 2001). Promoting the use of family-planning methods such as long-term contraceptives, injectables, and IUDs necessitated a skilled provider. The GSMP program was thus designed to incorporate social franchising to involve health care providers.

GSMP operates a franchise network of over 7,500 private independent health care providers. Partnerships are formed between the franchiser (Social Marketing Pakistan, or SMP) and selected providers (the franchisees) with the agreement that these providers will integrate a defined package of reproductive health services and deliver those services according to quality standards established by SMP. GSMP also provides demand-side vouchers that subsidize the costs of a package of reproductive health care services. Specifically, the franchise offers vouchers for maternal health (deliveries, ANC, PNC) and family-planning services (CHMI 2012). Poor women buy vouchers at a highly subsidized price, which entitles them to family planning and reproductive services from private providers in the social franchise managed by the GSMP network (Bashir et al. 2010). The vouchers help improve poor women's access to, and utilization of, family planning and reproductive services.

DKT Mozambique. Like GMSP, DKT Mozambique provides family planning and reproductive health services, but it has a focus on HIV/AIDS prevention. DKT Mozambique's Contraceptive Social Marketing program seeks to provide safe and affordable options for family planning and HIV prevention. Given that contraceptive prevalence in Mozambique is very low at 12 per cent, and only 60 per cent of women have knowledge of any method of family planning, social marketing is employed to increase awareness and encourage safe reproductive health activities. Another barrier to the treatment of HIV/AIDS in Mozambique is lack of access to family-planning methods for women. In response, DKT Mozambique launched a social franchising program that provides condoms, oral contraceptives, IUDs, implants, and misoprostol in nine clinics. The program is branded under the label Intimo and uses social media to increase access to its clinics. The program also contracts out with existing clinics to provide family-planning services. While vouchers are an established approach for GSMP, DKT Mozambique is currently in the process of initiating the use of coupons and voucher systems to improve poor womens' access to contraceptives (CHMI 2012; DKT International 2012).

Cluster Effect: Strengthening Access and Affordability. All three mechanisms – social marketing, social franchising, and vouchers – work together to strengthen access and affordability of health care services. By using social marketing, GSMP was able to combat the stigma associated with family planning and reproductive health issues, and increase the perceived value of such services in Pakistan. Employing a social franchising approach enables the two programs to increase the quantity of providers and health care services offered, and, as result, improve access. This approach also allows the programs to provide services at an equal or lower cost compared to other delivery options, thereby increasing cost-effectiveness. Costs containment is facilitated through bulk purchasing, which helps lower costs of drugs and supplies. Furthermore, franchising enables programs to reach out to underserved and widely dispersed populations. It also facilitates the integration of providers into a referral network. The Greenstar hub, for example, connects all the providers within a district to a referral network, which allows for a broader choice of reproductive health services to clients (McBride & Ahmed 2001). A referral system links the different levels of service providers and helps ensure that clients in need of more specialized interventions, such as IUDs or surgical contraception, are directed to the appropriate service delivery point.

Moreover, family planning and reproductive health concerns a significant portion of the population, and it is a relatively low-cost health service with limited skill required, making it possible to train and maintain many dispersed providers through the franchise model. This allows both GSMP and DKT Mozambique to take advantage of a growing channel for delivering family planning and reproductive health products and services. In doing so, both programs are demonstrating that health products and services can be delivered cost-effectively at increasing scale.

The use of vouchers helps target poor populations that may be unwilling or unable to pay for health services, and is one means of ensuring low-income groups are able to access such services. The voucher is either heavily subsidized or free. This ensures the poor do not have pay out of pocket or bear the total cost burden of health care services. While DKT Mozambique is still in the process of implementing a voucher scheme, GSMP has already been using vouchers in its goals to reduce financial barriers to care among the poor. The vouchers have aided poor clients in Pakistan to obtain family-planning health care in low-resource settings, and increased the utilization of family planning and reproductive health services.

Through their separate programs, GSMP and DKT Mozambique have combined social marketing, vouchers, and franchising in a synergistic manner to improve access, cost-effectiveness, quality, and equity. These three mechanisms help to increase the number of service delivery providers and health care services offered, provide services at an equal or lower cost compared to other service delivery options, provide services that adhere to quality standards, and strengthen equity by serving low-income population groups.

CLUSTER TWO: MICROINSURANCE, MHEALTH, AND SERVICE DELIVERY NETWORK
Sampled programs implementing innovative practices in microinsurance, mHealth, and membership in a service delivery network are able to improve availability and affordability of their services. These programs are Arogya Raksha Yojana (ARY), Karuna Trust, Pesinet, and CARE Rural Health Mission.

Microinsurance refers to insurance products that offer financial protection to low-income individuals. These products are tailored specifically for individuals who have little savings and offers compensation for illness, injury, or death. Low-income individuals enrolled in microinsurance plans are expected to pay regular monetary payments (premiums) that are risk-adjusted. Risk pooling under microinsurance allows many individuals or groups to pool risks and redistribute the costs of the risky events within the pool, eliminating significant variability in health costs (CGAP, 2012). mHealth refers to mobile-enabled business models that aim to leverage low-income ownership or use mobile devices to reduce program administrative burdens, or increase access by soliciting and providing essential information or transactions to low-income customers. A network refers to a group of providers that are loosely joined to deliver services to specific population groups. Each provider is a separate entity and retains its own branding. Membership in the network may entitle the provider to payments, patient volume, central services, or training. This cluster of practices aligns with several finance, process, and delivery innovations described by Ojha et al. (2011), including networking, enabling process, core process, channel, and brand. We'll now further explore the models of ARY and Pesinet.

Arogya Raksha Yojana (ARY). Natural disasters can exacerbate poverty and lead to worsening conditions among the rural poor. ARY is a program that aims to reduce the severity of poverty resulting from health-related catastrophes in rural India through a comprehensive health insurance plan that offers people affordable access to high-quality health care. Enrolees contribute a regular monthly fee that eliminates most cost variability, thus reducing the cost for those who could be forced into poverty through catastrophic medical expenses. By pooling risks upfront, ARY can provide affordable health care to members through its network of nine clinics and thirty-five hospitals, which provides them access to over 1,600 surgeries without having to pay out of pocket, and subsidize hospitalization not requiring surgery. The clinics are located in more remote regions for those unable to visit hospitals for minor ailments. With high numbers of enrolees, ARY is able to provide affordable health care while its network hospitals and clinics remain financially viable. While anyone can seek health care services at ARY clinics, only those who are ARY members are eligible for free outpatient services.

In addition, ARY uses mobile technology, specifically mobile phones, to manage its enrolment system. Details of each customer are entered on the mobile phone, and the member's photograph is captured on the phone. This data is sent directly from the mobile phone to the insurance company's server. While urban areas are attractive for insurance programs since administrative costs are lower due to bulk business from corporations, ARY is able to use mobile phones to increase efficiency and reduce administrative burden, which includes decreasing data entry errors and time between enrolment and delivery of cards to customers (CHMI 2012).

Pesinet. Mali is one of the poorest countries in the world and has one of the highest maternal mortality rates (Fournier, Dumont, Tourigny, Dunkley, & Dramé 2009). Many pregnant women and children die from benign illnesses that could easily be treated with locally available medical resources; however, barriers such as cultural, financial, and geographical reasons prevent people from visiting doctors in a timely manner. As a result, untreated diseases become complicated and difficult to treat, and local health structures are underused and experience economic difficulties. Pesinet, a not-for-profit organization, aims to overcome these barriers by implementing a program that uses mobile phones to deliver health care services to women and children in Mali's capital of Bamako. These services include regular home-based health monitoring, health insurance, education, and prevention, practices that are combined to provide early detection of disease and affordable access to health providers (CHMI 2012).

Pesinet maintains a network of existing primary health centres to provide its services, which involve the use of simple mobile technologies as well as the work of agents in the communities to enable remote monitoring by the local doctor. Health care agents directly visit the homes of children enrolled in the program so that families do not have to travel to a health care centre. Pesinet agents make home visits on a weekly basis to increase the chances of early detection of illnesses. An online application linked to a database allows for remote monitoring of health data by the local doctor, activity management, and tracking of key impact indicators. The system's early detection of disease creates an incentive for families to seek medical care, and primary health centres in Pesinet's network view this as a solution to their endemic underuse and helpful for securing their revenues. In addition, families pay approximately one euro a month to enrol in the service, which acts as microinsurance. The fee covers many services, including health care agent's visits, doctor's visits, remote consultations by doctors, and covers half the price of children's medication (CHMI 2012).

Cluster Effect: Improving Availability and Affordability. By using mobile phones, ARY and Pesinet can serve a large number of low-income individuals needing access to health care. ARY uses mobile phones as a management tool to keep track of its enrolees. Similarly, Pesinet uses mobile technology to both record and transfer health information and reduce the amount of time a doctor needs to access and analyse it (Pesinet 2012). The use of mobile technology is a means of decreasing administrative burden and improving the capacity of health systems in India and Mali to provide quality health care, while the use of microinsurance has made accessing these services more affordable for patients. Both ARY and Pesinet also employ networks of health care facilities to increase their outreach and provide their services to more communities.

These programs combine components of microinsurance, mHealth, and networks into their businesses to deliver both affordable and easily available services to their patients. Members benefit from the spread of risk and mobile technology that simplifies and eases interactions with programs, resulting in viable health care services that benefit both the patient and program.

CLUSTER THREE: HIGH-VOLUME LOW-COST, SPECIALIZATION, CROSS-SUBSIDIZATION, HEALTH OUTREACH, PRODUCT AND PROCESS RE-ENGINEERING, AND PARASKILLING

Another notable cluster of innovative practices involves a high-volume, low-cost approach, along with cross-subsidization, specialization of activities, health outreach, process and product re-engineering, and paraskilling. This cluster of practices tends to be employed by programs with a narrow health focus and a prominent use of procedure-based care like surgery. With regard to the high-volume, low-cost approach, Prahalad (2006, 28–30) notes that organizations like Aravind are able to be profitable with low margins per unit by serving large volumes of clients, resulting in the creation of economic value in a new way. This is often accomplished through specialization, which involves focusing on a narrow set of activities within a disease area. For example, Narayana Hrudayalaya allows individual doctors to specialize by focusing on one or two cardiac surgeries, which has led to improved quality of care (Bhattacharyya et al. 2010). Cross-subsidization involves achieving financial stability through charging higher rates for wealthier patients, who are more willing and able to pay for services, which offsets the costs of serving poorer patients (Bhattacharyya et al. 2010). As noted previously, poor populations in highly dispersed rural areas and dense urban markets present challenges to accessing this group, and it is essential to find low-cost approaches to reaching the poor (Prahalad 2006). Health outreach involves engaging with more clients by delivering services to remote populations using modes of transportation or providing infrastructure, such as the health camps and telemedicine internet kiosks Aravind provides in remote villages. Process or product re-engineering entails altering a process or product in a way that improves the efficiency, quality, and/or costs of a service or product for clients (CHMI 2012). For example, Aravind engages in this innovative activity by re-engineering operating rooms to allow eye surgeons to operate on two tables in alternation (Bhattacharyya et al. 2010). Aravind also engages in paraskilling, where surgeons are able to focus on diagnosis and operations, since other clinical processes in the operating room have been standardized so that staff with fewer specialized skills can perform them. This cluster of practices emphasizes providing affordable and accessible specialized care, and can be described as involving several finance, process, and delivery innovations outlined by Ojha et al. (2011), including business model, enabling process, channel, and brand. To understand how different programs combine these innovative practices, two programs are explored: SalaUno Salud and Sadguru Netra Chikitsalaya.

SalaUno Salud. SalaUno Salud is an eye clinic that has operated in Mexico since 2002, providing prescription glasses and surgeries for cataracts, photocoagulation laser for diabetic retinopathy, glaucoma treatment, and corneal transplants. SalaUno Salud specializes by focusing on cataract surgeries, and it has a high-volume, low-cost approach by taking advantage of economies of scale. As a result, it performs five times more surgeries per week than those carried out by the average doctor in Mexico, and cataract surgery prices are one-third the regular market price offered by other competitors; SalaUno Salud charges US$550 compared to the US$1,650 average market price. This is possible with process re-engineering through introducing small-incision cataract surgeries to Mexico, an approach that is less expensive and requires fewer post-operative visits for patients than traditional methods (Gogate et al. 2003). SalaUno Salud also seeks to provide affordable care by practicing cross-subsidization. It uses its profits from patients that pay full price to offset the costs of offering a subsidized price to an NGO partner that provides cataract surgeries to patients in extreme poverty. As a result, 64 per cent of cataract surgeries have been free of cost to these patients. SalaUno Salud also partners with a local cinema to provide 100 free surgeries per month to those unable to pay, offsetting the expenses with their income from those who are willing and able to pay for services. Furthermore, this program engages in health outreach, and it conducts weekend campaigns, where teams are sent to villages to offer free screenings for eye problems, clinic referrals, and inexpensive lenses. In addition to its clinic in Mexico City, SalaUno Salud is in the process of expanding by opening a number of satellite clinics as part of its service delivery chain (CHMI 2012). Engaging in health outreach and developing a service delivery chain helps SalaUno Salud reach more patients, which is vital for its high-volume, low-cost approach. Specialization ensures that the quality of treatments remains high despite focusing on efficiency and low costs.

Sadguru Netra Chikitsalaya. Sadguru Netra Chikitsalaya (SNC) is a rural hospital in India founded in 2000 that also focuses on performing eye surgeries (CHMI 2012; Kumar 2011). Unlike SalaUno Salud, which is situated in a larger urban centre, SNC is located in a remote area of India called Chitrakoot. Despite this location, it conducts over 100,000 eye surgeries a year (Kumar 2011). While SNC has added a range of health care services over time, its main clinical focus and specialty is comprehensive eye care and, more specifically, cataract surgeries, cornea replacement, vitreo/retina treatment, and occuloplasty. It engages in a high-volume, low-cost approach, performing 250–300 surgeries daily compared to 3–5 in a government hospital, and 40–50 refractions per day by an optometrist compared to an average of 15–20 in the public sector. Through these high volumes they are able to charge less, with cataract surgeries costing US$33 for middle-class patients versus US$50–60 for this surgery in larger cities (CHMI 2012). In order to perform this high volume of surgeries, SNC practices process re-engineering. This involves surgeons working on two tables in the operating room so that nurses and paramedical staff prepare the next patient while a surgery is being performed. As a result SNC can perform a cataract surgery in one-third of the standard industry time. This process also involves paraskilling and training of lay health workers, where SNC recruits local youth and trains them as ophthalmic assistants. By having these assistants perform other tasks, such as vision checking, tension tests, refraction, and blood pressure evaluation, surgeons can focus on core clinical activities and increase their productivity (Kumar 2011).

Cluster Effect: Operational Efficiency with a Narrow Clinical Focus. Both SNC and SalaUno Salud specialize in providing eye surgeries, which entails engaging in a narrow clinical focus. This approach allows for greater predictability of health problems and treatments, such that processes can be standardized and staff with less specialized training can carry out more tasks. Indeed, both programs use workers with less formal training for most clinical activities, allowing surgeons to focus on performing the operations. This approach of specialization, standardization, and paraskilling increases efficiency and productivity, reduces costs, and can improve quality (Bhattacharyya et al. 2010).

Ensuring there are enough clients who can financially and physically access the services is crucial. Both SalaUno Salud and SNC engage in cross-subsidization as one method to provide more affordable care. However, SNC's approach is to provide separate clinics for paying and non-paying patients, the former involving more peripherals, such as furnished rooms and no queues. The free surgeries are supplemented by those paying for surgeries. Like SalaUno Salud, SNC's cross-subsidization is also supported by a third party, although in SNC's case, this is not a local business or an NGO, but a government entity, the National Program for Control of Blindness. However, similar to SalaUno Salud, SNC engages in health outreach through its outreach camps in rural areas, which are also supported by state government and some private sector donors. These free eye camps involve doctors and ophthalmic assistants screening patients for common eye ailments, and referring those requiring further treatment to the SNC hospital. These approaches allow SNC and SalaUno Salud to serve more people who might otherwise not be able to afford and access eye surgery services, which is important for their ability to maintain high volumes.

Discussion

To identify effective models for improving the health of the poor, we need to understand the innovative practices used by high-performing organizations. We have defined and analysed innovative practices carried out by 80 well-documented health programs in LMICs and identified a number of interesting trends. Our findings suggest that reaching the poor who are often located in remote and difficult-to-reach locations is a priority for these programs, and they use health outreach to improve physical access. Ensuring that skilled practitioners are available is also important, and programs are addressing shortages of skilled labour in impoverished areas by training community members as health providers. As well, the growing accessibility of mobile technologies in LMICs has resulted in many health programs using mobile phones to connect with clients who may have been difficult to reach otherwise using a medium that is increasingly affordable and being adapted to a variety of health purposes. We also found that health awareness and education, and social marketing have emerged as important innovative practices for programs in Southeastern Asia and for programs focused on family planning and reproductive health. In addition, franchising appears to be a prominent innovative practice for programs in the field of maternal and child health, family planning and reproductive health, and those operating in East Africa. Microinsurance appears to be an important emerging innovative practice in West Africa. These findings suggest a number of interesting trends and areas that can be followed up for more in-depth analysis in the future.

Finally, our research also found that some programs are practicing similar clusters or combinations of innovative practices as part of their strategies. We described three notable innovative practice clusters, exploring how different programs combine these practices in similar and distinctive ways to serve poor populations. This is a promising area of future study, since it will be instructive to understand how certain innovative practices tend to be combined in particular contexts and health areas, and how these combinations shape their performance in terms of effectively and efficiently impacting the health of the poor.

It should be noted, however, that a limitation to this research and future studies is the limited data available on health programs. The publicly available data on the programs in our 80-program subset varies widely in terms of quality and quantity, and more detailed information is needed on the specific operational processes and practices of these programs, as well as their performance. CHMI's efforts to obtain additional quality data through its Reported Results initiative are an important advancement in this area. Yet in order to engage in a robust analysis of health programs, their innovative practices, and their performance, access to more complete, precise and detailed data from dependable sources is required.

Conclusion

Health programs in LMICs are pursuing a variety of innovative practices in their strategic approaches to better meet the needs of the poor and improve the health of this population. By analysing the innovative practices carried out by these programs, we found that some practices were more prominent in certain regions and health areas, and that health outreach, mHealth, and provider training were the most commonly pursued innovative practices. We also found that some programs are practicing similar clusters of innovative practices as part of their program strategies to provide accessible and affordable quality health care. Our findings point to a number of promising areas of future research, including a more in-depth exploration of the innovative practices pursued in specific health areas and geographic contexts, as well as further study of innovative practice clusters. This can involve considering how these practices are combined in productive ways in certain health areas and their impact on the health of poor populations.

Appendix A

Table 2.A1 List of innovative practices

Innovative Practice	Example	Source
Marketing Practices[18]		
Social Marketing: The application of marketing techniques to achieve behavioural changes. The focus is on achieving specific behavioural goals with specific audiences in relation to different topics relevant to a social good, i.e. health. The goal is to make potentially difficult and long-term behavioural change in target populations.	PDA has used Condom Nights and peer education programs that focus on behaviour change. PSI has campaigned for safe sexual behaviour through magazines, television spots, and radio drama.	Bhattacharyya et al. (2010); CHMI (2012)
Tailoring Services to the Poor: A marketing tool that involves tailoring how products and services are provided to meet the needs of the poor. It involves accommodating the needs of the poor, making them accessible and attractive. It can include indirectly making the treatment more affordable, but does not refer to a decreased price for the service/treatment itself.	BMVSS of Jaipur Foot allows patients to check in at any time, and provides free room and board, and free meals. Also, fittings are completed in one session.	Bhattacharyya et al. (2010)
Vouchers: A demand-side approach involving subsidized coupons and discounts distributed to a target population that can be used to purchase health services and products from approved providers.	Greenstar provides demand-side vouchers that subsidize the costs of a package of reproductive health care services.	CHMI (2012)

(Continued)

Table 2.A1 Continued

Innovative Practice	Example	Source
Mobile Money: Models that enable the poor to access and transfer cash outside of traditional financial services channels, often via mobile devices or alternatives to bank branch infrastructure.	Changamka helps the poor in Kenya better access health facilities by issuing Smart Cards, which allow them to slowly but steadily save money that can then be put towards visits to the doctor, medicine, and more.	Monitor Group (Kubzansky et al. 2011)
Microinsurance: Small-size insurance products designed to meet the needs and cash flow of those often excluded from formal insurance networks.	Families see their health spending decrease thanks to the regular health monitoring and microinsurance scheme provided by Pesinet.	Monitor Group (Kubzansky et al. 2011); CHMI (2012)
Franchising: A group of providers operating under the same brand. Outlets are operator-owned and services are standardized by a central franchisor.	Greenstar operates a franchise network of over 7500 private independent health care providers, signing franchising agreements with them and investing in developing a strong brand.	Bhattacharyya et al. (2010); CHMI (2012)
Health Awareness/Education: Programs that create social awareness and educate the public about specific health topics such as disease prevention and treatment, healthy behaviours, correct use of pharmaceuticals, etc.	With the Learning about Living program, three teachers per school are invited to take part in training about participatory teaching methods and sexual and reproductive health information for teenagers. They use this training to educate their students on reproductive health issues.	CHMI (2012)

Financial Practices (internal)

High Volume, Low Unit Costs: Programs describe themselves as high-volume, low-cost, or keeping costs low through high asset utilization.	BlueStar Healthcare Network is a social franchising strategy to improve access to quality sexual and reproductive health services through existing private providers. BlueStar has a mission to serve low-income women, and is committed to a strategy of lower-cost, higher-volume services.	Bhattacharyya et al. (2010); Monitor Group (Kubzansky et al. 2011); CHMI (2012)

(Continued)

Table 2.A1 Continued

Innovative Practice	Example	Source
Specialization: Focusing on a narrow scope of health offerings in a health focus area. (Note: often combined with high volume, low cost)	Narayana Hrudayalaya doctors specialize on one or two types of cardiac surgeries.	Monitor Group (Kubzansky et al. 2011)
Cross-Subsidization: Achieving financial sustainability through a cross-subsidization strategy, where a program exploits the greater willingness and ability to pay among the wealthier patients to subsidize expensive services for lower-income patients.	Paying customers of Dentista Do Bem indirectly subsidize the cost of caring for poorer patients at private, for-profit clinics.	Bhattacharyya et al. (2010); CHMI (2012)
Capital Funding: Involves providing capital funding for franchisees or service providers to start up or improve the quality of their health programs.	KMET provides microfinance loans to its franchisees.	Bhattacharyya et al. (2010)
Generating Revenue: Engaging in other market activities to generate revenue for the health program.	PDA has developed 16 for-profit companies that are mandated to put funds towards NGO activities.	Bhattacharyya et al. (2010)
Contracting: Programs where a government entity selects and pays one or several providers to deliver specific health services to specific populations.	Dial 108 Emergency is an emergency transport and response model that is delivered through a public private partnership with state governments and is provided either free or through user fees as mandated by the contract with the participating state government.	CHMI (2012)
Operating Practices		
Optimizing Human Resources: Organizations have trained lay health workers to work in new areas. They help less-skilled people acquire skills that were previously exclusive to trained professionals. This also involves training health professionals to provide higher quality care.	Aravind trains high school graduates from rural areas into paramedical staff like optical technicians. KMET trains existing health workers to enhance the quality of reproductive health care given by this group.	Bhattacharyya et al. (2010); Monitor Group (Kubzansky et al. 2011); CHMI (2012)

(Continued)

Table 2.A1 Continued

Innovative Practice	Example	Source
Process and Product Re-engineering: Altering a product or process in a way that improves the quality or efficiency of a service or product.	Sadguru Netra Chikitsalaya has re-engineered their operating rooms to allow surgeons to work on two tables in alternation; VisionSpring offers a new adjustable lens.	Bhattacharyya et al. (2010); CHMI (2012)
Paraskilling: Re-engineering complex systems into simplified tasks that can be performed by a larger, lower-skilled workforce.	To lower workforce costs, Aravind's doctors focus on diagnosis and surgery, while nurses perform tasks in the operating room that do not require a surgeon's skill.	Bhattacharyya et al. (2010); Monitor Group (Kubzansky et al. 2011); CHMI (2012)
mHealth: Mobile-enabled business models that aim to leverage low-income ownership or use of mobile devices to provide essential information or transactions to low-income customers.	The SMS for Life initiative uses a combination of mobile phones, SMS messages, and electronic mapping technology to generate information on stock availability of Artemisinin-Based Combination Therapy.	Monitor Group (Kubzansky et al. 2011); CHMI (2012)
Health Outreach: Activities to engage with more clients that involve providing mobile services. This involves practitioners physically going to see and provide services to patients or providing the physical tools/infrastructure for patients to access practitioners.	Aravind provides health camps to reach patients in rural areas. It also has internet kiosks in remote villages where pictures can be taken and sent to a doctor, who can also talk to the patient online.	Bhattacharyya et al. (2010); CHMI (2012)
Distribution through Dedicated Direct Sales Force: Recruiting local agents to sell and distribute products, bypassing shops and other channels to make it easier for the poor to have access they may otherwise not get.	Living Goods is an "Avon-like" network of franchised community health promoters who provide health education and earn a living selling essential health products door-to-door at prices affordable to the poor.	Monitor Group (Kubzansky et al. 2011)

(Continued)

Table 2.A1 Continued

Innovative Practice	Example	Source
Distribution through Improved Informal Channels and Shops: Using and upgrading existing informal distribution and sales channels to sell through multiple fragmented and unorganized shops.	World Health Partners uses SkyMeds/WHP-Approved Shops that provide low-cost, high-quality medicines for patients.	Monitor Group (Kubzansky et al. 2011)
Distribution through Shared Channels: Using shared channels and existing customer sales and distribution platforms to reach remote markets.	World Health Partners uses existing diagnostic laboratories to process its patients' lab tests.	Monitor Group (Kubzansky et al. 2011)
Network: A group of providers that are loosely joined to deliver services to specific population groups. Each provider is a separate entity and retains its own branding. Membership in the network may entitle the provider to payments, patient volume, central services, or training.	CARE Rural Health Mission has a delivery network that includes village health champions, primary health centres, and hospitals.	CHMI (2012)
Supply Chain Enhancements: Programs that reduce costs and improve the efficiency of supply chains that move medical products from manufacturer to retailer.	The RedPlan Salud business model is unique, providing its network of midwives with brand-name, reduced-priced products, which are obtained through negotiated volume discounts from four major pharmaceutical companies.	CHMI (2012)
Policy Development/Other Policy or Regulation: Programs and policies that incentivize quality and provide consumer protection by standardizing medical and institutional practices, regulating insurance packages and coverage, placing limitations on marketing, etc. It includes efforts to shape government policy regarding health care.	PATH is reprioritizing diarrhoeal diseases within the Vietnamese government by supporting the updating and strengthening of national diarrhoeal disease control policies and clinical management guidelines.	CHMI (2012)

(Continued)

Table 2.A1 Concluded

Innovative Practice	Example	Source
Service Delivery Chain: A group of providers that operates under the same brand, but where operators are paid employees of a sponsoring organization.	CARE is one of the fastest-growing hospital chains in India, currently operating 13 facilities.	CHMI (2012)
Integrated Delivery System: An organization that delivers a full continuum of care (prevention, primary care, secondary care, tertiary care, ancillary services, etc.) Some integrated models also incorporate financing by collecting prepaid premiums to cover the cost of care for members.	OTTET's Telemedicine network is an integrated health care service delivery model that has been established as a need-based communitycentric approach to promote and provide preventive health care and disease management services.	CHMI (2012)
Government Health Insurance: A health insurance scheme sponsored by government that pools resources, spreads risk across a broad population, and expands coverage.	RSBY is a state-managed national health insurance program designed to improve access to quality medical care for informal workers living below the poverty line in India.	CHMI (2012)
Monitoring Standards: Programs and policies that give credentials to select providers based on having met certain quality, structural, and managerial standards. Also, any program that mandates specific clinical practice guidelines, and/or monitors providers over time to ensure quality.	Initiative on Primary Healthcare has implemented policies and practices to ensure smooth and effective management of primary health care facilities for efficient delivery of all associated services.	CHMI (2012)
Pay for Performance: Programs or policies that incentivize quality by rewarding providers financially for meeting pre-established targets for the delivery of health care services.	Initiative on Primary Healthcare's goal was to drastically reorganize the system by employing innovative management techniques and performance-based incentives.	CHMI (2012)

Appendix B

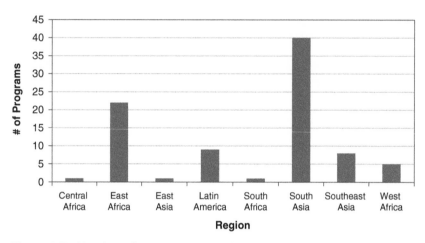

Figure 2.B1 Number of programs by region

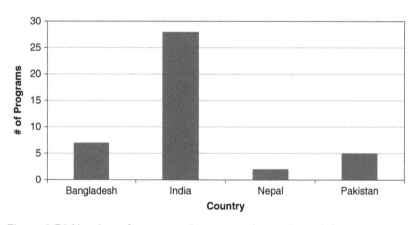

Figure 2.B2 Number of programs by country in southern Asia

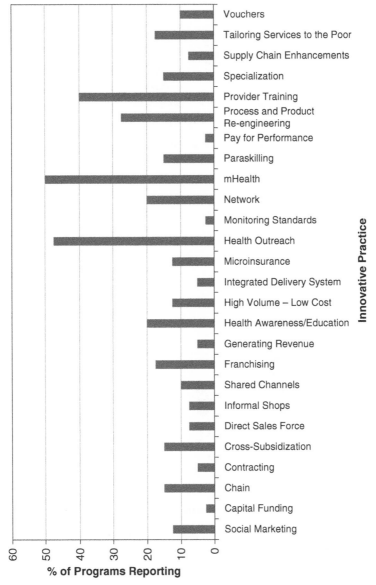

Figure 2.B3 Percentage of innovative practices pursued by programs in southern Asia

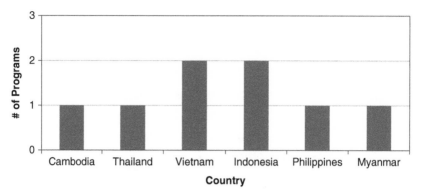

Figure 2.B4 Number of programs by country in southeastern Asia

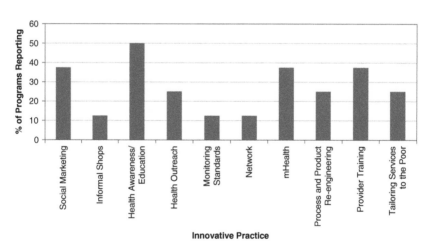

Figure 2.B5 Percentage of innovative practices pursued by programs in southeastern Asia

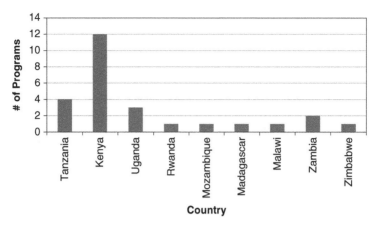

Figure 2.B6 Number of programs by country in eastern Africa

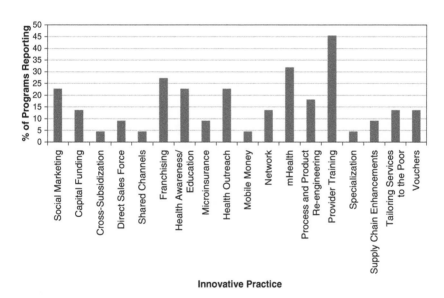

Figure 2.B7 Percentage of innovative practices pursued by programs in eastern Africa

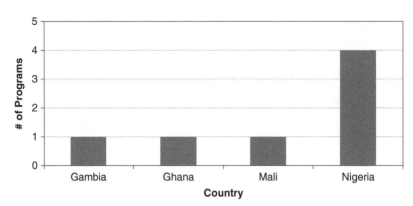

Figure 2.B8 Number of programs by country in western Africa

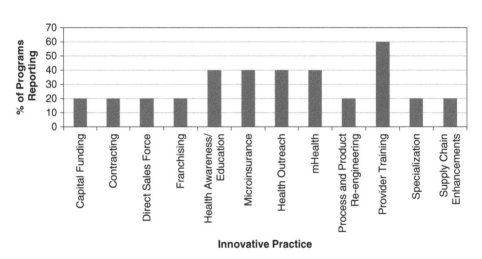

Figure 2.B9 Percentage of innovative practices pursued by programs in western Africa

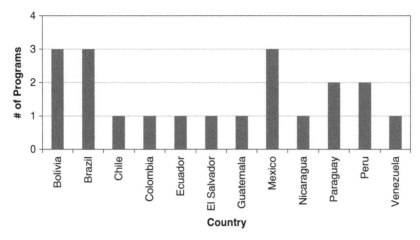

Figure 2.B10 Number of programs by country in Latin America

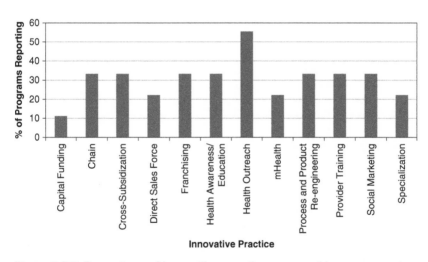

Figure 2.B11 Percentage of innovative practices pursued by programs in Latin America

NOTES

1   These 80 programs were selected from the CHMI dataset by focusing on pro-
    grams with available data in four important areas of health activity: the estab-
    lished fields of maternal, newborn, and child health (MNCH); general primary
    care; and infectious diseases, plus the emerging area of mHealth. We used the
    CHMI database and public sources to collect data on the performance and activi-
    ties of these 80 programs.

2   Table 2.A1 in Appendix A provides a list of these innovative activities, their defi-
    nitions, and their source.

3   Note that some programs operate in multiple countries and regions.

4   Countries were categorized based on the UN grouping of countries by region
    (United Nations Statistics Division 2011). For analysis purposes, the regions of
    South America and Central America have been combined into one region, Latin
    America.

5   Only regions with multiple programs were further analysed by looking at the
    innovative activities pursued by programs in these areas. The regions of Central
    Africa, South Africa, and East Asia each only had one program and were not
    included in this analysis discussion.

6   All figures regarding the number of countries per region and the frequencies
    of innovative practices by region can be found in Appendix B. Figure 2.B1
    in Appendix B shows the number of programs in each geographic
    region.

7   See Appendix B, Figure 2.B2.

8   See Appendix B, Figure 2.B3.

9   See Appendix B, Figure 2.B4.

10   See Appendix B, Figure 2.B5.

11   See Appendix B, Figure 2.B6.

12   See Appendix B, Figure 2.B7.

13   See Appendix B, Figure 2.B8.

14   See Appendix B, Figure 2.B9.

15   See Appendix B, Figure 2.B10.

16   See Appendix B, Figure 2.B11.

17   Note that maternal and child health was one of the subsets purposively selected
    from for the eighty publicly extracted programs.

18   Note that the broad categories of marketing practices, financial practices, and
    operating practices are based on the article by Bhattacharyya et al. (2010),
    and are used here to organize innovative practices. However, these categories
    should not be considered mutually exclusive, and there are cases where overlap
    occurs.

REFERENCES

Bashir, H., Sarfara, K., Eichler, R., Beith, A., & Brown, E. 2010. "Pay for Performance: Improving Maternal Health Services in Pakistan." *P4P Case Studies*.

Bhattacharyya, O., Khor, S., McGahan, A., Dunne, D., Daar, A.S., & Singer, P.A. 2010. "Innovative Health Service Delivery Models in Low and Middle Income Countries – What Can We Learn from the Private Sector?" *Health Research Policy and Systems* 8(24): 1–11. https://doi.org/10.1186/1478-4505-8-24.

Center for Health Market Innovations (CHMI). 2012. "Programs." http://healthmarketinnovations.org/programs.

Consultative Group to Assist the Poor (CGAP). 2012. "Microfinance Gateway: Microinsurance Overview." http://www.findevgateway.org.

DKT International. 2012. "Mozambique." http://www.dktinternational.org/country -programs/mozambique/.

Fournier, P., Dumont, A., Tourigny, C., Dunkley, G. & Dramé, S. 2009. "Improved Access to Comprehensive Emergency Obstetric Care and Its Effect on Institutional Maternal Mortality in Rural Mali." *Bulletin of the World Health Organization* 87: 30–8. https://doi.org/10.2471/BLT.07.047076.

Gogate, P.M., Deshpande, M., & Wormald, R.P. 2003. "Is Manual Small Incision Cataract Surgery Affordable in the Developing Countries? A Cost Comparison with Extracapsular Cataract Extraction." *British Journal of Ophthalmology* 87(7): 843–6. https://doi.org/10.1136/bjo.87.7.843.

Grier, S., & Bryant, C.A. 2005. "Social Marketing in Public Health." *Annual Review of Public Health* 26: 319–39. https://doi.org/10.1146/annurev.publhealth.26 .021304.144610.

Hardee, K., & Leahy, E. 2008. "Population, Fertility, and Family Planning: A Program in Stagnation." *Population Action International* 3: 1–12. Washington, DC: PAI. http://gsdl .ewubd.edu/greenstone/collect/admin-mprhgdco/index/assoc/HASH01e9.dir/P0071.pdf.

Howitt, P., Darzi, A., Yang, G., Ashrafi, H., Atun, R., Barlow, J., Blakemore, A., Bull, A.M.J., Car, J., Conteh, L., Cooke, G.S., Ford, N., Gregson, S.A.J., Kerr, K., King, D., Kulendran, M., Malkin, R.A., Majeed, A., Matlin, S., Merrifield, R., Penfold, H.A., Reid, S.D., Smith, P.C., Stevens, M.M., Templeton, M.R., Vincent, C., & Wilson, E. 2012. "Technologies for Global Health." *The Lancet* 380(9840): 507–35. https://doi.org/10.1016/s0140-6736(12)61127-1.

Hwang, J., & Christensen., C.M. 2008. "Disruptive Innovation in Health Care Delivery: A Framework for Business Model Innovation." *Health Affairs* 27(5): 1329–35. https://doi.org/10.1377/hlthaff.27.5.1329.

Kaplan, Robert S., & Norton, David P. 2001. *The Strategy-Focused Organization: How Balanced Scorecard Companies Thrive in the New Business Environment*. Boston: Harvard Business School Press.

Kubzansky, M., Cooper, A., & Barbary, V. 2011. "Promise and Progress Market-Based Solutions to Poverty in Africa." Cambridge, MA: Monitor Group.

Kumar, R.V. 2011. CARE Hospitals. "Access Health International and Results for Development Institute/Rockefeller Foundation." http://healthmarketinnovations.org/program/care-hospitals.

Lawn, J.E., Tinker, A., Munjanja, S.P., & Cousens, S. 2006. "Where Is Maternal and Child Health Now?" *The Lancet* 368(9546): 1474–7. https://doi.org/10.1016/s0140-6736(06)69387-2.

McBride, J., & Ahmed, R. 2001. "Social Franchising as a Strategy for Expanding Access to Reproductive Health Services: A Case Study of the Green Star Delivery Network in Pakistan." Commercial Market Strategies New Directions in Reproductive Health.

Melnick, G.A. 2007. "From Family Planning to HIV/AIDS Prevention to Poverty Alleviation: A Conversation with Mechai Viravaidya." *Health Affairs* 26(6): 670–7. https://doi.org/10.1377/hlthaff.26.6.w670.

Montagu, D. 2002. "Franchising of Health Services in Developing Countries." UC Berkeley: Bay Area International Group. http://escholarship.org/uc/item/2cz3k6hn.

Ojha, N.P., Ghosh, P., Khandelwal, S., & Kapoor, H. 2011. "What Global Winners Teach Us." *Business Today*, 53–6.

One Heart World-Wide. 2012. *News Releases*. Retrieved from http://www.oneheartworld-wide.org/.

Pesinet. 2012. "Pesinet: A New Approach to Healthcare in Africa." Accessed 14 September 2012. http://www.pesinet.org/wp/.

Porter, M.E. 1996. "What Is Strategy?" *Harvard Business Review*. November–December: 61–78.

– 1998. *Competitive Strategy: Techniques for Analyzing Industries and Competitors*. New York: The Free Press.

Prahalad, C.K. 2006. *The Fortune at the Bottom of the Pyramid: Eradicating Poverty through Profits*. Upper Saddle River: Pearson Education, Inc.

Prata, D., Montagu, D., & Jefferys, E. 2005. "Private Sector, Human Resources, and Health Franchising in Africa." *Bulletin of the World Health Organization* 83: 274–9.

Rangan, V.K., Quelch, J.A., Herrero, G., & Barton, B. 2007. *Business Solutions for the Global Poor: Creating Social and Economic Value*. San Francisco: John Wiley & Sons.

Roth, J., McCord, M.J., & Liber, D. 2007. *The Landscape of Microinsurance in the World's 100 Poorest Countries*. The Microinsurance Centre, LLC. www.microinsurancecentre.org.

Scortino, R. 2005. "Achieving Contraceptive Security and Meeting Reproductive Health Needs in Southeast Asia." Asia Pacific Alliance for Sexual and Reproductive Health and Rights. http://www.asiapacificalliance.org/

population-a-reproductive-health-archive/289-contraceptive-security-and-meeting -reproductive-health-needs-in-southeast-asia.html.

Social Franchising for Health. 2016. "About Social Franchises." http://sf4health.org/ about-social-franchises.

United Nations Statistics Division. 2011. "Composition of Macro Geographical (Continental) Regions, Geographical Sub-Regions, and Selected Economic and Other Groupings." http://millenniumindicators.un.org/unsd/methods/m49/m49regin .htm.

Van Rossem, R., & Meekers, D. 2007. "The reach and impact of social marketing and reproductive health communication campaigns in Zambia." *BMC Public Health* 7(352): 1–12. https://doi.org/10.1186/1471-2458-7-352.

Weberg, D. 2009. "Innovation in Healthcare: A Concept Analysis." *Nursing Administration Quarterly* 33(3): 227–37. https://doi.org/10.1097/naq .0b013e3181accaf5.

WHO (2006). The World Health Report 2006: Working Together for Health. http:// www.who.int/whr/2006/en/.

– (2011). "mHealth: New Horizons for Health through Mobile Technologies." *Global Observatory for eHealth Series* 3, World Health Organization.

3 The Future of Health Care Access

JOHN A. MACDONALD, ANITA M. MCGAHAN,
WILL MITCHELL, ONIL BHATTACHARYYA,
JOHN GINTHER, LEIGH HAYDEN, KATHRYN MOSSMAN,
HIMANSHU PARIKH, ILAN SHAHIN, AND RAMAN SOHAL

Introduction

For generations, the model of how people in the developed world access health care services has involved face-to-face encounters between doctors and patients in bricks-and-mortar medical facilities. The contours of that model are well-known. A patient arrives in a clinic, registers her insurance at the front desk, and waits. Then a nurse or an aide ushers her into a sterile room, takes her vital signs, and hands her a paper gown. Some minutes later, a doctor in a white coat enters the room, asks her questions for ten minutes or so, and conducts a brief physical examination. The doctor issues a diagnosis, writes a prescription, and sends the patient off to make a co-payment. Afterwards, the patient will drive to a local pharmacy to purchase medication. She is one of forty patients who the doctor will see that day.

In developing countries, that model of access is structurally untenable. According to the World Health Organization, there is a global shortage of 4 million health care providers; in 57 countries, by the WHO's reckoning, that shortage amounts to a "crisis" (Chen et al. 2004; World Health Organization 2006). The WHO also estimates that 30 per cent of the world's population lacks access to essential medicines (World Health Organization 2004). Rural clinics in the developing world are scarce and ill supplied, and patients are often required to make a two-day journey to receive care from better-equipped urban medical facilities. Even within cities, travel to and from a clinic through jammed streets can take several hours. Urban clinics, moreover, are typically overwhelmed by patient demand. Alternative providers such as local pharmacists are well meaning, but they tend to have limited training. In place of insurance, people must rely on family savings to cover health care expenses. Medications are often counterfeit, serving as placebos at best and causing considerable harm at worst. Across large swaths of the globe, a lack of supporting infrastructure and appropriately trained personnel undermines any hope of replicating the Western model of health care.

But a new breed of innovators who work in start-up companies, multinational corporations, NGOs, and government agencies are responding to this challenge by using information and communication technology (ICT) to reinvent health care access. Consider: in a remote area of a developing country, a patient walks not into a medical clinic, but into the home of a local woman. Trained as a health worker, the woman asks a few questions in the patient's native dialect, takes the patient's temperature and blood pressure, and then picks up a mobile phone. Within seconds, a paramedic is on the line. Using one of 70 algorithms in a clinical decision-making software package, the paramedic works through another, more targeted series of questions. The local health worker then holds the line as the paramedic, via the internet, sends a brief summary of the case to a physician for review. The summary includes a diagnosis and a proposed treatment plan. The physician agrees with the diagnosis but suggests a longer course of antibiotics, and signs off. The paramedic comes back on the line to explain the diagnosis and the treatment plan, and the local health worker offers to provide medications directly to the patient. Meanwhile, the physician turns his attention to the next case summary that appears on his screen – one of 400 that he will review that day. That's not a theoretical scenario. That's the reality for patients enrolled in eSwasthya, a program offered by the Health Management and Research Institute, a non-profit organization based in India.

ICT has the potential to topple or at least lower the geographic, financial, and cultural barriers to access that dominate the health care landscape in low-resource environments. Spurred by a rapid diffusion of mobile telephony and by a sharp increase in internet penetration, many organizations in the developing world are building health programs that hinge on the use of mobile phones, internet-enabled computers, and other ICT devices. In some cases, these programs complement existing hands-on health care services. In other instances, they present ambitious and innovative alternatives to traditional care.

The new frontier of health care access has many striking features: a radical reinterpretation of what it means to see a health care professional, a redefinition of skill on the front line of care, an amplification of each professional's productivity, and a vast extension of geographic reach. Yet by far the most significant feature is an intensive focus on the needs of the patient. Programs such as eSwasthya make significant use of ICT, but their primary focus is on providing members of their target population with access to needed care.

The Center for Health Market Innovations (CHMI), based in Washington, DC, has amassed data on 1,200 for-profit and non-profit health programs

(The Center for Health Innovations 2013). The Results for Development Institute launched CHMI in 2010 with funding from the Bill & Melinda Gates Foundation, the Rockefeller Foundation, and UKaid. Since then, the CHMI database has emerged as the world's leading repository of information on global health innovation. We are all members of the Toronto Health Organization Performance Evaluation (T-HOPE) team, and in that capacity we scoured the CHMI database for programs in the developing world that prominently feature the use of ICT. We focused our attention on programs for which detailed information on organizational strategy and operational results is publicly available. Ultimately, we identified 40 programs that meet those criteria. They cover a wide range of applications – from public outreach on sexual and reproductive health to the use of biometric identification cards in microinsurance plans. But all of them aim to extend and improve health care access.

A Framework of Innovation

To make sense of the many ICT-enabled health programs that have emerged in recent years – and to identify worthwhile candidates for investment or emulation – funders, government officials, and program managers need to have a clear analytical framework. In this article, we introduce a simple yet compelling classification scheme.

We believe that the best way to look at innovations in health care access is through the lens of demand: Who will benefit from implementing such programs, and what form will that benefit take? In that spirit, we focus first on the potential users of health technology and then on the uses to which that technology might be put.

When it comes to ICT-based health access, there are two groups of core users: patients and providers. The first group includes not only patients and their families, but also members of the general population who have an interest in disease prevention and wellness. The second group encompasses a wide variety of health care professionals. This category includes, for example, rural physicians in India who access continuing medical education through Narayana Hrudayalaya, a large hospital chain that delivers training via satellite and fibre-optic technology. But it also includes local entrepreneurs – many of them former tuberculosis patients – who run mini TB clinics under the auspices of Operation ASHA, a program that uses a biometric patient-record system. Operation ASHA began in India but now operates in Cambodia and Vietnam as well.

The uses of ICT in health care fall into two broad categories: educating people about healthy living or medical practice, and empowering people to access or deliver treatment. The first use category covers initiatives that aim to increase the knowledge of those who dispense or receive health services. It includes activities that range from issuing SMS bulletins about safe sex to producing online modules that teach new techniques to primary care providers. The second use category involves applications that directly or indirectly affect patient care. It includes (among others) telemedicine kiosks, clinical decision-making software, and supply-chain management tools that improve access to medication.

A dual focus on users and uses yields a two-by-two framework that encompasses four broad categories of ICT-based health care innovation (table 3.1). This framework brings order to the seemingly chaotic landscape of this growing sector. It serves as a map to a fast-changing terrain that will enable decision-makers to evaluate various innovations. ICT is changing what it means to be a user within a system of health care access, and it's changing the range of potential uses as well. Categorizing and comparing programs from around the world helps us identify where and how that transformation is unfolding globally.

Table 3.1 ICT in health care access: A survey of innovation

Educating Patients	Empowering Patients
Individuals use ICT to learn how to maintain health.	Individuals use ICT to access health care services.
Examples	**Examples**
• Using a mobile SMS platform to share information on preventing sexually transmitted diseases • Distributing preventive health information via culturally appropriate YouTube videos	• Using biometric smart cards to identify and register families for health insurance • Integrating mobile point-of-sale devices with microinsurance and health-savings plans
Programs	**Programs**
• mDhil (India) • Marie Stopes International (40 countries)	• Rashtriya Swasthya Bima Yojana (India) • Changamka Microhealth (Kenya)
Implications	**Implications**
Patients learn how to manage health issues proactively for themselves and their families. Public health services can roll out education programs quickly and cost-effectively, even in the face of pandemic disease.	Patients gain access to affordable health insurance and to efficiently delivered health care services. Health care workers reliably receive payment for their services.

(Continued)

Table 3.1 Concluded

Educating Providers	Empowering Providers
Health care professionals use ICT to improve their medical knowledge.	Health care professionals use ICT to improve access to their services.
Examples • Instruction of health workers via online and offline training modules • Provision of continuing medical education services via satellite or fibre-optic connection	**Examples** • Remote ECG analysis • Telemedicine services in which patients and providers engage remotely with skilled professionals via telephone or advanced telediagnostic software
Programs • Health[e] Foundation (Africa, Asia, Latin America) • Narayana Hrudayalaya (India, Africa)	**Programs** • World Health Partners (India) • SMS for Life (Tanzania)
Implications Remote providers receive up-to-date protocols and offer evidence-based care. Providers learn to think in terms not just of what they can offer, but also of what patients need.	**Implications** Remote providers can access specialized assistance instantly. Health professionals can remotely serve a vast number of patients from a single location. Patients no longer need to travel long distances to receive care.

A Survey of the Field

The framework has utility for investors, donors, policymakers, and program managers. For investors and donors, it offers a tool for comparing organizations that apply for funds with peer organizations that target a similar set of users and uses. Similarly, policymakers can deploy the users-and-uses framework to assess public health programming, to allocate scarce resources, and to encourage private investment in a given area (many of the examples in the CHMI database represent public-private partnerships, and many others began as private projects that government health departments then took over). Program managers can categorize their own efforts by referencing the framework. Doing so will help them with strategic planning, and it will also help them to avoid the pitfalls that other organizations have encountered in serving particular user groups or in implementing particular uses.

Now, with this framework in place, we can survey the rich variety of ICT-enabled health programs that populate the CHMI database. Several of these programs operate in multiple areas of the framework; they serve multiple users and uses. But we categorize them here according to the domain where their impact is most especially salient.

Educating Patients

Two programs in the database offer examples of using ICT to provide accessible health education to the general population.

mDhil, a venture-backed start-up based in Bangalore, India, leverages mobile telephony and the internet to reach its target audience – urban young adults in New Delhi and Mumbai – at a fraction of the cost of traditional education initiatives. In its first year in operation, mDhil attracted 150,000 paid subscribers to its SMS health messaging service. The service costs 5 cents per health tip or 60 cents per month by subscription. Since its founding in 2009, mDhil has aggressively expanded its internet presence. Its full-featured website covers health issues that range from weight loss to cancer. It also publishes a series of video clips on YouTube that has attracted more than 10 million views. The videos feature recurring personalities who answer questions about various topics; the most popular clips are those that address sexual health concerns. The ability of mDhil to conduct an internet-based marketing strategy on a large scale distinguishes it from most other programs that aim to broaden health care access.

Marie Stopes International (MSI), based in London, targets men and women in need of sexual health services. MSI has been in operation for more than 30 years, and it currently has centres in 40 countries. Its program in Bolivia, a country with limited communication infrastructure, offers mobile clinic services, finances health care for low-income families, distributes contraceptives, and provides public education on sexual health issues. To promote reproductive health education, MSI Bolivia established a confidential phone line through which adolescents and young adults can ask questions that they find too embarrassing to bring up in a public setting. Trained university students field questions on the line six days a week. If necessary, they refer callers to an MSI clinic for medical care. The cost of each call is about 21 cents, and MSI Bolivia and the caller share the cost equally. MSI plans to expand its service by creating a web portal for patients and providers, and by enabling patients to book clinic appointments through its confidential hotline.

Educating Providers

The database features two programs that expand access to care by using ICT to improve the training of local health care workers.

Health[e] Foundation, based in Amsterdam, has a simple mission: to deliver state-of-the-art medical information to resource-limited regions of the world. Founded in 2003 by the Dutch physician Fransje van der Waals, Health[e] Foundation offers a blended curriculum that combines brief, periodic on-site training sessions with three-month-long e-learning modules that participants can take online or offline (via USB memory stick). The modules address a broad range of topics, including HIV and AIDS, tuberculosis, and mental health. At the end of each module, participants receive a certificate, along with access to course updates and continuing-education materials. Medical experts from around the world help create and curate this educational content. Health[e] Foundation operates on every continent except North America and Antarctica, and it presents its course material in multiple languages. Each year, about 1,000 physicians, nurses, and other health workers receive training through the foundation.

Narayana Hrudayalaya, based in Bangalore, India, supplements its core health care services by operating a highly advanced provider education platform. The Narayana facility in Bangalore is one of the world's premier cardiac surgery centres. It has 5,000 patient beds, and it's best known for offering a low-cost ($2,000) coronary artery bypass procedure. Recently, Narayana began a less publicized venture into continuing medical education and telemedicine. It joined the PAN African e-Network, a multiorganizational initiative that uses satellite and fibre-optic technology to bring Indian expertise in education and health care to Sub-Saharan Africa. Initially, the network focused on providing remote consultations and ECG readings to in-country health care workers. But Narayana, which is leading the health care aspect of the project, quickly recognized the potential of the network to deliver educational content to African physicians. Today, Narayana offers remote educational services in sixteen African nations.

Empowering Patients

Several ICT-enabled programs in the database augment the ability of low-income patients to access standard health care services.

Rashtriya Swasthya Bima Yojana ("National Health Insurance Program"), based in India, uses portable biometric data collection and other ICT methods to support a nationwide insurance plan. The program has helped establish affordable access to care for about 34 million poor Indian families. It's a public-private partnership in which the Indian government serves as the payer, third-party insurers provide risk coverage, and contracted administrators manage enrolment and claims. The federal government covers 75 per cent of the cost of premiums, and state governments cover the remaining 25 per cent. Each participating family pays a one-time fee of 30 rupees (about 70 cents) at the time of enrolment. The head of each family and four other family members have their fingerprints and picture taken at a terminal that immediately adds them to a central database and generates a chip-enabled smart card. At that point, family members may use the card to access about $600 worth of hospital services. Several features of the plan help patients to avoid delays in care. The authentication, claims, and authorization processes are tied to a patient's smart card, and they are completely paperless. The plan also offers preapproval and fixed pricing for 750 procedures and claims. To participate in the service, hospitals must have a reliable internet connection, and they must install fingerprint and smart-card readers. The service closely monitors hospitals for possible fraud and quickly removes offending institutions from the program.

Changamka Microhealth, an insurer based in Nairobi, Kenya, that began operation in 2008, also issues smart cards. The organization targets people who have some income but are unable to open a savings account at a traditional financial institution. With a Changamka card, users can visit a doctor or buy medicine at more than thirty accredited establishments in Nairobi, Kikuyu, Mombasa, and Naivasha. Changamka has negotiated discount rates with each of those providers. Patients can use the cards for outpatient treatment, maternity care, third-party payment, or in-house services that their employers provide. The cards are available at supermarkets and other retailers, patients can add money to the cards at a cellular-connected terminal or through a mobile phone, and the cards do not expire. Changamka has partnered with GA Insurance, a Kenya-based company that acts as both underwriter and fund manager for the organization.

Empowering Providers

Finally, several programs in the database deploy ICT systems to enhance provider-side efficiency.

World Health Partners (WHP), based in New Delhi, offers an example of ICT-enabled remote primary care. WHP, a non-profit partnership, began as an eighteen-month pilot in the Indian state of Uttar Pradesh, and more recently it has expanded to Bihar, one of India's poorest states. WHP recruits pharmacists, local health workers, and other informal care providers and sets them up in franchised "clinics" under the WHP brand. The clinics mainly handle primary care concerns, but patients can visit them for preventive medicine, for tuberculosis treatment – or for anything in between. As with eSwasthya, patients first consult a local WHP franchisee and then connect via telephone or videoconference to a remote physician. After the consultation, the physician can send a prescription to the clinic via SMS. WHP maintains laboratories for blood work, X-rays, and ultrasound tests, and it runs WHP-branded pharmacies as well. Patients pay less than $1 per visit, of which 60 per cent goes to the franchisee and 40 per cent goes to WHP. There are 250 telemedicine centres in the

WHP network, and thus far WHP providers have served about 750,000 people. Today, WHP franchisees operate in 4,000 villages in Bihar. But the partnership is adding villages to its network at a pace of 400 per month, and its goal is to serve 20,000 villages by 2015.

SMS for Life, a system for improving supply-chain management, shows that provider-side ICT implementation can go well beyond enabling telemedicine. The project began as a pilot program in Tanzania, a country with endemic malaria. About 93 per cent of the population is at risk of malarial infection, and there are an estimated 60,000 deaths annually from this preventable illness. To prevent stock-outs of antimalarial medication (among other crucial supplies), the Tanzanian Ministry of Health and Social Welfare partnered with Novartis, IBM, and several multinational organizations to develop a system for monitoring supply levels across the country. Each Thursday, health facility workers receive an automated text message that asks them to report on their stock levels. If they don't reply within twenty-four hours, they receive a reminder message. The next Monday morning, a district officer receives a summary report of supply levels throughout a given region. The officer can then order additional supplies or redistribute supplies from one facility to another. Within six months of the pilot's start, the stock-out rate in Tanzania declined from 79 per cent to 26 per cent.

Assessing the Data

Sorting the ICT projects in the CHMI database in accordance with the users-and-uses framework helps shed light on areas of health care where the application of ICT has been fairly robust – and on areas where there are notable opportunities for further innovation. A large number of these projects, for example, focus on empowering either patients or providers. They target populations that traditional services have been unable to reach, and they do so by overcoming limitations related to geography, transportation, and the high cost of delivering on-site services. These examples provide other organizations with models for bringing together traditional and nontraditional providers to enable services that do not require brick-and-mortar facilities or face-to-face interaction.

There are also multiple entries in the CHMI database that fall within the patient education domain. These services, which often rely on cell phone and SMS technology, take advantage of the explosion in mobile telephony that is occurring in even the poorest communities around the world. These services have one other advantage: the organizational infrastructure needed to initiate them is relatively simple.

By contrast, we found notably few examples of ICT-based innovation in the provider-education domain. The reason for that gap is twofold, we believe. First, training providers is a highly technical undertaking – considerably more so than, say, launching a mass SMS campaign to teach the general public about condom use. It requires both medical and educational expertise, along with a deep understanding of local provider practices. Second, although many Western medical schools are working with schools and governments in the developing world to improve provider training, the standard approach continues to focus on delivering such assistance on-site and in person.

These barriers are surmountable. We expect to see slow but significant growth in ICT-enabled provider education, especially as ICT infrastructure becomes more prevalent in the developing world and as educational institutions there become more sophisticated. Established schools such as Stanford University and start-up ventures such as the Khan Academy (a non-profit video-based education service) are already demonstrating that educators can conduct large-scale knowledge transfers – even entire university courses – via the internet. It's only a matter of time before similar approaches to educating providers begin to take hold in developing countries.

Until recently, program managers with an interest in ICT-enabled strategies to improve health care access had few examples to follow. Fortunately, as the programs in the CHMI database indicate, promising examples are now emerging. The next challenge will be to evaluate the long-term viability and the outcomes of such programs, and that will require looking beyond simple metrics such as the number of people who have been treated or trained. A working group that includes CHMI, T-HOPE, and the Global Impact Investing Network is developing a set of metrics for investors and funders to use in assessing new health care projects. But that effort will take a significant amount of time to unfold. Meanwhile, tools such as the users-and-uses framework help to illuminate the variety and the depth of activity in this emerging field.

Assessing the Future

Numerous limitations continue to affect the implementation of ICT-based health care solutions. Internet connectivity is still nascent in much of the developing world. The instability of electrical supply in developing countries presents a massive challenge as well. And although mobile phone service is becoming ubiquitous, high rates of illiteracy limit the usability of SMS-based programs in many parts of the globe. In a recent post at SSIR online, Ken Banks noted that organizations continue to push technology – mobile technology, in particular – into low-resource settings without fully taking into account local needs (Banks 2013). The use of ICT in health care is still in its infancy, and we shouldn't let its novelty distract us from the need to assess its relevance to target communities. Health care technology, in short, cannot surmount all barriers to health care access.

Despite those obstacles, there are substantial opportunities to expand ICT-enabled health care services. Most developing countries now have the telecommunications infrastructure to support at least basic ICT services, and those services can readily improve access to health care treatment and education through the deployment of voice and SMS applications. More sophisticated services, meanwhile, are emerging in countries that have both a strong technical infrastructure and a sophisticated organizational infrastructure. Fortunately, more and more countries do have that combination of resources.

What's more, the potential scalability of ICT-based services offers an opportunity for organizations to extend their programs beyond individual countries. After all, many developing countries suffer from similar gaps in health care access and face similar infrastructure limitations. At least five of the forty programs that we identified in our survey are transnational in scope. We have already discussed four such programs: Operation ASHA, which sponsors TB clinics in multiple Asian countries; Health[e] Foundation, whose provider education platform reaches physicians in Asia, Africa, and South America; Marie Stopes International, which offers sexual and reproductive health services in 40 different countries; and Narayana, an Indian organization that participates in the PAN African e-Network. In addition, a program called Dentista do Bem coordinates the efforts of volunteer dentists in Portugal and in numerous countries throughout Latin America. Other ICT-enabled approaches – with due allowance for the need to make cultural and linguistic modifications – have the potential to extend across national borders as well.

The innovative programs in the CHMI database reflect a disruptive model of care that has not yet spread from developing countries to more resource-rich settings. The broad use of advanced telemedicine and clever smart card – enabled insurance schemes are rare or nonexistent in much of the developed world. Yet the potential benefits that those services could bring to the operation of, say, an American health maintenance organization (HMO) or a Canadian local health integration network (LHIN) are immediately apparent. Indeed, given their relative freedom from technical obstacles and their high literacy rates, developed countries present an environment in which ICT-driven health care clearly might flourish. One place to start would be in the use of long-established mobile technologies – an area where "advanced" countries have lagged behind their less-developed counterparts. SMS-based payment and health education applications have become commonplace in many developing countries, for example, even as people in the developed world focus on creating medical smartphone apps that have struggled to find broad utility.

In all parts of the world, the largest barrier to implementing ICT-based health care is not a lack of technology or a lack of medical skill. Instead, it is the belief – prevalent in both the developing world and the developed world – that high-quality health care services require hands-on, person-to-person engagement within a traditional brick-and-mortar medical facility. As that mindset changes and as organizational and logistical capabilities continue to improve, we are likely to see rapid growth in demand-focused, ICT-enabled services that address the needs of both patients and providers. Technology that can improve access to health care now exists, and it's becoming ever more widely available. We simply need the motivation and the courage to use it.

REFERENCES

Banks, K. 2013. "The Truth about Disruptive Development." *Stanford Social Innovation Review*. https://ssir.org/articles/entry/the_truth_about_disruptive_development.

Chen, L., Evans, T., Anand, S., Boufford, J.I., Brown, H., Chowdhury, M., ... Wibulpolprasert, S. 2004. "Human Resources for Health: Overcoming the Crisis." *The Lancet* 364(9449): 1984–90. https://doi.org/10.1016/s0140-6736(04)17482-5.

The Center for Health Market Innovations. 2013. http://healthmarketinnovations.org.

World Health Organization. 2004. "Equitable Access to Essential Medicines: A Framework for Collective Action." *WHO Policy Perspectives on Medicines*.

– 2006. *The World Health Report 2006: Working Together for Health*. Geneva: World Health Organization.

4 For-Profit Health Care Providers at the Bottom of the Pyramid

DAVID LEUNG, KATHRYN MOSSMAN, RAMAN SOHAL,
HIMANSHU PARIKH, JASON SUKHRAM,
ONIL BHATTACHARYYA, ANITA MCGAHAN,
AND WILL MITCHELL

Introduction

Accessing quality, affordable health care remains a significant challenge in many low- and middle-income countries (LMICs). Challenges arise from weak health systems, limited service availability and affordability, lack of skilled health workers, poor infrastructure, and weak supply chains (Bustreo, Okwo-Bele, & Kamara 2015), (World Health Organization 2014). Despite real strides in recent years, access to essential health services continues to be limited in LMICs. Disease burdens and ill health disproportionately afflict people in poorer countries.

Dismal differences in health outcomes are far too easy to find. In 2013, the maternal mortality rate in LMICs was 450 per 100,000 live births, compared to 17 in high-income countries, while only 46 per cent of births in LMICs are attended by skilled health personnel compared to almost all (99 per cent) in high-income countries (World Health Organization 2014). Stunting in children under five due to long-term undernutrition was at 40 per cent in Sub-Saharan Africa and South Asia in 2010 (Smith & Haddad 2015), while 98.6 per cent of the 6.3 million deaths of children under five years old from all causes in 2013 were in developing regions (You, Hug, & Chen 2014). Infectious diseases disproportionately affect developing countries; the mortality rate from HIV/AIDS was almost 12 times higher in LMICs than in high-income countries in 2010, while 90 per cent of the 627,000 malaria deaths in 2012 occurred in Africa (World Health Organization 2014).

Many initiatives have sought to address these complex challenges. Two themes in global health include the potential for information and communications technology (ICT) to address wicked problems in health care and growing interest in for-profit providers. Within strategy research, the role of for-profit health care in LMICs arises in the more general literature on bottom of the pyramid (BOP) enterprise (sometimes referred to as base of the pyramid). Several scholars have highlighted for-profit opportunities to serve the lowest income groups (e.g., Prahalad & Hart 2002; Hammond, Kramer, Katz, Tran, & Walker 2007; London & Hart 2004), although others are more sceptical (e.g., Karnani 2007; Tung & Bennett 2014).

This study compares how for-profit and non-profit providers use ICT-based services to address health care needs in LMICs. We start by identifying several relevant for-profit ventures. We then assess how the ventures use ICTs and how they generate income. We are particularly interested in whether for-profit programs primarily target the more limited, but still available, higher-income clients in LMICs or, instead, also use ICT to reach poorer segments, either independently or as partners of non-profit organizations. We seek to contribute to global health studies and to the strategy literature on bottom of the pyramid business activity.

Background

ICT-Based and For-Profit Health Care Services

ICT INNOVATION IN HEALTH

In the past decade, there has been a dramatic increase in the use of ICT-based services to address LMIC health care challenges. Just as mobile-based health applications are exploding in developed markets, a diverse range of ICT-based services is emerging in LMICs. Although they have yet to reach full potential, the fields of eHealth (using ICTs to help improve health system performance) and mHealth (using mobile technologies) are growing (Crean 2010). Examples of ICTs in health include telemedicine, mobile devices for connecting providers and patients, electronic medical records, e-learning tools, and decision support systems (Gerber, Olazabal, Brown, & Pablos-Mendez 2010). ICT health applications have been used for multiple health care purposes, including sending text message reminders to TB and HIV/AIDS patients to improve adherence to medical protocols (Interactive Research and Development & Stop TB Partnership 2012); using mobile phones and internet connections so local health workers and midwives can consult skilled providers (Ratzan & Gilhooley 2010); providing clinical decision support software on mobile phones to guide health workers through screening, examination, and treatment (Altman, Fogstad, Gronseth, & Kristensen 2011); developing mobile applications that help patients budget and pay for health care (PMNCH 2012); collecting patient data via mobile phones and using electronic medical records to track malaria and TB incidence and prevalence (Asiimwe et al. 2011) (Millard, Bru, & Berger 2012) (Khan et al. 2012); and tracking medical supplies such as bed nets, medications, and rapid diagnostic tests to ensure items are replenished before stock-outs (Githinji, Kigen, Memusi, Nyandigisi, & Mbithi 2013).

While ICTs appear to have great potential for increasing health access and otherwise improving health care in LMICs (Gerber et al. 2010; MacDonald, McGahan, Mitchell, & The T-HOPE Team 2013), many projects remain small-scale initiatives (World Health Organization 2011) often with uncoordinated implementation and limited scale up (Lewis, Synowiec, Lagomarsino, & Schweitzer 2012). Still, some emerging evidence suggests that ICTs provide benefits for LMIC health care. For example, mobile technologies have been found to improve local health worker access to more highly trained medical staff, increase the capacity of health workers, reduce response time in addressing medical complications (Chib 2010), promote timely collection of malaria surveillance data (Asiimwe et al. 2011), increase reported TB cases (Khan et al. 2012), improve antiretroviral therapy adherence (Da Costa, Barbosa, Sigulem, de Fatima Marin, & Pisa 2012), and reduce stock-outs of vital medical supplies (Barrington, Wereko-Brobby, Ward, Mwafongo, & Kungulwe 2010; Githinji et al. 2013). Electronic medical records have also shown to increase the number of patients started on appropriate medication, decrease patients lost to follow-up, improve medication delivery (Fraser et al. 2007), and reduce laboratory reporting errors compared to paper systems (Blaya et al. 2010).

The focal point for most discussions of ICT use in LMICs tends to be in the non-profit and public health care sectors. A 2011 WHO report on mHealth, for example, focuses on a survey of 114 member states on the adoption and status of public mHealth initiatives and barriers to implementation (World Health Organization 2011). A 2012 World Bank report states that most current and emerging mHealth initiatives are developed by non-profit NGOs, with for-profit mHealth models relatively rare in developing countries (Qiang, Hausman, Yamamichi, & Miller 2012). The World Bank report also notes that only 4 per cent of mHealth initiatives in Kenya are for-profit, concluding that such models often lack donor and government support received by non-profits and are also inhibited by bureaucracy, limited financing, and clients' ability and willingness to pay for services in LMIC markets (Qiang et al. 2012).

FOR-PROFIT HEALTH CARE VENTURES IN LMICS

Nonetheless, health care in LMICs is increasingly drawing for-profit enterprise (World Bank 2008). This activity in LMIC health care parallels more general discussion in the international management and strategy literatures, where we see for-profit firms playing a pivotal role in the use of new health information and communication technologies, as in other high-technology sectors. There is a wide range of examples: medical technology companies producing medical instruments, devices and electromedical equipment (Wei & Clegg 2014); firms developing new technologies for the global in vitro diagnostics market (Srai & Alinaghian 2013); Korean family businesses engaging in multiple high-technology sectors in emerging markets (Miller, Lee, Chang, & Le Breton-Miller 2009); Chinese commercial organizations innovating in ICT industries such as software, communications, and e-commerce (Gu & Tse 2010); and US medical device firms modifying their innovative activities in response to the market (Chatterji & Fabrizio 2014). As leaders in the technology field, for-profit actors may be well placed to facilitate the growth and application of ICTs in LMIC health care.

Literature is emerging on the role of the for-profit sector in harnessing innovative ICTs for health care in LMICs. mHealth initiatives have significant market potential, with IT companies such as Nokia, Vodaphone, and Microsoft showing interest (Interactive Research and Development & Stop TB Partnership 2012). A study of four health hotlines found that for-profit ventures often partner with mobile network operators or telecom firms (Ivatury, Moore, & Bloch 2009). Others have suggested that for-profit social enterprises are well placed to develop and market ICTs in health care, although this is dependent on access to long-term funding (Crean 2010). As well, mHealth initiatives starting as non-profits sometimes convert to commercial ventures; 60 per cent of mHealth enterprises that one study examined in India, for instance, are for-profit or hybrid models (Qiang et al. 2012). Hybrid business models can bring together non-profit and for-profit actors through partnering on implementation, financing, and provision of goods and services (Qiang et al. 2012). eHealth and mHealth may also be offered in LMICs through public-private partnerships that combine the capabilities of public and private entities (Schweitzer & Synowiec 2012).

QUESTIONS: FOR-PROFIT VERSUS NON-PROFITS AT THE BOTTOM OF THE PYRAMID

Despite the growing interest, we are only beginning to understand the use of ICTs in health provision by for-profit ventures. One basic question is whether for-profit health care ventures using ICT are at all common. Tung and Bennett (2014), for instance, found few substantive for-profit ventures in a global study of low-income health services. There is little information among those that do operate about how they use ICTs and how they generate income in the segments they target, especially in comparison with non-profits.

It is possible that for-profit ventures in LMICs focus on wealthier clients. A study of ICT kiosks for education services in India, for instance, found that the primary target was middle rather than bottom-income consumers (Kuriyan, Ray, & Toyama 2008). Basic profit maximization theory (Simon 1979; Miner 2006) suggests that for-profit firms are most likely to target higher-income segments. In contrast, since non-profits are prevented from distributing profits to those with control over the organization, non-profits have weaker incentives to maximize profit and more scope to focus on social goals (Glaeser & Shleifer 2001).

In providing health care in LMICs, the private sector has been found generally to serve more affluent groups than the public sector (Basu, Andrews, Kishore, Panjabi, & Stuckler 2012); this is considered particularly true for for-profit private providers. Bennett (1992) notes that "the for-profit sector has no equity concerns, and thus will focus its activities on those parts of the market which are likely to be most profitable." As a result, the private for-profit sector is often described as focused on serving urban populations and higher-income segments (Bennett 1992). Also, at least one study suggests that for-profit providers tend to require out-of-pocket payment; hence, they may focus on serving wealthier populations able to pay their fees (Patouillard, Goodman, Hanson, & Mills 2007).

More generally, there is growing interest in for-profit opportunities in bottom of the pyramid environments. Several scholars (e.g., Prahalad & Hart 2002; London & Hart 2004) argue that businesses can operate profitably by fine-tuning services to meet the needs and cash flow of low-income consumers. Interest has focused on for-profit microcredit (Mair, Marti, & Ventresca 2012), market-specific products that suit the needs and cash flow of low-income consumers (Prahalad 2006), branding (Rahman, Hasan, & Floyd 2013), partnerships between for-profit enterprise and public and/or private non-profit organizations (Hammond et al. 2007), pricing strategies (Jones Christensen, Siemsen, & Balasubramanian 2015), and other elements of creating profitable business opportunities in low-income environments.

However, bottom of the pyramid research has only begun to study for-profit health care models in LMICs. The study by Tung and Bennett (2014) that we mentioned earlier, which found few for-profit health care ventures, is one of the few such investigations. Moreover, this literature typically provides only limited comparison of for-profit and non-profit enterprises that target the poor with their services. Despite the lack of attention to date, it is possible that for-profit health care is making relevant in-roads in such environments, potentially in different ways than non-profits. We seek to generate greater understanding of such activity.

There is only limited theory to frame a study of for-profit health care in low-income countries, beyond the general expectation that for-profit providers are more likely than non-profit vendors to target opportunities with meaningful potential to earn profits. Therefore, we undertook an exploratory study that compares the activities of for-profit and non-profit health care providers in multiple LMICs. We conducted basic statistical comparisons complemented by field examples that illustrate emerging patterns in the activities. We believe that the analysis provides a basis both to understand an important phenomenon of global health care and to help advance the general understanding of business activity in low-income environments.

Methods and Data: For-Profit and Non-Profit Health Care Providers in LMICs

We used a database of health care programs operating in LMICs collected by the Center for Health Market Innovation (CHMI), based in Washington DC, to identify for-profit and not-for-profit programs that have provided ICT-based health care services (Center for Health Market Innovations 2016). This database contains information about more than 1,200 health programs in LMICs, with an emphasis on delivery by for-profit and non-profit private sector organizations. CHMI began collecting the data in 2010.

The CHMI data seeks to identify programs using innovative approaches to health care in LMICs. CHMI defines innovations as programs and policies – implemented by governments, non-governmental organizations (NGOs), social entrepreneurs, or private companies – that improve health care, including organizing delivery, financing care, regulating performance, changing behaviours, and enhancing processes. CHMI encourages programs to submit data about their organizations and also works with partner organizations in more than 20 countries to identify and collect information about health care programs.

These data provide the most encompassing collection of non-governmental health care programs operating in LMICs. While the data do not include all such programs, CHMI actively solicits listings by as many relevant organizations as possible, with an emphasis on organizations that seek to provide services to low-income populations. As a result, it provides a broad listing of programs for study, although it is most representative of programs and countries for which English is a common language, at least for reporting purposes (hence, for example, there is far more representation from India than from China).

The data include programs in multiple health areas, such as eye care, maternal and child health, tuberculosis, malaria, primary care, secondary/tertiary care, and family planning and reproductive health, among others. The programs use varied operational models, including social franchising, public private partnerships, clinic chains and networks, mobile clinics, social marketing, microinsurance, and mobile health technologies. Previous work in a broader project has used this data to study transnational scaling (Shahin et al. 2014), as well as a limited discussion of using ICT to increase access to health care (MacDonald et al. 2013).

For this study, launched in 2014, we began with detailed information about 683 programs in the CHMI database that offered enough information for detailed comparisons. From this set, we focused on programs that reported ICT-based activities. We identified relevant programs based on the criterion that the project reported using ICT as part of its approach to providing services.

Based on this criterion, we were able to undertake a multidimensional assessment of 175 programs that reported using ICT to support their services, including 125 not-for-profit (NFP) and 50 for-profit (FP) programs. Thus, 29 per cent of the programs (50/175) for this study of ICT use are FPs, somewhat higher than the average of for-profit programs in the overall CHMI data set (21 per cent). The large majority of the for-profit programs were independent operations, although about 10 per cent of the for-profit projects were operated by non-profits, governments, or multi-lateral organizations. Some programs were sponsored by international parents, though most were locally based (the data do not provide systematic information about parent location, so we cannot compare for-profit and non-profit ventures on that dimension). The programs in the study were founded between 1941 and 2012 (median of 2008 for FPs and 2007 for NFPs).

The smaller incidence of FP projects undoubtedly reflects the difficulty of operating profitably in low-income environments. Nonetheless, the fact that we found a substantial number of organizations seeking to operate for-profit ventures in these environments speaks to the potential draw of markets that may offer bottom of the pyramid business opportunities.

Table 4.1 reports the types of ICT in the data. Models involving computers and phones are by far the most common for both for-profit and not-for-profit programs, with non-profits being somewhat more likely to use phone technology – mainly basic cell phones for voice and SMS, based on our interviews and review of public information about the programs. A smaller number of programs use unique ID technology, tablets, and/or remote diagnostic tools. We introduce two examples below; throughout the paper, we provide additional examples of for-profit programs that operate in various income segments in multiple LMICs.

mDhil, founded in India in 2009, uses both phones and computers to support health services. mDhil is a for-profit that provides basic health care information to Indian consumers via text messaging, mobile web browsers, and interactive digital content. Text message subscribers receive three messages a day on their mobile phone for a fee of one rupee ($US0.02) per day. The health

Table 4.1 Types of information and communications technology (ICT)

ICT	For-profit (50 Programs)	Not-for-profit (125 Programs)
Computers	60%	50%
Phones	58%	72%
Unique ID	8%	10%
PDA/tablets	6%	8%
Remote diagnostic tools	6%	8%
Other (GPS)	4%	4%

alerts are written by public health professionals; the most popular topics are sexual health, weight management, and H1N1 information, along with information on general health, tuberculosis, diet, stress, skincare and beauty, and diabetes. mDhil also provides health information on Facebook and YouTube, emphasizing wellness, women's health, and medical expertise.

MediSmart is an example of a for-profit venture that uses unique ID technology. Founded in 1990 and now operating across Africa, MediSmart uses smart cards to capture a patient's complete electronic health record, and provides credentialing and authentication through similar cards for doctors and administrators, along with optional readers that identify patients. MediSmart sells its services to for-profit insurance programs to help reduce administration costs, call centre dependency, fraud, and unmanaged private reimbursements.

We used the data to assess several questions, including where the programs operate, what services they offer, what types of clients they target, and who they ally with. In doing so, we compared the tendencies of for-profit ventures to those of non-profit health care organizations operating in LMICs. In undertaking the research, we also interviewed people at 31 programs that use ICTs and reviewed public information about other programs. We believe that the patterns in the data and insights from the examples allow for greater understanding about the potential opportunities and limits of for-profit health care programs in providing health care services for low-income clients.

Results: Insights from the Data and the Field

Where Do For-Profit Programs Operate?

Table 4.2 summarizes the countries in which the programs operate, among the 28 countries in the sample. Several patterns stand out. First, India is the most common location for both FP and NFP programs, likely reflecting a

Table 4.2 LMICs in which ICT-based health care programs operate

Top 6 Countries: For-profit Programs (11 Total Countries)[a]	GNI/ Capita, 2013 ($US 2011)	FP (50 Programs)	Top 6 Countries: Not-for-profit Programs (27 Total Countries)[b]	GNI/ Capita, 2013 ($US 2011)	NFP (125 Programs)
India	$5,238	42%	India	$5,238	24%
Kenya	$2,193	16%	Kenya	$2,193	15%
Indonesia	$9,254	10%	Bangladesh	$2,476	7%
Pakistan	$4,549	8%	Indonesia	$9,254	7%
Bangladesh	$2,476	6%	Uganda	$1,365	7%
Vietnam	$5,125	6%	Pakistan	$4,549	4%
Mean GDP/ Capita: Top 6	**$4,806**		**Mean GDP/ Capita: Top 6**	**$4,179**	
Mean GDP/ Capita: Other	**$7,214**		**Mean GDP/ Capita: Other**	**$5,235**	

[a] Other countries for FP programs (all less than 5% of cases): Brazil, Philippines, South Africa, Tanzania, Uganda.
[b] Other countries for NFP programs (all less than 4% of cases): Afghanistan, Argentina, Benin, Bolivia, **Brazil,** Cambodia, Democratic Republic of the Congo, Ecuador, Ethiopia, Ghana, Haiti, Laos, Malawi, Mali, Nigeria, Peru, Rwanda, **South Africa, Tanzania,** Vietnam, Zimbabwe (cases in **bold** overlap with FP countries).
Note: GDP/capita is based on a purchasing power parity (PPP) in 2013.

country with a very large population, sufficient telecom infrastructure to support ICT-based services, and a public sector that supports active engagement in health care by domestic and international organizations. Owing to these factors, India is one of the countries in which CHMI has partners that help identify innovative health care organizations for the database. It is also possible that the program density in India reflects a form of aggregation benefit (Alcácer & Chung 2014), in which organizations learn from each other and spawn an ongoing series of new ventures, similar to Saxenian's (1996) description of Silicon Valley in California and Route 128 in Massachusetts.

We see evidence of such spillovers in South Asia, where several programs provide standardized high-volume, low-cost eye surgeries. Aravind Eye Care System, a chain of non-profit eye hospitals in India that is now the largest supplier of eye care in the world, was the pioneer. Launched in 1976, Aravind's model employs innovative operations processes to increase efficiency, such as allowing surgeons to operate on two patients in alteration, while medical staff prepares the next patient for surgery. This helps minimize the time needed for surgeries and enables high volumes of patients to be served. Aravind also uses telemedicine technology to expand their ability to reach more patients and follow up with those with chronic eye diseases. Cross-subsidization often accompanies this high-volume, low-cost approach, allowing programs to subsidize costs for poor patients with the revenues of higher income patients. While Aravind has been highly recognized for pioneering this approach in India, several other programs in the regions have learned from Aravind and also are pursuing this model, including LV Prasad (1987) and Sadguru Netra Chikitsalaya (2000) in India, the Lumbini Eye Institute in Nepal (1983), and Al-Shifa Trust Eye Hospitals in Pakistan (1990).

As well as depth of specialization within one particular ICT category such as in eye surgery, there is also a breadth of ICT usage that forms complementary ecosystems. Kenya has the second highest prevalence of programs. Of the eight for-profit organizations we identified in Kenya (Changamka Microhealth, Daktari 1525 Program, Faulu, Kenya Women Finance Trust, Kutana Cloud, Mamakiba, Penda Health, Viva Afya), the organizations operate in seven health care ICT categories (from a total of 23 categories). Of the organizations with overlapping functions, two are microinsurance companies and three are utilizing electronic medical records. This suggests that these aggregation benefits can not only support deep innovation within one particular activity (as in the case with Aravind and other eye surgery providers in South Asia) but also allow partnerships and synergies to form between the organizations.

Second, five of the top six countries are the same for FP and NFP (India, Kenya, Indonesia, Bangladesh, and Pakistan). This may suggest that similar ecosystems foster innovation for both types of providers, paralleling the implication concerning aggregation benefits. Key aspects of the ecosystem are likely to include availability of telecommunications infrastructure and a strong enough educational system to provide at least basic training of local staff. Figure 4.1 reports a comparative index of voids in market-based institutions (Dutt et al. 2016) for the five overlapping countries in the top six of FP and NFP programs. Each of the five countries faces substantial challenges in providing support for business activity, particularly in lack of transparency in contracts, rules, and corruption. At the same time, though, each offers at least a moderate degree of physical infrastructure (including telecommunications) and access to labour needed to support private enterprise, whether for-profit or non-profit.

Third, the FP programs have a more restricted range than the NFPs, with only 11 countries versus 27 countries. In part, this reflects the smaller number of FP programs. In addition, though, the coverage range of the FP programs differs from the NFPs, once one moves past the five common countries in the top six. As table 4.2 reports, FP programs tend to operate in countries with

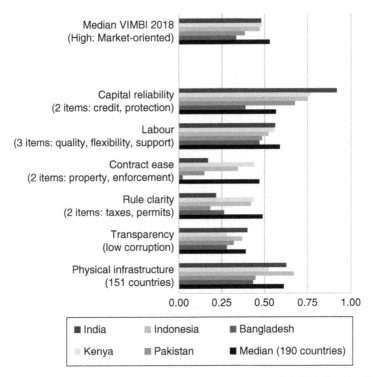

Figure 4.1 Index of voids in market-based institutions (VIMBI) for the five common countries in the top six of FP and NFP programs

Note: Will Mitchell provided the VIMBI indices, which use data from the World Bank (business and education level reports on capital availability, education levels and labour flexibility, contract reliability, and business rules), the World Economic Forum (physical infrastructure), and Transparency International (corruption).

higher mean GDP/capita, which offer greater ability to pay for services. It is unclear at this point in the analysis, though, whether the FP programs tend to target higher-income clients, whether in lower or middle-income locations; we will turn to that question later.

What Services Do For-Profit Health Care Programs Offer?

We next considered what types of services for-profit providers offer. We assess primary purposes as well as more fine-grained categories of ICT use and the types of medical needs the programs address. Table 4.3 reports the major patterns.

Table 4.3 ICT applications

A. Primary ICT purpose (50 FP; 125 NFP)	FP %	NFP %
Improve data management	60	51
Expand geographic access to services	42	42
Improve patient communications	36	42
Improve diagnosis and treatment	34	41
Streamline financial management	14	5
Mitigate fraud and abuse	8	4
B. ICT categories (47 FP; 96 NFP)		
Electronic medical records	38	26
Teleconferencing consultations and 24/7 phone/SMS consultations	30	35
ICT-supported microinsurance	13	7
Standardized clinical screening/decision-making support systems	9	13
Identification tools/smart cards	9	10
Patient education SMS services	6	6
Text reminder systems	4	9
Portable medical equipment	4	6
Stock-out reminder systems	4	3
Diagnostic lab services	4	0
Provider education	2	6
Home visits with technology	2	4
Emergency ambulance/paramedic call lines	2	3
Financial savings system with mobile reminders	2	1
Online clinical monitoring	2	0
On-site monitoring systems	0	22
Patient social media platforms	0	13
SMS clinical monitoring systems	0	9
Vaccination reminder systems	0	3
Broadcasted education	0	1
Online donations	0	1
ICT-base organizational processes	0	1
Electronic vouchers/coupons	0	1
C. General care services (50 FP; 125 NFP)		
General care: Primary	78	50
General care: Secondary/tertiary	36	16
D. Specialized care services (50 FP; 125 NFP)		
D1. Specialized areas with common public health mission and donor focus		
Maternal and child health	30	39
Family planning	6	31
Nutrition	4	10
HIV/AIDS	2	30

(Continued)

Table 4.3 Concluded

Tuberculosis	0	18
Malaria	0	10
D2. Other specialized care		
Emergency care	6	3
Non-communicable diseases	6	3
Eye care	2	5
Dentistry	0	4

Panel A shows that ICT both supports health care activities and helps provide direct care. Key support purposes include data management (60 per cent) and improving communications with patients (36 per cent). In parallel, direct care purposes include expanding geographic access to services (42 per cent), as well as improving diagnosis and treatment (34 per cent). The key point here is that multiple forms of ICT offer substantial potential across a wide range of health care services.

Panel B provides a more fine-grained comparison of the types of ICT categories that FP and NFP programs report using. We initially wondered whether FP ventures would use a broader range of ICT innovations than NFPs, potentially because of greater access to capital and/or knowledge. In practice, though, the most remarkable point of the comparison is that in almost all categories, FP and NFP organizations are equally likely to use the technology. Across twenty-three categories of ICT usage, ranging from electronic medical records to electronic vouchers, only three categories show a difference in usage. Both organizational forms commonly use electronic medical records and teleconferencing consultations. Both report moderate use of ICT-based micro-insurance and clinical screening tools. Neither commonly employ ICT-based organizational tools or electronic vouchers. Overall, FP and NFP ventures are drawing on ICT-based opportunities in similar ways.

Panel C of the table, though, reports a striking difference in general care services. FPs are more likely than NFPs to provide general care (primary and/or secondary/tertiary). Such for-profit services may provide more flexible access and sometimes higher quality than public health care facilities, offering revenue-generating opportunities for for-profit ventures by differentiating their services from public health care models (see Lindelow & Serneels 2006).

CARE Hospitals in India is an example of for-profit general care. CARE, founded in 1997 in Hyderabad, is one of the fastest growing hospital chains in India, providing primary and tertiary health care services across the country.

CARE was founded by a group of physicians, including physicians who had become frustrated with the bureaucracy in the public system. CARE's primary market is the middle-income segment, but it serves populations across geographic (rural and urban) and social (low- to high-income groups) spectra. Within the past decade, CARE has grown from 100 to 1,500 beds and from one to 13 units, now serving about half a million out-patients and 50,000 admissions annually, with cardiac care (about 4,000 cardiac surgeries a year) making up a key part of the patient load. CARE has three focus areas: the hospital, primary health clinics, and village health guides outfitted with point-of-care diagnostics and staff who perform education, data-collection, and basic care within the community. CARE's business model revolves around cost control. The hospital uses electronic data records to closely monitor costs of single procedures, emphasizes accurate diagnosis, and has developed clinical processes to limit unnecessary expensive invasive procedures. With the attention to cost, CARE is able to perform advanced procedures at a fraction of international costs while maintaining high quality, thereby promoting itself as a destination for foreign patients. For-profit CARE Hospitals also has a not-for-profit society (CARE Foundation) that invests in medical education and research. It also works to adopt technology to reach the poor in rural and urban communities. The CARE Rural Health Mission, supported by the CARE Foundation, is carrying out telemedicine programs in Maharashtra and Andhra Pradesh states. The hospital also has initiated a microinsurance program for basic primary care for $10/year for a family of four; this product complements government insurance that covers care in the hospital.

Launched in 2009, Viva Afya also uses ICT to support general primary care. Viva Afya primarily uses a hub-and-spoke model to serve densely populated low-income areas in Kenya. In this model, a main clinic (hub) is supported by several electronically connected satellite clinics (spokes). Viva Afya operates about twelve clinics in and around Nairobi, which are open seven days a week. Each clinic has a clinician, lab technician, pharmacy technician, and nurse on staff, thereby providing patients with a single stop for primary care. The anchor clinic is managed by a medical doctor, with a pharmacy run by a licenced pharmacist and a diagnostic laboratory run by a licenced laboratory technician. The anchor clinic provides consultation, diagnosis, and treatment for a wide range of illnesses. Satellite clinics, which are run by clinical officers and registered nurses, offer consultation services as well as weekly "Well Mother and Well Baby" clinics. Satellites are electronically linked to the anchor clinic for medical referrals. Clinical officers and nurses at the satellite clinics can seek advice from doctors at the anchor through telephone and instant messaging. Viva Afya, in conjunction with several microfinance organizations, offers bundled services based on annual subscription payments for safe motherhood, well baby, diabetes, and hypertension. Viva Afya uses two main types of ICT: an electronic medical record system and an early detection and prevention system (EDPS). The electronic medical record allows the satellite clinics to send patient information to anchor clinics, and its interoperability allows records to be transferred in from outside the Viva Afya network. The EDPS, which is available on both computer and phone platforms, can diagnose and suggest treatment for multiple diseases.

In turn, Panel D highlights a difference in specialized services. FPs are less likely than NFPs to provide targeted health-specific care, often called vertical services. FPs are particularly unlikely to engage in vertical services that are the traditional emphases of public health programs, such as family planning, HIV/AIDS, TB, and malaria services, which NFPs appear to offer as a public good consistent with a public health mission and donor preferences.

Nonetheless, some for-profit ventures do focus on more specialized care. Narayana Hrudayalaya, founded in India in 2000, for instance, is one of the world's largest paediatric heart hospitals, performing thirty-two heart surgeries a day, about eight times more than India's average. Almost half of the patients are children and babies. Narayana is able to keep treatment costs low while maintaining high quality of care by accepting donations and implementing cost-saving methods such as relying on digital X-rays rather than more expensive films, reducing inventory and processing times using comprehensive hospital management software, and increasing the volumes of patients served to maximize use of infrastructure. The hospital charges about half the price of average private hospitals in India, while almost 60 per cent of treatments are provided below cost or free. Narayana also launched the Care Companion program, which trains family members in basic tasks that support at-home care management. The hospital enjoys a high success rate – an average 1.4 per cent mortality rate within thirty days of coronary artery bypass graft surgery, compared to 1.9 per cent in the US. To address the 70 per cent of the population living in rural areas, the hospital has built a network of telemedicine centres, which provide free services to patients in remote rural areas; more than 21,000 cases have been referred using this service.

Marasin Stoa Kipas (MSK), founded in 2007, is another specialist for-profit venture. MSK trains and provides village health workers with rapid diagnostic kits and pre-packaged medication used for diagnosing and treating malaria in rural Papua New Guinea. MSK provides free diagnosis for all patients while charging a fee for malaria medication. The company operates through village kiosks operated by local women who are trained in basic malaria diagnosis and treatment. Based on the results of rapid diagnostic tests, patients are weighed on colour-coded scales that determine the pre-packaged medicine they receive for their three-day treatment.

Table 4.3 shows that FPs tend to offer a more limited range of services, primarily emphasizing general care and, to a somewhat lesser extent, maternal and child health services. This may reflect a limited set of profitable opportunities. At the same time, though, the differences could arise from market crowding by NFPs that are able to offer low cost or free services subsidized by donors and/or public agencies.

An example of market crowding is the case of insecticidal bed nets for preventing malaria. Approximately 1 million people in Africa die each year from malaria, making this a significant health challenge that many have tried to address. Many NFPs have provided antimalarial bed nets free through funding from international donors or government partners (Ahmed, Hossain, Kabir, & Roy 2011). However, some have raised concerns that this limits local markets because they cannot compete with free distribution of nets, preventing financially sustainable solutions for addressing malaria. Others are concerned about widespread coverage of nets sold by the private sector due to issues of affordability (Heierli & Lengeler 2008). The World Health Organization recommends finding ways to combine mass and targeted distribution so bed nets are available free of charge or at highly subsidized rates (World Health Organization 2012).

One for-profit approach to dealing with crowding involves working with partners to subsidize the nets. Based in Tanzania, A to Z Textile Mills is a for-profit company that produces low-cost, long-lasting bed nets to prevent malaria transmission from mosquitos. Founded in 2004, this private-public partnership brings together A to Z Textile Mills with Sumitomo Chemical, Exxon Mobil, the World Health Organization, Roll Back Malaria, Population Services International, and UNICEF, which supply materials and provide funding. The nets, which are effective for up to five years instead of the typical six months, are sold via direct marketing and online sales. Nets retail at US$5, but those subsidized and sold through the partnership are bought at the market price from A to Z and sold for US$2.15 to vulnerable groups. Each year, the company produces 29 million bed nets and employs 7,000 people.

How Do FPs Raise Money?

Table 4.4 reports patterns in how FPs generate their income. The large majority of FPs use revenue from services to a much greater extent than non-profits (88 per cent v. 32 per cent), and are particularly likely to use service revenue as their primary income source (66 per cent v. 12 per cent), through a mix of

Table 4.4 Income sources

A. Income Source	FP: Any Income (50 Programs)	NFP: Any Income (125 Programs)	FP: Primary Income	NFP: Primary Income
Revenue for service	88%	32%	66%	12%
Donor	28%	90%	10%	70%
Investor capital	24%	3%	10%	1%
Government	8%	20%	2%	5%
In-kind	2%	14%	0%	1%
B. Revenue Model	**FP**	**NFP**		
Memberships/ subscriptions	42%	9%		
Out-of-pocket payments	52%	24%		

memberships and/or out-of-pocket payments (Panel B). A substantial minority of FPs target donor funding, though to a much lesser extent than non-profits (28 per cent v. 90 per cent) and much less commonly as their primary income source (10 per cent v. 70 per cent). A moderate number of FPs, meanwhile, have raised investor capital, again substantially more commonly than non-profits (24 per cent v. 3 per cent). Few FPs rely on government support or in-kind contributions. Thus, for-profit ventures are substantially more likely than non-profits to be self-supporting.

The Mobile Cardiac Catheterization Laboratory in India provides an example of self-supporting direct revenue. The lab was launched in Karnataka in 2005 by the Vivus Group of hospitals to help treat heart disease in rural and peri-urban areas. The mobile cath lab is housed in a forty-foot sterile air-conditioned trailer, which can travel throughout the state on regular roads. A mobile unit can be set up for about one-quarter of the Rs 40 million (US$650,000) that is required for a regular cath lab, while the mobile service charges patients Rs 5000 (US$80), about half of what a comparable procedure would cost at an urban cath lab. The lab uses remote diagnostic tools that provide support from the company's home facilities. Patients are screened for heart problems by their family doctor and then, if needed, referred to a local facility, where a cardiologist from Vivus Group examines the patient and decides on the need for a coronary angiogram. Once a month, usually on a weekend, the mobile cath lab comes to the local facility and a cardiologist from the Vivus Group together with the family doctor conducts the angiogram inside the trailer. Patient recovery occurs in local hospitals or in nursing homes with basic recovery facilities. Patients needing further treatment are typically sent to Bangalore, while patients with milder needs can be managed locally.

As another example, Microcare has grown into the largest provider of group health insurance in Uganda since its launch in 2000. Burial societies, microfinance institutions, vendor associations, and other groups need to have at least 25 members to qualify. Microcare's insured base is composed of 70 per cent formal sector workers and 30 per cent informal sector workers, in both urban and rural communities. For annual fees per person of $90–$250 for formal sector groups, $10 for rural informal sector groups, and $25–$35 for urban informal sector groups, Microcare offers coverage through contracts with selected public and private health care providers. Microcare keeps premiums low by providing preventive health services to community members that target malaria, HIV/AIDS, waterborne diseases, and maternal and child health. These services also help increase renewal rates by keeping members engaged with tangible products. Microcare uses electronic identification systems to reduce fraud, along with extensive electronic medical records technology and claims processing via a networked hospital check-in system.

Some for-profits use memberships and/or subscriptions in their revenue model. MeraDoctor, launched in India in 2011, uses an Android app to connect patients with doctors who give health advice via instant messages. Doctors join the platform to gain income and build reputation. A subscription of Rs 2,000 per year (about US$35) provides 24/7 access to advice. MeraDoctor was founded by an Indian doctor who had worked for a social investment fund in New York and then relocated to Kenya before returning to India, together with a former World Bank executive. By 2013, about 10,000 families had subscribed. Many of MeraDoctor's users are young people using shared phones or facing scrutiny from family members, so the app now offers a delete feature for private medical information.

In parallel, some for-profits leverage donor funding as part of their income stream in the low-income segment. Founded in 2011, Swasth Health Centres is a for-profit primary care clinic chain operating in the slums of Mumbai, India. Its ICT use involves developing an electronic medical record system that is user friendly for clinicians and staff to enter and review data. One of the cofounders previously worked for McKinsey with a focus on the health care and development sectors, while another cofounder worked for KPMG; both have used their experiences to shape their business operations and interactions with investors and funders. The program is a for-profit social enterprise with a charitable arm, Swasth Foundation, which allows them to raise money from donors to open and operate new clinics until they break even. The program is also a member of the International Partnership for Innovative Healthcare Delivery (IPIHD) network, as well as the Social Entrepreneurship Accelerator at Duke (SEAD), receiving guidance on their models through business and strategy support, peer learning, and connections with the international investor community. Swasth participates in the CHMI Primary Care Learning Collaborative, which provides a forum for primary care programs operating in different countries to share insights and knowledge on improving their health care models.Launched in 2011, as of publication, Swasth has over 150,000 families registered at its clinics.

Penda Health is an example of a for-profit that complements client payment with support from donors and investors. Penda, founded in 2012, is a social enterprise operating primary care clinics for hard to reach populations in the bottom three income quintiles in Nairobi, Kenya. This for-profit chain uses online programs for shift planning and to train staff on clinical practices. Two of Penda's cofounders were Americans inspired to provide affordable, accessible, high-quality health services for women and their families in Kenya. The program has several Kenyan and American medical and business experts as advisors. Penda obtained seed funding from family and friends in the US and has received support from international donors and investors, including USAID, the Mulago Foundation, the Eleos Foundation, and the Robert Wood Johnson Foundation. The program is a member of IPIHD's innovator network and the CHMI primary care learning collaborative. Started in 2012, as of publication, Penda serves 25,000 patients a year.

NationWide is a for-profit in India that relies heavily on international investor funding. Launched in 2010, NationWide is a chain of primary care clinics with a family doctor model that target a full range of income groups. The clinics are open to both walk-in patients and subscribers of the clinic. Subscriptions include a personal physician, access to electronic health records, and 24/7 access to doctors though an on-call hotline. NationWide also operates a family physician training program and supports its physician staff in obtaining internationally recognized certification from the UK, which improves the respect of the general public towards family physicians, an under-appreciated specialty in India. By mid-2014, NationWide had grown to 36 clinics (15 full-service clinics and 21 satellite clinics in Bangalore and the Delhi region). This growth has been supported by Norwest Venture Partners and other international investors, which supply more than 90 per cent of NationWide's funding.

What Types of Clients Do FPs Target?

We next turned to market segmentation, wanting to assess whether for-profit ventures heavily emphasized segments with particularly high profit potential or, instead, whether they also operate at the bottom of the pyramid. Comparisons include urban versus rural populations, demographic targeting, and income targeting. Table 4.5 reports the patterns.

Table 4.5 Market segmentation

A. Geographic targeting (47 FP; 122 NFP)	FP	NFP
Urban	79%	56%
Peri-urban	62%	60%
Rural	66%	83%
B. Demographic targeting (50 FP; 125 NFP)	**FP**	**NFP**
Gender-specific	16%	34%
Young (children or YA)	6%	37%
C. Income targeting (41 FP; 108 NFP)	**FP**	**NFP**
C1. Quintiles		
Bottom 20%	68%	88%
Lower-middle income (20–40%)	93%	76%
Middle income (40–60%)	93%	73%
Higher-middle income (60–80%)	54%	33%
High income (80–100%)	49%	31%
C2. Income mix	**FP**	**NFP**
Bottom 40% income segment only	7%	26%
Bottom 40% and over 40% income segments	90%	73%
Over 40% segment only	2%	1%

Panel A addresses geographic targeting, showing that FPs are more likely than NFPs to be urban (79 per cent v. 56 per cent) and less likely to be rural (66 per cent v. 83 per cent). This distribution may reflect the fact that urban populations in LMICs tend to have greater income and offer a more concentrated and easier to serve market. Nonetheless, it is striking that almost two-thirds of the FP programs offer rural coverage, though often in combination with urban and/or peri-urban operations.

TeleSehat, founded in Pakistan in 2008, is an example of a for-profit service that targets the rural population while also providing urban coverage. TeleSehat seeks to overcome the rural-urban health care divide by providing quality health care services to rural Pakistan by using advanced telemedicine systems. TeleSehat expands the patient base of existing clinics without significantly expanding infrastructure and incurring large investments. With over 3,000 clients, the service provides real-time, remote clinical examination, diagnosis, and treatment, along with a centralized clinic management system with patient records that is accessible from anywhere. TeleSehat is assisting large hospitals in the cities to establish telemedicine cabins in their buildings and increasing health care accessibility for the poor. In addition to providing 24/7 access to health care practitioners, TeleSehat trains health care workers and other staff members.

The HealthLine service in Bangladesh, founded in 2006, is another example of a program that serves both urban and rural clients. HealthLine is an interactive teleconference between a Grameenphone mobile user and a licenced physician that is available at any time of the day. Grameenphone subscribers may seek medical advice on emergency, non-emergency, or regular medical situation by dialling 789. In Bangladesh, where the ratio of patients to doctors is 4,000:1, there are even fewer physicians in rural areas. HealthLine utilizes Grameenphone's ability to cover 95 per cent of the geographic area of the country, especially rural areas where 80 per cent of the population lives. These rural areas lack hospitals, clinics, and health facilities as well as qualified doctors. HealthLine provides access to health care that was not available before, including information on doctors, drugs, laboratory reports, and disease conditions. Call charges are fixed at Tk 15 for three minutes (about US$0.21), which make it accessible for the poor. The service is available to the 20 million Grameenphone mobile phone subscribers in Bangladesh. Those who do not have a Grameenphone subscription can access HealthLine services through community information centres and village phones. Callers range from common citizens to professionals. Village doctors also find it useful to consult the doctors at the HealthLine call centre when they need advice. By late 2014, the doctors had received and answered a total of about 3.5 million calls on as many as 79 different medical complaints from across the country.

Panel B of table 4.5 turns to demographic targeting. Unlike NFPs, which commonly target the young and/or specific genders, FPs are less likely to have a specific target demographic. This suggests that FPs seek as wide a market as possible to achieve higher revenue.

Clinic Africa, founded in 2007, is a for-profit chain of primary care clinics that serves the general population in Uganda. The chain has opened five clinics: three urban and two rural. The clinics, which operate on a fee-for-service basis supplemented by donor support, are centrally owned but individually operated by local physicians. The central organization is affiliated with an NGO that facilitates donor funding and helps oversee quality control for the network. Physicians retain most of the profits, with a portion of the revenues being paid to cover central costs. The urban clinics are profitable, although the rural clinics have struggled to break even.

Panel C addresses income targeting. Not surprisingly, the patterns in Panel C1 show that FPs are less likely than NFPs to target poorest clients (68 per cent v. 88 per cent) and more likely to target the highest income quintile (49 per cent v. 31 per cent). Nonetheless, it is striking that more than two-thirds of the FPs provide services to the bottom income quintile.

Panel C2 helps determine how many of the for-profit programs can afford to address the lower income segment. Far fewer FPs than NFPs provide services only in the bottom 40 per cent of the market (7 per cent v. 26 per cent). In turn, FPs are more likely than NFPs to seek clients across lower- and higher-income segments (90 per cent v. 73 per cent), possibly as a means of cross-subsidizing their service and, potentially, seeking efficiencies from greater scale. At the same time, though, many NFP programs also seek income-spanning segments. Moreover, both FP and NFP programs rarely target only the upper-income segment, possibly because the segment typically is not large enough to support viable operations. This pattern also likely reflects the goal of the CHMI to gather information from programs that serve poorer populations.

ASEMBIS Health, founded in Costa Rica in 1991, is a program that successfully operates across income segments. ASEMBIS is a for-profit social enterprise that provides medical services through call centres, technology, and affordable pricing. ASEMBIS uses a multi-tiered pricing model in which higher revenues earned from wealthier patients cross-subsidize low-income patients. In doing so, they have created a self-sustaining network of clinics that provides full eye care, from basic eye examinations to sophisticated surgical procedures, at a 40–70 per cent discount from market rates. ASEMBIS has a 60 per cent market share for sales of corrective glasses. ASEMBIS's integrated network includes non-traditional health professionals for vision testing and preventive care, cost-efficient and high-volume clinics, and mobile rural clinics (it is the only player in many rural areas). ASEMBIS redesigned the eye care process to maximize utilization of the scarcest resource: optometrists. In its clinics, optometrists care for an average of seventy patients per day. The model is sustainable and profitable, as ASEMBIS generated one hundred thousand dollars in profits in 2010 out of $5.7 million in sales. A new clinic typically breaks even within about a year.

So far, the patterns suggest that for-profit health care ventures in LMICs commonly target segments and services that offer the greatest opportunities to generate profitable revenue. At the same time, though, a substantial proportion of for-profit ventures operate in seemingly low-profit environments, including rural communities and low-income segments. As we noted above, part of the route to this pattern appears to arise from cross-subsidization across segments.

We now turn to another possible route to profitability in low income segments, which considers complementary sources of revenue. It is possible that for-profit providers turn to governments or donors to subsidize their services for the poorest part of the population.

Table 4.6 compares income sources of for-profit programs that operate in the lowest 20 per cent income segment to those that operate only above that

Table 4.6 For-profit income sources for the lowest income segment

FP Operates in Bottom 20% Income Segment	Yes (28 Programs)	No (13 Programs)
A. Source of Income		
Donor funding	21%	31%
Government funding	7%	8%
In-kind funding	4%	0%
Investment capital	25%	38%
Revenue for service	96%	77%
B. Revenue Model		
Memberships/subscriptions	46%	31%
Out-of-pocket payments	64%	38%

segment. Counter to the suggestion above, donor and government funding are no more likely in the lowest income segments than they are for higher-income clients. Thus, it appears that for-profit health care providers seek to provide services that even the poorest clients are willing to pay for, most commonly receiving revenue at the time of service via out of pocket payments (96 per cent and 64 per cent in Panels A and B in table 4.6).

iKure in India is an example of a for-profit venture that uses ICT to help tailor its services for people with limited income. iKure is a health social enterprise that reaches the rural poor by providing affordable primary care services through 28 rural health centres located in West Bengal. Founded in 2010, iKure's centres are staffed by doctors, pharmacists, and trained health workers, and are open seven days a week. iKure operates a mobile medical unit that can reach people living farther from the centres, and also provides health camps for diabetes, eye care, and gynaecology. The program partners with several urban hospitals, which provide expertise on critical cases at the centres, facilitating a hub-and-spoke model. iKure has developed wireless health incident software that monitors key metrics including prescriptions, stock management, and doctor performance. The software helps connect centres, hospitals, and doctors, while increasing operational efficiency. The high-volume, low-cost business model is funded by patient fees. Patients save at least US$2 per visit compared to equivalent health services at the nearest other provider. Moreover, 80 per cent of patients only have to travel 500 metres to one kilometre to access iKure's services, compared to the typical 10 kilometres required to reach equivalent providers. The low cost and close location provide an attractive option for people with limited income in rural areas who are seeking quality health care.

Who Do For-Profit Health Care Ventures Partner with?

Partnerships offer another potential means for sharing the load of providing services in low-income segments. Table 4.7 reports partnership patterns. Panel A shows that FP ventures are less likely than NFPs to have partners (49 per cent v. 72 per cent). Nonetheless, partnerships are common, as the numbers show that almost half of the FPs use allies in their services.

TeleDoctor, launched during 2007, is a for-profit venture that uses partnerships to target low-income clients in Pakistan. TeleDoctor is a health hotline that operates through Telenor, a mobile service provider that covers rural and underserved areas of the country. The service connects Telenor subscribers with certified doctors who provide advice on health questions, discuss lab results, and help access emergency medical response. The TeleDoctor service will also send prescriptions to patients by SMS, as well as SMS and pre-recorded voice messages on healthy living. Callers can choose from multiple languages and can speak with male or female physicians. TeleDoctor was launched in 2007 and receives approximately 1,500 calls per day.

Panel B shows similar distributions in numbers of partners among FP and NFP ventures that have at least one ally. The only significant difference is that FPs are less likely to be part of large coalitions (four or more partners). There is some indication, then, that many for-profit ventures use partnerships in their services, but typically with a focused set of allies.

Table 4.7 Health care partnerships

A. Partners (50 FP; 125 NFP)	FP	NFP
Has partner(s)	50%	71%
B. Number of Partners (25 FP; 90 NFP)	FP	NFP
One	48%	37%
Two	20%	23%
Three	20%	18%
Four or more	12%	22%
C. Types of Partner (25 FP; 90 NFP)	FP	NFP
FP	88%	38%
NFP/multilateral organization (MLO)	40%	76%
Government	16%	34%
D. Partnerships by Programs in Bottom 40% Income Segment (40 FP; 107 NFP)	FP	NFP
D1. At least one partner	45%	74%
D2. Type of partner (18 FP, 79 NFP)		
FP partner	83%	41%
NFP/government/MLO partner	50%	85%

Nonetheless, some for-profit ventures are part of larger coalitions. MicroEnsure, founded in 2002 and now operating in Sub-Saharan Africa and Asia, is an example of a for-profit venture that uses multiple partnerships to help provide services in low income segments. MicroEnsure is an insurance intermediary with a focus on introducing affordable insurance protection for poor populations. It partners with organizations that serve the poor, such as rural banks, microfinance organizations, and humanitarian organizations, as well as telecommunications companies. In Nigeria, for example, it partners with Airtel and Cornerstone Insurance to provide free home and life insurance to low- and middle-income Airtel subscribers. Customers sign up for the service through their mobile phones; if they recharge their Airtel line with a minimum of 1,000 Nigerian naira (about US$6) before the last day of each month, they receive insurance coverage for the next month; the more they recharge, the more coverage they receive. This approach provides MicroEnsure with access to Airtel's clients while also building loyalty and a customer base for their telecom partner. Started in 2002, MicroEnsure currently serves 11 million clients, including 6 million in Africa, with 85 per cent of customers never being insured before.

In Tanzania, meanwhile, MicroEnsure supports the KNCU Health Plan, launched in the Kilimanjaro area of Northern Tanzania in 2011. This plan offers affordable health care to members of the Kilimanjaro Native Cooperative Union, a union of coffee growers with more than 60 cooperatives and 50,000 families. The plan operates as a partnership between the non-profit PharmAccess Foundation and Mission for Essential Medical Supplies and the for-profit MicroEnsure. The KNCU plan covers members and their families for primary health care and limited secondary care for chronic diseases (e.g., diabetes, hypertension, asthma, arthritis, rheumatism), maternity care such as delivery and caesarean section, and neonatal care. The annual premium for the plan is 40,500 Tanzanian shillings (about US$25) per person, although subsidies from the cooperative mean that members pay about 12,000 shillings (US$7.50) per year. Penetration rates are typically between 35 per cent and 55 per cent per community. Membership contributions can be deducted from coffee sales or paid in cash.

Panel C of table 4.7 shows a separation of partnerships. FPs are more likely than NFPs to partner with other FPs, while NFPs are more likely to partner with other NFPs or government agencies. Nonetheless, more than 50 per cent of the FPs that form partnerships do so with NFP allies, again suggesting a route to sharing the burden in meeting the needs of low-income populations.

Mediphone, founded in 2011 in India, is an example of a for-profit partnership. Mediphone is an alliance of Airtel and Healthfore (Religare Technologies) that provides advice over the phone for non-acute and minor ailments. To access this service, a client calls 54445 from a mobile phone and is connected to a medical practitioner who has access to a clinical decision support system. Mediphone is available to Airtel telecom customers, who are charged 50 paise (US$0.01) per call for connection charges and Rs 35 (US$0.60) per consultation irrespective of call duration. The call is answered by a Healthfore health officer, who is an accredited nurse or doctor. Services include psychological counselling, first-level medical advice, family planning, and nutrition guidance, as well as advice on self-care, doctor's consultation, and medication. When needed, the service can transfer the call to emergency services. In 2014, Mediphone received 2,000 calls per day.

Some FPs do ally with non-profits or government actors. Beginning in 2006, for instance, IGE Medical Systems (IGEMS) contracted with the Indian state of Bihar to provide radiology services in health care facilities across Bihar, from primary health centres to district hospitals. Although services in government hospitals were provided free to patients in Bihar, important diagnostic infrastructure for the services was lacking. To help provide the infrastructure, the government contracted with private providers to set up and operate within the public facilities, paid based on the number of tests performed. The private provider is paid Rs 50–Rs 75 (about US$1 to $1.50) per X-ray screening. Initially, the charges were paid by patients, but the state revised the agreement so that the charges are now paid by the government. The units include a range of radiology services: X-rays in all hospitals, plus ultrasound units and hysterosalpingogram (HSG) facilities for fertility tests in subdistrict hospitals. X-ray films are generated by the private provider and then are reported by doctors in the hospitals, with overall monitoring by district health societies. As an expansion of the initial partnership, a central reporting system is being established in Patna district, with connections to the ultrasound and X-ray centres in individual hospitals, which are then connected via teleradiology. About 450 X-ray units are functional across the 38 districts of Bihar and have provided services to more than 225,000 patients, while 30,000 patients have been serviced through ultrasound centres. IGEMS reports that the volume helps in negotiating prices for raw materials and gaining profits in spite of low prices (although reporting that payments are sometimes delayed). To build out the program, IGEMS developed an innovative business model of franchising in which more than 500 local entrepreneurs were encouraged to operate radiology centres with technical support from IGEMS.

We further investigated whether for-profit programs that target the lower-income segments tend to rely on partnerships to do so. We found that FP programs that target the lowest-income segment are no more likely than FP programs that do not target that segment to use partnerships (just under half in both cases).

Panel D of table 4.7 next compares FPs and NFPs operating in the bottom 40 per cent income segment (we found similar results when limited the comparison to the bottom 20 per cent segment). Almost half of the FPs operating in the lower-income segment have partners, including a mix of FP and NFP partners. However, FPs are less likely than NFPs operating in those segments to use partners (45 per cent v. 74 per cent), particularly non-profit partners (30 per cent v. 56 per cent). Thus, partnerships appear to help many for-profits operate in low-income segments, but they are more likely than non-profits to operate independently, possibly because they tend to have stronger operating skills.

Discussion: For-Profit Health Care in LMICs

Our goal for this research was to explore the role of for-profit providers in using ICT-based services to address health care needs in LMICs. We found substantial engagement, both in the patterns of the data and the nuance of the examples. Several characteristics of a "typical" for-profit venture in this study stand out. While India is the most common location, the ventures operate in a varied mix of countries, though often in countries above the very poorest (table 4.2). The ventures most commonly use computers and phones, and occasionally other ICT platforms, to support health care services (table 4.1). ICT supports a wide range of services, with electronic medical records and teleconferencing being most common; FPs tend to emphasize general care, along with a meaningful presence in maternal and child health services, together with a limited amount of other specialty services (table 4.3). They provide coverage in a range of income segments, typically for a wide demographic range, and commonly for multiple income groups (table 4.5). The for-profit ventures commonly gain their income directly from their clients, including both memberships and out-of-pocket payment, although some programs gain complementary support from donors and investors, especially for the lowest income segment (tables 4.4 and 4.6). Finally, for-profits use a mix of independent and partnership models, with varied number and types of partners (tables 4.7 and 4.8).

Together, these patterns generate a summary set of implications. For-profit ventures are less likely than NFPs to serve the poorest clients but, nonetheless, many for-profits do target the bottom of the pyramid. Partnerships with both for-profit and non-profit organizations help some for-profit ventures spread the cost of serving the poor, though many operate independently. For-profits that operate in LMICs, including within the lowest income segments of those countries, seek revenue by providing general care to a broad population in multiple settings. This is typically paid for by direct patient payment that is sometimes supplemented by donor and government support. The general care services and broad populations help create scale, while direct patient payment requires fine-tuning the business model to fit patients' available cash flow.

Several findings align with previous studies of for-profit health ventures in LMICs. Tung and Bennett (2014) found most of their limited set of for-profit ventures in South Asia, which is consistent with India as the most common location of ICT-based services in our study. In line with Bennett (1992) and Patouillard et al. (2007), we found that FPs commonly serve urban populations and/or at least middle-income segments, and often require out of pocket payments.

We also find key contrasts with prior work. A substantial proportion of the FPs in the study serve rural and/or bottom income communities, which contradicts assertions that FPs primarily target more affluent groups (e.g., Bennett 1992; Kuriyan et al. 2008). Our study suggests that FPs are finding ways to serve this population, including using ICT-based health care to reduce costs, often combined with cross-subsidization and strategic partnerships, as well as microinsurance and subscription models. Moreover, some discussions have suggested that ICT, despite its benefits, could dilute quality of care (e.g., Sarhan); while systematic implications about performance are beyond the scope of this study, many of the examples suggest that ICT can help improve access and quality of care.

Our research also explores areas that prior work has not studied in depth, including the types of ICT models that FPs use to serve lower-income populations and the partnerships they have formed. The study compares these characteristics of for-profit ventures with non-profits, highlighting similarities along with notable differences. Although FPs tend to focus more on general care services than NPFs, for-profit and non-profit programs are largely using the same ICT technologies and engaging in similar ICT models, contradicting the idea that FPs are more likely to engage in some models, such as health hotlines (Ivatury et al. 2009).

While a 2012 World Bank report (Qiang et al. 2012) describes mHealth in LMICs as dominated by NFPs, suggesting that for-profit mHealth models are relatively rare in these contexts, almost one-third of our sample of ICT-based health care programs were for-profit ventures. The same report describes a lack of donor and government support for for-profit mHealth projects compared to non-profits. Although NFPs in our study are, indeed, far more likely to receive donor funding than FPs, we still find that more than a quarter of the for-profit ventures do supplement patient revenues with donor funding.

In addition, while FPs are less likely to engage in partnerships than NFPs, half of the for-profit ventures are developing alliances to support their operations, with more than 60 per cent of the FPs that create partnerships do so, at least in part, with governments and/or NFPs. This supports Schweiter and Synoweic's (2012) suggestion that partnerships may be one of the most effective ways for mHealth and eHealth projects to operate, combining the capabilities of both public and private entities. Our research suggests that a closer look at the ICT health sector in LMICs provides important nuances that indicate both overlap and complementarity between the activities of NFPs and FPs, with increasing potential for both to engage in this field.

More generally, we contribute to bottom of the pyramid research. Health care is one of the key frontiers at the intersection of social welfare in business opportunity. We highlight the active interest in this area by for-profit ventures while identifying approaches that they undertake in order to be financially viable when offering services in the lowest income segments.

Intriguingly, almost all the for-profit health care activity in this study involves local ventures, sometimes with knowledge and financial support from foreign partners. We found only limited engagement by MNEs, most commonly by telecom companies that saw opportunities to leverage their infrastructure while also seeking to expand their customer base. Two reasons likely underlie the limited engagement by MNEs. First, most firms face strong challenges in their core segments, having only limited time and funds for expansion to lower-income tiers. Second, MNEs often have only limited understanding of the nuances of local markets in LMICs, particularly in low-income segments. Local ventures often have greater knowledge that they can use to tailor their services, so as to have the potential to operate profitably despite the low income of their customers. A striking example from beyond this study is the India pharmaceutical firm Cipla's success in low-income markets where established Western pharmaceutical companies have not been able to operate (Mitchell & Capron 2015).

Together, these points about attention and knowledge reflect Husted's (2013) question about how much engagement at the bottom of the pyramid we should expect from MNEs. Rather, entry by innovative local actors may be more likely. Clearly, this point merits attention.

The study has limits that suggest avenues for ongoing research. First, the sample of the study is based on self-reported data and data gathered by partners of the CHMI. Nonetheless, the data are by far the most extensive set of information about non-profit and for-profit private health care ventures in LMICs. The range and depth of the information provides important insights, in the minimum as a platform for ongoing research.

Second, we focus on the activities of for-profit and non-profit ventures without comparing their performance. Unfortunately, the data provide very limited information about performance. Fewer than a third of the programs in the study provide any form of performance information and, moreover, much of the available data is not comparable, covering a diverse set of outcome factors, including numbers of visits, clinicians, patient trials, and condoms distributed. Certainly, not all ventures have succeeded. First Micro Insurance Agency in Pakistan, for instance, introduced life and health insurance products for low-income communities in 2006, but had to discontinue the program in 2011. Further research is needed to study the sustainability and comparative impact of for-profit and non-profit health care ventures.

This study highlights the point that for-profit health care ventures are highly relevant actors in low-income health care. Clearly, there is and will continue to be a critically important role for non-profit and government health services in all markets. Still, this research is part of the growing recognition of the role of for-profit ventures to serve even the poorest communities in low-income settings. Further research and practice are needed to extend these insights.

REFERENCES

Ahmed, S.M., Hossain, S., Kabir, M.M., & Roy, S. 2011. "Free Distribution of Insecticidal Bed Nets Improves Possesion and Preferential Use by Households and Is Equitable: Findings from Two Cross-Sectional Surveys in Thirteen Malaria Endemic Districts of Bangladesh." *Malaria Journal*: 10(1) 357. https://doi.org/10.1186/1475 -2875-10-357.

Alcácer, J., & Chung, W. 2014. "Location Strategies for Agglomeration Economies." *Strategic Management Journal* 35(12): 1749–61. https://doi.org/10.1002/smj.2186.

Altman, D., Fogstad, H., Gronseth, L., & Kristensen, F. 2011. "Innovating for Every Woman, Every Child." Oslo: The Global Campaign for the Health Millennium Development Goals.

Asiimwe, C., Gelvin, D., Lee, E., Ben Amor, Y., Quinto, E., Katureebe, C., ... Berg, M. 2011. "Use of an Innovative, Affordable, and Open Source Short Message Service Based Tool to Monitor Malaria in Remote Areas of Uganda." *The American Journal of Tropical Medicine and Hygiene* 85(1): 26–33. https://doi.org/10.4269/ajtmh .2011.10-0528.

Barrington, J., Wereko-Brobby, O., Ward, P., Mwafongo, W., & Kungulwe, S. 2010. "SMS for Life: A Pilot Project to Improve Anti-malarial Drug Supply Management in Rural Tanzania Using Standard Technology." *Malaria Journal* 9(1): 298. https:// doi.org/10.1186/1475-2875-9-298.

Basu, S., Andrews, J., Kishore, S., Panjabi, R., & Stuckler, D. 2012. "Comparative Performance of Private and Public Healthcare Systems in Low- and Middle-Income Countries: A Systematic Review." *PLoS Medicine* 9(6): e1001244. https://doi.org/ 10.1371/journal.pmed.1001244.

Bennett, S. 1992. "Promoting the Private Sector: A Review of Developing Country Trends." *Health Policy and Planning* 7(2): 97–110. https://doi.org/10.1093/heapol/7.2.97.

Blaya, J.A., Shin, S.S., Yale, G., Suarez, C., Asencios, L., Contreras, C., ... Fraser, H. S. F. 2010. "Electronic Laboratory System Reduces Errors in National Tuberculosis Program: A Cluster Randomized Controlled Trial." *International Journal of Tuberculosis and Lung Disease* 14(8): 1009–15.

Bustreo, F., Okwo-Bele, J.-M., & Kamara, L. 2015. "World Health Organization Perspectives on the Contribution of the Global Alliance for Vaccines and Immunization on Reducing Child Mortality." *Archives of Disease in Childhood* 100 Suppl (Suppl 1): S34–7. https://doi.org/10.1136/archdischild-2013-305693.

Center for Health Market Innovations. 2016. CHMI Programs. http://healthmarketinnovations.org/programs.

Chatterji, A.K., & Fabrizio, K.R. 2014. "Does the Market for Ideas Influence the Rate and Direction of Innovative Activity? Evidence from the Medical Device Industry." *Strategic Management Journal* 37(3): 447–65. https://doi.org/10.1002/smj.2340.

Chib, A. 2010. "The Aceh Besar Midwives with Mobile Phones Project: Design and Evaluation Perspectives Using the Information and Communication Technologies for Healthcare Development Model." *Journal of Computer-Mediated Communication* 15(3): 500–25. https://doi.org/10.1111/j.1083-6101.2010.01515.x.

Crean, K.W. 2010. "Accelerating Innovation in Information and Communication Technology for Health." *Health Affairs* 29(2): 278–83. https://doi.org/10.1377/hlthaff.2009.0795.

Da Costa, T.M., Barbosa, B.J.P., Sigulem, D., de Fatima Marin, H., & Pisa, I. 2012. "Results of a Randomized Controlled Trial to Assess the Effects of a Mobile SMS-Based Intervention on Treatment Adherence in HIV/AIDS-Infected Brazilian Women and Impressions and Satisfaction with Respect to Incoming Messages." *International Journal of Medical Informatics* 81(4): 257–69. https://doi.org/10.1016/j.ijmedinf.2011.10.002.

Dutt, N., Hawn, O., Vidal, E., Chatterji, A., McGahan, A., & Mitchell, W. 2016. "How Open System Intermediaries Address Institutional Failures: The Case of Business Incubators in Emerging Market Countries." *Academy of Management Journal* 59(3): 818–40. https://doi.org/10.5465/amj.2012.0463.

Fraser, H.S.F., Allen, C., Bailey, C., Douglas, G., Shin, S., & Blaya, J. 2007. "Information Systems for Patient Follow-up and Chronic Management of HIV and Tuberculosis: A Life-Saving Technology in Resource-Poor Areas." *Journal of Medical Internet Research* 9(4): e29. https://doi.org/10.2196/jmir.9.4.e29.

Gerber, T., Olazabal, V., Brown, K., & Pablos-Mendez, A. 2010. "An Agenda for Action on Global e-Health." *Health Affairs* 29(2): 233–6. https://doi.org/10.1377/hlthaff.2009.0934.

Githinji, S., Kigen, S., Memusi, D., Nyandigisi, A., & Mbithi, A.M. 2013. "Reducing Stock-outs of Life-Saving Malaria Commodities Using Mobile Phone Text-Messaging: SMS for Life Study in Kenya." *PLoS One* 8(1): e54066. https://doi.org/10.1371/journal.pone.0054066.

Glaeser, E.L., & Shleifer, A. 2001. "Not-for-Profit Entrepreneurs." *Journal of Public Economics* 81(1): 99–115. https://doi.org/10.1016/S0047-2727(00)00130-4.

Gu, M., & Tse, E. 2010. "Building Innovative Organizations in China: The 'Execution+' Organization." *Asia Pacific Journal of Management* 27(1): 25–53. https://doi.org/10.1007/s10490-008-9115-2.

Hammond, A.L., Kramer, W.J., Katz, R.S., Tran, J.T., & Walker, C. 2007. *The Next 4 Billion: Market Size and Business Strategy at the Base of the Pyramid.* Washington, DC: World Resource Institute-International Finance Corporation.

Heierli, U., & Lengeler, C. 2008. *Should Bednets Be Sold or Given Free? The Role of the Private Sector in Malaria Control. Poverty Allieviation as a Business Series.* Berne, Switzerland: Swiss Agency for Development and Co-operation.

Husted, B.W. 2013. "Global Environmental and Social Strategy." *Global Strategy Journal* 3(2): 195–7. https://doi.org/10.1111/j.2042-5805.2013.01057.x.

Interactive Research and Development & Stop TB Partnership. 2012. "mHealth to Improve TB Care." Geneva: Switzerland.

Ivatury, G., Moore, J., & Bloch, A. 2009. "A Doctor in Your Pocket: Health Hotlines in Developing Countries." *Innovations: Technology, Governance, Globalization* 4(1): 119–53. https://doi.org/10.1162/itgg.2009.4.1.119.

Jones Christensen, L., Siemsen, E., & Balasubramanian, S. 2015. "Consumer Behavior Change at the Base of the Pyramid: Bridging the Gap between For-Profit and Social Responsibility Strategies." *Strategic Management Journal* 36(2): 307–17. https://doi.org/10.1002/smj.2249.

Karnani, A. 2007. "The Mirage of Marketing to the Bottom of the Pyramid." *California Management Review*: 49(4): 48–109. https://doi.org/10.2307/41166407.

Khan, A., Khowaja, S., Khan, F.S., Qazi, F., Lotia, I., Habib, A., ... Keshavjee, S. 2012. "Engaging the Private Sector to Increase Tuberculosis Case Detection: An Impact Evaluation Study." *The Lancet Infectious Diseases* 12(8): 608–16. https://doi.org/doi: 10.1016/S1473-3099(12)70116-0.

Kuriyan, R., Ray, I., & Toyama, K. 2008. "Information and Communication Technologies for Development: The Bottom of the Pyramid Model in Practice." *The Information Society* 24(2): 93–104. https://doi.org/10.1080/01972240701883948.

Lewis, T., Synowiec, C., Lagomarsino, G., & Schweitzer, J. 2012. "E-health in Low- and Middle-Income Countries: Findings from the Center for Health Market Innovations." *Bulletin of the World Health Organization* 90(5): 332–40. https://doi.org/10.2471/blt.11.099820.

Lindelow, M., & Serneels, P. 2006. "The Performance of Health Workers in Ethiopia: Results from Qualitative Research." *Social Science & Medicine* 62(9): 2225–35. https://doi.org/10.1016/j.socscimed.2005.10.015.

London, T., & Hart, S.L. 2004. "Reinventing Strategies for Emerging Markets: Beyond the Transnational Model." *Journal of International Business Studies* 35(5): 350–70. https://doi.org/10.1057/palgrave.jibs.8400099.

MacDonald, J.A., McGahan, A.M., Mitchell, W., & The T-HOPE Team. 2013. "The Future of Health Care Access." *Stanford Social Innovation Review*, 48–54.

Mair, J., Marti, I., & Ventresca, M.J. 2012. "Building Inclusive Markets in Rural Bangladesh: How Intermediaries Work Institutional Voids." *Academy of Management Journal* 55(4): 819–50. https://doi.org/10.5465/amj.2010.0627.

Millard, P., Bru, J., & Berger, C. 2012. "Open-Source Point-of-Care Electronic Medical Records for Use in Resource-Limited Settings: Systematic Review and Questionnaire Surveys." *BMJ Open* 2(4): e000690. https://doi.org/10.1136/bmjopen-2011-000690.

Miller, D., Lee, J., Chang, S., & Le Breton-Miller, I. 2009. "Filling the Institutional Void: The Social Behavior and Performance of Family vs Non-family Technology Firms in Emerging Markets." *Journal of International Business Studies* 40(5): 802–17. https://doi.org/10.1057/jibs.2009.11.

Miner, J.B. 2006. *Organizational Behavior 2: Essential Theories of Process and Structure*. Armonk, New York: M.E. Sharpe.

Mitchell, W., & Capron, L. 2015. "Filling the Missing Middle: Emerging Market Multinationals are Profiting in Tough Environments by Becoming Institutional Intermediaries. Lessons from Cipla in India and Beyond." Toronto: Rotman Teaching Note.

Patouillard, E., Goodman, C.A., Hanson, K.G., & Mills, A.J. 2007. "Can Working with the Private For-Profit Sector Improve Utilization of Quality Health Services by the Poor? A Systematic Review of the Literature." *International Journal for Equity in Health* 6(1): 17. https://doi.org/10.1186/1475-9276-6-17.

PMNCH. 2012. *Private Enterprise for Public Health. Opportunities for Business to Improve Women's and Children's Health: A Short Guide for Companies*. Geneva, Switzerland.

Prahalad, C.K. 2006. *The Fortune at the Bottom of the Pyramid: Eradicating Poverty through Profits*. Upper Saddle River, New Jersey: Wharton School Publishing.

Prahalad, C.K., & Hart, S.L. 2002. "The Fortune at the Bottom of the Pyramid." *Strategy+Business* First quarter(26): 1–15.

Qiang, C.Z., Hausman, V., Yamamichi, M., & Miller, R. 2012. "Mobile Applications for the Health Sector." Washington, DC: World Bank.

Rahman, M., Hasan, M.R., & Floyd, D. 2013. "Brand Orientation as a Strategy That Influences the Adoption of Innovation in the Bottom of the Pyramid Market." *Strategic Change* 22(3–4): 225–39. https://doi.org/10.1002/jsc.1935.

Ratzan, S.C., & Gilhooley, D. 2010. "Innovative Use of Mobile Phones and Related Information and Communication Technologies." In *Every Woman, Every Child: Investing in Our Common Future*. Geneva, Switzerland: Global Strategy for Women's and Children's Health.

Sarhan, F. "Telemedicine in Healthcare. 2: The Legal and Ethical Aspects of Using New Technology." *Nursing Times* 105(43): 18–20.

Saxenian, A. 1996. *Regional Advantage: Culture and Competition in Silicon Valley and Route 128*. Boston, MA: Harvard University Press.

Schweitzer, J., & Synowiec, C. 2012. "The Economics of eHealth and mHealth." *Journal of Health Communication* 17(Suppl 1): 73–81. https://doi.org/10.1080/10810730.2011.649158.

Shahin, I., Sohal, R., Ginther, J., Hayden, L., MacDonald, J.A., Mossman, K., ... Perriëns, J. 2014. "Trans-national Scale-Up of Services in Global Health." *PLoS ONE* 9(11): e110465. https://doi.org/10.1371/journal.pone.0110465.

Simon, H.A. 1979. "Rational Decision Making in Business Organizations." *The American Economic Review* 69(4): 493–513. https://www.jstor.org/stable/1808698.

Smith, L.C., & Haddad, L. 2015. "Reducing Child Undernutrition: Past Drivers and Priorities for the Post-MDG Era." *World Development* 68: 180–204. https://doi.org/10.1016/j.worlddev.2014.11.014.

Srai, J.S., & Alinaghian, L.S. 2013. "Value Chain Reconfiguration in Highly Disaggregated Industrial Systems: Examining the Emergence of Health Care Diagnostics." *Global Strategy Journal* 3(1): 88–108. https://doi.org/10.1111/j.2042-5805.2012.01047.x.

Tung, E., & Bennett, S. 2014. "Private Sector, For-Profit Health Providers in Low- and Middle-Income countries: Can They Reach the Poor at Scale?" *Globalization and Health* 10(1): 52. https://doi.org/10.1186/1744-8603-10-52.

Wei, T., & Clegg, J. 2014. "Successful Integration of Target Firms in International Acquisitions: A Comparative Study in the Medical Technology Industry." *Journal of International Management* 20(2): 237–55. https://doi.org/10.1016/j.intman.2013.05.003.

World Bank. 2008. *The Business of Health in Africa: Partnering with the Private Sector to Improve People's Lives*. Washington, DC: World Bank.

World Health Organization. 2011. *mHealth: New Horizons for Health through Mobile Technologies: Global Observatory for eHealth Series*. (Vol. 3). Geneva: World Health Organization.

World Health Organization. 2012. *World Malaria Report 2012*. Geneva: World Health Organization. https://doi.org/10.1071/EC12504.

World Health Organization. 2014. *WHO | World Health Statistics 2014*. Geneva: World Health Organization.

You, D., Hug, L., & Chen, Y. 2014. *Levels & Trends in Child Mortality*. New York: United Nations Children's Fund.

5 Criteria to Assess Potential Reverse Innovations: Opportunities for Shared Learning between High- and Low-Income Countries

ONIL BHATTACHARYYA, DIANE WU,
KATHRYN MOSSMAN, LEIGH HAYDEN, PAVAN GILL,
YU-LING CHENG, ABDALLAH DAAR, DILIP SOMAN,
CHRISTINA SYNOWIEC, ANDREA TAYLOR,
JOSEPH WONG, MAX VON ZEDTWITZ, STANLEY ZLOTKIN,
WILL MITCHELL, AND ANITA MCGAHAN

Background

There has always been an imperative to do more with less in low- and middle-income countries (LMICs) in general, but particularly in health care (Syed et al. 2012). While investment in health care has been increasing for many of these countries, the needs and challenges faced by LMICs are greater than in high-income countries (HICs), and the resources are much more limited (Jakovljevic & Getzen 2016; Jakovljevic 2016).[1] The ability of LMIC organizations to innovate is facilitated by the absence of constraining legacy systems, a flexible regulatory environment, low performance of standard approaches, and an urgency to do things better and cheaper (Immelt, Govindarajan, & Trimble 2009). As a result, many innovations that originate in LMICs have been shown to reduce cost, improve quality, and enhance access (Bhattacharyya et al. 2010). The relevance of these innovations to HIC settings has only recently been acknowledged, due to a growing pressure to control costs and improve access for marginalized groups (Immelt et al. 2009; Syed, Dadwal, & Martin 2013; Harris 2013). This has increased interest in shared learning about innovations between low- and high-resource settings (Crisp 2014). The adaptation of LMIC innovations to HICs has been described as "reverse innovation" (Immelt et al. 2009; Trimble & Govindarajan 2012). While the use of the term reverse is controversial, the opportunities for HICs to learn from LMIC innovation are compelling. This novel approach to harness LMIC inventions in health care and life sciences could rapidly generate promising options for developed countries, overcoming some constraints to innovation in high-income settings.

The potential for LMIC innovations in HICs in medical-device and health product development, process-of-care improvements, and policy innovations is starting to be realized. This is evidenced by such cases as General Electric India's US$800 electrocardiogram, now sold in 194 countries around the world (Trimble & Govindarajan 2012); the construction of Health City Cayman Islands, a 104-bed hospital using low-cost, high-throughput methods based on Narayana Hrudayalaya's model in India (Health City Cayman Islands 2015); adaptation of a community health worker model from Kenya to New York City by City Health Works (Singh 2012; City Health Works 2015); and implementation of the Opportunity NYC – Family Rewards program in New York, inspired by Mexico's Oportunidades conditional cash transfer program (Riccio 2010). Many of these initiatives have taken hold, but some have struggled; the initial Opportunity NYC program was discontinued, for instance, because of high cost and marginal effects (Bosman 2010).

While the impact of specific innovations has varied, their potential has garnered attention from a variety of stakeholders in HICs. They seek improvements involving efficiency in discovery (Singh & Chokshi 2013), implementation of low-cost innovations to manage rising costs and a shrinking tax base, and reduction of barriers to moving products and services across national boundaries. Those interested in adapting LMIC innovations to HIC contexts include funders such as the Robert Wood Johnson Foundation and the Commonwealth Fund in the US, (Robert Wood Johnson Foundation 2015; The Commonwealth Fund 2013) and the Tekes Finnish Funding Agency for Innovation (Tekes 2015).

Despite the limited number of current examples, the pace of development of new products, processes, and policies from LMICs that are relevant to HICs can only increase, as disease patterns converge and health care coverage in low-resource settings increases (Jamison et al. 2013). With increased opportunities for funding and more LMIC-HIC partnerships, the capacity to develop and test new approaches from LMICs is rapidly growing (Crisp 2014). However, replicating any innovation is challenging, and replicating in a very different context even more so; therefore, many factors must be considered in deciding to implement a new health model. Unsuccessful efforts such as the Opportunity NYC program underline such risks. The literature on reverse innovation describes examples and processes for how to develop reverse innovations (Radjou, Prabhu, & Ahuja 2012; Trimble & Govindarajan

2012), with one article describing a competition for selecting LMIC innovations to test in HIC settings developed on an ad hoc basis (Snowdon, Bassi, Scarffe, & Smith 2015). This presents a critical opportunity for standardizing an approach to the evaluation of potential reverse innovations. To this end, we propose a screening mechanism to identify and promote those innovations from low- and middle-income markets with the greatest potential for application in HICs.

Methods

Using an iterative, qualitative approach involving literature review, primary case study testing, secondary database review, and a modified Delphi process, we developed a two-part screening tool to identify innovations with the potential to improve care and/or reduce costs in HICs.

Literature Review and Initial Criteria Development

Initial development of the tool began with review of the relevant literature around reverse innovation, using search terms such as "reverse innovation," "frugal innovation," "embedded innovation," and "global health innovation," From this, we developed a candidate set of 11 criteria to test further and refine. We then shared these initial criteria with six key informants in the global health field, including researchers, funders, and clinicians based in HICs with extensive experience engaging with and assessing Canadian and LMIC health innovations. Based on their feedback, we revised the initial categories, resulting in eight refined criteria.

Primary Testing on Case Studies of Innovative Programs

Next, we applied the criteria to brief case studies we had developed for four LMIC health programs in the Center for Health Market Innovations (CHMI) database (Center for Health Market Innovations 2015) that our team had previously identified as having potential for adaptation in HICs. This allowed us to explore the relevance and utility of the eight criteria, and from this case study review, we developed a basic scoring system and divided the eight criteria into two steps:

1. Evaluation of the program's success within the LMIC context.
2. Evaluation of the program's likelihood to be a reverse innovation in an HIC.

Secondary Testing with Expanded Sample of Programs

We then tested the criteria on 60 programs in the CHMI database randomly sampled within five categories: innovative products, services, organizational structures, information and communication technologies, and financial models. Through this testing, along with discussion and review of our findings, we developed a set of nine criteria with revised definitions and refined cut-off scores to identify likely and unlikely reverse innovations.

Expert Consultation in Modified Delphi Process

The resulting nine criteria were reviewed by a Reverse Innovation Working Group comprised of 31 experts in medicine, engineering, management, and political science, as well as representatives from government and industry, all with an expressed interest in reverse innovation. Many of the members were judges in a national reverse innovation competition held in Canada in 2014 (Snowdon et al. 2015). Feedback was solicited using a modified Delphi process, an approach used to facilitate communication and build consensus among a group of experts on a particular topic (Shelton & Creghan 2014). This involved a first round of feedback with the group convening in a teleconference to provide open-ended feedback on the criteria. Afterwards, input on specific questions was solicited electronically from the working group. This feedback was used to revise the criteria, which were then shared again along with another set of focused questions that were discussed at an in-person meeting with the working group. Feedback from this group was again incorporated into the criteria, and these revised criteria, including the scoring system and suggested cut-offs scores, were shared with working group members electronically, at which point we achieved consensus.

Results

The resulting tool consists of eight criteria divided into two steps with a simple scoring system. Figure 5.1 presents the final scoring system, which consists of two parts: success in the LMIC and the potential for success in an HIC. The first part includes assessments of accessibility, cost-effectiveness, scalability, and overall effectiveness in the LMIC. The total cut-off score of 10 is low to act as a coarse screen leading to the second phase. The second part reviews the health challenge addressed by the innovation, the compatibility with infrastructure and regulations, the novelty of the innovation, and the receptivity for the innovation in the HIC. The scores for this second part indicate whether the innovation is likely or unlikely to be a successful reverse innovation, or requires further investigation.

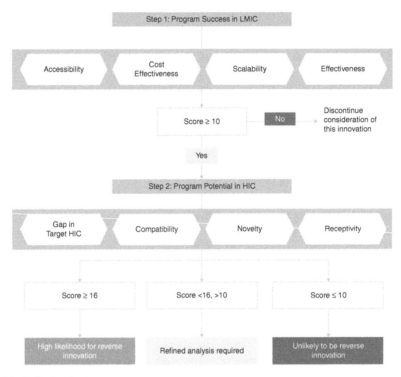

Criteria Scoring System

0: No information exists, or the criterion is not applicable.
1: Demonstration that this has not been achieved.
2: Uncertain or conflicting demonstration.
3: Some demonstration of achievement.
4: Strong demonstration of achievement.
5: Significant demonstration of achievement.

Definitions of Individual Criteria

Accessibility: Innovation increases access of products or services through increasing financial, geographic, and/or social access.
Cost-Effectiveness: Innovation improves cost-effectiveness to payer, provider, or end user.
Scalability: Innovation increases scope, geographic cover, or customer base.
Effectiveness: Documentation of effectiveness of innovation using appropriate evaluative methods.
Gap in Target HIC: Creating solutions for unsolved (or imperfectly solved) challenges or unaddressed health issues or service gaps.
Compatibility: Compatible with health care infrastructure in the target HIC country.
Novelty: Innovation is a novel approach or is an established innovation used in a new way that has great promise.
Receptivity: Openness and engagement of partners as well as those not considered partners but who may be impacted by the innovation.

Figure 5.1 Criteria to assess potential reverse innovations

Case Examples

Tables 5.1 and 5.2 provide examples of application of the criteria to two different programs drawn from the CHMI database (Center for Health Market Innovations 2015).

Table 5.1 Applying the reverse innovation criteria: Uganda Health Information Network (UHIN)

Criteria	Score	Rationale
Accessibility	4	The program provides community health workers with PDAs that automatically load public health data to a centralized databank. This helps with disease surveillance to ensure the right medicines and services are directed where needed.
Cost-Effectiveness	5	A study by independent consultants reported a savings of 25% per unit compared to traditional manual paper data collection.
Scalability	4	There are 700 health workers in the program. There are 175 remote health facilities in the country that now have PDA capability, serving 1.5 million people.
Effectiveness	3	The cost-effectiveness of the program has been evaluated by independent consultants. The program is currently evaluating its health impact on health care planning, resource allocation, and delivery.
	16	Conclusion: Move to Step 2
Criteria	Score	Rationale
Gap in Target HIC	5	Information integration and digitalization, with particular attention to cost control, are extremely important challenges for the Canadian health system.
Compatibility	3	It is unclear how this information system would be regulated in the Canadian context, particularly with privacy considerations. However, the system could likely be adapted to meet Canadian regulations.
Novelty	4	PDAs and smartphones remain a relatively innovative, uncommon tool for health data collection in Canada.
Receptivity	4	The International Development Research Centre and former Canadian International Development Agency (now Global Affairs Canada) are the primary funders of this initiative, suggesting strong connections to Canada.
	16	Conclusion: Score is ≥16. Likely to be a reverse innovation.

Table 5.2 Applying the reverse innovation criteria: Bloomberg Philanthropies
Maternal Health Initiative (BPMHI)

Criteria	Score	Rationale
Accessibility	5	The program has upgraded 9 remote health centres, increasing geographic access to services provided locally; prior to the program, patients had to travel 3–4 hours to the nearest hospital.
Cost-Effectiveness	4	Indirectly, the program has improved cost-effectiveness by "up-training" midwives to perform more complex tasks such as C-sections, reducing the need for more costly health care providers.
Scalability	4	Since inception, the program has increased its coverage from 9 sites to 12, and has been expanding to e-learning platforms in 2013. Deliveries at all intervention hospitals have increased from 3,500 deliveries per year before the program to 9,000 deliveries per year after the program launch.
Effectiveness	3	One district where the program operates experienced a 32% decline in maternal deaths after the program was implemented. However, information on evaluation techniques and reporting on impact for all sites is limited.
	16	Conclusion: Move to Step 2
Criteria	Score	Rationale
Gap in Target HIC	4	Access to quality maternity care services, particularly in rural and northern areas, is an important health care issue in Canada.
Compatibility	1	Midwives and physician assistants play a limited role in Canada as of present. Implementation of such a program would be challenging given current regulations and staffing levels.
Novelty	3	Midwifery and physician assistant–performed C-sections are quite a novel concept; however, refurbishing rural hospitals is not.
Receptivity	1	This initiative does not involve Canadian partners or Canadian stakeholders.
	9	Conclusion: Score is ≤10. Unlikely to be a reverse innovation.

Canada is chosen as the target HIC for these examples, as Canada was the primary location for the majority of the authors.

The first program, the Uganda Health Information Network (UHIN), provides community health workers with an online information system and personal digital assistants for recording health information (Shinyekwa 2010). The Bloomberg Philanthropies Maternal Health Initiative (BPMHI), on the other hand, trains health workers in performing life-saving procedures in maternal health in rural and remote areas of Tanzania (CHMI 2016).

UHIN has proved to be effective at improving health workers' capabilities to access information remotely through a handheld digital device, leading to a score of 4 in Accessibility. It also has a proved ability to scale, having expanded successfully to 175 health facilities, therefore scoring 4 in Scalability. The program has demonstrated impact through an independent evaluation, which reported a 25 per cent savings per patient visit unit through the new information system, compared to the original paper-based system, leading to a 5 in Cost-Effectiveness. Thus, it has demonstrated some impact in this area, and it is in the process of evaluating its organizational performance and health system outcomes, leading to a 3 for Effectiveness.

Moving to Step 2, UHIN's main mandate, health information integration and access to maternal health care, is highly relevant to the current Canadian policy environment, leading to a score of 5 in Gap in Target HIC. Given the general historical uncertainty of success associated with IT-based health care initiatives, however, UHIN scores a 3 in Compatibility with existing Canadian infrastructure. Mobile phone technology to record and store patient data in health care is relatively novel in the Canadian context, leading to a 4 in Novelty. Finally, UHIN is well connected to Canadian partners such as the International Development Research Centre and the former Canadian International Development Agency, leading to a 4 in Receptivity. This leads to an overall score of 16, with the conclusion that the program is likely to be worth testing as a reverse innovation in Canada.

Similarly, the Bloomberg Philanthropies Maternal Health Initiative scores well in Step 1. The initiative has improved access to health care for patients by upgrading remote health centres while expanding the skill set of midwives to include caesarean sections, ostensibly improving the access to this much-needed procedure, and others, in rural areas, leading to a 5 in Accessibility. Through task shifting, the initiative has lower costs compared to staffing with physicians or long-distance ambulance transportation, leading to a 4 in Cost-Effectiveness. The program has also expanded from nine to 12 sites, giving it a 4 in Scalability. At the same time, unlike the first initiative's independent evaluation, BPMHI lacks specific data that measures the program's impact, leading to a score of 2 in Effectiveness.

However, through Step 2, we find that UHIN has a much higher likelihood of success as a reverse innovation compared to BPMHI. The initiative certainly addresses an important gap in Canada, the accessibility of maternal health care in remote rural areas, scoring 4 on Gap in Target HIC, and uses a novel approach, scoring 3 on Novelty. Despite these positives, current Canadian regulation on scope of practice precludes midwives from doing surgery, leading to a rating of 1 on Compatibility. The program also lacks connections with existing Canadian partners, giving it a 1 on Receptivity. Given its overall rating of 9, the Bloomberg Philanthropies Maternal Health Initiative does not pass final-round screening, and thus would not be considered for further testing and adaptation into Canada.

Discussion

The increasing pace of innovation in LMICs and the rising interest in cost control of HICs suggests that the value of systematically screening promising ideas from one setting for implementation in the other will rise over time. This paper describes a screening tool to rapidly assess promising LMIC innovations for adaptation in HICs and identify those with high potential for more in-depth review and evaluation. It highlights (but does not resolve) the trade-off between high-potential radical innovations, which are difficult to implement, and incremental innovations that provide "easy wins." It also highlights challenges in adapting LMIC innovations to HICs, including differences in scope of practice, quality concerns, and regulatory issues. It was developed with a broad range of experts from different sectors, and field tested for relevance to products, organizational processes, and policies. While our tool does not solve the challenge of adaptation from a low- to high-resource setting, it can help decide whether an approach is worth pursuing despite the barriers. It does so by including criteria for impact, cost, access, technical feasibility, and alignment with public policy.

Screening for reverse innovations may be useful for public, private for-profit, and non-profit organizations, particularly those that are interested in affordable approaches to meet the needs of marginalized or hard-to-reach groups. We envision that the metrics incorporated in the tool may be useful to a variety of stakeholders, including multinational corporations, such as the Innovation Managers at Xerox, who canvass Indian start-ups for innovations that may be implemented in their global operations (Radjou, Prabhu, Kaipa, & Ahuja 2010); health care institutions, such as the Commonwealth Fund's Innovation Collaborative, which brings together large health systems seeking novel approaches to increase efficiency; and governmental bodies, such as the New York City Council, which adapted Mexico's conditional cash transfer program. For these stakeholders, the process of reverse innovation could be accelerated by using the criteria to screen databases for low-cost, high-yield innovations like the 1,300 programs listed in the CHMI database (Center for Health Market Innovations 2015), the over 600 groups identified by Grand Challenges Canada (Grand Challenges Canada 2015), or the almost 100 examples in the World Innovation Summit for Health Innovation Network database (World Innovation Summit for Health 2016). Having a standard screening tool can help to proactively obtain the appropriate information from potential innovations and inform the further development of these databases. To this end, these criteria were tested for inter-rater reliability using a detailed data set on innovations compiled by Imperial College in the United Kingdom for consideration by US delivery systems.

The strengths of this study include its multidisciplinary perspective, and its iterative development using numerous case examples, which contrast with the more ad hoc nature of previous work. The limitations include the narrow focus on application to the Canadian context, which may limit generalizability to other settings; the use of abstract concepts like compatibility, which may be subjective and limit agreement on how to assess each parameter; and the limited data on the programs under study. While the scoring system and the cut-off scores were developed through several rounds of testing and feedback, there is some subjectivity in determining the scores for programs. The scores for each category are based on how strongly a program has demonstrated achievement in each area. The tool can be strengthened through further testing and standardization, which is currently ongoing at Imperial College. Next steps in this area would include testing in a country context other than Canada, and prospectively assessing the success of implementing innovations that scored higher with this tool, with others having lower scores. The work of the Innovation Collaborative in the US, which has chosen three innovations to implement, can help to further this area of research, but more examples will be needed to assess the validity of the tool.

Summary screening of potential innovations is an important first step, but replication also requires identifying the key ingredients or efficiency core of an intervention, a process requiring more in-depth investigation (Wong, Zlotkin, Ho, & Perumal 2014). CHMI has a tool to assist with this that looks at what makes the intervention work and its key contextual factors (Results for Development (R4D) 2014). The University of California at Los Angeles's Global Lab for Innovation has also drafted elaborate criteria to evaluate cost-saving innovations from across the globe with the aim of identifying and piloting these innovations within their health care system (UCLA Health 2014). Together, these tools help map the first steps in a complex process that draws on the ingenuity of people in low-resource settings as a source of new ideas for high-income settings, increasing the likelihood that they could have an impact.

Conclusion

Diligent application of a tool to identify innovations from low-resource settings that improve affordability, access, or quality could provide a range of options to improve the economics of health care in high-cost countries. As experience grows and more data becomes available, the tool can be refined and made more generalizable for the benefit of health organizations and decision-makers worldwide. Once promising strategies are identified, the challenge of adapting innovations from LMICs to HICs remains, with opportunities for future research into the approaches that generate performance differences in translation itself. As the number of potential reverse innovations increase, a rapid screen should be followed by efforts to identify key components and contextual factors to increase their uptake and impact both in high- and low-income countries.

NOTE

1   We use the terms HIC and LMIC as described by the World Bank (https://datahelpdesk.worldbank.org/knowledgebase/articles/906519), which provides country categories based on gross national income (GNI) per capita. At the time of this research in 2016, we distinguish between HICs (those with a GNI per capita of US $12,476 or more), and LMICs (those with a GNI per capita below US$12,476).

REFERENCES

Bhattacharyya, O., Khor, S., McGahan, A., Dunne, D., Daar, A.S., & Singer, P.A. 2010. "Innovative Health Service Delivery Models in Low and Middle Income Countries – What Can We Learn from the Private Sector?" *Health Research Policy and Systems* 8(24). https://doi.org/10.1186/1478-4505-8-24.

Bosman, J. 2010. "City Will Stop Paying the Poor for Good Behavior." http://www.nytimes.com/2010/03/31/nyregion/31cash.html.

Center for Health Market Innovations. 2015. "CHMI." Accessed 5 September 2013. http://healthmarketinnovations.org.

CHMI. 2016. "Bloomberg Philanthropies Maternal Health Initiative (BPMHI)." Accessed 1 November 2015. http://healthmarketinnovations.org/program/bloomberg-philanthropies-maternal-health-initiative.

City Health Works. 2015. "Ambassadors of Health." Accessed 2 July 2015. http://cityhealthworks.com/.

Crisp, N. 2014. "Mutual Learning and Reverse Innovation – Where Next?" *Globalization and Health* 10(1): 14. https://doi.org/10.1186/1744-8603-10-14.

Grand Challenges Canada. 2015. "Grand Challenges." Accessed 12 February 2015. http://www.grandchallenges.ca/.

Harris, M. 2013. "Correspondence: Community Health Workers: An Opportunity for Reverse Innovation." *The Lancet*, 382(9901): 1326–7. https://doi.org/10.1016/s0140-6736(13)62135-2.

Health City Cayman Islands. 2015. "Our Caribbean Hospital." Accessed 10 December 2015. http://www.healthcitycaymanislands.com/about/our-hospital/.

Immelt, J.R., Govindarajan, V., & Trimble, C. 2009. "How GE Is Disrupting Itself." *Harvard Business Review* 87(10): 56–65.

Jakovljevic, M.M. 2016. "Comparison of Historical Medical Spending Patterns among the BRICS and G7." *Journal of Medical Economics* 19(1): 70–6. https://doi.org/10.3111/13696998.2015.1093493.

Jakovljevic, M., & Getzen, T.E. 2016. "Growth of Global Health Spending Share in Low and Middle Income Countries." *Frontiers in Pharmacology* 7(21): 21. https://doi.org/10.3389/fphar.2016.00021.

Jamison, D.T., Summers, L.H., Alleyne, G., Arrow, K.J., Berkley, S., Binagwaho, A., ... Yamey, G. 2013. "Global Health 2035: A World Converging within a Generation." *The Lancet* 382(9908): 1898–955. https://doi.org/10.1016/S0140-6736(13)62105-4.

Radjou, N., Prabhu, J., & Ahuja, S. 2012. *Jugaad Innovation: Think Frugal, Be Flexible, Generate Breakthrough Growth*. San Francisco: Jossey-Bass.

Radjou, N., Prabhu, J., Kaipa, P., & Ahuja, S. 2010. "How Xerox Innovates with Emerging Markets' Brainpower." Accessed 10 January 2016. https://hbr.org/2010/08/how-xerox-innovates-with.

Results for Development. 2014. *Identifying the Active Ingredient: Promoting Adaptation and Global Exchange of Innovation*. Washington, DC: Results for Development.

Riccio, J. 2010. "Sharing Lessons from the First Conditional Cash Transfer Program in the United States." *National Poverty Center Policy Brief*, 22. http://www.npc.umich.edu/publications/policy_briefs/brief22/policybrief22.pdf.

Robert Wood Johnson Foundation. 2015. "Grants: Supporting the International Partnership for Innovative Healthcare Delivery's Mission to Improve Access to Quality and Affordable Care Worldwide." Accessed 8 May 2015. http://www.rwjf.org/en/library/grants/2014/07/supportingtheinternationalpartnershipforinnovativehealthca.html.

Shelton, K., & Creghan, K.A. 2014. "Demystifying the Delphi Method." In V.C.X. Wang (ed.), *Handbook of Research on Scholarly Publishing and Research Methods* (375–95). Hershey, Pennsylvania: IGI Global.

Shinyekwa, I. 2010. "Cost Effectiveness Assessment of Uganda Health Information Network." Kampala, Uganda: Uganda Health Information Network, Phase IV.

Singh, P. 2012. "Bringing the Concepts of Peer Coaches and Local Health Workers from Africa to Harlem." *Health Affairs* 31(12): 2801–2. https://doi.org/10.1377/hlthaff.2012.1109.

Singh, P., & Chokshi, D.A. 2013. "Community Health Workers: An Opportunity for Reverse Innovation. Authors' Reply." *The Lancet* 382(9901): 1327. https://doi.org/10.1016/S0140-6736(13)62136-4.

Snowdon, A.W., Bassi, H., Scarffe, A.D., & Smith, A.D. 2015. "Reverse Innovation: An Opportunity for Strengthening Health Systems." *Globalization and Health* 11(2). https://doi.org/10.1186/s12992-015-0088-x.

Syed, S.B., Dadwal, V., & Martin, G. 2013. "Reverse Innovation in Global Health Systems: Towards Global Innovation Flow." *Globalization and Health* 9(1): 36. https://doi.org/10.1186/1744-8603-9-36.

Syed, S.B., Dadwal, V., Rutter, P., Storr, J., Hightower, J.D., Gooden, R., ... Pittet, D. 2012. "Developed-Developing Country Partnerships: Benefits to Developed Countries?" *Globalization and Health* 8(1): 17. https://doi.org/10.1186/1744-8603-8-17.

Tekes. 2015. "Tekes Provides Funding for Two New Strategic Research Openings." Accessed 8 May 2015. https://nakedapproach.fi/2015/02/19/tekes-funds-three-new-strategic-research-openings-with-5-8-million.

The Commonwealth Fund. 2013. "A New Agenda for a Post–Health Reform Landscape." https://www.commonwealthfund.org/publications/publication/2013/sep/new-agenda-post-health-reform-landscape.

Trimble, C., & Govindarajan, V. 2012. *Reverse Innovation: Create Far from Home, Win Everywhere.* Boston: Harvard Business Review Press.

UCLA Health. 2014. "The Global Lab for Innovation: Building Sustainable Healthcare." https://globalhealth.ucla.edu/projects/global-lab-innovation-building-sustainable-healthcare.

Wong, J., Zlotkin, S., Ho, C., & Perumal, N. 2014. "Replicating Parts, Not the Whole, to Scale." Accessed 10 March 2016. http://ssir.org/articles/entry/replicating_parts_not_the_whole_to_scale.

World Innovation Summit for Health. 2016. "WISH Innovation Catalogue." Accessed 10 January 2016. http://www.wish.org.qa/innovation/innovation-catalogue.

SECTION B

Understanding the Contributions
of Private Sector Health Care Services

In this section, we explore how private sector organizations develop innovative models to provide health care services that aim to increase access, quality, and efficiency of health care in low- and middle-income countries (LMICs) in ways that can be measured and improved. It includes an overview of the Toronto Health Organization Performance Evaluation (T-HOPE) framework, which provides a way of assessing program performance in terms of three categories: health status, access, and operations/delivery. This framework synthesized performance measurement frameworks from the health care and management literature and compared them to what is routinely reported by organizations engaged in a wide range of activities. We then developed a set of metrics that balance credibility, feasibility, and comparability to inform reporting standards. The research in this section also provides more detail on measures for quality, efficiency, and scale and considers characteristics of programs able to achieve greater scale. These concepts and tools can help assess and compare innovative programs for funders or groups who want to replicate them, while identifying opportunities for managers to improve or expand their services.

Chapter 6 ("Assessing Health Program Performance in Low- and Middle-Income Countries: Building a Feasible, Credible, and Comprehensive Framework") outlines the T-HOPE framework, which was designed to assist researchers, policymakers, funders, and program managers to feasibly and credibly assess the performance of private sector health care organizations.

Chapter 7 ("Performance Measurement for Innovative Health Programs: Understanding Efficiency, Quality, and Scale") provides a deeper discussion of relevant metrics to assess private sector services in terms of efficiency, quality, and scale. Efficiency evaluates time and resource use, quality focuses on the degree to which services meet accepted standards and increase likelihood of desired outcomes, and scale reflects the breadth and depth of coverage of services.

Chapter 8 ("Transnational Scale Up of Services in Global Health") identifies characteristics that support the ability to operate in multiple countries, comparing programs that operate in single countries to those that cross borders in terms of four categories: health focus, activities, legal status, and funding source. Programs achieving transnational scale most commonly focus on vertical health services, engage in a range of consumer outreach and delivery support activities, are private rather than public in status, and are more likely than single-country programs to use direct revenues such as out-of-pocket payments in their financial mix.

While there are many promising innovative programs emerging in LMICs, there has been a lack of comprehensive assessment of which models are having a real impact. We need a set of rigorous yet feasible measures to evaluate and understand these programs and help make decisions about which should be further supported and scaled up. We have attempted to provide a set of such measures, explaining the process of researching and constructing them to optimize their credibility and practicality to encourage their use. We also provide a number of examples of their application to compare programs, including examining ways to understand and measure scale with a comparison of programs achieving different levels of scale. Although we recognize that there continue to be constraints in applying some of these measures, particularly health outcomes, it is important to encourage more robust, consistent, and feasible performance measurement of these innovative programs to support more sophisticated modes of analysis and advance the field of global health more broadly.

6 Assessing Health Program Performance in Low- and Middle-Income Countries: Building a Feasible, Credible, and Comprehensive Framework

ONIL BHATTACHARYYA, KATHRYN MOSSMAN, JOHN GINTHER, LEIGH HAYDEN, RAMAN SOHAL, JIEUN CHA, AMEYA BOPARDIKAR, JOHN A. MACDONALD, HIMANSHU PARIKH, ILAN SHAHIN, ANITA MCGAHAN, AND WILL MITCHELL

Background

Adapting health services to meet the rising demand and evolving health burden in low- and middle-income countries (LMICs) is key to improving health outcomes. Interest in the potential for health innovations to improve quality and access of health care for LMIC populations is growing rapidly (Bloom, Henson, & Peters 2014; Dandonoli 2013; Binagwaho et al. 2013). Many organizations, including private providers, governments, donors, and social impact investors, have developed and supported innovative approaches to health services delivery for the poor. In particular, the private health sector, which includes for-profit and not-for-profit, formal and non-formal entities (Hanson & Berman 1998), plays a significant innovative role in influencing health policy and providing health care and supplies in LMICs (Swanson et al. 2015; Bhattacharyya et al. 2010). However, our evidence on what works, particularly in the private health sector of developing regions, is relatively weak (Bennett, Lagomarsino, Knezovich, & Lucas 2014), and greater understanding of the effectiveness, scale, and scope of private sector initiatives is needed (Hanson et al. 2008). Innovative programs are seldom evaluated in a way that allows for meaningful comparisons (Schweitzer & Synowiec 2012; Mills, Brugha, Hanson, & McPake 2002; Howitt, Darzi, Yang, Ashrafian, & Atun 2012), and in rapidly changing health markets, formal evaluations are often too time consuming and costly for new interventions or rapidly evolving organizations (Bennett, Lagomarsino, et al. 2014). We need new approaches to improve the knowledge base on health markets in LMICs, which will be crucial for improving health policy and practice (Bennett, Bloom, Knezovich, & Peters 2014). This requires a cohesive set of measures that balance credibility (relevant aspects of performance), comparability (across different organizations), and feasibility (available data).

Performance measurement frameworks seek to determine the activities and success of a program's strategy and provide insights for future improvements (Kalinichenko, Amado, & Santos 2013). Multiple performance frameworks have been designed to assess health systems (World Health Organization 2010; De Savigny, Campbell, & Best 2010), health service delivery organizations (Bradley, Pallas, Bashyal, Berman, & Curry 2010; Kalinichenko et al. 2013), and health quality (Kelly & Hurst 2006; Donabedian 2005). Additional frameworks measure the impact of socially responsible businesses and social enterprises (Clark, Rosensweig, Long, & Olsen 2004; (Global Impact Investing Network (GIIN) 2012).

While some of the performance measures in existing frameworks have been rigorously tested to determine their credibility, they face substantial challenges in comparability and feasibility. They are often specific to certain practices and health areas, making them difficult to apply across health areas and models. They also often do not consider whether programs have the capacity to collect and report the necessary data, imposing burdens that may detract from service delivery, particularly for smaller and newer health programs.

Performance measures are relevant for multiple stakeholders. Funders and researchers must compare health programs to determine what activities they are undertaking and which are performing well. Program managers are interested in the minimum data set that is relevant to operations and to assess their performance relative to their peers. Meeting the goals of stakeholders requires that performance measures are credible in assessing relevant aspects of performance, comparable in evaluating programs across different health areas and models, and feasible for programs. The measures need to achieve a balance among these three elements of assessment.

This study presents a balanced framework for assessing the performance of health care programs in LMICs and elsewhere. This framework integrates important existing approaches and supplements them with novel operational criteria. The result is a template that organizations can use for reporting purposes and may also serve as a practical tool for policymakers, funders, and researchers to assess programs for investment and scaling to maximize their health impact.

Methods

The Toronto Health Organization Performance Evaluation (T-HOPE) framework was developed using an iterative, qualitative process. Our aim was to develop a set of performance dimensions that balance what is theoretically desirable and what is empirically viable, with an emphasis on identifying measures that are credible, feasible, and comparable across health programs.

Literature: Credibility and Comparability

We began by consolidating 11 existing performance frameworks on health service evaluation (Donabedian 2005; Bradley et al. 2010; Kelly & Hurst 2006; De Savigny et al. 2010; World Health Organization 2010), social impact investment (Kaplan & Norton 1992; Clark et al. 2004; Global Impact Investing Network 2012), and business process innovation (CHMI 2015; Ojha, Ghosh, Khandelwal, & Kapoor 2011; Bhattacharyya et al. 2010). This yielded an initial composite framework of 12 performance dimensions. In this process, we identified credible dimensions vetted by scholars and practitioners that were relevant for comparing a variety of health and business models. In consolidating frameworks from different disciplines, we focused on selecting robust dimensions applicable to a broad range of programs.

Practice: Feasibility

We next considered the performance measures that health programs are already reporting. We reviewed performance data reported by a purposive sample of 80 diverse, data-rich programs from the Center for Health Market Innovations (CHMI) database. This database catalogues over 1,400 innovative health programs in LMICs, with an emphasis on private sector delivery (this includes for-profit, not-for-profit, and public-private partnership initiatives that serve poor populations in LMICs), and displays reporting provided by the programs. We determined the 80 programs for the sample by focusing on programs with available data in four important areas of health activity: the established fields of maternal, newborn, and child health (MNCH), general primary care, infectious diseases, and the emerging area of mHealth. We supplemented the data available on these 80 programs in the CHMI database by collecting data from publicly available sources through an online search of program websites and reports, journal articles, and news websites.

In our review of these 80 programs, our aim was to determine the types of measures programs are already reporting to assess feasibility, while maintaining comparability by identifying common measures reported by a range of programs from different health areas with different models. The assessment included programs operating in diverse health areas, such as MNCH, eye care, tuberculosis, primary care, family planning, and reproductive health. The programs commonly employ innovative operational models, such as social franchising, public-private partnerships, clinic chains and networks, mobile clinics, social marketing, microinsurance, and the use of mHealth technologies. Through this review, we identified performance dimensions in our initial composite framework that a variety of innovative health programs are also reporting data on, updating our framework to reflect this aspect of feasibility.

We then refined our initial framework by reviewing the relevant literature on each of the performance dimensions, including academic publications and technical reports. This review sought to strengthen the definitions and measurement approaches in a way that provides a relevant balance of our three desired characteristics:

- *Credibility*: Consistent with ideas commonly presented in the literature
- *Feasibility*: Based on existing reporting, requiring limited time and effort to provide data
- *Comparability*: Programs engaging in different health areas and models could report on the dimension

Results and Discussion

Through this process, we developed the T-HOPE framework, which includes three categories of performance: health status, health access, and operations/ delivery. Within the three categories, there are 14 subcategories of performance: three fields with definitions for health status, three for health access, and eight for operations/delivery. Table 6.1 summarizes the framework, providing definitions, indictors, and examples of each dimension. We also drew from the literature to identify seven descriptive fields, which table 6.2 summarizes. The descriptive fields are useful for building profiles and understanding the context of specific programs.

Table 6.1 T-HOPE framework: Performance dimensions

Performance Dimension	Example Indicators	Examples from CHMI Profiles: healthmarketinnovations.org
A. Health Status		
A1. Population Coverage: Volume of clients served as a percentage of a defined target population per reporting period.	• Percentage of the target population using program services or products per reporting period.	**Bangladesh Urban Primary Health Care Project (Bangladesh):** Between 1998 and 2011, the primary care program had covered 82.6% (approximately 7.78 million) of the target population in Bangladesh.
A2. Health Output: Quantitative evidence about the number of health services/products provided and/or clients served/trained per reporting period.	• Number of clients served per reporting period. • Number of products provided per reporting period.	**World Health Partners (WHP) (India, Kenya):** 25,836 patient visits conducted by WHP providers between January 1, 2013, and December 31, 2013.
A3. Health Outcome: Quantitative evidence of impact on intermediate or long-term health outcomes demonstrated by changes in learning, actions, and/or health status of clients/target population per reporting period.	• Change in mortality rate in target population per reporting period. • Change in disease incidence in target population per reporting period. • Change in uptake of healthy behaviours in target population per reporting period.	**Deepak Foundation Gujarat (India):** Initiated in 2005 to save lives and promote institutional deliveries, the foundation's Safe Motherhood and Child Survival Project observed a 38.7% decline in maternal mortality from 430 cases per 100,000 live births in 2005 to 263 in 2011.
B. Health Access		
B1. Affordability: Quantitative evidence about the price of services and products compared to the average price of similar services and products in the local context, or as a proportion of income at a given time period.	• Price of service/product compared to price of the same service of a local competitor at a given period. • Price of product/service as a proportion of average household income at a given period. • Product/service provided for free.	**PROSALUD (Bolivia):** Charges approximately US$4 for an appointment with a general practitioner, compared to US$28 in the private sector.

(Continued)

Table 6.1 Continued

Performance Dimension	Example Indicators	Examples from CHMI Profiles: healthmarketinnovations.org
B2. Availability: Quantitative evidence about the ability of clients/patients to access health services at the needed place and time per reporting period.	• Number of providers, facilities, or hospital beds per target population per reporting period. • Average geographic distance or time needed for the target population to reach the facility. • Percentage of health care workers absent from the facility per reporting period. • Change in stock-outs of medications or supplies per reporting period. • Hours of facility operation per reporting period.	**Hygeia Community Health Plan (Nigeria):** Hygeia has achieved a 95% reduction in stock-outs of antimalarials and other essential drugs among its network of providers between January 2007 and December 2010.
B3. Pro-poor Targeting: Proportion of clients that are economically disadvantaged and criteria used to identify and target the poor; includes whether the program is targeting a poor area or targeting the most disadvantaged group within a population.	• Percentage of a program's clients that are in the bottom 20% income quintile. • Percentage of a program's clients living on less than US$2 per day. • Percentage of a program's clients that live in a predominantly poor area.	**HealthyBaby/HealthyLife Vouchers (Uganda):** A 2010–11 survey found that 29.3% of women using the HealthyBaby voucher were in the poorest quintile of the household wealth index.
C. Operations/Delivery		
C1. Clinical Quality: Quantitative evidence of providing safe, evidence-based care, which can include comparisons to other providers of similar services, and/or demonstrating change over time.	• Medical error rate per time period. • Surgical complication rate compared to providers of similar services. • Percentage of cases meeting predetermined quality standards.	**Aravind Eye Care System (India):** Aravind has managed to keep its infection rates low, with an average of about 4 cases per 10,000 patients, compared to an average of 6 per 10,000 in the UK.

(Continued)

Table 6.1 Continued

Performance Dimension	Example Indicators	Examples from CHMI Profiles: healthmarketinnovations.org
	• Percentage of patients receiving appropriate care according to approved guidelines. • Readmission rate per time period.	
C2. User Satisfaction: Quantitative or qualitative evidence that is collected using a systematic methodology and reflects the clients' perceptions of the quality of services provided.	• Client renewal rates. • Client retention rates. • Percentage of patients satisfied with services based on patient survey. • Percentage of patients who would recommend the program to others.	**Red Segura Nicaragua (Nicaragua):** In a customer satisfaction survey conducted in 2011, the average score women of reproductive age gave to the medical attention they received at Red Segura clinics was 4.8, on a scale of 1 to 5, with 5 being the highest quality of care.
C3. Management Quality: The procedures, systems, and processes the program has implemented to strengthen quality in key aspects of operations and delivery.	• Description of implementing a monitoring and evaluation system. • Description of establishing a board of governors to provide guidance and oversight. • Description of internal audit conducted on regular basis • Description of accreditation or certification by a reputable organization. • Description of receiving international awards for excellence and/or achievement.	**Mahila Swahsta Sewa (Nepal):** Quality assurance mechanisms include: 1) Quality assurance visits focused on the service delivery of intrauterine devices (IUDs) using the Lot Quality Assurance Sampling Method; 2) Development and use of quality monitoring checklists; 3) Quality action plans to address issues.

(Continued)

Table 6.1 Continued

Performance Dimension	Example Indicators	Examples from CHMI Profiles: healthmarketinnovations.org
C4. Economic Efficiency: Quantitative evidence about the cost of delivering the product/ service to patients/ clients.	• Unit cost of providing a service/product for a single client/patient. • Average total cost to provide services/ products to clients/ patients.	**Operation ASHA (Cambodia, India):** Operation ASHA has developed a model in which the cost of providing complete TB treatment to a patient is US$80, compared with the cost of US$300 among other not-for-profit organizations.
C5. Non-economic Efficiency: Quantitative evidence about how long it takes for a program to deliver a product/ service compared to a previous reporting period or providers of similar services.	• Patient or procedure volume per time period compared to a previous reporting period. • Patient or procedure volume per time period compared to providers of similar products/ services.	**Rapid SMS Malawi (Malawi):** The RapidSMS mHealth data collection system results in a significant reduction in data transmission delay. While Malawi's current paper-based system takes 1–3 months to transmit child nutrition data, the RapidSMS system takes only two minutes.
C6. Human Resources Supply: Description of the program's human resources supply and strategy to recruit, retain, and train staff.	• Description of initiatives that seek to promote recruitment or retention of staff. • Description of staff training programs. • Turnover or retention rate per reporting period. • Description of staff satisfaction and/or factors contributing or detracting from recruitment and retention.	**Living Goods (Kenya, Uganda):** Community health promoters are trained to provide basic health counselling on a variety of topics to their communities and make a modest living by selling health products. All health promoters are trained to give basic public health counselling on the use of products and to facilitate referrals to acutely ill patients. Field agents meet community health promoters at least once a month to resupply, collect payments, communicate current promotions, and provide ongoing health education and business coaching.

(Continued)

Table 6.1 Concluded

Performance Dimension	Example Indicators	Examples from CHMI Profiles: healthmarketinnovations.org
C7. Political Support: Qualitative evidence of a relationship or partnership with a local, regional, or national government entity.	• Description of financial or technical support from a local, regional, or national government entity. • Description of authorization of activities by a government entity. • Description of successful advocacy resulting in policy change. • Description of providing training for government officials.	**Chiranjeevi Yojana (India):** This program aims to reduce maternal and infant mortality through government contracts with private providers. Qualified providers sign a memorandum of understanding with the district government and are financially compensated for deliveries provided to eligible patients.
C8. Financial Management: Financial data related to the program's balance sheet, income statement, and cash flows, as well as ratios, concepts, and calculations.	• Value of total assets at the end of the reporting period. • Net income resulting from all business activities during the reporting period. • The net cash flow of the organization during the reporting period, which is calculated by subtracting outflows from inflows of cash and cash equivalents. • Value of equity and/ or other financial contributions in the organization provided by the entrepreneur(s) at the time of investment.	**Naya Jeevan (Pakistan):** The operational revenue of this microinsurance program in Pakistan increased by 350% between 2010 and 2011; earned income increased from US$2,850 in 2010 to US$10,500 in 2011.

Table 6.2 T-HOPE framework: Descriptive fields with examples

A. Program Profile:

Description of several operational aspects of the program.

Example: Marie Stopes International (MSI) Bolivia

Summary (100-word overview): MSI Bolivia approaches the subjects of sexual and reproductive health in men and women through the provision of established and mobile services, aiding in the financing of services for low-income families, social marketing, and participative, inclusive education.

Implementing organization: Marie Stopes International.

Health focus: Family Planning & Reproductive Health.

Type of product/service: Reproductive service delivery at medical centres and mobile clinics; a call centre to provide info and make referrals; social marketing about new contraceptive products; and education in regards to sexual and reproductive rights, as well as sexual violence.

Client type: Young adults (13–24); men; women; general population

Program type: Country office of an international organization.

Country registered and legal status: Bolivia, private (not-for-profit).

Country of Operation: Bolivia.

Geographic location (within the country): La Paz, Santa Cruz, Cochabamba, Potosi, Chuquisaca, Oruro, Beni. Operates in 4 of 9 states, and reaches more than 110 municipalities with 5 mobile units.

Stage: Existing/expansion stage.

Year launched: 1995.

Number of facilities: 11 (6 established health centres, 5 mobile clinics).

Number of employees: 50–99; MSI Bolivia manages a staff of 70 professionals, including doctors, drivers, health promoters and social marketing experts.

Target population: Approximately 800,000 people.

Operational and technical partners: None

B. Problem:

Brief description of the problem that the program is trying to address, including the rationale and/or justification for the program.

Example: MotoMedics (Vietnam)

In a city like Hanoi where traffic is a critical problem, traditional ambulance vans struggle to reach patients within 30 or 45 minutes after the call for assistance is made. By then, the chance to provide life-saving medication or procedures significantly decreases. The introduction of a medical first responder program using motorbikes would improve response times and could significantly increase medical emergency survival rates as well as lower the costs of medical care for the patient.

(Continued)

Table 6.2 Continued

C. Goal:
Description of the program's theory of change or what the program aims to achieve through its interventions.

Example: Ziqitza – Dial 1298 for Ambulance (India)
Dial 1298 for Ambulance, delivered by Ziqitza Health Care Limited (ZHL), strives to deliver a nationwide network of life support ambulance services accessible to anyone, anytime, and anywhere through an easy-to-remember four-digit telephone number. The program is committed to meeting international quality standards in emergency medical services and aims to extend the availability of emergency transportation and care to lower-income populations.

D. Process:
Description of how the program achieves its goals. This field should outline the processes and steps that are used to deliver the program's products and/or services and the relationships between them.

Example: Piramal eSwasthya (India)
Local literate women are recruited to undergo a rigorous training program in which they are trained to collect simple diagnostic information and to provide preventive medicine, first aid, and customer service.

These women are given a medical kit, marketing material, and a mobile phone. They are then assisted in setting up a teleclinic (Piramal e-Swasthya Center) at their own homes.

Villagers who feel ill come to the Piramal eSwasthya Center or are given a home visit. After talking to and examining the patient, the health care worker communicates this diagnostic data through their mobile phone to a centralized call centre.

A call centre paramedic enters the information provided into a simple e-diagnosis system, which generates an automated response with the recommended prescription and treatment. Doctors manning the call centre also validate this.

If the ailment appears serious, the call centre recommends that the patient visit a secondary or tertiary health care facility immediately.

The health care worker also conducts preventive health workshops, which generate awareness about issues such as sanitation, nutrition, and first aid.

E. Challenges/Opportunities:
Description of the obstacles the program faces in delivering its products or services, and/or any opportunities the program has discovered and plans to leverage.

Example: Aceh Besar Midwives with Mobile Phones (Indonesia)
This 2006 World Vision project leveraged mobile phone communication technology in Indonesia by distributing cell phones and developing an SMS data collection system, which helped to facilitate patient data collection by midwives and voice communication between midwives and obstetrician-gynaecologists. Challenges faced in the use of these technologies included high cost of adoption, inadequate health care facilities, and poor infrastructure support.

(Continued)

Table 6.2 Concluded

F. Strategic Planning:
Description of how the program sets its plans for identifying and achieving future goals, including scaling-up or plans for growth. This section should include plans for engaging in activities to obtain resources and assigning responsibilities to attain these goals. This section should also provide information on the future plans of the program.

Example: LifeNet International (Burundi, East Africa)
Through their efficient social franchising model, which involves medical training, management training, pharmaceutical supply, and growth financing for existing clinics, LifeNet plans to double the quality of care received in 10 million patient visits to 1,000 partner clinics in 10 East African countries by 2020.

G. Innovative Practices:
Description of innovative practices used by the program to meet its goals.

Example: APOPO (Tanzania and Mozambique)
Using process re-engineering, APOPO trains African giant pouched rats in Tanzania and Mozambique to provide second-line screening of TB samples from collaborating TB diagnostic centres.

All examples are taken from CHMI program profiles.

Table 6.3 reports the frequency of reporting for each performance dimension by the 80 CHMI programs in our sample (i.e., the proportion of the 80 programs that report data for each framework dimension). The table also disaggregates the frequency of reporting based on subgroups for health area, type of innovation, and legal status. While there is substantial variation across subgroups, a large majority falls within the 50 per cent range around the mean reporting frequency value for each of the fourteen performance dimensions.

IMPLICATIONS

Despite substantial variance, most subgroups provide similar frequency coverage, almost all falling within the 50 per cent range around the mean frequency value for each category. The "for-profit" legal status subgroup is the most likely to fall below the 50 per cent coverage range (four of 14 categories). No other subgroup has more than two categories that fall below the 50 per cent coverage range. For-profit programs may have lower reporting rates due to weaker incentives to disclose data that is not considered relevant to their bottom line.

This framework can be used to understand a program's performance, including its activities, goals, and organizational context. The dimensions are framed and defined in a manner that balances comprehensiveness with comparability across diverse programs. By systematically applying the criteria in the

Table 6.3 Frequency of reporting by 80 CHMI programs for 14 performance dimensions (% reporting), including subgroups based on health area, innovation, and legal status

Performance Dimension	Total (% Reporting)	Subgroup: Health Area				Subgroup: Innovation			Subgroup: Legal Status		
		MNCH	Primary Care	Family Planning and Reproductive Health	Infectious Disease (Malaria, TB, HIV/AIDS)	Financial	Provider Training	mHealth	Not-for-profit	For-profit	PPP
A. Health Status											
A1. Population Coverage	13%	14%	9%	12%	19%	18%	16%	11%	17%	0	11%
A2. Health Output	88%	77%	92%	92%	89%	100%	84%	86%	91%	94%	72%
A3. Health Outcome	45%	64%	28%	65%	56%	49%	46%	40%	59%	13%	39%
B. Health Access											
B1. Affordability	54%	55%	56%	58%	44%	67%	57%	60%	63%	63%	22%
B2. Availability	30%	23%	31%	38%	33%	33%	41%	31%	30%	38%	22%
B3. Pro-poor Targeting	23%	41%	28%	31%	22%	36%	19%	17%	26%	25%	11%
C. Operations/Delivery											
C1. Clinical Quality	26%	45%	9%	42%	41%	36%	30%	17%	33%	19%	17%
C2. User Satisfaction	33%	23%	38%	35%	33%	38%	30%	31%	39%	31%	17%
C3. Management Quality	30%	45%	41%	42%	26%	44%	30%	29%	30%	31%	28%
C4. Economic Efficiency	21%	14%	19%	27%	30%	28%	22%	20%	26%	13%	17%

(Continued)

Table 6.3 Concluded

Performance Dimension	Total (% Reporting)	Subgroup: Health Area				Subgroup: Innovation			Subgroup: Legal Status		
		MNCH	Primary Care	Family Planning and Reproductive Health	Infectious Disease (Malaria, TB, HIV/AIDS)	Financial	Provider Training	mHealth	Not-for-profit	For-profit	PPP
C5. Non-economic Efficiency	15%	9%	6%	8%	7%	18%	19%	17%	15%	25%	6%
C6. Human Resources Supply	58%	73%	41%	77%	70%	62%	100%	57%	74%	25%	44%
C7. Political Support	40%	41%	34%	50%	44%	49%	41%	37%	39%	6%	72%
C8. Financial Management	84%	82%	84%	81%	74%	87%	84%	91%	80%	94%	83%
Summary Statistics											
Cases (a)		22	32	26	27	39	37	35	46	16	18
Minimum	13%	14%	6%	8%	7%	18%	16%	11%	17%	0%	6%
Maximum	88%	82%	92%	92%	89%	100%	100%	91%	91%	94%	83%
Mean	40%	44%	37%	47%	42%	47%	44%	39%	45%	34%	33%
No. in bottom 25% (b)	0	0	2	0	1	0	0	0	0	4	2
No. in top 25% (b)	2	2	0	1	1	1	1	0	0	1	1

(a) Numbers within the "health area" and "innovation" subgroups sum to more than 80 cases because some programs engage in multiple activities.
(b) "No. in bottom (top) 25%" indicates number of cases in the fourteen performance dimensions in each column that are less than half (more than 1.5 times) the mean percentage in the performance dimension.

framework, diverse stakeholders including program managers, funders, and researchers may achieve an understanding of relative program performance.

Illustrative Comparisons

To illustrate the framework, tables 6.4, 6.5, and 6.6 compare 10 programs, two providing eye care services, five in mHealth, and three in MNCH. Together, the 10 cases provide comparison for all 14 categories in the T-HOPE framework. We summarize the comparisons here, in terms of their implications for funders, researchers, and program managers.

EYE CARE SERVICE COMPARISONS

Table 6.4 compares the performance dimensions for two facilities that provide cataract surgeries, including Eye Care Program 1, a for-profit program in Latin America, and Eye Care Program 2, a not-for-profit program in South Asia. Several implications arise for different types of stakeholders.

Funders. Funders can use the comparisons to help determine high-opportunity investments, based on the strength of the factors that a given funder believes are most relevant for its goals. In this example, a funder focused on primarily serving disadvantaged populations may choose to fund Eye Care Program 1 given that a greater proportion of its patients are poor or, instead, might provide funding to Eye Care Program 2 to help it serve a larger number of poor people, even if the proportion is smaller.

Researchers. Scholars can use the comparison to research innovation and performance, such as exploring how different aspects shape program performance, including the operating context (Latin America v. South Asia, rural v. urban), legal status (for-profit v. not-for-profit), and model infrastructure (hub and spoke v. hospital).

Program Managers. Program managers, meanwhile, can use the comparison to identify opportunities to learn new skills and techniques. For instance, Eye Care Program 1 might seek to understand how Eye Care Program 2 grew its population coverage and learn from Eye Care Program 2's efficiency in performing cataract surgeries.

MHEALTH COMPARISONS

Table 6.5 compares the performance dimensions of five programs using mHealth, including mHealth Program 1, a for-profit hospital using management

Table 6.4 T-HOPE framework: Comparison of eye care programs (two programs)

	Comparative Features	Eye Care Program 1 (Latin America)	Eye Care Program 2 (South Asia)
Overview		Eye Care Program 1 is a for-profit program that provides eye care services and specializes in cataract surgeries using a high-volume, low-cost approach. It operates several vision centres, a surgical hub, and provides outreach activities in the national capital.	Eye Care Program 2 is a not-for-profit rural hospital that focuses on performing high-volume, low-cost eye surgeries in the country. The hospital is located in one major city, with a satellite facility in a second city.
Population Coverage (A1)	Eye Care Program 2 has 80% market share for its operations compared to 2.5% for Eye Care Program 1.	In 2012, the program's market share was estimated at 2.5% in the urban part of the country.	In 2011, the program had approximately 80% of the market share within its catchment area.
Health Output (A2)	Eye Care Program 2 provides more than 30 times as many eye surgeries a year as Eye Care Program 1.	5,400 cataract surgeries were performed from 2010 to 2012.	95,243 surgeries were performed from 2010 to 2011.
Affordability (B1)	Both programs are providing eye surgeries that are much lower in cost and performed more efficiently than their private and public competitors. Indeed, both programs provide surgeries that are approximately half the cost of similar services in the local context.	As of 2013, cataract surgeries cost approximately US$465, half the national average of US$1,240.	The cost of cataract surgery is US$33 for a middle-class patient compared to around US$50–US$60 in bigger cities.

Pro-poor Targeting (B3)	Both programs focus on serving the poor, although a higher proportion of Eye Care Program 1's patients are from an economically disadvantaged group.	85% of patients treated are living at the bottom of the pyramid.	The program focuses on serving impoverished, rural communities. Over 50% of the services it delivers are free or subsidized for poor patients.
Clinical Quality (C1)	Both have surpassed the WHO's recommended guidelines for visual acuity after cataract surgery, suggesting quality is high.	While 53% of patients had visual acuity less than 20/200 before surgery, 87% ended up with best corrected visual acuity (BCVA) greater than 20/60 (equivalent to the WHO benchmark of 6/18).	From 2007 to 2008, 81% of patients receiving small incision cataract surgery operations had BCVA <3/60 (blinding cataract) before surgery; BCVA at 6 weeks after operation was ≥6/18 in 87% of operated eyes. (The WHO recommends that after cataract surgery, at least 85% of operated eyes should have visual acuity ≥6/18 and less than 5% of operated eyes should have BCVA <6/60) (Sixty-Second World Health Assembly, 2009).
Non-economic Efficiency (C5)	Eye Care Program 2's surgeons are able to perform 100 times as many surgeries as their local competitors, while Eye Care Program 1 performs 10 times as many as their local competitors. While these differences seem substantial, with the comparison in Eye Care Program 2's favour, it should be noted that Eye Care Program 2 is more established than Eye Care Program 1, having launched 10 years earlier.	Program surgeons perform 100 cataract operations per month, compared to an average of 7–10 per month conducted in private hospital settings.	On average, 250–300 cataract surgeries are performed per day, compared to 3–5 surgeries a day performed by the nearby government hospital. Due to its innovative operational practices, its surgeons can perform a cataract surgery in one-third of the industry standard time.

Table 6.5 T-HOPE framework: Comparison of programs using mHealth (five programs)

Comparative Features	mHealth Program 1 (South Asia)	mHealth Program 2 (South Asia)	mHealth Program 3 (Sub-Saharan Africa)	mHealth Program 4 (South America)	mHealth Program 5 (South Asia)
Overview	A for-profit hospital using management software and a high-volume, low-cost approach to provide heart surgeries.	A not-for-profit program using a telemedicine call centre and CHWs to provide primary care services.	A not-for-profit program where community health workers collect children's health data on mobile phones, with monitoring by a primary care doctor.	A not-for-profit program that provides reproductive service delivery at medical centres and a call centre.	A public-private partnership with a charitable organization operating government primary health centres, some of which provide telemedicine services.
Health Output (A2)	mHealth Programs 1, 2, 4, and 5 serve several thousands of patients a year, while mHealth Program 3 is more focused.	From 2001 to 2007, the program performed over 23,000 surgeries and 34,000 catheterization procedures.	From 2008 to 2011, the program treated 40,000 patients in 200 villages.	From 2009 to 2012, over 1,400 children were enrolled in the program by their parents; 900 children are actively being served.	In 2010, the program had 15,000 monthly average clients, providing consultations, lab services, vasectomy, tubal ligation, intrauterine devices (IUDs), injectables, implants, pills, condoms, and emergency contraception.	In 2012, the program reached 1 million people through its primary health centres.

Health Outcome (A3)	mHealth Programs 3, 4, and 5 report strong levels and gains in health outcomes that merit study on how the programs and/or other sources achieved them.			Behaviour change and improved access increased the rate at which subscribers visit health facilities; a subscriber to the program visits the health care centre at least 3 times per year on average, whereas the average user rate in the district is 1.05.	In 2010, with 71,454 couple-years of protection (CYPs), it achieved 31% increase in CYP's over the previous year.	From 1996 to 2007, in states served by the organization's primary health care centres, infant mortality dropped from 75% to 24%; still birth from 38% to 10%; perinatal mortality from 68% to 17%; neonatal mortality from 70% to 10%; child mortality (1–5 years) from 12% to 3%; under-5 mortality from 88% to 27%.
Affordability (B1)	All five programs offer more affordable services than other options available locally.	In 2012, the program charged US$2,400 for heart surgery, compared to US$5,500 charged at an average private hospital in the country.	In 2012, the program provided free consultations.	In 2012, families paid a monthly subscription fee of about US$1 for the package of services per child. This is the equivalent of a kilo of onions, a price affordable to low-income families in the urban areas.	In 2012, the cost of a medical consultancy in facilities is US$4.30 against US$10 in the local market.	All services at primary health centres are provided free of cost.

(Continued)

Table 6.5 Continued

Comparative Features	mHealth Program 1 (South Asia)	mHealth Program 2 (South Asia)	mHealth Program 3 (Sub-Saharan Africa)	mHealth Program 4 (South America)	mHealth Program 5 (South Asia)
Availability (B2) mHealth Programs 3, 4, and 5 provide models for gains in availability of health care services.			In 2012, the program improved access to immediate health care for 20% of the local families by an average of 15 km; travel time was reduced by 4 hours or more.	In 2012, the call centre operated Monday to Friday 8:30 a.m. to 7 p.m. and Saturday 9 a.m. to 1 p.m. The call centre has a national number, and can be called by individuals anywhere in the country.	In 2012, all primary health centres operated 24 hours a day, 7 days a week.
Pro-poor targeting (B3) mHealth Program 3 has a particularly high proportion of poor patients, while mHealth Program 1 provides subsidies to a meaningful share of its patients.	The program has subsidized poor patients to the tune of US$2.5 million, which benefited close to half of the patients that came to the program for treatment.		90% of the program's subscribers report having unstable earnings.		
User Satisfaction (C2) mHealth Programs 2 and 3 have high patient satisfaction rates, with mHealth Program 3		The program has received an 85% patient satisfaction rating consistently	A 2009 evaluation survey carried out by a PhD student under the supervision of a national agency	Market research found that clients were intimidated by white-coated doctors and sterile environments, which	

	having a slightly higher rating. mHealth Program 4 provides an example of how to increase patient ease.		over the last year from patient feedback surveys.	showed that 96% of the enrolled families are satisfied with the service.	they associated with illness rather than health. With trained staff performing most consultations and providing advice in friendlier environments, clients report feeling more at ease.
Management Quality (C3)	mHealth Programs 2, 3, 4, and 5 offer examples of activities that can strengthen management, operations, and delivery.	The program is an ISO 9001:2008 certified company.	The program uses a qualitative health monitoring system to ensure that both low- and higher-income populations are served.	The program uses a standardized assessment tool for all regional programs. The evaluations improve technical and financial performance, while creating transparency and accountability.	The program uses a hospital management information system developed by a major university to improve to hygiene and good maintenance.
Economic Efficiency (C4)	mHealth Programs 1, 3, and 4 offer models of achieving different aspects of financial efficiency.	The program brought down the cost of electrocardiogram machines from US$750 to less than US$300.		The operational cost to provide call centre services is US$0.21 per minute per call to the call centre, which allows the non-profit to provide affordable services.	The operating cost of each primary health centre is about US$50,000, lower than comparable facilities.

(Continued)

Table 6.5 Concluded

	Comparative Features	mHealth Program 1 (South Asia)	mHealth Program 2 (South Asia)	mHealth Program 3 (Sub-Saharan Africa)	mHealth Program 4 (South America)	mHealth Program 5 (South Asia)
Non-economic efficiency (C5)	mHealth Programs 1 and 2 serve more patients in a day than other local options, while mHealth Program 4 provides faster service than other local options.	The program performs 32 heart surgeries a day, about eight times more surgeries per day than the average for other comparable hospitals.	In traditional models, a doctor could treat up to a 100 patients per day. The program's model allows each doctor to diagnose over 400 patients per day spread across 100 villages.		The program's tubal ligation procedure takes 20 minutes compared to 2 hours observed in other facilities.	
Human Resources Supply (C6)	mHealth Programs 2, 3, 4, and 5 provide models of training for health workers.	The program has trained over 200 local village women to become health workers.		The program started offering training sessions in 2011 for its teams as well as medical teams in the partnering health centre.	The program offers ongoing training to staff to assure quality of care.	The medical officer, staff nurse, pharmacist, and laboratory technician are required to stay in the same town/village where the primary health care centre is located. Auxiliary nurses and midwives are trained to do pap smears.

Political Support (C7)	All programs partner with governments actors, using multiple models to gather support and gain contact with clients.	The program developed microinsurance schemes with state governments, which work on flexible payments, and have helped thousands coming from low-income groups to procure services.	The program partners with the state government.	The program organized an informational event for the surrounding population in front of the District Chief's home. Counsellors presented to the District Chief, and then the program's employees followed suit with an information session. The program also partners with the Ministry of Health.	The program negotiated agreements with the national Ministry of Health and with local governmental units that enable them provide services at municipal health centres. The municipality schedules visits from program staff, organizes clients, and provides places for services.	The program operates as a PPP, with the charitable organization managing government primary health centres in several states.
Financial Management (C8)	The programs offer models to learn about varied mixes of fee, donor, and government sources of revenues.	Over 50% of revenue came from heart surgeries, while 9% came from coronary care charges and 8% from outpatient fees. In the financial year that ended in March 2005, the hospital earned 20% operating profits before interest, depreciation, and taxes.		The program receives 50% of operating costs from subscription fees, while the other 50% is sought from donors. The program reports that it has not yet found a sustainable economic model.	The program works with an annual revenue of about US$1.5 million; of this, 50% is raised from fee revenue from clinic services.	90% of operating costs are covered by state governments; the charitable organization covers 10% of costs through donations from individual donors.

Table 6.6 T-HOPE framework: Comparison of programs using MNCH (three programs)

Comparative Features	MNCH Program 1 (South Asia)	MNCH Program 2 (South East Asia)	MNCH Program 3 (South Asia)
Overview	A for-profit hospital chain providing health care to women and children.	A not-for-profit network of franchised clinics providing maternal and child health services and family planning, reproductive health, and HIV/AIDS services.	A not-for-profit clinic franchise offering services for maternal and child health, family planning and reproductive health, general primary care, tuberculosis, and malaria.
Health Output (A2)	MNCH Programs 2 and 3 serve millions of clients a year, while MNCH Program 1 serves about 10,000 patients a year.	Since its inception in 2005 through the summer of 2007, the program served over 21,271 outpatients and 1,810 inpatients, of which 1,043 were there for deliveries. The program has become the largest chain in the region, treating more than 70,000 patients and delivering more than 7,000 healthy babies.	In 2010 alone, the program's 629 centres, across 40 countries, provided seven million couples with high-quality health services, including: family planning; safe abortion and post-abortion care; maternal and child health care, including safe delivery and obstetrics; diagnosis and treatment of sexually transmitted infections; and HIV/AIDS prevention.	In 2010, the program served 9.5 million clients needing services for diarrhoea, pneumonia, immunization, and child delivery in the hospital and at home.
Health Outcome (A3)	Both MNCH Programs 1 and 2 show improvements in health outcomes due to their interventions, with MNCH Program 1's	Of all the women who deliver their second or third child at the program, over 50% had their previous delivery	The program provided 49,619 IUDs in 2011, which was the major contributor to its 283,571 CYPs generated during the period.	

	impact involving changes in healthy prenatal and delivery behaviours, and MNCH Program 2's showing an impact in reproductive health.	at home or in an under-resourced government hospital; between 2011 and 2012, the average antenatal visits by the pregnant women increased from 2.5 to over 4.	In 2012, prices for services ranged between free (for the poor) and US$0.38.
Affordability (B1)	MNCH Program 3 provides free services for the poor, while MNCH Programs 1 and 2 provide services for less than other similar local offerings. MNCH Program 1 provides services for approximately one-fifth the cost of similar services elsewhere, while MNCH Program 2 provides services for approximately one-third to one-sixth the cost of similar services elsewhere.	In 2012, the price of a normal delivery at the program was approximately US$40, compared to the standard US$200, which includes all doctor and nurse visits, all medicines, and the complete stay in the hospital.	In 2012, the program had both mandatory and recommended pricing. For example, the price for an IUD is set at US$2. Competitive prices for an IUD in private clinics range from US$6.60–US$13. Deliveries by midwives range from US$33–US$77, whereas private doctor and hospital prices range from US$220–US$330.
Availability (B2)	Both MNCH Programs 1 and 2 are roughly within walking distance of the communities they serve.	In 2012, families who patronized the hospital typically lived within a 5 km radius of the hospital. Strong word-of-mouth recommendations extended this radius up to 20 km.	In 2012, 81% of the program's facilities were within walking distance for community women.

(Continued)

Table 6.6 Continued

	Comparative Features	MNCH Program 1 (South Asia)	MNCH Program 2 (South East Asia)	MNCH Program 3 (South Asia)
Pro-poor Targeting (B3)	All programs serve poor clients. For MNCH Programs 2 and 3, approximately one third to one half of their clients are impoverished. MNCH Program 1 serves clients that are disadvantaged but not at the bottom of the pyramid.	The program targets customers from a key tier in the national population: not the very bottom of the pyramid, but those that are low on the pyramid. Monthly family income of customers is as follows: 40% earn below US$90 per month; 30% earn between US$91 and US$130 per month; 20% earn between US$131 and US$220 per month; and 10% earn above US$220 per month. The poverty line in the region is US$31 per month.	In 2011, 46% of the program's clients were members of households whose incomes fell below the poverty line; 66% were unemployed and 78% had at least 2 children.	One of the primary goals of the program is to serve poor patients; therefore, all clinics have what is known as a poorest-of-the-poor fund. Clients that qualify as poor receive a card, which entitles them to receive free services. The official qualification process for the card is based on criteria used by the national public health department to identify lower socio-economic status, but if a client indicates that they are poor, they are provided with the card. The program reports that 27% of its patients are poor.
Clinical Quality (C1)	All programs show impact in clinical quality in provision of clinical services.	Through the program's long-standing partnership with a US health care institute, its clinical quality indicators have shown	Through the program's Quality Technical Assessment, 100% of franchised midwives were found adhering	As of 2011, there were almost 6,000 safe deliveries per quarter. Only one woman had died while giving birth

	significant improvement. For example, its "culture of safety" ratings increased from 35% in January 2010 to 77% in December 2010.		to service provision standards and having maintained confidence in their delivery of program services.	under the care of a franchised facility since the program's inception.
User Satisfaction (C2)	MNCH Programs 2 and 3 show approximately 60–70% of patients are satisfied with services. In addition, 98% of MNCH Program 2's patients expressed loyalty, suggesting high user satisfaction. Only 0.3% of MNCH Program 1's patients have filed complaints regarding services, also suggesting a high level of patient satisfaction.	Only 18 complaints from about 6,000 users of inpatient services were received through the program's complaint registration system between 2011 and 2012.	61% of the program's clients identified themselves to be satisfied with regard to price and 68% in regard to the feeling of comfort. In addition, 58% expressed satisfaction equivalent to that of the evaluation's highest scale in terms of feeling security against conception. 98% expressed loyalty to the program, which was primarily based on quality of services.	The clients are typically loyal users of the program's services, and the franchise found that 71% of customers are repeat users.
Management Quality (C3)	All programs conduct monitoring protocols to ensure high quality management and operations.	The flagship hospital was ISO 9001:2000 certified in 2007. Customer-focused service is embodied in the program's protocol and approach whereby each employee is expected to be polite, attentive, and respectful to patients.	Clinical compliance audits, business systems audits, and franchisee and customer satisfaction surveys are conducted regularly through site visits at each franchisee.	Not-for-profit organizations monitor clinical quality of the clinics and report findings and progress on resolving performance gaps to the program head office. A clinic-level quality

(Continued)

Table 6.6 Concluded

Comparative Features	MNCH Program 1 (South Asia)	MNCH Program 2 (South East Asia)	MNCH Program 3 (South Asia)
		Team members help franchisees correct problems with entering data.	circle is in place, and all clinic staff members are responsible for maintaining the quality of the services they provide. A clinical quality council reviews clinic performance indicators.
Economic Efficiency (C4)	Both MNCH Program 2 and 3 report on cost per CYP, with MNCH Program 3's costs at less than half that of MNCH Program 2.	The cost per CYP dropped to US$16 after two years – roughly on par with other franchises at similar stages of development.	The cost per CYP generated is about US$7.
Human Resources Supply (C6)	All programs report on their human resources situation. MNCH Program 1 describes efforts to attract doctors and employ other types of health workers to keep costs low. MNCH Program 2 describes training for franchisees, and MNCH Program 3 describes reasons for staff turnover.	Talent recruitment: doctors earn fixed salaries so they can focus on care of existing patients as opposed to the need to attract new customers. The program typically employs auxiliary nurse midwives who undergo significantly less training than graduate nurse midwives, reducing costs and attrition.	As part of staff training, franchisees must complete a minimum of 10 supervised IUD insertions, 5 IUD removals, and 10 pap smears.	Within the franchisors' headquarters, 35% of staff turnover was due to releasing staff for performance reasons, while 65% of staff turnover was due to career advancement either for opportunities outside the country or in-country promotions.

software in South Asia; mHealth Program 2, a not-for-profit telemedicine program in South Asia; mHealth Program 3, a not-for-profit mobile monitoring program in Sub-Saharan Africa; mHealth Program 4, a not-for-profit medical centre and call centre in South America; and mHealth Program 5, a PPP operating clinic with telemedicine services in South Asia.

Funders. Funders such as investors may be particularly interested in partnering with mHealth Program 1, which has shown strong revenue and profits through its financial model, as well as strong performance in noneconomic efficiency and management quality as evidenced by its ISO 9001:2008 certification. Donors may want to support the efforts of mHealth Programs 2 and 4, which have achieved substantial scale in providing affordable and efficient health services. Donors interested in helping a medically successful program that needs financial support may be drawn to mHealth Program 3. Public agencies and policymakers looking for PPP models may want to explore mHealth Program 5's successful approach to partnership.

Researchers. Researchers may be interested in exploring how mHealth Programs 1 and 2 are able to serve many more patients per day than other local options and the types of procedures that are amenable to this. They may want to study how these programs, both for-profit and not-for-profit, have been able to develop relationships with government entities to deliver their programs, and the advantages and challenges of doing so. Researchers may also want to study how mHealth Program 5 has contributed to improvements in local health outcomes.

Program Managers. Program managers may be interested in learning how mHealth Programs 2 and 3 are able to achieve high satisfaction ratings with patients, and how to scale up services to serve the large numbers of patients mHealth Programs 1 and 2 are able to serve. Program managers may also be interested in learning about the value proposition that mHealth Program 5 has used to gain substantial financial support from public bodies.

MATERNAL, NEWBORN, AND CHILD HEALTH (MNCH) COMPARISONS

Table 6.6 compares the performance of three MNCH programs, including MNCH Program 1, a for-profit hospital chain serving women and children in South Asia; MNCH Program 2, a not-for-profit clinic franchise focusing on MNCH and reproductive health in South East Asia; and MNCH Program 3, a not-for-profit clinic franchise offering MNCH and general primary care services in South Asia.

Funders. Funders may be particularly interested in the CYPs generated by programs and the ability for MNCH Program 3 to provide CYPs at a relatively low cost, choosing to support programs that are able to produce health outcomes most cost-effectively.

Researchers. Researchers may be interested in understanding how MNCH Program 1 has influenced the health behaviours of pregnant women. Given that MNCH Programs 2 and 3 are franchises, scholars may also want to explore how Health Outcome, Clinical Quality, User Satisfaction, and Management Quality compare with non-franchised MNCH programs.

Program Managers. Program managers may find the data on Human Resources Supply particularly relevant, including MNCH Program 1's efforts to employ non-physician health workers to keep costs low, the types of training provided by MNCH Program 2 for its franchisees, and reasons for staff turnover in MNCH Program 3's franchise model.

In these examples, the framework data give a snapshot of performance information about each program, and provides an entry point for funders, researchers, and program managers to conduct preliminary comparisons and identify avenues for further investigation. Applied at regular intervals, these performance dimensions can also help track program performance over time, providing a richer understanding of the program's capabilities and potential. As well, to understand program performance, one must have knowledge of program operations, goals, challenges, and processes that shape this performance; the descriptive fields framework offers relevant information that complements the T-HOPE performance framework.

General Implications

One of the key strengths of this framework is the integration of established approaches for measuring the performance of health programs and organizations. The wide variety of tools used today creates confusion, puts an inappropriate burden on delivery organizations, and fails to achieve comparability. Delivery organizations in LMICs with limited resources often have difficulty meeting the monitoring and evaluation demands placed on them by different donors, suggesting the need for greater coordination on reporting requirements and simplified measures (Ebrahim 2005; Bornstein 2006). By harmonizing measurement requirements, funders may implement more effective pan-organizational strategies for achieving targeted health outcomes while reducing the reporting burden on the organizations they fund (Yang, Farmer, & McGahan 2010).

This framework can be used to highlight and compare the performance of innovative health programs for various stakeholders. However, while providing a snapshot of program performance at a moment in time, it will be of greatest value when combined with descriptive information about program activities, goals, and context that shapes this performance. It can provide an even richer understanding of program performance if applied over time to track progress. Also, while the framework can facilitate comparison of performance among programs and over time, given the diversity of innovative models emerging, we have not included benchmarks for the example indicators of our performance dimensions. Benchmarks will vary by health area and operational model, and program managers and others can identify whether their programs are meeting accepted standards.

While we have endeavoured to develop credible, feasible, and comparable performance measures, some of the framework criteria are structurally more difficult to measure than others, as table 6.3 highlights. For example, Population Coverage requires an accurate, quantified measure of a program's target population, which may not be readily available in resource-limited settings without birth registration and accurate census information. Measuring Pro-poor Targeting may involve complex and multidimensional considerations for identifying poor patients (Hulme, Moore, & Shepherd 2001). Assessing Health Outcome, meanwhile, may be challenging and time consuming, involving tracking patient health status after the intervention (Kalinichenko et al. 2013); this may involve impact evaluations, requiring advance planning, additional funding, and rigorous research designs to ensure the results are attributable to the program, a research approach relatively few social development programs have been able to carry out (Savedoff, Levine, & Birdsall 2006).

We have included these performance dimensions in the framework because they are considered critical for assessing impact in the literature (Jee & Or 1999; Shengelia, Murray, & Adams 2003; Patouillard, Goodman, Hanson, & Mills 2007). We have aimed to provide simple and straightforward definitions and example indicators based on the reporting of programs in the CHMI database. However, some dimensions may require additional information and knowledge that is not as easily accessible for new and small-scale programs as it is for large-scale established ones. Greater technical and financial support is needed from stakeholders such as funders and researchers to assist program managers with reporting on this valuable data (Bennett, Lagomarsino, et al. 2014; Savedoff et al. 2006). In addition, further field testing of the framework can help to refine these performance dimensions so they are more attainable for program managers, and also help to identify more feasible methods for program managers to access this information in resource-constrained contexts.

Despite these limitations, the development of an integrative framework that acknowledges and balances the trade-offs between credibility, feasibility, and comparability is urgently needed. This could benefit programs interested in understanding and communicating their activities and accomplishments, funders making decisions on which programs to support, and researchers seeking to better understand performance of innovative health care delivery models and programs. This framework also aims to encourage greater discussion on the types of metrics needed to meaningfully and cost-effectively understand program performance, identifying areas for improvement and opportunities for further collaboration and discourse among different groups with shared interests in global health.

Conclusions

The T-HOPE framework is designed to cultivate the adoption of performance measures that meet the needs of diverse programs, while encouraging collaboration, coordination, and sharing of knowledge among programs, funders, and researchers. In doing so, the framework provides an important step towards accurately and realistically assessing the health impact and sustainability of programs aiming to meet the needs of the poor.

In practice, this framework has been incorporated into CHMI's Reported Results initiative (CHMI 2015). Through this initiative, programs can display public profiles with reporting on selected performance dimensions. The T-HOPE approach has also informed the Impact Reporting and Investment Standards's (IRIS) (Global Impact Investing Network (GIIN) 2015) health working group of the Global Impact Investment Network in the development of a core set of health metrics for social enterprises. The resulting IRIS metrics, while focused on a small number of process measures that are pertinent to clinics and hospitals, have been selected to enhance comparability. In parallel, the more comprehensive T-HOPE framework allows for comparisons across a wider range of program types, and may be used to describe trade-offs between quality, cost, and accessibility. Thus, the approaches are complementary: IRIS metrics may be used to scan for promising activities among hospitals and clinics, while the T-HOPE framework can be used to structure in-depth analyses and comparison of health programs.

The collection of credible, feasible, and comparable information on health organization performance is essential for identifying effective and innovative approaches to delivery. By understanding and comparing the performance of health programs, we can better determine which models are generating innovations that create health impact and real value in LMICs. Such understanding is crucial to progress.

REFERENCES

Bennett, S., Bloom, G., Knezovich, J., & Peters, D.H. 2014. "The Future of Health Markets." *Globalization and Health* 10(1): 51. https://doi.org/10.1186/1744-8603-10-51.

Bennett, S., Lagomarsino, G., Knezovich, J., & Lucas, H. 2014. "Accelerating Learning for Pro-poor Health Markets." *Globalization and Health* 10(1): 54. https://doi.org/10.1186/1744-8603-10-54.

Bhattacharyya, O., Khor, S., McGahan, A., Dunne, D., Daar, A.S., & Singer, P.A. 2010. "Innovative Health Service Delivery Models in Low and Middle Income Countries – What Can We Learn from the Private Sector?" *Health Research Policy and Systems* 8(24). https://doi.org/10.1186/1478-4505-8-24.

Binagwaho, A., Nutt, C.T., Mutabazi, V., Karema, C., Nsanzimana, S., Gasana, M., ... Farmer, P.E. 2013. "Shared Learning in an Interconnected World: Innovations to Advance Global Health Equity." *Globalization and Health* 9(1): 37. https://doi.org/10.1186/1744-8603-9-37.

Bloom, G., Henson, S., & Peters, D.H. 2014. "Innovation in Regulation of Rapidly Changing Health Markets." *Globalization and Health* 10(1): 53. https://doi.org/10.1186/1744-8603-10-53.

Bornstein, L. 2006. "Systems of Accountability, Webs of Deceit? Monitoring and Evaluation in South African NGOs." *Development* 49(2): 52–61. https://doi.org/10.1057/palgrave.development.1100261.

Bradley, E.H., Pallas, S., Bashyal, C., Berman, P., & Curry, L. 2010. *Developing Strategies for Improving Health Care Delivery: Guide to Concepts, Determinants, Measurement, and Intervention Design*. Health, Nutrition, and Population (HNP) Discussion Paper. Washington: World Bank.

Center for Health Market Innovations. 2015. "Performance Measurement." https://healthmarketinnovations.org/chmi-themes/performance-measurement.

Clark, C., Rosensweig, W., Long, D., & Olsen, S. 2004. *Double Bottom Line Project Report: Assessing Social Impact in Double Bottom Line Ventures*. Berkeley: Center for Responsible Business.

Dandonoli, P. 2013. "Open Innovation as a New Paradigm for Global Collaborations in Health." *Globalization and Health* 9(1): 41. https://doi.org/10.1186/1744-8603-9-41.

De Savigny, D., Campbell, A.T., & Best, A. 2010. "Systems Thinking: What It Is and What It Means for Health Systems." In D. De Savigny & T. Adam, eds, *Systems Thinking for Health Systems Strengthening: Alliance for Health Policy and Systems Research*. 37–48. Geneva: World Health Organization.

Donabedian, A. 2005. "Evaluating the Quality of Medical Care." *Millbank Quarterly* 83(4): 691–729. https://doi.org/10.1111/j.1468-0009.2005.00397.x.

Ebrahim, A. 2005. *NGOs and Organizational Change: Discourse, Reporting, and Learning.* Cambridge: Cambridge University Press.

Global Impact Investing Network. 2012. "IRIS Metrics: Framework Structure." Accessed 20 October 2012. https://iris.thegiin.org/metrics.

Global Impact Investing Network. 2015. "Healthcare Delivery." Accessed 12 January 2015. https://iris.thegiin.org/health-metrics.

Hanson, K., & Berman, P. 1998. "Private Health Care Provision in Developing Countries: A Preliminary Analysis of Lvels and Composition." *Health Policy and Planning* 13(3): 195–211. https://doi.org/10.1093/heapol/13.3.195.

Hanson, K., Gilson, L., Goodman, C., Mills, A., Smith, R., Feachem, R., ... Kinlaw, H. 2008. "Is Private Health Care the Answer to the Health Problems of the World's Poor?" *PLoS Med* 5(11): e233. https://doi.org/10.1371/journal.pmed.0050233.

Howitt, P., Darzi, G., Yang, G., Ashrafian, H., & Atun, R. 2012. "Technologies for Global Health." *The Lancet* 380(9840): 507–35. https://doi.org/10.1016/S0140-6736(12)61127-1.

Hulme, D., Moore, K., & Shepherd, A. 2001. *Chronic Poverty: Meanings and Analytical Frameworks: CPRC Working Paper 2.* Manchester: Chronic Poverty Research Centre.

Jee, M., & Or, Z. 1999. *Health Outcomes in OECD Countries.* Paris: OECD Publishing. https://doi.org/10.1787/513803511413.

Kalinichenko, O., Amado, C.A.F., & Santos, S.P. 2013. *Performance Assessment in Primary Health Care: A Systematic Literature Review.* Faro: CEFAGE-UE.

Kaplan, R.S., & Norton, D.P. 1992. "The Balanced Scorecard: Measures That Drive Performance." *Harvard Business Review* January-February: 71–9.

Kelly, E., & Hurst, J. 2006. *Health Care Quality Indicators Project: Conceptual Framework Paper.* OECD Health Working Papers No. 23. Paris: OECD Publishing.

Mills, A., Brugha, R., Hanson, K., & McPake, B. 2002. "What Can Be Done about the Private Health Sector in Low-Income Countries?" *Bulletin of the World Health Organization* 80(4): 325–30.

Ojha, N.P., Ghosh, P., Khandelwal, S., & Kapoor, H. 2011. "Innovation Overview." *Business Today*, 3–56.

Patouillard, E., Goodman, C.A., Hanson, K.G., & Mills, A.J. 2007. "Can Working with the Private For-Profit Sector Improve Utilization of Quality Health Services by the Poor? A Systematic Review of the Literature." *International Journal for Equity in Health* 6(1): 17. https://doi.org/10.1186/1475-9276-6-17.

Savedoff, W., Levine, R., & Birdsall, N. 2006. *When Will We Ever Learn? Improving Lives through Impact Evaluation.* Washington, DC: Center for Global Development.

Schweitzer, J., & Synowiec, C. 2012. "The Economics of eHealth and mHealth." *Journal of Health Communication* 17(Suppl 1): 73–81. https://doi.org/10.1080/10810730.2011.649158.

Shengelia, B., Murray, C., & Adams, O. 2003. "Beyond Access and Utilization: Defining and Measuring Health System Coverage." In C. Murray & D. Evans (eds), *Health Systems Performance Assessment: Debates, Methods, and Empiricism.* 221–34. Geneva: World Health Organization.

Sixty-Second World Health Assembly. 2009. *Prevention of Avoidable Blindness and Visual Impairment: Report by the Secretariat.* Geneva: World Health Organization.

Swanson, R.C., Atun, R., Best, A., Betigeri, A., de Campos, F., Chunharas, S., ... Van Damme, W. 2015. "Strengthening Health Systems in Low Income Countries by Enhancing Organizational Capacities and Improving Institutions." *Globalization and Health* 11(1): 5. https://doi.org/10.1186/s12992-015-0090-3.

World Health Organization. 2010. *Monitoring the Building Blocks of Health Systems: A Handbook of Indicators and Their Measurement Strategies.* Geneva: World Health Organization.

Yang, A., Farmer, P.E., & McGahan, A.M. 2010. "'Sustainability' in Global Health." *Global Public Health* 5(2): 129–35. https://doi.org/10.1080/17441690903418977.

7 Performance Measurement for Innovative Health Programs: Understanding Efficiency, Quality, and Scale

ONIL BHATTACHARYYA, ANITA MCGAHAN, WILL MITCHELL,
KATE MOSSMAN, RAMAN SOHAL, JOHN GINTHER,
JIEUN CHA, AMEYA BOPARDIKAR, JOHN A. MACDONALD,
LEIGH HAYDEN, HIMANSHU PARIKH, AND ILAN SHAHIN

Introduction

In recent years, growing attention has been paid to innovative programs in low- and middle-income countries that use market-based approaches to provide for the health care needs of impoverished populations. These programs have the potential to transform health care systems by offering quality care on a large scale for a reasonable cost. In order to assess which programs work well, we need to understand their efficiency, quality, and scale. In doing so, we can determine which types of programs have the greatest potential to improve the health of the poor. Understanding organizational performance also exposes tensions between efficiency, quality, and scale that may be overcome through organizational innovation.

The most promising programs will provide affordable care of high quality to a large number of people, but efficiency, quality, and scale are complex concepts, and optimizing them may require trading one off against another. The available literature narrowly defines these topics, yet it is important to understand these three areas and their interrelationships to assess a program's overall performance. Emerging markets are a source of disruptive innovations in health care and other areas, using strategies such as providing products or services that are of slightly lower quality, but also much lower in cost, and able to operate at a larger scale, thus serving more people and having greater impact. Stakeholders, such as program managers, investors, donors, and researchers, need adequate measures of efficiency, quality, and scale to understand the underlying trade-offs in these strategies. For program managers, monitoring their performance in these key areas informs strategic decisions key to their success. As well, by understanding the performance of other programs, program managers can adopt activities that can improve their own operations. Investors and funders (including large health insurers) can measure the performance of health programs to gain information on which programs are efficiently and effectively meeting the health care needs of a population, helping them decide which programs to support. For researchers, assessing these elements of performance allows for comparison of which strategies are performing well to create generalizable knowledge to advance the field.

To assist these stakeholders in assessing the performance of innovative health programs, we developed the T-HOPE framework with credible, feasible, and comparable metrics (Bhattacharyya et al. 2015). In this chapter, we focus on a more in-depth discussion of the development of the following dimensions in our T-HOPE framework: efficiency, quality, and scale. This involves exploring the relevant literature to determine how these concepts are defined and the key components of each measure. We also consider how these dimensions are reported in a subset of 80 well-documented organizations from the CHMI dataset. We then present our recommended definitions for efficiency, quality, and scale, and the key components of these measures. We attempt to reconcile recommendations from the academic literature with the practices of organizations in the field to optimize the credibility, feasibility, and comparability of performance measures to identify promising innovations in health care delivery targeting the poor.

Background

What Works: Optimizing Efficiency, Quality, and Scale

According to prior researchers, the world needs novel approaches that are affordable, of acceptable quality, and can be provided on a large scale in order to address the needs of the 2.5 billion people living on less than US$2 a day (Chen & Ravallion 2012). Developing nations are eager for innovative approaches offering decent performance at an ultralow cost, described as models that can offer a 50 per cent solution for 15 per cent of the price (Trimble & Govindarajan 2012). Indeed, Radjou et al. (2012) advocate developing "good enough" solutions that get the job done, optimizing the use of scarce natural and financial resources to make basic services like health care affordable for more people. The scaling-up process can be thought of as comprising of three successive stages: 1) effectiveness, developing a solution that works;

2) efficiency, finding a way to deliver the solution at an affordable cost; and 3) expansion, developing a strategy to provide solutions on a larger scale (Korten 1988, as cited in Cooley & Khol 2006). Though this is described as a linear process, once a program is operating, optimizing these three dimensions may require strategic trade-offs.

A variety of strategic choices are made for different program strategies. For example, SMS for Life is an SMS-based monitoring system that aims to eliminate stock-outs of antimalarial medication in medical facilities. The intervention was successful at reducing stock-outs at facilities in three target districts, and even eliminated stock-outs altogether in one district. Achieving these results required the adoption of a strategy that uses emergency orders where inventory dropped too low. While this approach may not be the most cost-effective, the system in place focuses on quality by improving the likelihood that the medication will be available for those in need of it.

In contrast, the Greenstar Social Marketing Pakistan (GSMP) program emphasizes efficiency by providing affordable and integrated family planning and reproductive health services to low-income clients at a nationwide scale. Through its franchise business model, the GSMP network has grown over time to encompass a broader set of service providers and has expanded its network to include more types of service delivery packages and service providers (McBride & Ahmed 2001). Since GSMP lacks the resources needed to ensure rigorous site supervision and monitoring, this growth has occurred without any explicit emphasis on quality. While the social franchising model enables Greenstar to maximize efficiency and lower its costs, it is more difficult to regulate and monitor compliance within quality standards using this model.

Alternatively, Aravind, which provides surgery for cataracts, is a rare example of a program that performs well on all three dimensions. Aravind provides higher-quality eye surgeries that are performed quicker and at a reduced cost compared to its competitors, which is in part due to a strategy towards greater specialization of staff.[1] Understanding the performance of these programs and the underlying strategic choices taking place entails measuring efficiency, quality, and scale.

Conceptualizing Performance and Productivity

In order to assess health programs, one must measure their performance in terms of their ability to efficiently provide quality care to an optimal number of clients. Smith (2002, 145) identifies two main functions for performance data: "to identify in general 'what works' in promoting the objectives of the health system and to identify the functional competence of specific practitioners or organizations." Performance is a relative concept, where one can measure performance of an organization relative to the performance of another organization in the same time period, or measure the performance of an organization at different time periods (Coelli et al. 2005).

Measuring performance entails a consideration of productivity, a complex concept that has also been associated with efficiency, quality, economic growth, surplus value, profitability, and need, among other factors (Saari 2006). For Coelli et al. (2005, 1), "A natural measure of performance is a productivity ratio: the ratio of outputs to inputs, where larger values of this ratio are associated with better performance". The literature on productivity and the related concept of efficiency tends to be very narrowly defined and focused on the micro level. Our more practical aim in this chapter is to broadly discuss efficiency, quality, and scale as important measures in assessing program performance. In the following sections, we explore these concepts more generally and trace their connections with each other.

Productivity, Scale, and Efficiency

Scale and efficiency are important components for understanding productivity. Examining change in productivity over time is known as total factor productivity growth (Grosskopf 1993) or productivity change (Hollingsworth 2008). Productivity change is a result of technical changes (advances in technology), scale economies (achieving optimal scale), and allocative efficiency (selecting a mix of inputs that produces a given quantity of output at minimum cost given input prices) (Coelli et al. 2005). Overall efficiency encompasses both technical and allocative efficiency (Hollingsworth 2008), concepts that are further explored in the section on measuring efficiency.

Ensuring that a health program is operating at an optimal size and volume is significant to improving productivity, and scaling up to appropriate levels is crucial to meet the health needs of a larger portion of the population. Indeed, the World Bank (2003) notes that the process of scaling up involves efficiently increasing impact from a small scale to a large scale of coverage. However, depending on the demand and impact of the provided health services, some health programs may find themselves operating at a large scale that is no longer optimal in terms of efficiency, known as diseconomies of scale. Serving more people and having a greater health impact may supersede the importance of efficiently operating at optimal scale.

Another consideration when assessing efficiency is the domain of quality, an important concept in understanding performance. The relationship between efficiency and quality is further explored in the next section.

Efficiency and Quality

In order to understand a program's performance, one must go beyond simply looking at efficiency and scale and consider dimensions of quality. Measures of economic efficiency address the question of whether the product or service was delivered cheaply; however, they do not reflect the quality of the product or service. For instance, doctors at SalaUno Salud perform five times more eye surgeries per week than the average doctor in Mexico, yet the program provides no measures of quality or outcome. In absence of this complementary data, these relative efficiencies may also compromise clinical quality or patient outcome. Ideally, when measuring efficiency in the health field, measuring the final output^2 would involve capturing the impact of the service or product, such as the health gains of individual patients (Hollingsworth 2008). However, dimensions of quality and outcome in relation to efficiency are not well developed in the health care literature. As a result, most research published on this issue has used some form of intermediate outputs, such as looking at the number of treated patients (Hollingsworth 2008). However, Hollingsworth (2008) notes that this method is not ideal given that it does not inform us of whether the patient's health has actually improved.

An overemphasis on measuring efficiency while ignoring quality can risk skewing the assessment of a health program's performance, promoting approaches that are low cost but also low impact. As Smith (2002, 146) points out, "what is measured and how it is measured can introduce powerful incentives into health care." For example, Smith (2002) suggests that an emphasis on cost data with little reference to clinical outcome in early UK performance measurement initiatives has resulted in a low-cost, low-quality system. As follows, measuring efficiency assuming or absent of quality data may create an unintended incentive and valuation of efficiency at the cost of quality. Consequently, both economic and non-economic measures of efficiency should be presented alongside quality figures. Efficiency measurement should be considered only a partial measure of overall performance, and the objectives of health service actors should also be considered, which may include improving quality (Hollingsworth 2008). Porter and Kaplan (2011) recommend that evaluations of efficiency include a measure of quality. After costing the service, data on health outcomes should be compared to the cost, looking at the cost per outcome (Porter & Kaplan 2011). Thus, in assessing the performance of innovative health programs, we consider performance to entail dimensions of scale and efficiency, as well as quality (which is expanded to include outcomes and impacts), in an effort to provide a more comprehensive approach to understanding how well these programs efficiently provide quality health services to meet the needs of their target populations.

Methods

The overall process for developing the T-HOPE framework is discussed in chapter 6. Here, we focus more in-depth on the development of three measures for the framework: efficiency, quality, and scale.[3] Their development first involved a literature review to identify the key dimensions of each measure. We then collected data on 80 diverse and data-rich CHMI programs (Bhattacharyya et al. 2015). These programs were selected by focusing on programs operating in four important health areas: the established fields of maternal, newborn, and child health (MNCH); general primary care; infectious diseases; and the emerging area of mHealth. To supplement the data on programs in the CHMI database, we also collected data on these programs using publicly available sources, including program websites and reports, journal articles, and websites located through an online search. We assessed the frequency of reporting by these 80 programs of key dimensions in our T-HOPE framework (see table 7.1). Based on a review of the literature and reported data, we refined our definitions of efficiency, quality, and scale to ensure this program data is appropriately captured.

Results

Efficiency

LITERATURE REVIEW

Efficiency can be assessed at a macro or micro level, where macro-level efficiency refers to allocation of resources made at a health system level and micro-efficiency looks at value of outputs realized with given inputs (Kelley & Hurst 2006). Our focus here is a micro-efficiency lens to monitor programs.

Economic Efficiency. Efficiency is dichotomized into economic and non-economic efficiency. Economic efficiency has been further categorized as technical or allocative efficiency. Hollingsworth (2008, 1108) defines technical efficiency as "producing the maximum amount of output from a given amount of input or alternatively, producing a given output with minimum input quantities." Allocative efficiency refers to an input/output mix that avoids waste, minimizing cost/maximizing revenue respectively (Hollingsworth 2008). While the literature has general agreement on the theoretical concepts of economic efficiency, measuring it remains elusive. As reported in a typology on efficiency in health care by a US Department of Health and Human Services study (McGlynn et al. 2008, 3): "We found little overlap between the peer-reviewed literature that

Table 7.1 Frequency of reporting by 80 CHMI programs for 14 performance dimensions (% reporting)

T-HOPE Framework Performance Dimension	Total (% Reporting)
A. Health Status	
A1. Population Coverage	13
A2. Health Output	88
A3. Health Outcome	45
B. Health Access	
B1. Affordability	54
B1. Availability	30
B3. Pro-poor Targeting	23
C. Operations/Delivery	
C1. Clinical Quality	26
C2. User Satisfaction	33
C3. Management Quality	30
C4. Economic Efficiency	21
C5. Non-economic Efficiency	15
C6. Human Resources Supply	58
C7. Political Support	40
C8. Financial Management	84

describes the development, testing, and application of efficiency measures and the vendor-based efficiency metrics that are most commonly used."

Many studies use econometric analyses when examining economic efficiency in health care, such as Data Envelopment Analysis (DEA) and Stochastic Frontier Analysis (SFA), which estimate the production possibility frontier of an operation (Hollingsworth 2008). These approaches, while credible, are not feasible for program managers to report in due to the high degree of expertise and resources required to conduct these studies.

Still, any cost-to-service ratio requires some computation to produce accurate figures. Porter and Kaplan (2011) outline a seven-step cost measurement system for developing accurate, credible measures of cost to service. It involves mapping the process needed in delivering the service (the T-HOPE framework already includes this component under the descriptive field's process category), estimating the time and resources involved at each step, and attributing the appropriate cost per resource per client or patient to compute the total cost for delivering the product or service to a single client or patient. Using this activity-based costing method, costs of service can be appropriately attributed to given services rather than aggregating all costs at a higher level.

The amount of work required to compute cost-to-service figures may still be too demanding for some program managers. Moreover, if the framework only accepts cost-to-services figures at a client or patient level, then program managers may simply divide total costs by total output, claiming it as a patient-level cost-to-service figure. It would be difficult to verify which method was used to compute the figure; however, scaling the cost figure in exact proportion to the total costs may not reflect the relative use of fixed costs in the process. This form of patient-level reporting will have less credibility than the activity-based costing method described above, but it will have better comparability across programs compared to aggregate cost figures. In another approach, which is more credible but has limited comparability across programs, program managers may provide total cost figures in aggregate, comparing them to quality measures in this form when the quality measures are reported on the same client and/or population base.

Non-economic Efficiency. Non-economic measures of efficiency are less reported in the health care literature. Bradley et al. (2010) measures organizational performance by considering facility utilization rate by clients and client and patient volume per time period. Bradley et al. (2010) also considers facility utilization rate in comparison to organizational capacity as a measure of organizational performance. Additionally, Impact Reporting and Investment Standards (IRIS) (GIIN 2012) captures facility or product utilization rates and records patient wait times. High utilization rates and quicker flow times are considered drivers of efficiency: "High throughput/high asset utilization in which high customer volume drives capacity utilization, pushes down unit costs of key human or physical assets, and provides economies of scale for purchasing, marketing, and other functions" (Karamchandani 2009, 47). Non-economic efficiency measures the relative ability of a program to deliver a product or service. These figures should compare programs with similar processes, revealing which programs can achieve better asset utilization or quicker delivery of service.

MEASURING EFFICIENCY

In assessing the reporting of efficiency, we explored how programs reported key components of both economic efficiency (consisting of cost-to-service/ product and total cost), and non-economic efficiency (consisting of product or service delivery time, rate of delivery of product or service, and client and patient utilization rate of product or facility). Table 7.2 provides an overview of the frequency of reporting on these measures.

EXAMPLES OF EFFICIENCY REPORTING

Two programs reporting on their efficiency are Narayana Hrudayalaya (NH) and APOPO. NH incurs a cost of US$2,000 to perform an open-heart surgery. The organization was recognized for performing 27 surgeries in one day in a single facility, the second-highest number in a single facility globally. APOPO, a program that trains rats to provide TB sample screenings, reports that it costs them about 6,000 euros over nine months to train a HeroRAT. These rats can evaluate 40 samples, an average lab technician's daily workload, in just seven minutes.

REFINING THE EFFICIENCY DIMENSION

In assessing the program reporting of efficiency measures, we found that frequency of reporting ranged from 1.2 per cent for client/patient utilization rate of product/facility to 21.4 per cent for total cost. This suggests that the existing reporting on this dimension is currently lacking. Generally, reporting could be improved for all efficiency measurement dimensions, and we have refined our recommended definitions for these dimensions to clarify the required data.

Table 7.2 Summary of reported efficiency data

Efficiency Measures	% Reporting
Economic Efficiency Measures	
Cost-to-service/product: cost of providing a single client/patient the service/product	6.0
Total cost: total cost to provide a given number of products/services	21.4
Non-economic Efficiency Measures	
Flow, service, and/or wait times: time required to deliver a client a single product/service (Cachon 2009, 15)	9.6
Throughput: rate that a product/service is delivered to a client/patient (Cachon 2009, 15)	13.1
Client/patient utilization rate of product/facility: how many clients served/products produced relative to capacity[a] (Cachon 2009, 41)	1.2

[a]Capacity refers to the maximum output possible within a given period of time (Cachon 2009, 32).

Efficiency indicators were developed while keeping in mind their credibility, feasibility, and comparability among program managers, donors, investors, and researchers. While econometric models of economic efficiency are more credible in the literature, they are not practical for most program managers. Accordingly, measures were developed that slightly reduce credibility but significantly increase reporting feasibility.

Special training is not required for the costing methods we recommend, though the complexity of the cost-to-product/service calculations will directly correlate with the complexity and variability in the program process model. Reporting on this measurement requires data on the cost of each resource used in the process (e.g. nurse) and the expected time with each resource during the delivery of the product or service. The difficulty of collecting this information will again directly correlate with the complexity and variability in the process model. In addition, reporting on non-economic efficiency measures requires programs to track numbers of patients served in a given time period. This will require resources to incorporate into the monitoring system, but does not require special training to collect.

Comparing non-economic efficiency measures across multiple reporting periods provides insight into program performance. It allows programs to track changes in operational efficiency without the limitations of comparing disparate delivery models across programs. In assessing the reporting of efficiency measures, we also noted the frequency of reporting on change over time for these dimensions. We found that reporting on changes in a program's delivery time and rate were recorded by 4.76 per cent of programs. While this is infrequently reported, we have included a change-over-time component in our recommended definition of non-economic efficiency to encourage programs to provide more than one time point, which will allow for analysis of a program's ability to carry out core tasks efficiently over time.

Staff-to-service ratios are recommended by Bradley et al. (2010) as measures of efficiency. Since each program will have adopted its own delivery chain, the credibility of comparison will be limited due to less standardized delivery models across programs. For instance, Piramal eSwasthya and CARE Hospitals are general primary care providers with 1:4 and 1:1.2 patient to health worker ratios respectively. This comparison does not offer insight on their relative efficiencies because the health care workers use their time differently between the two delivery models. For example, under the Piramal eSwasthya model, health workers visit ill patients in their homes or in the health care centres workers operate out of their homes, whereas at CARE Hospitals, all patients must seek care at the hospital facility. Measuring patient or procedure volume per time period presents a similar challenge when making comparisons across programs. Therefore, we add the caveat that measures of non-economic efficiency should include comparisons with other programs as long as they are using similar models and providing similar products or services.

Based on this review, we developed and refined definitions of economic and non-economic efficiency for the T-HOPE framework (see table 7.3).

Quality

LITERATURE REVIEW

It is important to include measures of quality in assessing the performance of a health program to understand its impact. In the literature, quality measures can be found under performance dimensions such as health outcome and impact, clinical quality, and management quality.

Health Outcome and Impact. Health outcomes are intermediate observable and measurable changes, which include specific change in behaviours, knowledge, attitudes, status, skills, or level of functioning due to a program's activities (Clark et al. 2004; Twersky & Ratcliffe 2010). Health impact refers to long-term health outcomes as well as changes in the social, economic, civic, and environmental conditions as a consequence of the program (Mills & Bos 2011; Taylor-Powell et al. 2003). Many sources in the literature lack more precise definitions of each, instead providing examples in its place.

Clinical Quality. The Institute of Medicine (Lohr 1990, 21) defines clinical quality as "the degree to which health services for individuals and populations increase the likelihood of desired health outcomes and are consistent with current professional knowledge." Bradley et al. (2010) more specifically outlines clinical quality as how well a provider's care conforms to best clinical practice, noting that it does not refer to population health outcome measures where the denominator is the population, such as antenatal care or vaccination coverage.

Table 7.3 Recommended operational definition for efficiency

Efficiency: A measure of the relationship between inputs consumed and outputs produced. It consists of the following components:

Economic Efficiency: Quantitative evidence about the cost of delivering the product/service to patients/clients. Measures include cost-to-service/product for a single client/patient, or, where not feasible, total costs to provide services/products.

Non-economic Efficiency: Quantitative evidence about how long it takes for a program to deliver a product/service compared to a previous reporting period or providers of similar services.

Thus, clinical quality indicators include the ability of providers to deliver best-practice care, which is context-sensitive to the resources and the setting where they practice. For example, the International Diabetes Federation's guidelines for diabetes in childhood and adolescence vary based on a region's ability to provide standards of care with limited resources (International Diabetes Foundation 2011). The particular dimensions of clinical quality that are relevant here refer specifically to indicators that measure the quality of a health service provision that results in safe and appropriate evidence-based care.

Management Quality. Management quality focuses on the processes of managing health delivery, processes that are indirectly connected to higher quality care. The conceptual and empirical literature notes that there are several legitimate and possible domains comprising management quality. For simplicity and comparability, management quality will be defined as a binary and qualitative category, involving presence or absence of a management mechanism that has been associated with high-quality care. Management refers to the means to achieve product or service quality. In outlining elements of management quality, Bradley et al. (2010) identify three important dimensions that aid in operationalizing this category: 1) quality assurance mechanisms; 2) information systems quality; and 3) governance quality – leadership.

Management quality is a worthwhile category to include in the analysis of quality since it allows for an understanding of the process that informs the realization of health outcomes. Organizations such as NH and Aravind, for example, employ robust monitoring and evaluations systems that enable them to systematically track performance of their respective programs (e.g. infection rates). This enables NH and Aravind to innovate in care processes while tracking the impact on quality of care and patient outcomes. While the linkages between management quality and health outcomes are difficult to define precisely, programs embedded in well-managed organizations are more likely to be able to implement strategies successfully without compromising results.

MEASURING QUALITY

In assessing the reporting of quality measures, we explored how programs reported on key components of health outcome and impact, clinical quality, and management quality. The frequency of reporting of these dimensions is described in table 7.4 below.

EXAMPLES OF QUALITY REPORTING

Aravind and Mahila Swahsta Sewa (MSS) are two examples of programs reporting on quality. Aravind, which provides eye cataract surgeries, reports it

Table 7.4 Summary of reported quality data

Quality Measures	% Reporting
Health Outcome and Impact Measures	
Health outcome and impact	45.0
Clinical Quality Measures	
Safety of intervention	6.3
Adherence to clinical guidelines/standards	10.0
Management Quality Measures	
Existence of a monitoring and evaluation system	12.5
Existence of a performance review process	6.3
Existence of audit	1.3
Existence of data management system	1.3
Existence of standards and guidelines	2.5
International organization for standardization certification	2.5

has managed to keep its infection rates low, an average of about four cases per 10,000 patients, compared to an average six per 10,000 in the UK. MSS reports that in 2011, 67 out of 78 of its reproductive health clinics met the best-practice quality standards set by Population Services Institute.

REFINING THE QUALITY DIMENSIONS

The review of the literature and reporting in the database helped us refine three dimensions in our T-HOPE framework: health outcome, clinical quality, and management quality. The recommended definitions for the dimensions were developed in an effort to create measures that were an optimal balance of feasibility, credibility, and comparability.

For greater precision, we have tried to make clear distinctions between health outcome, clinical quality, and management quality in our dimension definitions. Whereas health outcome focuses on intermediate or long-term health outcomes of clients and populations, clinical quality refers to the ability to provide safe, evidence-based care by following best practice guidelines. It captures error rates, complication rates, and readmissions as an indication of this adherence. Aspects of a program's effectiveness are captured under health outcomes rather than clinical quality to reduce duplication. Management quality focuses on non-clinical operational processes that can contribute to the ability of the program to deliver its services and products.

Reporting on outcome and quality dimensions ranged from 1.3 per cent for existence of audit and existence of a data management system to 45 per cent for health outcome and impact. Health outcome is an important measure of how well a program actually contributes to the health of its clients and the population. While it can be difficult to measure, sometimes involving time-consuming and rigorous research designs (Bhattacharyya et al. 2015), almost half of the 80 programs are reporting on health outcome, indicating that they recognize the importance of collecting and sharing this data to convey their impact. For our dimension definition, we have focused on capturing a program's health outcome through changes in learning, actions or health status of clients, and, if possible, the broader population targeted for the intervention.

In our analysis, clinical quality was not frequently reported; only 21 out of 80 programs reported a clinical quality measure. This may speak to the challenges program managers face in measuring clinical quality given the resources required for this assessment, which can include access to current knowledge of best clinical practices and sophisticated measurements and calculation of adherence to these standards.

The credibility of the clinical quality dimension is strengthened when it captures a change over time or provides clinical quality performance in comparison to another program. Performance compared to other organizations or compared to another reporting period can display the robustness of a systematic clinical process that yields quality, or conversely, identify if a result was due to chance. While it may be more challenging to capture the comparator, we have included the option to add either comparison to another point in time or to the clinical quality of similar providers.

While reporting on management quality measures was quite low among the 80 programs, the process of collecting this data can be considered highly feasible since it does not necessitate studies or evaluations but rather requires descriptions of the processes, procedures, or mechanisms an organization has established. A program manager can easily collect this data, although the data is difficult to compare across programs due its qualitative and non-standardized nature. Table 7.5 provides a summary of the revised operation definitions for quality measures.

Scale

LITERATURE REVIEW

The need to scale up health services has taken on an increasing sense of urgency in the current context given the multitude of low-cost, high-impact interventions to address the burden of diseases and the demand from populations in need.

Table 7.5 Recommended operational definition for quality

Health Quality: Evidence of the quality of care provided and the health impact obtained through the provision of a health service/product. This includes the following dimensions:

Health Outcome and Impact: Quantitative evidence of impact on intermediate or long-term health outcomes demonstrated by changes in learning, actions, and/or health status of clients/target population per reporting period.

Clinical Quality: Quantitative evidence of providing safe, evidence-based care, which can include comparisons to other providers of similar services, and/or demonstrating change over time. Measures include error rates, complication rates, readmission rates, percentage of cases meeting predetermined quality standards, and percentage of patients receiving appropriate care according to approved guidelines.

Management Quality: The procedures, systems, and processes the program has implemented to strengthen quality in key aspects of operations and delivery. It can include descriptions about the following management processes associated with higher quality care:

1. Quality assurance mechanisms
   a. Audit
   b. Performance assessment
   c. Monitoring and evaluation system
   d. Standards and guidelines
   e. Oversight bodies
2. External recognition of quality standards
   a. Accreditation or certification by a reputable organization
   b. International awards for quality and excellence
3. Governance quality
   a. Board of governors
   b. Management committees

Despite it being a widely used term, there is lack of consensus on the precise definition of scale. The term is often used synonymously with going to scale, replication, spread, expansion, adaptation of techniques, ideas, approaches and concepts (i.e., means), and to increased scale of impact (i.e., ends) (WHO & Expand Net 2009; World Bank 2003). Ryan (2004, iv) provides a useful starting point for thinking about scale: "Scaling up is a necessary response to a situation where an action which needs to be carried out should be undertaken at greater speed and/or to provide a greater volume of output than is the prevailing situation. Whatever it is, more of it is needed; and probably at lower unit input."

In the context of health services delivery, scaling up is used to describe an increase in the coverage of health interventions that have been tested in pilot and experimental projects to benefit more people and support policy and program development at a larger or national scale (Mangham & Hanson 2010). Scale is commonly used to describe the objective or process of either increasing the coverage of health interventions or increasing the financial, human, or capital resources that are required to expand coverage (Mangham & Hanson 2010). The term can refer to either the coverage of an intervention or the function dimension of an intervention, in which case the term refers to an increase in the scope of activities (Mangham & Hanson 2010).

Strategies to Scaling Up. Understanding scalability, or the ability for a program to scale up, necessitates an examination of the strategies being employed by organizations to manage the growth of their health services. There are a number of strategies that have been used successfully to address human resources supply challenges that can limit growth, including standardization and simplification of procedures, and the use of paraskilling, whereby low-skilled staff are trained to perform tasks that are typically performed by more skilled or qualified staff. The lack of trained health worker personnel, for example, is identified in the literature as a key constraint to scaling up efforts of health services. CARE Hospitals uses a paraskilling process whereby functions of higher-level personnel are repackaged and assigned to less-trained individuals capable performing the job. With this task shifting, more highly trained staff are allowed to optimize their potential by focusing on higher-skill functions, while more routine or less demanding tasks are carried out by individuals with less education or training. Assessing scalability requires a consideration of strategies to overcome human resource constraints.

In addition, the use of mechanisms such as contracting, franchising, or social marketing by non-state actors like private for-profit organizations have been identified as ways to address deficiencies of the public sector in providing health services at a larger scale (Mangham & Hanson 2010). For example, Greenstar Social Marketing Pakistan franchises a range of family planning services through its network of over 18,000 private doctors. A franchise structure allows Greenstar to scale up much more rapidly. In the commercial sector, franchising is an effective way for systematic replication. Franchising allows for the implementation of tested and successful concepts by franchisees in a decentralized manner (Meuter n.d.).

Scaling Up and Optimal Size. The decision to scale up a health services program demands consideration of its optimal size. The desirable size of a program may limit scaling-up efforts due to diseconomies of scale and quality or scale trade-off constraints. It is important to consider whether a program should be scaled up at all and whether scaling should occur along horizontal, vertical, or functional dimensions (Hartmann & Linn 2007). Lifebuoy Friendship Hospital, for example, is a highly contextual program targeting marginalized and isolated char communities. In such a context, the scope for expansion may be limited along horizontal lines (i.e. covering more people) but may be possible along functional dimensions (i.e. offering a broader range of health services) to a defined target population.

Scaling Health Impact and Health Programs. While scaling up a health program and a health impact are distinct concepts, increasing reach is one way of increasing impact either directly or indirectly. For example, a health program implemented by an NGO or private health provider that is replicated by the public sector has the potential to create wider health impact without itself growing. In Thailand, the Population and Community Development Association (PDA) used awareness raising and information dissemination mediums in its campaign efforts to combat the spread of HIV and AIDS (PDA 2012). PDA was able to influence the government of Thailand to establish a national AIDS education program. In cooperation with the Ministry of Interior, PDA also trained government officers, district officers, governors, and community leaders, such as monks, to inform the wider community about AIDS. The ability of PDA's programs to influence actors at a national level demonstrates how scaling up can extend beyond the program to create health impact without the organization itself growing.

Assessing Scale Up and Scalability. There are a number of aspects that need to be considered in conceptualizing scale, and the Scaling Up Management (SUM) framework (Cooley & Kohl 2006) identifies several useful dimensions, methods, and critical ingredients for assessing scale up and scalability. Table 7.6 below describes five of key dimensions that are relevant for understanding the past scale up and current scale of health services delivery (Cooley & Kohl 2006).

Table 7.6 Dimensions of current scale and past scale up

Geographic coverage	Extending to new locations
Breadth of coverage	Extending to more people in the currently served categories and localities
Depth of services	Extending additional services to current clients
Client type	Extending to new categories of clients
Problem definition	Extending current methods to new problems

The SUM framework (Cooley & Kohl 2006) offers a useful classification for scale that is ultimately premised on the two key dimensions comprising scale: 1) expansion of experience, scaling up impact within an area or country on the basis of one or more existing initiatives; and 2) transfer of experience, scaling up impact in new and unassociated areas on the basis of one or more existing initiatives (World Bank 2003). Expansion and replication can involve pursuing a number of different scale up methods. These methods are further described in table 7.7.

The SUM framework (Cooley & Kohl 2006) also operationalizes scaling up by outlining the critical ingredients that are relevant for assessing scalability (see table 7.8).

Table 7.7 Scaling up methods

Expansion (scope)	Growth	The most common form of expansion, which occurs when the organization extends to new locations.
	Franchising	When agents or clones of the organization operate using the same business model.
	Spin-Off	When aspects or parts of the originating organization go on to operate independently.
Replication (use)	Policy Adoption	When a model is scaled up from a pilot run by an organization to a program or practice mandated and often run by the public sector.
	Grafting	Where a model – or one component of a model – is incorporated into another organization's array of services or methods of service delivery.
	Diffusion and Spillover	Tend to be spontaneous in nature and occur when a model spreads by informal networking with new or existing organizations or through the use of more deliberate dissemination efforts.
Collaboration (falls between expansion and replication)	Formal Partnerships/ Joint Ventures/ Strategic Alliances Networks/ Coalitions	Collaboration mechanisms range from formal partnerships to informal networks and encompass innovative structures and governance arrangements.

Table 7.8 Assessing scalability

Financial strength	Refers to a non-profit's organizational strength and sustainability, often secured by endowment or operating budgets with dependable revenue streams.
Program expansion	Describes the scope of service, usually measured by the number of clients served. When a program demonstrates positive outcomes for its participants, the goal is often to provide more funding and bring it to more people. To a funder, enabling an organization with a proved track record to expand its operations represents a high-return, low-risk activity.
Multisite replication	Refers to attempts to dissect the essential elements of a successful initiative or service model in order to reconstruct the effort elsewhere with different personnel and under different circumstances. Replication can proceed in two ways: (1) within the organization, through a set of chapters or a franchise system linking independent organizations; or (2) outside the organization, through independent efforts to create similar programs.
Political commitment	Political commitment entails support for a program from local, regional, or national governments. Nationwide scale ups of intervention programs generally require several key factors, ranging from political commitment to sequenced work plans and to long-term predictable funding. There are innumerable instances where developing countries harnessed these elements to deliver interventions that have dramatically improved the lives of the poor at a national scale.
Theory of change	If an organization has a clearly articulated theory of change, or an understanding of how and why certain elements will achieve the desired change, the potential for replication is likely to rest on the degree to which its key activities and the key components of its operating model can also be articulated and standardized. As a general principle, the greater the number of elements that can be standardized, the more likely it is that replication will succeed.

MEASURING SCALE

Based on a literature review, we identified key measures of scale, which include an assessment of past scale up and current scale (including past growth and current figures on the number of people served, services provided, and geographic coverage); current scalability (including operational process, political commitment, operational and technical partners, finances, stage, and theory of change); and future plans for scale up (including strategic planning). We identified where these measures are being collected in the T-HOPE framework, including the descriptive fields. For example, in examining scale in terms of geographic coverage, this data is most readily obtained from the framework's availability dimension and program profile: summary field. These categories contain information indicating where the program is currently being implemented. In considering scale in terms of the people served, breadth can be derived from the health output field, which already captures results indicating the number of clients served or services delivered. Data on client type is most easily obtained from the program profile field under the summary category. In examining scale in terms of the services provided, depth of services, which involves understanding the program's offerings, can be ascertained from the program profile field under the summary and type of products and services categories. Problem definition involves understanding the problem the service or program seeks to address, a dimension that is captured under goals. For all of these measures of scale, it is also valuable to understand how programs have changed over time in order to assess past scale up, which can indicate potential for future scale up. Table 7.9 indicates the key measures of scale and the T-HOPE framework performance dimensions and fields where these measures are captured, along with the frequency of reporting on this data.

EXAMPLES OF REPORTING FOR SCALE MEASURES

PROSALUD and ACQUIRE Tanzania Project are examples of programs that were able to report on change over time regarding past scale up. PROSALUD has been able to increase the breadth of coverage over time. This includes increasing the number of male condoms distributed nationwide from 28,082,134 (2000–2004) to 30,398,484 (2004–2009), increasing the number of Depo-Provera shots distributed nationwide from 717,490 (2000–2004) to 2,006,790 (2004–2009), and increasing the number of IUDs distributed nationwide from 4,936 (2000–2004) to 74,425 (2004–2009). In terms of extending geographic coverage, the ACQUIRE Tanzania Project has been able to increase its coverage from 2008–2009, expanding comprehensive post-abortion care services from 10 to 16 districts in the regions of Mwanza and Shinyanga, and to five districts of Zanzibar.

Table 7.9 Summary of reported scale data

Scale Categories	Components	T-HOPE Framework Dimensions or Fields	% Reporting	
Current Scale and Past Scale Up (up to last 10 years)				
			Current Data Point	Change Over Time
People	**Breadth of coverage:** Extending to more people in the currently served categories and localities	Health Output	42.5	17.5
	Client type: Extending to new categories of clients	Program profile: Summary	28.8	0
Services	**Depth of services:** Extending additional services to current clients	Program profile: Summary; Type of products/ services	90.0	0
	Problem definition: Extending current methods to new problems	Goal	75.0	0
Coverage	**Geographic coverage:** Extending to new locations	Availability; Program profile: Summary	40.0	16.3
Current Scalability				
	Operational process: Extent to which components of the process can be standardized and replicated	Process	77.5	
	Political support: Political partnerships with government entities	Political support	40.0	
	Operational and technical partners: Refers to formal partnerships, joint ventures, strategic alliances, and networks/ coalitions	Program profile: Operational and technical partners	76.3	

(Continued)

Table 7.9 Concluded

Scale Categories	Components	T-HOPE Framework Dimensions or Fields	% Reporting
	Finances: Refers to a program's sustainability as evidenced by sufficient and consistent revenue flows	Financial Management	66.3
	Stage: Refers to maturity of program	Program profile: Stage	97.5
	Theory of change: Extent to which theory of change has elements that can be standardized	Goal	50.0
	Future Scalability		
	Strategic planning: How the program sets its plans for identifying and achieving future goals including scaling up or plans for growth	Strategic Planning	48.8

REFINING SCALE MEASURES

Reporting on dimensions of scale in the T-HOPE framework ranged from 0 per cent for client type (change over time reporting), depth of services (change over time reporting), and problem definition (change over time reporting), to 97.5 per cent for stage. Dimensions with the highest levels of reporting tended to be those that involved descriptive data that were very feasible to report, along with dimensions that were already well developed in the original CHMI data collection process. For example, the three highest reported dimensions all involved reporting readily available descriptive data for well-defined categories in the original CHMI database: stage, at 97.5 per cent; depth of services, which at a single point involves the current services offered, at 90 per cent; and operational processes at 77.5 per cent. Those with the lowest reporting included all of the dimensions with a change over time component, including client type (0 per cent), depth of services (0 per cent), problem definition (0 per cent), geographic coverage (16.3 per cent), and breadth of people served (17.5 per cent). This suggests that while including change is important for understanding how programs have scaled over time, it might not be feasible for many program managers. As a result, program managers should be requested to provide data on these categories for the current reporting period, and encouraged to report data on a previous time point in the last ten years for comparison purposes. In addition, developing clear definitions for these scale dimensions will assist with reporting in these areas.

Furthermore, the initial version of the T-HOPE framework captured both client type and geographic coverage under program profile: summary. To more precisely collect and organize this data, we added subcategories to the program profile for client type and geographic location (the latter refers to where the program is operating at the sub-country level, such as villages, cities, districts, and regions). In addition, health programs, such as those listed in the CHMI database, may be referring to different organizational structures or levels, such as those operating as international organizations, local organizations, or country offices of international NGOs. For example, Marie Stopes Bolivia is a country office for Marie Stopes International. Determining the scalability of a program entails understanding the unit of analysis of the listed program and their organizational structure. As a result, we have added a subcategory for program type under program profile in order to understand the operating level of the listed program. This will aid in identifying programs that have been the result of expansion and replication through larger organizational processes. Table 7.10 provides a summary of the recommended definitions for measuring scale.

Table 7.10 Recommended operational definition for scale

Scale: Evidence of the ability of a program to expand and replicate. Assessing scalability involves examining a program's past, current, and future programming activities.

Current Scale and Past Scale Up: Current reporting period data on a program's breadth, client type, depth of services, problem definition, and geographic coverage; optional data can also be provided from a reporting period within the last ten years. This will provide useful information about the current scale of the program and how it has expanded or replicated along these components in the past.

Current Scalability: An assessment of the current ability to scale is obtained by looking at a program's finances, operational process, partnerships, and stage and theory of change.

Future Scalability: A program's future activities for expansion and replication as derived from its strategic planning.

Discussion

Efficiency, quality, and scale are ineluctably linked and allow for a robust assessment of performance. They are important measures in assessing how well the strategies being employed by programs are able to deliver needed health services to the poor. Examining efficiency makes it possible to gauge whether processes are completed using the least resources and in the shortest time possible. Efficiency, as a measure, helps us understand whether a health program is making good economic use of resources. Quality is a measure that aids in evaluating whether a program is achieving the desired results. The case for scale is becoming increasingly urgent as shared concern amplifies among stakeholders in both the public and private spheres that the global health needs of the poorest and most marginalized are not being addressed at an acceptable pace.

Performance measurement is key for the stakeholders of innovative health programs. For program managers, measures for efficiency, quality, and scale provide tools for self-reporting and monitoring, which helps gauge their model's performance and identify high-performing models elsewhere. These measures provide investors and donors with intelligence to screen programs, allowing them to investigate and fund those most likely to succeed and achieve impact. Researchers gain insight from these composite measures, enabling them to evaluate effective strategies and identify the salient factors responsible for their success.

Efficiency and Quality

In examining the concept of efficiency, we found that there is general theoretical agreement on this topic but little harmony about methods for its measurement. Moreover, the most common means to estimate economic efficiency are not feasible for most managers in low- and middle-income settings. Accordingly, the recommended measure of economic efficiency has been based on the need to balance the measure's credibility and feasibility. We suggest that efficiency measures should not be presented in isolation, so as to avoid unintended incentive towards valuing efficiency at the cost of quality. Accordingly, quality measures should be presented alongside efficiency indicators.

Scale

Scaling up health services in low- and middle-income countries to address the HIV/AIDS crisis, maternal mortality, and the burden of disease in the poorest countries, is a matter of increasing importance. The magnitude of global health challenges demands solutions capable of reaching a vast number of people. A critical challenge and goal of health service delivery models is to increase the impact they have, and increasing impact requires discrete programs that are proved to be successful and replicable models to operate at a large scale.

Scale is an inherently complex concept that presents some challenges for evaluation. In our T-HOPE framework, scale is incorporated as a secondary measure comprising a number of dimensions including: geographic coverage (extending to new locations); breadth of coverage (extending to more people in the currently served categories and localities); depth of services (extending additional services to current clients); client type (extending to new categories of clients); and problem definition (extending current methods to new problems). The components of scale are derived from pre-existing fields in the framework.

Scaling up health services means that programs are not only expanding their coverage but also providing services and products in a cost-efficient manner such that they are effectively reducing prices and yielding healthier margins (Credit Suisse & Schwab Foundation for Social Entrepreneurship 2012). The ability of scalable health service programs to concomitantly generate a social and financial return is what is ultimately attractive to investors and donors.

Conclusion

In this chapter, we developed measures for efficiency, quality, and scale, key components in measuring performance. In this process, we reviewed the relevant literature to ascertain the key components of each measure. We then determined which of the dimensions and descriptive fields in our T-HOPE framework cover these dimensions, and assessed the frequency of reporting in a subset of well-documented programs. Using this information, we refined definitions for these framework dimensions and added several subcategories to the program profile descriptive fields, including client type, program type, and geographic location. This has improved our T-HOPE framework, helping to ensure that data relevant to efficiency, quality, and scale will be appropriately captured for assessment. Our aim in developing these measures is to provide the tools for evaluating program performance, which is integral to assessing which programs and strategies should be supported to address the pressing health care needs of populations around the world.

Appendix

Table 7.A1 Aravind Eye Care System: Reporting on scale, efficiency, and quality

---

Scale

Depth of services

- Eye care surgery

Geographic coverage

- India
- Hospitals opened in Coimbatore and Pondicherry in 2003

Breadth

- Aravind now performs more than 1,000 procedures each day across all its hospitals.
- From inception until January 2012, Aravind served 32 million outpatients with four million surgeries performed.
- In 2006 AECS was performing approximately 270,000 surgeries per year and serving over 2 million patients.
- April 2007 to March 2008: about 2.4 million people received outpatient eye care and over 285,000 have undergone eye surgeries.
- April 2010 to March 2011, over 2.6 million people received outpatient eye care and over 315,000 have undergone eye surgeries.
- In the year ending March 2011: outreach department conducted over 2,600 camps through which over seven lakh patients were screened and over 76,000 patients underwent surgery. Over 6,500 candidates from 94 countries have undergone some form of training at Aravind.
- More than 300 ophthalmologists and 600 paramedical workers are trained every year in different subspecialties of ophthalmology.

Strategies

- *Paraskilling*: the hospital allows nurses to perform tasks in the operating room that do not require a surgeon's skill.
- *Gains from specialization*: to lower workforce costs, Aravind focuses on letting doctors do what they are best at – diagnosis and surgery.
- *Cross-subsidization:* Aravind uses a cross-subsidy model to maintain financial sustainability as well as offers free services to the majority of patients.

Finances

- Aravind maintains a surplus through primarily earned revenue. In 2009–10 it enjoyed a surplus of US$13 million, on US$29 million in revenues. Only 6 per cent of its operating budget is grant subsidized.

(Continued)

Table 7.A1 Concluded

Strategic planning: Future plans for scaling up

- Aravind aims to perform 1 million surgeries and grow to 100 hospitals by 2015.
- The organization plans to sustain the growth and double the service delivery capacity in the next 10 years by expanding to new locations and expanding the telemedicine technology-based primary eye care model for universal coverage and follow-up of patients with chronic eye diseases.
- Better systems for the diagnosis and management of chronic diseases like glaucoma, diabetic retinopathy and age-related muscular degeneration would be created.
- There will be different centres of excellence in specialty eye care services through pioneering clinical and basic science research.

Economic Efficiency

- Aravind has been able to reduce the cost of cataract surgeries through a high volume, vertically integrated delivery model.
- Intraocular lenses are produced in its Aurolab facility, which allows Aravind to produce the lenses at a per unit cost of US$2.
- By 2006, the cost of providing cataract surgery for a patient was about $18, compared to about US$1,800 for the same procedure in the US.
- Total costs for Aravind in 2002–3 were INR 204.6 million, which resulted in 1,447,575 outpatient visits and 202,066 surgeries in 2003.

Non-economic Efficiency

- The Aravind delivery model has two operating tables in use within one operating room. By allowing surgeons to work on two tables in alteration, Aravind is able to improve operation efficiency.
- While one surgery is progressing, a team of nurses and paramedical staff prepare the next patient for surgery. This process allows Aravind to perform cataract surgery in 10 minutes, about one-third of the industry standard.
- Surgeons perform six to eight operations per hour on an assembly-line basis with the support of internally trained mid-level ophthalmic personnel.
- The average ophthalmologist in India performs about 400 cataract surgeries a year; in comparison an Aravind doctor performs about 2,000. This is attributed to several factors, including steady flow of patients with minimal wait times (steady patient/surgical flow), well-trained staff, and high utilization rates of supplies and equipment.
- Once they could do 200 to 300 surgeries per day, rather than 20 or 30, their fixed costs drastically dropped. Aravind now performs more than 1,000 procedures each day across all hospitals.

Clinical Quality

- Despite the shared spaces, Aravind manages to keep its infection rates low, an average of about 4 cases per 10,000 patients, compared to an average 6 per 10,000 in the UK.

NOTES

1 A detailed profile of Aravind, including its reporting on measures of efficiency, quality, and scale, can be found in the appendix.
2 Output, in this case, refers to the products or services produced and is used in conceptualizing productivity.
3 Scale is not explicit performance dimension in the T-HOPE framework, but components of scale are included in a number of performance dimensions and descriptive fields in the framework.

REFERENCES

Bhattacharyya, O., Mossman, K., Ginther, J., Hayden, L., Sohal, R., Cha, J., Bopardikar, A., MacDonald, J.A., Parikh, H., Shahin, I., McGahan, A., Mitchell, W. 2015. "Assessing Health Program Performance in Low- and Middle-Income Countries: Building a Feasible, Credible, and Comprehensive Framework." *Globalization and Health* 11: 51. https://doi.org/10.1186/s12992-015-0137-5.

Bradley, E., Pallas, S., Bashyal, C., Berman, P., Curry, L. 2010. *Developing Strategies for Improving Health Care Delivery: Guide to Concepts, Determinants, Measurement, and Intervention Design.* Washington, DC: World Bank. http://siteresources.worldbank.org/HEALTHNUTRITIONANDPOPULATION/Resources/281627-1095698140167/DevelopingStrategiesforImprovingHealthCareDelivery.pdf

Cachon, G., & Terweisch, C. 2009. *Matching Supply with Demand: An Introduction to Operations Management.* Boston: McGraw-Hill/Irwin.

Chen, S., & Ravallion, M. 2012. "More Relatively Poor People in a Less Absolutely Poor World." *Review of Income and Wealth* 59(1): 1–28. https://doi.org/10.1111/j.1475-4991.2012.00520.x.

Clark, Catherine et al. 2004. *The Double Bottom Line Project Report: Methods Catalogue.* Columbia: Columbia Business School.

Coelli, T.J., Prasada Rao, D.S., O'Donnell, C.J., Battesse, G.E. 2005. *An Introduction to Efficiency and Productivity Measurement.* New York: Springer.

Cooley, L., & Kohl, R. 2006. *Scaling Up – From Vision to Large-scale Change: A Management Framework for Practitioners.* Washington, DC: Management Systems International.

Credit Suisse & Schwab Foundation for Social Entrepreneurship. 2012. *Investing for Impact: How Social Entrepreneurship Is Redefining the Meaning of Return.* Zurich: Credit Suisse and Schwab Foundation for Social Entrepreneurship.

Global Impact Investing Network. 2012. "IRIS Metrics: Framework Structure." Accessed 20 October 2012. https://iris.thegiin.org/metrics.

Grosskopf, S. 1993. "Efficiency and Productivity." In Fried, H.O., Lovell, C.A.K., Schmidt, S., eds, *The Measurement of Productive Efficiency: Techniques and Applications*. 160–94. New York: Oxford University Press.

Hartmann, A., & Linn, J.F. 2007. "Scaling Up: A Path to Effective Development." In *2020 Focus Brief on the World's Poor and Hungry People*. Washington, DC: International Food Policy Research Institute.

Hollingsworth, B. 2008. "The Measurement of Efficiency and Productivity of Health Care Delivery." *Health Economics* 17(10): 1107–28. https://doi.org/10.1002/hec.1391.

International Diabetes Foundation. 2011. *Global IDF/ISPAD Guideline for Diabetes in Childhood and Adolescence*. Brussels: International Diabetes Foundation.

Karamchandani, A., Kubzansky, M., & Frandano, P. 2009. *Emerging Markets, Emerging Models: Market-Based Solutions to the Challenges of Global Poverty*. Cambridge, MA: Monitor Group.

Korten, F.F. & Siy, Jr, R.Y., eds. 1988. "Sharing Experiences – Examples of Participatory Approaches in Philippines Communal Irrigation Projects." In *Transforming Bureaucracy: The Experience of the Philippine National Irrigation Administration*. West Hartford, CT: Kumarian Press. http://www.worldbank.org/wbi/sourcebook/sb0215.htm.

Kelley, E., & Hurst, J. 2006. "Health Care Quality Indicators Project, Conceptual Framework Paper." OECD Health Working Papers #23. https://doi.org/10.1787/440134737301.

Lohr, K.N., ed. 1990. *Medicare: A Strategy for Quality Assurance*. Washington, DC: National Academy Press.

Manghan, L.J., & Hanson, K. 2010. "Scaling Up in International Health: What Are the Key Issues?" *Health Policy and Planning* 25(2): 85–96. https://doi.org/10.1093/heapol/czp066.

McBride, J., & Ahmed, R. 2001. "Social Franchising as a Strategy for Expanding Access to Reproductive Health Services: A Case Study of the Green Star Service Delivery Network in Pakistan." Commercial Market Strategies.

McGlynn, E.A., Shekelle, P.G., Chen, S.S., Timmer, M., Goldman, D., Romley, John., Carter, J., Hussey, P., de Vries, H., Wang, M.C., Shanman, R.M. 2008. *Identifying, Categorizing, and Evaluating Health Care Efficiency Measures*. Santa Monica: RAND Corporation.

Meuter, J. (n.d.) *Social Franchising*. Berlin: Berlin Institute Worldwide. http://www.berlin-institut.org/online-handbookdemography.html.

Mills, S. & Bos, E. 2011. "Guidelines for Monitoring and Evaluating World Bank Projects Aimed at Improving Reproductive Health Outcomes." http://siteresources.worldbank.org/INTPRH/Resources/376374-1278599377733/ReproductiveHealthMEFinalMarch22011.pdf.

PDA. 2012. "The Population and Community Development Association." http://site. pda.or.th/.

Porter, M.E., & Kaplan, R.S. 2011. "How to Solve the Cost Crisis in Health Care." *Harvard Business Review* 89: 46–64.

Radjou, N., Prabhu, J., Ahuja, S. 2012. *Jugaad Innovation: Think Frugal, Be Flexible, Generate Breakthrough Growth*. San Francisco: Jossey-Bass.

Ryan, P. 2004. *Scaling Up – A Literature Review*. The Hague: IRC International Water and Sanitation Centre.

Saari, S. 2006. "Productivity: Theory and Measurement in Business." Espoo, Finland: European Productivity Conference. http://www.mido.fi/Index_tiedostot/ Productivity%202006.htm.

Smith, P.C. 2002. "Measuring Health System Performance." *The European Journal of Health Economics* 3(3): 145–8. https://doi.org/10.1007/s10198-002-0138-1.

Taylor-Powell, E., Jones, L. and Henert, E. 2003. *Enhancing Program Performance with Logic Models*. Wisconsin: University of Wisconsin-Extension.

Trimble, C., & Govindarajan, & V. 2012. *Reverse Innovation: Create Far from Home, Win Everywhere*. Boston: Harvard Business Review Press.

Twersky, F., Nelson, J. and Ratcliffe, A. 2010. *A Guide to Actionable Measurement*. Seattle: Bill and Melinda Gates Foundation.

World Bank. 2003. *Scaling Up the Impact of Good Practices in Rural Development: A Working Paper to Support Implementation of the World Bank's Rural Development Strategy*. Washington, DC: World Bank.

World Health Organization & Expand Net. 2009. *Practical Guidance for Scaling Up Health Service Innovations*. Geneva: World Health Organization.

8 Transnational Scale Up of Services in Global Health

ILAN SHAHIN, RAMAN SOHAL, JOHN GINTHER,
LEIGH HAYDEN, JOHN A. MACDONALD, KATHRYN MOSSMAN,
HIMANSHU PARIKH, ANITA MCGAHAN, WILL MITCHELL,
AND ONIL BHATTACHARYYA

Introduction

Many effective and inexpensive health interventions could address the burden of disease in low- and middle-income countries (LMICs), but population coverage is poor due to major gaps in delivery (Global Forum for Health Research & WHO 2004; Jamison et al. 2006). Health systems in many LMICs include a large private sector, comprised of a mix of licenced for-profit and non-profit organizations as well as informal providers (Saksena, Xu, Elovainio, & Perrot 2012). Some of these private sector organizations have developed viable approaches to provide affordable, accessible, and quality health care (Bhattacharyya et al. 2010; Karamchandani, Kubzansky, & Frandano 2009). Understanding the potential of these approaches to be replicated and scaled up is important but as yet unclear, both within health systems and across different countries (Bloom & Ainsworth 2010).

Understanding scaling up is critical to extending the reach of health services programs with clinically effective models that are cost-efficient and financially sustainable for people who have limited purchasing power, live in underserved areas, and have low health literacy (Credit Suisse 2012; Karamchandani et al. 2009). The medical and economic value of health services programs that have scaled can also make them attractive to governments, donors, and investors in search of solutions to address urgent global health problems. This paper describes more than 100 health care programs that operate in multiple countries, seeking to identify common characteristics of such programs. The study focuses on one dimension of scale, geographic coverage, which is the ability of a program to replicate its model in another country. The study provides a starting point for investigating other aspects of scale as well as when scaled-up programs are able to provide high-quality health care services.

Subramanian, Naimoli, Matsubayashi, & Peter (2011) observe that the predominant focus in the global health field is on achieving high coverage rates of health services and reducing mortality, to the neglect of understanding the processes for how to scale up. Scaling health care services involves multiple potential dimensions. The Scaling Up Management (SUM) framework from Management Systems International, perhaps the most general framework for assessing scale, suggests that a program can scale its services in several ways, including: breadth of coverage (expanding to cover more people in the currently served area); depth of services (offering additional services to current clients); client type (expanding services to new categories of clients); problem definition (expanding current methods to new problems and health areas); and geographic coverage (expanding to new locations) (Cooley & Kohl 2006). Research has only begun to examine the nature and determinants of these forms of scaling; while some literature addresses scaling in the public and private health care sectors, much of this work assesses specific disease areas, and it is unclear how to generalize the findings (Simmons, Fajans, & Ghiron 2009).

This paper examines expansion of geographic coverage in the form of transnational scale, which we define as health programs that operate in more than one country. Transnational scale indicates broader replicability compared to programs that operate within one country, demonstrating that a program and its innovations can be implemented in heterogeneous settings.

Our goal in this paper is to help identify factors that contribute to scaling up, both to determine current patterns and to identify potential routes to new opportunities for scaling. Clearly, achieving transnational scale does not necessarily match to health quality and/or outcomes, which need to be the focus of additional research. Nonetheless, multicountry replication warrants examination, because the ability of a program to transplant its model from one context to another context, which typically includes different socio-economic, cultural, and political aspects, signals relevant aspects of the replicability of the model and its ability to address health challenges on a larger scale as compared to single-country initiatives.

The study draws on the Center for Health Market Innovations (CHMI) database of nearly 1,200 private health services providers in LMICs. CHMI defines innovations as "programs and policies – implemented by governments, non-governmental organizations (NGOs), social entrepreneurs, or private companies – that improve privately delivered health care," including organizing delivery, financing care, regulating performance, changing behaviours, and enhancing processes (Center for Health Market Innovations 2008). We examine programs in the CHMI database that have achieved transnational scale (TNS) and compare them to single country programs (SCPs). In cataloguing cases of transnational scale, our research identifies key characteristics of programs that are able to operate in multiple countries. These findings illuminate factors that have facilitated or constrained transnational scale and offer insights for scholars, policymakers, funders, investors, and program managers seeking to identify scalable solutions capable of providing broader health impact.

Methods

CHMI is managed by the Results for Development Institute, which curates a database of organizations dedicated to improving privately delivered health care for the poor in LMICs. Sixteen regional partners recruit organizations in LMICs to submit data. The data include information about programs offered by organizations in LMICs that attempt to improve access, quality, and/or affordability of health services through activities such as direct patient contact, financial interventions, and supply chain support. Although it provides cross-sectional rather than longitudinal information, the CHMI data provide the most general available set of comparative data about private sector health care organizations operating in LMICs. This study uses programs as the unit of analysis, where a program is an operating entity that functions with a particular scope of objectives. For most cases in the dataset, each parent organization (in some cases, a partnership of multiple organizations) operates a single program.

This study examines selected programs in the CHMI database that reported a presence in two or more countries, and contrasts their characteristics with programs that operate within only one country. We extracted information from the database based on four main program characteristics: health focus, activity, legal status, and funding source. Health focus refers to the health needs a program targets (e.g., family planning and reproductive health, HIV/AIDS); activity refers to the program's service offerings, wherein lies its innovation (e.g., provider training, information technology, consumer outreach); legal status refers to how a program's parent organization is registered for ownership status (e.g., private for-profit, private not-for-profit, government); and funding source refers to the sources of capital for the program (e.g., donor, government, revenue generation). Within the CHMI reporting framework, programs may provide one or more responses for health focus and funding source; they report a single category for activity and legal status. The database has extensive coverage of these four characteristics; the rate of reported results for health focus, activity, legal status, and funding sources ranged from 88 per cent to 100 per cent. We assessed differences for the four characteristics between TNS and single-country programs based on descriptive statistics and t-tests of subsample means. We examined the characteristics of outlier programs that operated in ten or more countries. We also examined whether TNS status is associated with country and regional location, rural/urban coverage, or founding year.

Thus, in examining TNS programs, the study focuses on replication of a health care model beyond a single country. We stress that the study provides insight into *what* TNS programs are doing, without being able to assess *why* and *how* TNS programs scale. Nonetheless, understanding the characteristics of health care programs that achieve TNS scale is of interest to program managers who seek to expand their activities, as well as to donors and investors who seek to identify and invest in programs able to reach as many people as possible, working across a range of resource-constrained settings (Karamchandani et al. 2009). Further research with additional data can examine other important aspects of scale, such as program scope and quality of service.

Results

Screening for programs in the CHMI database that operate in two or more countries identified 116 distinct programs operating in 90 unique countries; transnational programs operated in a median of three countries, with a range of two to 22 countries. The African continent (Sub-Saharan and North Africa) had the largest share, with 95 programs (i.e., 82 per cent of the 116 TNS programs operated in at least one African country), while Asia had 49 (42 per cent of the TNS programs) and the Americas (Latin America and the Caribbean) had 25 (22 per cent) programs. The majority (65 per cent) of the TNS programs operated in a single continent, but 25 per cent operated in two continents and another 10 per cent operated across the three continental areas. The 116 TNS programs were founded as early as 1952 (the Sightsavers program, which provides eye care in Kenya, Sudan, Tanzania, and Uganda) and as late as 2012, with a median founding year of 2006.

Figure 8.1 shows the distribution of TNS programs by TNS breadth, i.e., the number of countries they operate in: 38 (33 per cent) operate in two countries, another 36 (31 per cent) operate in three or four countries, 28 (24 per cent) operate in five to 10 countries, and the remaining 14 (12 per cent) operate in more than 10 countries. Thus, most TNS programs are limited to a few countries, but a meaningful number achieve substantial international breadth, across countries and continents.

Health Focus

Figure 8.2 compares the health focus of the 116 TNS programs with the 1,068 single-country programs (SCPs) we identified in the database. The key implication of the comparison is that TNS programs are particularly likely to target specific health needs, while SCPs are more likely than TNS programs to provide more general care.

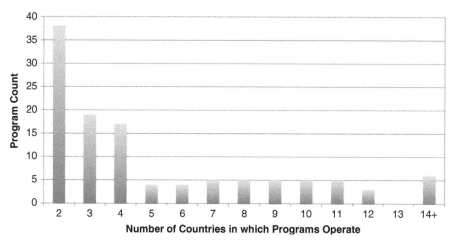

Figure 8.1 Program count for number of countries of operation

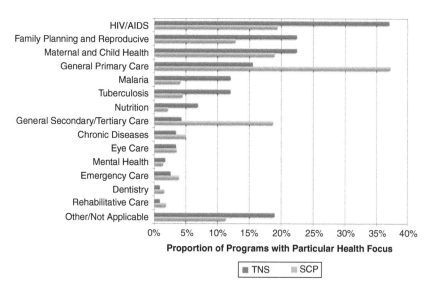

Figure 8.2 Distribution of health focus of transnational scale (TNS) and single-country programs (SCP)

The figure shows that more than a third of the TNS programs offer HIV/ AIDS services (37 per cent), followed by family planning and reproductive health (22 per cent) and maternal and child health (22 per cent). This contrasts with SCPs, where general primary care leads with 37 per cent of responses (v. 16 per cent in TNS), while HIV/AIDS represents the focus for only 19 per cent of single-country programs.

The data demonstrate that more than half of the TNS programs target specific health needs such as malaria, TB, HIV/AIDS, and family planning. For instance, D-Tree International, which was founded in 2004, has expanded from Tanzania to Malawi, South Africa, and India, providing clinical protocols via decision support software on mobile phones for use by clinic staff and community health workers to help them assess, diagnose and treat patients. The protocols address a substantial range of targeted services (e.g. HIV/AIDS, family planning, maternal and child health (MCH), TB, malaria, and chronic diseases).

We also examined whether programs offered single or multiple services. Single-service programs are most common: 65 per cent of TNS programs report a single focus out of 15 possible categories in the survey (mean of 1.65 health focus responses); 66 per cent of SCPs report a single focus (mean of 1.47 health focus responses). Among multiservice programs, TNS programs are most likely to offer combinations of HIV/AIDS, MCH, family planning and reproductive health, TB, and/or malaria services (73 per cent of the 41 multiservice TNS v. 58 per cent of the 366 multiservice SCPs), whereas multiservice SCPs are most likely to offer combinations that include general primary care and/or secondary or tertiary care (66 per cent of the multiservice SCPs v. 10 per cent of the multiservice TNS programs). This comparison reinforces the distinction in which TNS programs address targeted needs, while SCPs address more general clinical care.

Activities

Table 8.1 shows which types of support activities SCP and TNS programs have adopted for their health services. Among TNS programs, the most common activities included information technology (35 per cent) and consumer outreach (34 per cent), as well as multiple forms of delivery support (48 per cent), including provider training, operational processes, equipment, and supply chain enhancement. SCPs provide similar levels of IT (27 per cent) and consumer outreach (28 per cent), but significantly lower levels of delivery support (25 per cent). TNS programs were also more likely to provide diagnostic testing (8 per cent v. 2 per cent) and to expand via franchising (9 per cent v. 4 per cent).

Table 8.1 Frequency of SCP and TNS program activities

Activities	SCP	TNS
A. Information technology (IT)	27%	35%
B. Consumer outreach (education, social marketing)	28%	34%
C. Delivery support (at least one subcategory)	25%	48%**
C1. Provider training	17%	28%*
C2. Innovative operational processes	6%	15%**
C3. Products/equipment	4%	14%**
C4. Supply chain enhancements	2%	11%**
D. Diagnostics/lab testing	2%	8%*
E. Franchise	4%	9%*
F. Clinics/hospitals (mobile and/or stand-alone)	18%**	7%
F1. Stand-alone clinic/hospital	10%**	0%
F2. Mobile clinics	9%	7%
G. Health insurance (community, public, or private)	16%**	3%

Cases: SCP=1,068; TNS=116
** p <0.01; * p <0.05 (difference of mean t-tests, different populations and variances)
Note: The data include thirty types of program activities; Table 8.1 reports categories that achieve at least 8% for SCP and/or TNS programs (80% of all SCP activities; 74% of TNS activities).
Acronyms: MCH=maternal and child health; FPRH=family planning and reproductive health; TB-Malaria combines tuberculosis and malaria services; PC=primary care

By contrast, SCPs were more likely to provide clinical care through standalone clinics or hospitals (10 per cent v. none of the TNS programs) and/or health insurance (16 per cent v. only 3 per cent of TNS programs). The key point here is that TNS programs tend to emphasize support services, while SCPs are more likely than TNS programs to provide clinical care.

Several examples illustrate IT, consumer outreach, and provider training activities. 100% Jeune, for instance, is a not-for-profit program founded in 2000 that uses media and interpersonal communications to promote reduction of risk-taking behaviour among youth, initially in Cameroon and now also in Chad, and the Central African Republic. The Helping Babies Breathe non-profit program of the American Academy of Pediatrics, launched in 2010, meanwhile, teaches neonatal resuscitation techniques to MCH providers in India, Bangladesh, Pakistan, Kenya, and Tanzania.

Legal Status

Table 8.2 reports legal status. The summary point is that TNS programs are more likely to be private non-profits (72 per cent v. 51 per cent of SCPs) and

Table 8.2 Legal status of SCP and TNS programs

Legal Status	SCP	TNS
Private (not-for-profit)	51%	72%**
Private (for-profit)	14%	10%
Private (unspecified)	3%	4%
Public-private partnership	21%	19%
Public: State/government	10%**	3%
Corporate program	1%	1%

Cases: SCP=995 (93% reporting); TNS=106 (91% reporting)
** p<0.01 (difference of mean t-tests, different populations and variances)

less likely than SCPs to be public entities (3 per cent v. 10 per cent). We also checked the correlations of for-profit, non-profit, and public private partnership legal status with TNS breadth (the number of countries in which programs operated), finding no meaningful relationship.

Several examples of non-profit programs are intriguing. The non-profit AAD Telemedicine Project, launched in 2010 by the American Academy of Dermatology, for instance, electronically connects primary care physicians with dermatologists in Kenya, Botswana, Egypt, and Ghana to assist with diagnoses. Total Health Village, founded in 2008, meanwhile, is a non-profit that trains community-based health promoters to help facilitate self-empowerment within communities in eight countries in Latin America, Africa, and Southeast Asia.

Although for-profit TNS ventures are less common, several examples are noteworthy. Sproxil, for instance, enables consumers to text a barcode number on a drug's packaging and receive a response indicating whether it is genuine or counterfeit; by early 2012, this service, free to consumers, had been used over 1 million times in Nigeria and India (Center for Health Market Innovations 2008; Sproxil 2018). Other examples include Project Shakti, which distributes Unilever health care hygiene products in Bangladesh, India, and Sri Lanka, as well as the SAHEL venture that offers a satellite-based eHealth telemedicine network to health care professionals and hospitals in Kenya and Senegal.

Although unusual, the few public TNS programs also are interesting. The West Africa Drug Regulatory Authority Network (WADRAN), for instance, is a multinational collaboration that has had notable success in removing counterfeit and substandard drugs from the market. The Tanzania-Ghana Health Partnership, meanwhile, is a collaboration of the health service ministries in the two countries to exchange and implement health systems strengthening and delivery models.

Although public entities rarely take on transnational scale on their own, there is a substantial set of public-private partnerships among the

TNS programs (19 per cent, similar to 21 per cent for SCPs). One example is the Affordable Medicines Facility, which distributes drugs for Malaria in several countries in Africa. Another case is the East Africa Public Health Laboratory Networking Project, set up by public health agencies in Kenya, Uganda, Tanzania, and Rwanda to establish a network of public health laboratories serving as surveillance sites to monitor disease transmission.

Funding Source

Table 8.3 reports funding sources. The key implication is that donor funding is the primary means of support for the majority of all programs, while being particularly important for programs that achieve transnational scale.

Funding among TNS programs is mostly donor-led, with 82 per cent reporting donors as their primary funding source and 90 per cent receiving at least some donor funding; that is, only 10 per cent received no donor funding. In contrast, 32 per cent of SCPs operate independently of donors. Government funding, out-of-pocket payments, and membership fees are less common for TNS programs than for SCPs.

Table 8.3 Funding sources of SCP and TNS programs

Funding Source	SCP Any	TNS Any	SCP Primary	TNS Primary #
Donor	68%	90%**	56%	82%**
Government	31%*	22%	16%**	6%
Individual: Out-of-pocket payments	24%**	14%	13%	9%
Individual: Membership/subscription fees	15%**	5%	11%**	0%
In-kind contributions	9%	9%	1%	1%
Revenue (e.g., interest on loans)	4%	6%	1%	4%
Other third party (e.g., debt, equity)	6%	6%	3%*	1%

Cases: SCP=939 (88% reporting); TNS=105 (91% reporting)
** $p<0.01$, * $p<0.05$ (difference of mean t-tests, different populations and variances)
# Note: "Primary" is largest source of funding; "Any" is one of potential multiple funding sources (61% of TNS programs report having only one source of funding, compared to 33% of SCPs).

Other Possible Relationships with Transnational Scale

We investigated possible differences among the "outlier" programs that achieve substantial transnational scale, focusing on those that operated in more than 10 countries. Six programs operated in 14 or more countries: Zain Corporate AIDS Program (22 countries), Supply Change Management Systems (16), DKT International (15), Strengthening Laboratory Management Accreditation (15), AIDS Empowerment and Treatment International (14), and Venture Strategies Innovations (14). Zain is a global telecommunications company based in Kuwait that provides employees and their dependents with comprehensive HIV/AIDS counselling and care. Strengthening Laboratory Management Accreditation (SLMTA), operated by the Centers for Disease Control (CDC), offers a training approach in laboratory management and quality management systems with the goal to produce measurable improvement and prepare laboratories for accreditation based on international clinical laboratory standards. Supply Change Management Systems (SCMS), administered by the USAID, ensures reliable, cost-effective and secure supply of products for HIV/AIDS programs in developing countries. AIDS Empowerment and Treatment International (AIDSETI) is a non-profit network of community-based associations founded and managed by people living with HIV/AIDS in Africa and the Caribbean; the program is affiliated with US Doctors for Africa, which provides volunteer medical personnel who educate regional staff while providing care for people in the individual country associations. Venture Strategies Innovations (VSI) is a non-profit organization based in California that works with ministries of health, professional medical associations, and in-country experts to achieve regulatory approval of products that will improve women's health to integrate the products into the health system. DKT International is a non-profit organization based in Washington, DC, that serves as one of the largest private providers of family planning and reproductive health products and services in the developing world.

A few patterns stand out in the outlier analysis. Zain is a multinational corporation, which facilitates replication across countries through existing infrastructure, while SLMTA and SCMS have the support of major governmental and quasi-governmental organizations. Among the other three programs in 14 or more countries, the primary common point is they typically provide only limited clinical services, which are more difficult to scale across countries than operational or logistical activities. Five of the six programs emphasize support for targeted health needs, most commonly HIV/AIDS.

Another eight programs operate in more than 10 countries. Similar to the six largest outlier TNS programs, all eight focused on targeted health needs areas (e.g., HIV/AIDS, TB, malaria, MCH, dentistry, eye care). The focus on specific health needs by programs with greater TNS breadth might be due to donor priorities, which we address in the discussion section.

We also calculated correlations of the number of countries, numbers of continents, and specific continents (Africa, Asia-Middle East, and the Americas) with both health foci and health activities, finding no meaningful patterns. The implication here is that programs that manage to extend to multiple countries can do so with a wide range of health services and activities.

We investigated two other factors that might have affected the extent of TNS breadth (number of countries): urban-rural coverage and founding year. We examined rural-urban coverage, finding that 94 per cent of TNS programs covered rural communities, 86 per cent covered urban communities, and 80 per cent covered both urban and rural; hence, there was very little geographic specialization.

By contrast, founding year had a moderate relationship with TNS breadth. There was a limited positive relationship between earlier founding year and number of countries, though it was far from a dominant relationship. In addition, there was a moderate positive correlation between later founding year and provision of general clinical care (primary or secondary) by TNS programs (r=0.20), perhaps suggesting a more recent emphasis on TNS within general care.

Discussion

This study analysed a database of 1,184 low- and middle-income country health programs and identified 116 programs that have scaled across more than one country, offering more than 20 different types of activities in 14 health service areas in 90 different countries. These 116 TNS programs were compared to 1,068 single-country health programs. The study focuses on scale in terms of programs replicated by a single entity, as opposed to programs being replicated by different parent organizations. Program replication in different countries helps spread key health interventions – it is notable that almost 10 per cent of a large sample of programs covering a range of health areas was able to achieve transnational scale (Center for Health Market Innovation 2008).

The study suggests strategies and barriers to scaling up. Much of the literature offers conceptual frameworks (Waddington 2012)or cases focused on specific disease areas such as malaria, mental health, and neonatal care (Kamal-Yanni, Potet, & Saunders 2012; Knippenberg et al. 2005; Lunk, Boyce, Flisher, Kafaar, & Dawes 2009). Even the most systematic overview of scaling focuses on one aspect: the costs of scaling health interventions (Johns & Torres 2005). This study is the most general comparison of scaling activity that we know of. At the same time, we recognize that we address one aspect of scale, transnational activity, and focus on identifying the characteristics of programs that achieve TNS status without being able to reach conclusions about how or why they were able to reach multicountry status.

The characteristics of programs in the study that have achieved transnational scale differ from single-country programs for reasons that may reflect relevant drivers for and constraints to geographic replication. TNS programs most commonly emphasize targeted health needs rather than more comprehensive care, provide health care delivery support rather than direct clinical care, are private non-profits, and rely particularly heavily on donor funding. Single-country programs are more likely than TNS programs to provide comprehensive primary and secondary clinical care and, while they also commonly rely on donor funding, they are also more often able to draw on public financing or membership fees.

We draw on the broader literature to consider several factors that may underlie these patterns, including capital and skills intensity, as well as funder preferences. Prior studies suggest that capital-intensive interventions and those that require complex human resource interventions are difficult to scale (Cooley & Kohl 2006; Johns & Torres 2005; Mangham & Hanson 2010). Many of the reported scaled programs in our study conduct activities related to marketing and consumer education that require relatively low financial investment and limited human resource needs to achieve increases in output. General primary care, in contrast, is not easily standardized and thus is more difficult to scale due to the complexity.

Nonetheless, despite the common difficulties in scaling complex activities, this study found that some programs that provide sophisticated clinical services are able to achieve transnational scale. One example is Operation Asha, which provides TB treatment in India and Cambodia. Operation Asha focuses on a single disease area, using highly repetitive processes. The broader literature supports the idea that service standardization advances scalability (Cooley & Kohl 2006; Tung & Bennett 2014; World Bank 2003; Yamey 2011).

Preferences of funders, including donors and governments, as well as for-profit status, also undoubtedly shape the patterns. Several studies suggest that achieving scale, including transnational scale, requires financial sustainability (Cooley & Kohl 2006; Yamey 2011). Donors are by far the primary source of funding for the TNS programs in our study. Typically, donors emphasize non-profit rather than for-profit or public ventures. In turn, donors commonly have strong preferences for their support. Between 2001 and 2007, one-third of all donor funding was targeted for HIV/AIDS, malaria, and tuberculosis (Bloom & Ainsworth 2010), which reflect easily measurable Millennium Development Goals (United Nations 2002). By inference, this implication helps explain why HIV, TB, and malaria, as well as other targeted needs, such as family planning and maternal and child health, are the most reported health foci among programs scaled internationally.

Thus, the implications of the results suggest that donor funding can help programs surmount capital barriers so that they can operate in multiple countries, either from the outset or via expansion. The expansion can leverage teachings from one country to help support health care activities in multiple settings.

At the same time, donor funding commonly has substantial limits, which can constrain the ability to invest in more general care and capital-intensive activities. The emphasis on targeted health needs and lesser involvement in general primary care reflects a limit in the scope of impact of many of the transnational scaled programs. Changes in disease conditions and more general health needs are demonstrating an increased health burden stemming from non-communicable disease and more years lived with a disability (Murray et al. 2012), advancing the need for robust national health systems with broad scope of primary care and universal coverage. At this point, though, it appears that programs that achieve transnational scale are often vertical approaches that most commonly target particular health care needs and/or support rather than carry out clinical activities.

Clearly, these targeted efforts have high potential value in filling critical gaps in specific health services. Nonetheless, it is possible that the vertical approaches may contribute to fragmentation of health services among national health systems (McIntyre et al. 2008; Yu, Souteyrand, Banda, Kaufman, & Perriëns 2008), with potentially adverse impacts on quality, cost, and outcomes (Enthoven 2009). There is also a risk that pressures to scale up health programs may lead to trade-offs and compromise pro-poor targeting, equity, and/or quality (Mangham & Hanson 2010; Waddington 2012), which may be particularly problematic in vertical programs. These issues require additional research.

The limited involvement by government health agencies in TNS programs undoubtedly reflects their local priorities. Public agencies, which are often most central to providing primary care (World Health Organization 2005; World Health Organization 2008), have mandates to improve health services within their own countries. Nonetheless, the examples of public involvement in transnational scale, such as the WADRAN and Tanzania-Ghana Health partnerships and the Strengthening Laboratory Management Accreditation program of the CDC, which we noted earlier, demonstrate paths that are consistent with country-specific mandates. These points, too, require further study.

In parallel, we found only limited involvement of for-profit entities in TNS programs. This may reflect the difficulty of achieving profitable operations from complex organizations, particularly when targeted at relatively poor populations. Nonetheless, as we noted earlier, some for-profit ventures have expanded into niches in multiple countries, also meriting further attention.

Despite the constraints, the study suggests that, in addition to the more common targeted support, there are potential paths to achieving transnational scale of general care. The TNS programs providing general primary care tended to be founded more recently (median of 2010/2011 v. 2006 in the full set of programs), often as donor-supported non-profits, possibly reflecting a growing willingness to invest in broader care. The general care programs existed across all three continents, with a slightly higher median number of countries than the overall TNS population (four v. three). Underlying this ability to achieve greater TNS breadth, programs providing and supporting general care often involved telemedicine and other telecom-supported services. Examples include the Heberden Telemedicine System that connects providers in Africa and Haiti with physicians in the US, Israel, and Europe, as well as the Africa Teledermatology Project in six countries in Sub-Saharan Africa. Such programs reflect increasing ability to apply information technology to health care services.

Strengths and Limitations

This study has both strengths and limitations. The research is based on a large data set with substantial information about nearly 1,200 programs, of which 116 have achieved transnational scale. This allows for statistical power to make comparisons to single-country programs, covering focal health areas, program activities, funding sources, and legal status, as well as country locations, urban-rural coverage, and founding years.

At the same time, several limits point to the need for future research. Potential selection biases may affect inclusion in the database. The study does not examine replication of innovations across organizations. The analysis cannot distinguish between a presence in a country and high-impact operations in that country. In turn, it was not possible to examine the quality of TNS and single-country programs to understand whether trade-offs were being made between scale and quality, or to determine whether programs were replicated equally in all countries. We cannot determine the number of patients treated or population coverage. The cross-sectional design provides a snapshot of programs at one point in time, without providing trend information. Further research is needed to understand the goals of the programs, as well as structures and processes that must be in place to support successful multicountry replication, the major determinants of successes and failures in scaling up, and the trade-offs and strategic choices involved in achieving TNS status. Such research will need to examine the influence of politics and socio-cultural norms on the scale process as well as the trade-offs in program mandates and pro-poor targeting that may be necessitated as programs attempt to scale.

Conclusions

Understanding TNS is important conceptually, empirically, and in practice. Conceptually, TNS is a meaningful indicator of how broadly a program is able to spread its reach. For empirical health care measurement, TNS is an objective measure of scale that is comparable across hundreds of organizations. For health care practice, TNS is a relevant measure of replicability, demonstrating which program models are conducive to being transplanted in different contexts.

Program managers and donors can benefit from knowing the characteristics of health care programs that achieve transnational scale. The study suggests that certain processes can help advance TNS, such as provider training, logistics support, and supply chain enhancements. The study also offers insights on the kinds of health care activities that are more amenable to scale up.

At its core, the study offers two contrasting implications for health services policies and practices when targeting the poor in LMICs. First, most TNS programs in the study deliver disease-specific vertical interventions rather than more comprehensive clinical care. Second, though, the data demonstrate that some TNS programs have been able to scale clinical care and thus, while it is challenging, it is possible. Examining how clinical care can be scaled up warrants further examination, as it is an integral component of health services delivery. Most generally, this study is part of global efforts to understand how scale is achieved in practice, with the goal of helping health services scale effectively to improve population health.

REFERENCES

Bhattacharyya, O., Khor, S., McGahan, A., Dunne, D., Daar, A., & Singer, P.A. 2010. "Innovative Health Service Delivery Models in Low and Middle Income Countries – What Can We Learn from the Private Sector?" *Health Research Policy and System* 8(24). https://doi.org/10.1186/1478-4505-8-24.

Bloom, G., & Ainsworth, P. 2010. "Beyond Scaling Up: Pathways to Universal Access to Health Services." STEPS Centre. http://opendocs.ids.ac.uk/opendocs/bitstream/handle/123456789/2278/Beyond%20Scaling%20Up.pdf?sequence=1.

Center for Health Market Innovations. 2008. "Sproxil." http://healthmarketinnovations.org/.

Cooley, L., & Kohl, R. 2006. *Scaling Up – From Vision to Large Scale Change: A Management Framework for Practitioners*. Management Systems International. http://www.msiworldwide.com/files/scalingup-framework.pdf.

Credit Suisse. 2012. "Investing for Impact: How Social Entrepreneurship Is
    Redefining the Meaning of Return." https://www.issuelab.org/resource/investing
    -for-impact-how-social-entrepreneurship-is-redefining-the-meaning-of-return.html.
Enthoven, A.C. 2009. "Integrated Care Delivery Systems: The Cure for
    Fragmentation." *American Journal of Medical Care* 15: 284–90. http://www.ncbi
    .nlm.nih.gov/pubmed/20 088632.
Global Forum for Health Research, WHO. 2004. "Strengthening Health Systems: The Role
    and Promise of Policy and Systems Research." Alliance for Health Policy and Systems
    Research. http://www.who.int/alliance-hpsr/resources/Strengthening_complet.pdf.
Jamison, D.T., Breman, J.G., Measham, A.R., Alleyme, G., Claeson, M., Evans, D.B.,
    Jha, P., Mills, A., Musgrove, P. 2006. *Disease Control Priorities in Developing
    Countries Project*, 2nd Edition. New York: Oxford University Press; Washington,
    DC: The International Bank for Reconstruction and Development/The World Bank.
Johns, B., & Torres, T.T. 2005. "Costs of Scaling Up Health Innovations: A Systematic Re-
    view." *Health Policy and Planning* 20(1): 1–13. https://doi.org/10.1093/heapol/czi001.
Kamal-Yanni, M.M., Potet, J., & Saunders, P.M. 2012. "Scaling Up Malaria
    Treatment: A Review of the Performance of Different Providers." *Malaria Journal*
    11(414). https://doi.org/10.1186/1475-2875-11-414.
Karamchandani, A., Kubzansky, M., & Frandano, P. 2009. "Emerging Markets,
    Emerging Models: Market-Based Solutions to the Challenges of Global Poverty."
    Cambridge, MA: Monitor Group. https://community-wealth.org/sites/clone
    .community-wealth.org/files/downloads/report-karamchandani-et-al.pdf.
Knippenberg, R., Lawn, J.E., Darmstadt, G.L., Begkoyian, G., & Fogstad, H.,
    Walelign, N., Paul, V.K., Lancet Neonatal Survival Steering Team. 2005.
    "Systematic Scaling Up of Neonatal Care in Countries." *The Lancet* 635(9464):
    1087–98. https://doi.org/10.1016/S0140-6736(05)71145-4.
Lund, C., Boyce, G., Flisher, A.J., Kafaar, Z., & Dawes, A. 2009. "Scaling Up Child
    and Adolescent Mental Health Services in South Africa: Human Resource Require-
    ments and Costs." *Journal of Child Psychology and Psychiatry* 50: 1121–30.
    https://doi.org/10.1111/j.1469-7610.2009.02078.x.
Mangham, L.J., & Hanson, K. 2010. "Scaling Up International Health: What Are the
    Key Issues?" *Health Policy and Planning* 25(2): 85–96. https://doi.org/10.1093/
    heapol/czp066.
McIntyre, D., Garshong, B., Mtei, G., Meheus, F., Thiede, M., Akazili, J., ... Goudge,
    J. 2008. "Beyond Fragmentation and towards Universal Coverage: Insights from
    Ghana, South Africa, and the United Republic of Tanzania." *Bulletin of the World
    Health Organization* 86(11): 871–6. https://doi.org/10.2471/blt.08.053413.
Murray, C.J.L., Vos, T., Lozano, R., Naghavi, M., Flaxman, A.D., Michaud, C., ...
    Lopez, A.D. 2012. "Disability-Adjusted Life Years (DALYs) for 291 Diseases and
    Injuries in 21 Regions, 1990–2010: A Systematic Analysis for Global Burden of

Disease Study 2010." *The Lancet* 380(9859): 2197–223. https://doi.org/10.1016/S0140-6736(12)61689-4.

Saksena, P., Xu, K., Elovainio, R., & Perrot, J. 2012. "Utilization and Expenditure at Public and Private Facilities in 39 Low-Income Countries." *Tropical Medicine & International Health* 17: 23–35. https://doi.org/10.1111/j.1365-3156.2011.02894.x.

Simmons, R., Fajans, P., & Ghiron, L., eds. 2009. "Scaling Up Health Services Delivery: From Pilot Innovations to Policies and Programs." World Health Organization. http://whqlibdoc.who.int/publications/2007/9789241563512_eng.pdf.

Sproxil. 2018. "Boosting Sales through Consumer Engagement." https://www.sproxil.com/.

Subramanian, S., Naimoli, J., Matsubayashi, T., & Peter, D.H. 2011. "Do We Have the Right Models for Scaling Up Health Services to Achieve the Millennium Development Goals?" BMC Health Services Research 11(336). https://doi.org/10.1186/1472-6963-11-336.

Tung, E., & Bennett, S. 2014. "Private Sector, For-Profit Health Providers in Low and Middle Income Countries: Can They Reach the Poor at Scale?" *Globalization and Health* 10(52). https://doi.org/10.1186/1744-8603-10-52.

United Nations. 2002. "Millennium Development Goals." http://www.un.org/millenniumgoals/.

Waddington, C. 2012. "Scaling Up Health Services: Challenges and Choices." HLSP Institute. http://www.hlsp.org/LinkClick.aspx?fileticket=kZ4sevUUp0g%3D&tabib=1570.

World Bank. 2003. "Up the Impact of Good Practices in Rural Development. A Working Paper to Support Implementation of the World Bank's Rural Development Strategy." http://documents.worldbank.org/curated/en/203681468780267815/pdf/260310White0co1e1up1final1formatted.pdf.

World Health Organization. 2005. "Sustainable Health Financing, Universal Coverage, and Social Health Insurance." *World Health Assembly Resolution WHA* 58.33. http://www.who.int/health_financing/documents/cov-wharesolution5833/en.

World Health Organization. 2008. "The World Health Report 2008: Primary Health Care: Now More Than Ever." https://www.who.int/whr/2008/en/.

Yamey, G. 2011. "Scaling Up Global Health Interventions: A Proposed Framework for Success." *PLOS Medicine* 8(6). https://doi.org/10.1371/journal.pmed.1001049.

Yu, D., Souteyrand, Y., Banda, M.A., Kaufman, J., & Perriëns, J.H. 2008. "Investment in HIV/AIDS Programs: Does It Help Strengthen Health Systems in Developing Countries?" *Globalization and Health* 4(1): 8. https://doi.org/10.1186/1744-8603-4-8.

SECTION C

Vertical Cases – The Role of the Private Sector in Addressing Major Diseases

In this section, we examine how innovative private sector health care organizations are targeting vertical health areas, addressing specific health conditions such as tuberculosis (TB), malaria, diabetes, and mental health. By taking an active role in critical health areas, these organizations are addressing major disease burdens through experimentation with an extensive set of innovative activities, such as those involving financing, ICTs, marketing, and education. They are serving a wide range of social strata, including the poor, and addressing both infectious and chronic diseases. Most of the chapters in this section not only explore the innovations emerging to address specific vertical disease areas, but also consider the available evidence in the literature on the effectiveness, availability, and quality of these models in serving LMIC populations.

Chapter 9 ("Innovations in Tuberculosis Health Care: Exploring the Evidence on Emerging Practices in Low- and Middle-Income Countries") describes private sector health organizations that use innovative delivery mechanisms and ICT innovations to improve TB diagnostic and treatment services. Key examples include social franchises such as the Smiling Sun Franchise Program in Bangladesh, as well as SMS-based models used by On Cue Compliance and Uganda Health Information Network.

Chapter 10 ("Innovations in Malaria Health Care: Exploring the Evidence on Emerging Practices in Low- and Middle-Income Countries") focuses on private sector health organizations engaged in marketing, financing, and ICT innovations for improving malaria health care delivery. Key examples include Malaria Control in Cambodia's efforts to increase access to rapid diagnostic tests in remote areas and SMS for Life, an mHealth program in Tanzania that uses SMS to track malaria medication stock information.

Chapter 11 ("Innovative Practices in Global Health to Manage Diabetes Mellitus") describes innovative approaches for diabetes care delivered by the private sector. Examples include Amcare in Bangladesh, which runs call centres with medical staff that respond to patient queries, and interactive online games for self-monitoring through the Aged Diabetic Assistant in China.

Chapter 12 ("Innovations in Global Mental Health Practice") explores innovative mental health services provided by private sector health care organizations. These services focus on four activity areas: educating providers (e.g., BasicNeeds, which operates across Asia and Africa), advocacy and research (e.g., Anjali in India and APOE Sao Paulo in Brazil), decentralizing care via strategies such as mobile mental health camps, and comprehensive care (e.g., Instituto Prove in Brazil).

In exploring the innovative approaches to vertical disease areas in LMICs, we find that these models tend to focus on new delivery methods and ICTs to expand access, efficiency, and quality of care in the diagnosis and treatment of these diseases. Models that support consumer education and provider training are also important in ensuring patients are receiving appropriate and timely care and making healthy decision. Some innovative approaches, such as social franchising and collaborations with the public sector involving subsidies and disease surveillance, have preliminary evidence that they can improve care in these vertical areas. However, emerging ICT models require much more study. Still, our studies find ICTs can facilitate the flow of data about patients and medical supplies and help improve communications between patients and caregivers.

9 Innovations in Tuberculosis Health Care: Exploring the Evidence on Emerging Practices in Low- and Middle-Income Countries

ONIL BHATTACHARYYA, KATHRYN MOSSMAN,
ANITA MCGAHAN, WILL MITCHELL, DAVID LEUNG,
JOHN GINTHER, RAMAN SOHAL, LEIGH HAYDEN,
JOHN A. MACDONALD, HIMANSHU PARIKH,
AND ILAN SHAHIN

Introduction

Tuberculosis (TB) is one of the world's biggest health problems. It is the second leading cause of death from an infectious disease after HIV. One-third of the world's population is infected with latent TB, and in 2011, there were an estimated 8.7 million new cases of infection, and 1.4 million lives were lost due to this treatable and curable disease (WHO 2012a; WHO 2013). Progress is being made, particularly through the WHO's DOTS/Stop TB strategy: the mortality rate associated with TB, excluding HIV-positive cases, has decreased 41 per cent since 1990 (WHO 2012a).

However, substantive barriers still exist to managing TB, including underfunded TB initiatives, insufficient diagnosis and reporting infrastructure, and slow progress in development of treatments for multidrug resistant TB (MDR-TB) (WHO 2012a). Indeed, with the threat of MDR-TB and extensively drug-resistant TB (XDR-TB), and the increased vulnerability of those with HIV to TB, both private and public sector efforts are needed to combat TB and improve the health outcomes of the poor (WHO 2012a; WHO 2001).

In this chapter, we describe the current role of the private sector in delivering care to those with TB, and explore the innovative approaches they are engaging in, examining those with evidence as well as emerging approaches. These approaches were identified through a review of TB programs in the CHMI database along with academic and gray literature on TB. We conclude with a discussion of combining innovative activities and its potential to achieve health impact and organizational sustainability, while pointing to areas for future research.

Background

The Role of the Private Sector in TB

The private sector delivers care for a large proportion of TB cases. For most of the twenty-two countries with the highest levels of TB prevalence, a substantial proportion of total health expenditure is due to private expenditure, and out-of-pocket expenditure for health ranged from 23.2 per cent in Russia to 90.6 per cent in Cambodia in 2001 (Uplekar, Pathania, & Raviglione 2001). Indeed, many seek TB treatment from private providers, as this sector often provides greater flexibility, value, convenience, and privacy (Lönnroth, Tran, Thuong, Quy, & Diwan 2001). For example, experts suggest that private practitioners manage a large proportion of the TB cases that go unreported, and it is estimated that only 40 per cent of TB cases are reported worldwide (Uplekar et al. 2001). In western India, a study found that 86 per cent of TB patients first consulted private practitioners upon the appearance of symptoms, and two-thirds of patients that continued treatment remained in the private sector (Uplekar, Juvekar, Morankar, Rangan, & Nunn 1998). Additionally, in Vietnam and Pakistan half of patients initially chose a private provider for treatment of the current TB episode. These providers included private physicians, private nurses, traditional practitioners, and private pharmacies (Lönnroth, Thuong, Linh, & Diwan 2001; Khan, Walley, Newell, & Imdad 2000). Furthermore, a study in the Philippines found that 46 per cent of those who sought care for TB symptoms consulted a private medical practitioner (Tupasi et al. 2000). Thus, in low- and middle-income countries (LMICs), the private sector is a significant provider of tuberculosis care.

Tuberculosis at a Glance: Exploring TB Program Activities in the CHMI Database

Many LMIC health programs are innovating in the detection and treatment of tuberculosis. Innovation is defined as something new, or perceived as new by a population, that has the potential to redefine the economic and/or social context of health care and drive change (Weberg 2009). In this chapter, we focus on innovations in the delivery and financing of TB care for populations in LMICs. There are 62 programs in the CHMI database that focus on TB, and they operate in nine regions, with almost half located in East Africa (30; 48 per cent). Most of these TB programs operate as private, not-for-profit (35; 56 per cent) (see the appendix to this chapter). Among the 62 TB programs, the most frequently reported health market innovations are: information and communication technology (20; 32 per cent); provider training (15; 24 per cent); consumer education (12; 19 per cent); service delivery network (12; 19 per cent); and franchising (11; 18 per cent).

Combating TB effectively requires early diagnosis of TB; access and adherence to high-quality, standardized treatment; and the availability of well-trained health workers to provide services, including treatment supervision and patient support (Fitzpatrick, Floyd, Baena, Glaziou, & Sismanidis 2010). Innovative activities such as ICTs can increase geographic access to screening and speed up diagnosis while also encouraging adherence by providing consumer education and reminders to take medications. Provider training can increase the skills and competency of practitioners in providing appropriate, standardized treatment. Service delivery networks and franchising organize providers to expand the geographic access of TB services and monitor the quality of care provided.

The next sections explore innovative approaches to delivering TB services, some with established evidence of impact and other emerging approaches with potential to improve health outcomes.

Exploring the Evidence on Innovative TB Models

Approaches with Evidence: Exploring the Impact of Innovative Models in TB

There are number of innovative approaches in the private sector that have been studied for their health impact and have shown promising results.

DEVELOPING PUBLIC-PRIVATE PARTNERSHIPS TO IMPROVE DIAGNOSTIC AND TREATMENT PRACTICES

The large and growing role of the private sector in detecting, treating, and monitoring TB highlights a need to ensure that providers are providing effective care (Lönnroth, Thuong, et al. 2001). Concerns have been raised about private care provision involving inadequate diagnostic and treatment practices (Uplekar et al. 1998; Singla, Sharma, & Jain 1998) and lower treatment success rates (Lönnroth, Thuong, Lambregts, Quy, & Diwan 2003). There has also been evidence of distrust between the public and private sector in the provision of TB care (Vyas, Small, & Deriemer 2003). Given these concerns, the emergence of public-private partnerships (PPPs) and public-private mix (PPM) projects suggest a promising direction for TB control through greater collaboration and synergy. PPPs and PPMs tend to focus on encouraging private providers to follow the diagnostic and treatment principles of public national tuberculosis programs (NTPs), providing free or subsidized medications, strengthening referral systems between public and private sectors, and seeking greater supervision of private providers by the NTP (Quy, Lan, et al. 2003). This can involve training and monitoring, providing financial incentives for case detection and successful treatment, and implementing a standardized information and referral system (Quy, Lönnroth, Lan, & Buu 2003). PPPs are fairly widespread, and are found in South Asia, Southeast Asia, Africa, and Latin America (Malmborg, Mann, & Squire 2011). Sixteen TB programs in the CHMI database are PPPs.

PPPs have shown evidence of improvement in case detection and high rates of successful treatment (Quy, Lan, et al. 2003; Murthy, Frieden, Yazdani, & Hreshikesh 2001), suggesting the PPP model can improve the quality and access in TB care (Naser et al. 2012). These partnerships can be a pragmatic way to achieve high cure rates and increase coverage, although it is suggested that strong national TB programs are needed to coordinate PPP programs (Newell, Pande, Baral, Bam, & Malla 2004). A systematic assessment of PPM projects found that while this approach has had success in improving treatment outcomes and case detection, it is difficult to draw conclusions about cost reduction for patients and equity in access to services (Malmborg et al. 2011).

Example of a Program Reporting Results: Public Private Mix for Tuberculosis, Malaria, and Reproductive Health. This Cambodian program aims to improve TB case management and early case detection in the public and private sectors through strengthening the capacity of health providers and the linkages and referral mechanisms between these sectors. This PPM program project has helped identify an additional 2 per cent of TB cases per year, and a higher percentage of smear-positive cases to the national total (CHMI 2013d).

WORKPLACE TB PROGRAMS TARGETING WORKERS

Workplace TB programs are designed to improve the availability and accessibility of TB diagnosis and treatment for those who work in areas with high HIV rates and/or environments that facilitate TB transmission. These programs may provide medical treatment on site, or refer to nearby clinics (Zafar Ullah et al. 2012). For many workers in industrial settings, such as plantations and factories, getting screened or treated for TB is difficult because clinics are often only open during work hours (Zafar Ullah et al. 2012). In addition, workplace programs are designed to increase drug adherence, which increases TB cure rates and prevents new cases of MDR-TB. Employers benefit from these programs through fewer sick days and lower staff turnover (Private Sector Program-Ethiopia 2009; WHO 2012b). Such programs are growing among many low-income areas, including Kenya (WHO 2010), Ethiopia (Private Sector Program-Ethiopia 2009), and Bangladesh (Zafar Ullah et al. 2012). Often workplace TB programs are combined with workplace HIV programs (WHO 2010; Private Sector Program-Ethiopia 2009). Three TB programs in the CHMI database provide TB services at workplaces.

There is moderate evidence available on workplace TB programs. Studies have found that these programs can offer a high quality of care (Sinanovic & Kumaranayake 2006), and can be an effective way to deliver TB treatment (Bechan, Connolly, Murray, Standing, & Wilkinson 1997). Where there are fewer social barriers to TB/HIV treatment, there is good service utilization, cure rates are high, and default rates are low (WHO 2010; Zafar Ullah et al. 2012). In areas where receiving HIV/TB treatment is stigmatized, the programs have low usage rates, although excellent success among users (Private Sector Program-Ethiopia 2009).

Example of a Program Reporting Results: Anglo Gold Ashanti Health – TB. This South African workplace initiative is a comprehensive TB control program focused on rapidly identifying and diagnosing infectious cases of TB through occupational health chest X-ray screening of employees twice a year, and providing appropriate treatment with quality combination drug therapy using DOTS. In 2011 the incidence of occupational TB among workers was 1.8 per cent. In 2012, the incidence of occupational TB among workers was 1.4 per cent, and the TB cure rate in was 94 per cent, compared to the WHO target of 85 per cent (CHMI 2013a).

SOCIAL FRANCHISING: ORGANIZING DELIVERY TO INCREASE ACCESS TO TB CARE

Social franchises are networks of private health providers that provide products and services under a common brand (Schlein & Montagu 2012). Increasing access to standardized services for the early detection and treatment of TB is necessary for improving TB control, and the franchise model is intended to increase access, quality (through standardization, training, and monitoring), cost-effectiveness, and equity (Schlein & Montagu 2012; Population Services International 2012). Social franchises can fit within a national TB program (NTP) through notifying the NTP when a patient is diagnosed with TB or initiates TB treatment; some also diagnose and treat TB (WHO 2010; Population Services International 2012). The number of social franchises offering TB diagnosis and/or treatment has more than tripled between 2008 and 2011 (Schlein & Montagu 2012). TB services have been franchised in a number of countries, primarily in Africa, southeast Asia, and south Asia, with varying levels of services and health care providers (Schlein & Montagu 2012). Eleven TB programs in the CHMI database use social franchising to deliver care.

There is moderate evidence on the social franchising of TB services, most of which involves studies of the Sun Quality Health Franchise in Myanmar (CHMI 2013f). This franchise delivers highly subsidized, quality TB care and has achieved greater treatment success than the government-run program (Lönnroth, Aung, Maung, Kluge, & Uplekar 2007). Their patients, who perceive the franchise as offering relatively affordable and attentive care (O'Connell, Hom, Aung, Theuss, & Huntington 2011), are also slightly more likely to be in the lowest-income bracket, suggesting that social franchising can help to reach the poor and increase health equity (Montagu et al. 2013). However, employing user charges may limit access to the poor (Lönnroth et al. 2007), and further efforts are needed to target lower socioeconomic groups in rural areas (Montagu et al. 2013). In addition, research on social franchising in reproductive health and HIV/AIDS has found that this approach can increase quality of care (Shah, Wang, & Bishai 2011) and client satisfaction (Agha, Karim, Balal, & Sosler 2007), while its success is context dependent (Stephenson et al. 2004).

Example of a Program Reporting Results: Smiling Sun Franchise Program (SSFP). The Smiling Sun Franchise network of Bangladesh is composed of 325 franchisee-owned clinics and 6,000 community service providers. The network provides a number of services in line with the National Tuberculosis Control Program, including DOTS treatment and microscopy services. Smiling Sun has achieved significant cost reductions for drugs: discounts have dropped from 16 per cent to 25 per cent, improving affordability for the poor (CHMI 2013e).

EMPLOYING ELECTRONIC MEDICAL RECORDS TO IMPROVE TB DATA MANAGEMENT
Electronic recording and reporting systems can help strengthen TB surveillance and monitoring (Fitzpatrick et al. 2010). Electronic medical records (EMRs)

allow for improved management of patients, reporting of investigation results, and program evaluation (Millard, Bru, & Berger 2012). They help address issues affecting resource-poor settings, such as the lack of health care providers and geographic barriers (Blaya et al. 2007). In TB management, EMRs are beneficial for providing laboratory results, enhancing medication adherence, and decreasing clinical record duplication (Fraser, Blaya, Choi, Bonilla, & Jazayeri 2006). The increase in MDR-TB has spurred the development of EMRs in resource-limited settings, and a recent review found six open-source EMRs suitable for use in such contexts (Millard et al. 2012). There are seven TB programs in the CHMI database using electronic medical records to assist providers with TB care.

Studies of tuberculosis-targeted, patient-oriented EMRs in LMICs show increased numbers of patients started on appropriate medication, fewer patients lost to follow-up, and improved medication delivery (Fraser et al. 2007). They are associated with significant decreases in medical error rates and the reduction of data entry delays (Fraser et al. 2006). From a utilization standpoint, surveys of clinical users have indicated satisfaction with functionality and ease of use (Fraser et al. 2006; Blaya et al. 2007). In addition, EMRs used in laboratories have resulted in economic benefits and increased coverage, as well as timely access of results (Blaya et al. 2007; Blaya et al. 2010).

Example of a Program Reporting Results: World Health Partners. World Health Partners (WHP) operates a network of over 5,500 rural social franchises, branded as the Sky network, in Bihar, India. The network provides TB services as part of their infectious disease coverage package. EMRs paired with a TB patient tracking and adherence monitoring system developed on the MOTECH platform allow for real-time patient management, including web or voice-based treatment, adherence reporting, and alerts and reminders for providers. Since 2012, the Sky network has identified over 5,100 new TB cases with over 2,800 patients placed on DOTS (CHMI 2013n).

Approaches with Less Evidence: Emerging Models with the Potential for Impact

There are a number of emerging approaches to the delivery of TB care that show promise, but for which there is little available evidence. In particular, programs are increasingly using innovative ICTs to overcome geographic barriers and improve the efficiency and quality of diagnostic and treatment processes.

DATA COLLECTION, TRACKING, AND MONITORING WITH ICTS

While TB detection rates are improving, it is estimated that about one-third of cases remain undiagnosed and unreported (WHO 2012). Paper-based data collection is labour-intensive, and later aggregation and analyses of these data are difficult (mHealth Alliance & Stop TB Partnership 2012). ICTs, predominately mobile phones, can enhance health workers' ability to collect information on and track patients. Health workers log basic patient data and send the information directly to a server, most commonly through SMS. Some of these programs use customized software (Khan et al. 2012), PDAs, and GPS coordinates (Interactive Research and Development & Stop TB Partnership 2012) to help track additional information. There are eight TB programs in the CHMI database that collect patient data using mobile technologies.

The evidence base for this approach is limited. One program using phone-based data collection found a significant increase in reported TB cases; however, the impact assessment noted that several program components were modified to evaluate for potential impact (Khan et al. 2012). Greater research is needed on the ability for ICTs to increase the efficiency and quality of data collection, and whether it can improve the tracking of patients.

Example of a Program Reporting Results: Health at Home/Kenya. Health at Home/Kenya is a public-private partnership that brings TB screening, HIV counselling and testing, and malaria bed nets to remote areas in western Kenya with difficulty accessing health care. Counsellors and nurses visit homes with GPS-enabled Android phones to collect health data, record test results, and document the household location for future follow-ups. Collected data is then entered into the AMPATH medical record system. In 2011, Health at Home/Kenya reported it had screened 514,636 people for TB (CHMI 2013b).

ENSURING TREATMENT ADHERENCE WITH MOBILE TECHNOLOGIES

Adherence to TB treatment programs is critical – the disease carries a high mortality rate if not treated (WHO 2012) and breaks in regimen can lead to drug resistance (mHealth Alliance & Stop TB Partnership 2012). Directly Observed Treatment, short-course (DOTS) is widely used to improve treatment adherence, though it requires medical professionals to directly observe treatment, which is labour intensive (Barclay 2009). Mobile technology has the potential to streamline this process, and programs are sending SMS reminders to patients, encouraging them to take their medication, or requesting that patients send an SMS to their provider after taking medication. Other programs attach a sensor to medication containers that notify providers via SMS when opened (Interactive Research and Development & Stop TB Partnership 2012) or require patients to SMS codes revealed on positive urinalysis strips testing for medication (Sandhu 2011). There are six TB programs in the CHMI database that ensure adherence to treatment programs with ICTs.

There is currently little evidence available on the effectiveness of these interventions in TB (Interactive Research and Development & Stop TB Partnership 2012), and some question the appropriateness of this model as a replacement for person-to-person DOTS interventions (Barclay 2009). However, SMS reminders for HIV-infected adults have shown improved antiretroviral therapy adherence (Da Costa, Barbosa, Sigulem, de Fatima Marin, & Pisa 2012) and rates of viral suppression (Lester, Ritvo, Mlls, Kariri, & Karana 2010), as well as lower likelihood of treatment interruption exceeding 48 hours (Pop-Eleches et al. 2011). Further study is needed on these initiatives in TB and whether this approach has rates of treatment success comparable with face-to-face DOTS programs.

Example of a Program Reporting Results: On Cue Compliance. This program uses specially designed pill bottles equipped with a SIM card and transmitter (known as SIMpill) to ensure TB drug adherence. When the pill bottle is opened, an SMS message is sent to a designated health care worker. If the pill bottle is not opened, the patient receives a reminder text message. The pilot demonstrated promising results: with SIMpill, 90 per cent of patients complied with their medication regimen, compared to the 22–60 per cent compliance rate without the system (CHMI 2013c).

USING MOBILE TECHNOLOGY TO IMPROVE THE SUPPLY CHAIN OF MEDICATIONS AND REDUCE STOCK-OUTS

Ensuring effective drug management and reliable drug supply is essential for high-quality TB treatment (Fitzpatrick et al. 2010). Stock-outs of TB medicines cause interrupted or delayed treatment, which can increase drug resistance and prolong illness (mHealth Alliance & Stop TB Partnership 2012; Fitzpatrick et al. 2010). Stock-outs in low-resource settings continue to be a challenge. For example, in 2009, numerous stock-outs (some as long as three months) of first-line TB drugs were reported at Mulago Hospital, one of Uganda's biggest hospitals, located in Kampala (Clinton Health Access Initiative & Bill & Melinda Gates Foundation 2010). To counteract this, programs are using mobile technologies to collect information on drug usage and stock, sending electronic messages to administrators when drugs need to be refilled (Interactive

Research and Development & Stop TB Partnership 2012). There are two TB programs in the CHMI database using mobile technologies to monitor and manage stocks of TB medication.

There is little evidence on mobile technology solutions for stock-outs in TB. Most evidence on this approach comes from malaria research, particularly involving a program called SMS for Life, which aims to reduce stock-outs in malaria treatment in the Tanzanian Public Health System using SMS, internet, and mapping technology (Interactive Research and Development & Stop TB Partnership 2012). Studies have found that this approach decreased stock-outs in the study area compared to others not using this model (Barrington, Wereko-Brobby, Ward, Mwafongo, & Kungulwe 2010; Githinji, Kigen, Memusi, Nyandigisi, & Mbithi 2013). More research is needed on whether this approach also decreases stock-outs for TB medications and its ability to improve efficiency of reporting.

Example of a Program Reporting Results: UHIN. Through this program, different levels of health centres send health reports and data on drug usage and stocks to district health offices using mobile technologies, with the aim of increasing efficiency and ensuring sufficient supplies of TB drugs and other medications. An independent study found that the network delivered a 24 per cent savings per unit of spending over the traditional manual data collection and transmission approaches (CHMI 2016).

INCREASING DIAGNOSTIC EFFICIENCY USING MOBILE DEVICES
Early, rapid, and accurate TB diagnosis is important in improving health outcomes, minimizing the spread of infection, and preventing additional suffering and expense (WHO 2012). Mobile technology is being used in novel ways to speed the diagnosis process and make it more accessible in areas outside of laboratories and health centres (mHealth Alliance & Stop TB Partnership 2012). This often involves using applications and accessory attachments with mobile phones and tablets that can turn them into diagnostic tools, such as a low-cost stethoscope made by attaching an egg cup to a mobile phone (mHealth Alliance & Stop TB Partnership 2012). It also can involve using phones to connect specialists and lab technicians with patients, such as having community health workers (CHWs) take pictures of sputum smear slides or X-rays and sending these images through their phones to diagnostic hubs. Results are sent back to the CHWs with minimal delay, and they are able to give a diagnosis to the patient in person, preventing unnecessary long-distance travel for diagnostic services (mHealth Alliance & Stop TB Partnership

2012). There are two TB programs in the CHMI database using mobile devices for diagnostic purposes.

There is little research available on the use of mobile phones in TB diagnosis. One study examined the accuracy of sending images of microscopic observation drug susceptibility (MODS) cultures containing TB bacteria by mobile phone to a remote site for expert analysis (Zimic et al. 2009). It found 99 per cent agreement between the readings of the mobile phone image and direct observation through a microscope. Another study developed a mobile phone-mounted light microscope, finding that resolution exceeds that necessary to assess TB sputum samples (Breslauer, Maamari, Switz, Lam, & Fletcher 2009). Greater research is needed on the feasibility of implementing these technologies and their accuracy in the field.

Example of a Program Reporting Results: World Health Partners. This program not only employs EMR technology, but also uses a range of plug-and-play devices that operate through a tablet with a technology platform (World Health Partners 2017). Offline, the devices can be used to conduct screenings of patients, and online, they can be used to communicate remotely with doctors. This allows World Health Partners to operate in rural areas with underserved populations; 80 per cent of their clients in 2013 were from the poorest two quintiles (CHMI 2013g).

Evidence Gaps and Research Opportunities in TB Health Care

There are a variety of innovations practiced in the private sector to better address the challenges of TB, including innovative approaches with evidence, and those that are still emerging. Innovative activities may have even more potential when combined in mutually beneficial ways to increase efficiency, quality, and scale. An example of one such approach in TB involves combining ICTs, service delivery networks, and provider training. ICTs can increase efficiency by speeding diagnosis and data collection, and by reducing the human resources required to observe medication adherence. They can also improve data quality by decreasing data entry errors. Provider training can increase quality by ensuring providers can use the ICT correctly and are aware of TB guidelines for diagnosis and treatment. Service delivery networks connect and support providers, organizing delivery and expanding geographic access, which is needed to increase the scale of services. Innovative activities are needed fight the global TB epidemic, and combining innovations may be an important strategy to improve the health impact of TB programs.

There are many innovative programs in the area of TB, and their most frequent innovative activities involve information and communication technology (ICT), provider training, consumer education, service delivery network, and franchising. PPPs, workplace TB programs, social franchising, and EMRs have some evidence for their impact, while emerging approaches such as data collection with mobile devices, monitoring adherence through mobile technologies, using mobile technologies for drug supply management, and employing mobile phones as diagnostic tools are promising but require further research. The combination of innovative activities may hold potential, but greater study of these emerging approaches is needed in order to understand their ability to efficiently address TB on a large scale.

Appendix

Geographic Region of TB Programs

There are 62 TB programs in the CHMI database operating in nine regions, namely East Africa, South Asia, and Southeast Asia.

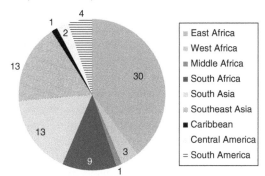

Legend:
- East Africa
- West Africa
- Middle Africa
- South Africa
- South Asia
- Southeast Asia
- Caribbean
- Central America
- = South America

Figure 9.A1 TB programs by region

Legal Status of TB Programs

The largest area of operation of TB programs in the CHMI database is in the private, not-for-profit sector (35; 35 per cent), followed by public-private partnerships (16; 62 per cent).

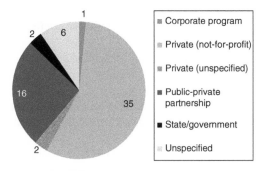

Legend:
- Corporate program
- Private (not-for-profit)
- Private (unspecified)
- Public-private partnership
- State/government
- Unspecified

Figure 9.A2 Legal status of TB programs

REFERENCES

Agha, S., Karim, A.M., Balal, A., & Sosler, S. 2007. "The Impact of a Reproductive Health Franchise on Client Satisfaction in Rural Nepal." *Health Policy and Planning* 22(5): 320–8. https://doi.org/10.1093/heapol/czm025.

Barclay, E. 2009. "Text Messages Could Hasten Tuberculosis Drug Compliance." *The Lancet* 373(9657): 15–16. https://doi.org/10.1016/s0140-6736(08)61938-8.

Barrington, J., Wereko-Brobby, O., Ward, P., Mwafongo, W., & Kungulwe, S. 2010. "SMS for Life: A Pilot Project to Improve Anti-malarial Drug Supply Management in Rural Tanzania Using Standard Technology." *Malaria Journal* 9(1): 298. https://doi.org/10.1186/1475-2875-9-298.

Bechan, S., Connolly, C., Murray, G.M., Standing, E., & Wilkinson, D. 1997. "Directly Observed Therapy for Tuberculosis Given Twice Weekly in the Workplace in Urban South Africa." *Transactions of the Royal Society of Tropical Medicine and Hygiene* 91(6): 704–7. https://doi.org/10.1016/S0035-9203(97)90532-0.

Blaya, J.A., Shin, S.S., Yale, G., Suarez, C., Asencios, L., Contreras, C., ... Fraser, H.S.F. 2010. "Electronic Laboratory System Reduces Errors in National Tuberculosis Program: A Cluster Randomized Controlled Trial." *International Journal of Tuberculosis and Lung Disease* 14(8): 1009–15.

Blaya, J., Shin, S., Yagui, M., Yale, G., Suarez, C.Z., Asencios, L.L., ... Fraser, H.S.F. 2007. "A Web-Based Laboratory Information System to Improve Quality of Care of Tuberculosis Patients in Peru: Functional Requirements, Implementation, and Usage Statistics." *BMC Medical Informatics and Decision Making* 7(1): 33. https://doi.org/10.1186/1472-6947-7-33.

Breslauer, D.N., Maamari, R.N., Switz, N.A., Lam, W.A., & Fletcher, D.A. 2009. "Mobile Phone-Based Clinical Microscopy for Global Health Applications." *PloS One* 4(7): e6320. https://doi.org/10.1371/journal.pone.0006320.

CHMI. 2013a. "AngloGold Ashanti – TB." http://healthmarketinnovations.org/.

– 2013b. "Health at Home/Kenya." http://healthmarketinnovations.org/.

– 2013c. "On Cue Compliance." http://healthmarketinnovations.org/.

– 2013d. "Public Private Mix for Tuberculosis, Malaria, and Reproductive Health." http://healthmarketinnovations.org/.

– 2013e. "Smiling Sun Franchise Program." http://healthmarketinnovations.org/.

– 2013f. "Sun Quality Health Network-Myanmar." http://healthmarketinnovations.org/.

– 2013g. "World Health Partners." http://healthmarketinnovations.org/.

– 2016. "Uganda Health Information Network (UHIN)." http://healthmarketinnovations.org/.

Clinton Health Access Initiative & Bill & Melinda Gates Foundation. 2010. *Falling Short: Ensuring Access to Simple, Safe, and Effective First-Line Medicines for Tuberculosis.* http://apps.who.int/medicinedocs/documents/s18389en/s18389en.pdf.

Da Costa, T.M., Barbosa, B.J.P., Sigulem, D., de Fatima Marin, H., & Pisa, I. 2012. "Results of a Randomized Controlled Trial to Assess the Effects of a Mobile SMS-Based Intervention on Treatment Adherence in HIV/AIDS-infected Brazilian Women and Impressions and Satisfaction with Respect to Incoming Messages." *International Journal of Medical Informatics* 81(4): 257–69. https://doi .org/10.1016/j.ijmedinf.2011.10.002.

Fitzpatrick, C., Floyd, K., Baena, I.G., Glaziou, P., & Sismanidis, C. 2010. *The Global Plan to Stop TB 2011–2015: Transforming the Fight towards Elimination of Tuberculosis*. Geneva: World Health Organization.

Fraser, H.S.F., Allen, C., Bailey, C., Douglas, G., Shin, S., & Blaya, J. 2007. "Information Systems for Patient Follow-up and Chronic Management of HIV and Tuberculosis: A Life-Saving Technology in Resource-Poor areas." *Journal of Medical Internet Research* 9(4): e29. https://doi.org/10.2196/jmir.9.4.e29.

Fraser, H.S.F., Blaya, J., Choi, S.S., Bonilla, C., & Jazayeri, D. 2006. "Evaluating the Impact and Costs of Deploying an Electronic Medical Record System to Support TB Treatment in Peru." *AMIA Annual Symposium Proceedings*, 264–8.

Githinji, S., Kigen, S., Memusi, D., Nyandigisi, A., & Mbithi, A.M. 2013. "Reducing Stock-Outs of Life-Saving Malaria Commodities Using Mobile Phone Text Messaging: SMS for Life Study in Kenya." *PLoS One* 8(1): e54066. https://doi.org/ 10.1371/journal.pone.0054066.

Interactive Research and Development, & Stop TB Partnership. 2012. *mHealth to Improve TB Care*. Geneva: World Health Organization.

Khan, A., Walley, J., Newell, J., & Imdad, N. 2000. "Tuberculosis in Pakistan: Socio-cultural Constraints and Opportunities in Treatment." *Social Science & Medicine* 50(2): 247–54. https://doi.org/10.1016/S0277-9536(99)00279-8.

Khan, A., Khowaja, S., Khan, F.S., Qazi, F., Lotia, I., Habib, A., ... Keshavjee, S. 2012. "Engaging the Private Sector to Increase Tuberculosis Case Detection: An Impact Evaluation Study." *The Lancet Infectious Diseases* 12(8): 608–16. https://doi .org/10.1016/S1473-3099(12)70116-0.

Lester, R.T., Ritvo, P., Mills, E.J., Kariri, A., & Karana, S. 2010. "Effects of a Mobile Phone Short Message Service on Antiretroviral Treatment Adherence in Kenya (WelTel Kenya1): A Randomized Trial." *The Lancet* 376(9755): 1838–45. https://doi.org/ 10.1016/S0140-6736(10)61997-6.

Lönnroth, K., Aung, T., Maung, W., Kluge, H., & Uplekar, M. 2007. "Social Franchising of TB Care through Private GPs in Myanmar: An Assessment of Treatment Results, Access, Equity, and Financial Protection." *Health Policy and Planning* 22(3): 156–66. https://doi.org/10.1093/heapol/czm007.

Lönnroth, K., Thuong, L.M., Lambregts, K., Quy, H.T., & Diwan, V.K. 2003. "Private Tuberculosis Care Provision Associated with Poor Treatment Outcome: Comparative Study of a Semi-private Lung Clinic and the NTP in Two Urban Districts in Ho Chi Minh City, Vietnam." *The International Journal of Tuberculosis and Lung Disease* 7(2): 165–71.

Lönnroth, K., Thuong, L.M., Linh, P.D., & Diwan, V.K. 2001. "Utilization of Private and Public Health Care Providers for Tuberculosis Symptoms in Ho Chi Minh City, Vietnam." *Health Policy and Planning* 16(1): 47–54. https://doi.org/10.1093/heapol/16.1.47.

Lönnroth, K., Tran, T.U., Thuong, L.M., Quy, H.T., & Diwan, V. 2001. "Can I Afford Free Treatment: Perceived Consequences of Health Care Provider Choices among People with Tuberculosis in Ho Chi Minh City, Vietnam." *Social Science and Medicine* 52(6): 935–48. https://doi.org/10.1016/S0277-9536(00)00195-7.

Malmborg, R., Mann, G., & Squire, S.B. 2011. "A Systematic Assessment of the Concept and Practice of Public-Private Mix for Tuberculosis Care and Control." *International Journal for Equity in Health* 10(1): 49. https://doi.org/10.1186/1475-9276-10-49.

mHealth Alliance, & Stop TB Partnership. 2012. *Pushing the Frontier: The Role of mHealth in the Fight Against Tuberculosis.* Geneva: World Health Organization.

Millard, P., Bru, J., & Berger, C. 2012. "Open-Source Point-of-care Electronic Medical Records for Use in Resource-Limited Settings: Systematic Review and Questionnaire Surveys." *BMJ Open* 2(4): e000690. https://doi.org/10.1136/bmjopen-2011-000690.

Montagu, D., Sudhinaraset, M., Lwin, T., Onozaki, I., Win, Z., & Aung, T. 2013. "Equity and the Sun Quality Health Private Provider Social Franchise: Comparative Analysis of Patient-Survey data and a Nationally Representative TB Prevalence Survey." *International Journal for Equity in Health* 12(1): 5. https://doi.org/10.1186/1475-9276-12-5.

Murthy, K.J., Frieden, T.R., Yazdani, A., & Hreshikesh, P. 2001. "Public-Private Partnership in Tuberculosis Control: Experience in Hyderabad, India." *The International Journal of Tuberculosis and Lung Disease* 5(4): 354–9.

Naser, A., Zafar Ullah, A.N., Huque, R., Husain, A., Akter, S., Islam, A., & Newell, J.N. 2012. "Effectiveness of Involving the Private Medical Sector in the National TB Control Program in Bangladesh: Evidence from Mixed Methods." *BMJ Open* 2(e001534): 1–8. https://doi.org/10.1136/bmjopen-2012-001534.

Newell, J.N., Pande, S.B., Baral, S.C., Bam, D.S., & Malla, P. 2004. "Control of Tuberculosis in an Urban Setting in Nepal: Public-Private Partnership." *Bulletin of the World Health Organization* 82(2): 92–8.

O'Connell, K., Hom, M., Aung, T., Theuss, M., & Huntington, D. 2011. "Using and Joining a Franchised Private Sector Provider Network in Myanmar." *PloS One* 6(12): e28364. https://doi.org/10.1371/journal.pone.0028364.

Pop-Eleches, C., Thirumurthy, H., Habyarimana, J.P., Zivin, J.G., Goldstein, M.P., de Walque, D., ... Bangsberg, D.R. 2011. "Mobile Phone Technologies Improve Adherence to Antiretroviral Treatment in a Resource-Limited Setting: A Randomized Controlled Trial of Text Message Reminders." *AIDS* 25(6); 825–34. https://doi.org/10.1097/QAD.0b013e32834380c1.

Population Services International (PSI). 2012. *Social Franchising for TB Care and Control. PPM Subgroup Meeting, Kuala Lumpur, Malaysia, 11 November.* Kuala Lumpur.

Private Sector Program-Ethiopia. 2009. *Increasing Access to TB/HIV Services through Workplace Programs.* Washington, DC: USAID.

Quy, H.T., Lan, N.T.N., Lönnroth, K., Buu, T.N., Dieu, T.T.N., & Hai, L.T. 2003. "Public-Private Mix for Improved TB Control in Ho Chi Minh City, Vietnam: An Assessment of Its Impact on Case Detection." *The International Journal of Tuberculosis and Lung Disease* 7(5): 464–71.

Quy, H.T., Lönnroth, K., Lan, N.T.N., & Buu, T.N. 2003. "Treatment Results among Tuberculosis Patients Treated by Private Lung Specialists Involved in a Public-Private Mix Project in Vietnam." *The International Journal of Tuberculosis and Lung Disease* 7(12): 1139–46.

Sandhu, J. 2011. "Opportunities in Mobile Health." *Stanford Social Innovation Review* Fall: 14–17.

Schlein, K., & Montagu, D. 2012. *Clinical Social Franchising Compendium: An Annual Survey of Programs, 2012.* San Francisco: Global Health Group.

Shah, N.M., Wang, W., & Bishai, D.M. 2011. "Comparing Private-Sector Family Planning Services to Government and NGO Services to Government and NGO Services in Ethiopia and Pakistan: How Do Social Franchises Compare across Quality, Equity, and Cost?" *Health Policy and Planning* 26 Suppl 1: i63–71. https://doi.org/10.1093/heapol/czr027.

Sinanovic, E., & Kumaranayake, L. 2006. "Quality of Tuberculosis Care Provided in Different Models of Public-Private Partnerships in South Africa." *The International Journal of Tuberculosis and Lung Disease* 10(7): 795–801.

Singla, N., Sharma, P.P., & Jain, R.C. 1998. "Survey of Knowledge, Attitudes, and Practices for Tuberculosis among General Practitioners in Delhi, India." *International Journal of Tuberculosis and Lung Disease* 2(5): 384–9.

Stephenson, R., Tsui, A.O., Sulzbach, S., Bardsley, P., Bekele, G., Giday, T., ... Feyesitan, B. 2004. "Reproductive Health in Today's World: Franchising Reproductive Health Services." *Health Services Research* 39(6): 2053–80. https://doi.org/10.1111/j.1475-6773.2004.00332.x.

Tupasi, T.E., Radhakrishna, S., Co, V.M., Villa, M.L.A., Quelapio, M.I.D., & Mangubat, N.V. 2000. "Bacillary Disease and Health-Seeking Behavior among Filipinos with Symptoms of Tuberculosis: Implications for Control." *International Journal of Tuberculosis and Lung Disease* 4(12): 1126–32.

Uplekar, M., Juvekar, S., Morankar, S., Rangan, S., & Nunn, P. 1998. "Tuberculosis Patients and Practitioners in Private Clinics in India." *International Journal of Tuberculosis and Lung Disease* 2(4): 324–9.

Uplekar, M., Pathania, V., & Raviglione, M. 2001. "Private Practitioners and Public Health: Weak Links in Tuberculosis Control." *The Lancet* 358(9285): 912–16. https://doi.org/10.1016/S0140-6736(01)06076-7.

Vyas, R.M., Small, P.M., & Deriemer, K. 2003. "The Private-Public Divide: Impact of Conflicting Perceptions between the Private and Public Health Care Sectors in India." *International Journal of Tuberculosis and Lung Disease* 7(6): 543–9.

Weberg, D. 2009. "Innovation in Healthcare: A Concept Analysis." *Nursing Administration Quarterly* 33(3): 227–37. https://doi.org/10.1097/NAQ .0b013e3181accaf5.

World Health Organization (WHO). 2001. *Involving Private Practitioners in Tuberculosis Control: Issues, Interventions, and Emerging Policy Framework*. Geneva: World Health Organization.

– 2010. *Public-Private Mix for TB Care and Control: A Toolkit*. Geneva: World Health Organization.

– 2012a. *Global Tuberculosis Report 2012*. Geneva: World Health Organization.

– 2012b. *Working Together with Businesses – Guidance on TB and TB/HIV Prevention, Diagnosis, Treatment, and Care in the Workplace*. Geneva: World Health Organization.

– 2013. "Media Centre: Tuberculosis." http://www.who.int/mediacentre/factsheets/ fs104/en/.

– 2017. "WHP Technology." Accessed 8 February 2017. http://worldhealthpartners .org/technology/.

Zafar Ullah, A.N., Huque, H.R., Husain, A., Akter, S., Akter, H., & Newell, J.N. 2012. "Tuberculosis in the Workplace: Developing Partnerships with the Garment Industries in Bangladesh." *International Journal of Tuberculosis and Lung Disease* 16(12): 1637–42. https://doi.org/10.5588/ijtld.12.0378.

Zimic, M., Coronel, J., Gilman, R.H., Giannina, C., Curioso, W.H., & Moore, D.A.J. 2009. "Can the Power of Mobile Phones Be Used to Improve Tuberculosis Diagnosis in Developing Countries?" *Transactions of the Royal Society of Tropical Medicine and Hygiene* 103: 638–40. https://doi.org/10.1016/j.trstmh.2008.10.015.

10 Innovations in Malaria Health Care: Exploring the Evidence on Emerging Practices in Low- and Middle-Income Countries

ONIL BHATTACHARYYA, KATHRYN MOSSMAN,
ANITA MCGAHAN, WILL MITCHELL, JOHN GINTHER,
RAMAN SOHAL, LEIGH HAYDEN, JOHN A. MACDONALD,
HIMANSHU PARIKH, AND ILAN SHAHIN

Introduction

In 2010, there were approximately 219 million cases of malaria and 660,000 deaths, with 3.3 billion people at risk of malaria, particularly children and pregnant women (World Health Organization 2012). Up to 90 per cent of deaths occur in Africa (World Health Organization 2012). Mortality has decreased by 25 per cent in the last decade due to increased coverage of effective strategies like insecticide-treated nets (ITNs) and artemisinin-based combination therapies (ACTs), but most at-risk groups still do not have access to these (World Health Organization 2012; Seidel et al. 2012). The private sector plays a significant role in delivering care in these countries, and many are developing innovative approaches to improve access to efficient, high-quality health care. In this chapter, we describe the current role of the private sector in the care of malaria, and then describe the innovative approaches they use, considering those with evidence as well as emerging approaches. They were identified through a review of malaria programs in the CHMI database along with academic and grey literature on malaria. We conclude with a discussion of how combining innovative activities can increase the potential for programs to achieve health impact and organizational sustainability, while pointing to areas for future research.

Background

The Role of the Private Sector in Delivering Malaria Care

The private sector in low- and middle-income countries (LMICs) is an important provider of health services in the prevention, diagnosis, and treatment of malaria. The global data on the provision of malaria medications by the private sector are striking. For example, worldwide, as much as 50 per cent of antimalarial medications are distributed by the informal private sector (Seidel et al. 2012). Furthermore, an estimated 400 million of the total 550 million treatments delivered in 2006 were distributed through the private sector (Schellenberg 2010). In rural Tanzania, the private sector supplies 58 per cent of antimalarial drugs, mostly through the retail sector, which supplied 39 per cent of all antimalarial drugs (Goodman, Kachur, Abdulla, Bloland, & Mills 2009). The private sector also plays a significant role in providing bed nets and diagnosing and treating malaria. For example, in Kenya, 58 per cent of bed nets are purchased from a private retailer (Noor, Omumbo, Amin, Zurovac, & Snow 2006), and in the malaria-endemic district of Sre Ambel in Cambodia, 22 per cent of residents seek treatment for malaria at private practitioners and 63 per cent seek treatment at drug vendors (Denis 1996; Yeung, Damme, Socheat, White, & Mills 2008). Thus, the private sector is playing an important role in the provision of malaria health care in LMICs.

Malaria at a Glance: Exploring Malaria Program Activities in the CHMI Database

Many private providers of malaria care are innovating in this area, which involves generating new activities that have the potential to drive change and deliver value in health care (Weberg 2009). There are 63 malaria programs in the CHMI database,[1] and they operate in eight regions, most notably East Africa (42; 67 per cent). Most of these programs are private, not-for-profit (40; 63 per cent) (see the appendix to this chapter). Among the 63 programs listed as having a focus on malaria the most frequently reported health market innovations are: consumer education (24; 38 per cent); provider training (23; 37 per cent); information and communication technology (ICT) (16; 25 per cent); social marketing (13; 21 per cent); franchising (11; 17 per cent); and supply chain enhancements (10; 16 per cent).

Malaria can be controlled and even eliminated, but this requires widespread access to effective prevention, diagnosis, and treatment methods and their appropriate use (WHO 2012). Consumer education and social marketing are important tools for increasing health awareness and demand for these products. Also, provider training is necessary to ensure informed practitioners and distributors are available to provide appropriate interventions. ICTs can help monitor the prevalence of malaria to better target interventions and efficiently track the supply of malaria products, while franchising can increase the availability of providers and health services. Finally, supply chain enhancements can improve access to necessary prevention tools and medications by increasing efficiency and widening distribution of these products, while ensuring that they remain affordable through financial and technical support for suppliers and distributors.

Exploring the Evidence on Innovative Malaria Models

Approaches with Evidence: Exploring the Impact of Innovative Models in Malaria

Innovative malaria programs are seeking to increase the quality and availability of health care needed to improve prevention, diagnosis, and treatment of the disease. The innovative models in malaria care in the CHMI database have been reviewed, and some approaches are becoming more widespread and have evidence on their effectiveness in serving LMIC populations.

INCREASING COVERAGE OF ITNS USING SOCIAL MARKETING AND VOUCHERS
Social marketing of ITNs can complement free ITN distribution campaigns to maximize bed net coverage (Schellenberg 2010; Khatib et al. 2008). Social marketing involves selling a branded and subsidized health product, such as ITNs, and using the marketing mix – price, product, place, and promotion – to ensure the product corresponds with consumer values so that they are more likely to purchase and use the product (Seidel et al. 2012). However, financial barriers are one of the largest challenges to accessing ITNs (Heierli & Lengeler 2008), and programs need to take measures to ensure the ITNs are affordable (Agha, Van Rossem, Stallworthy, & Kusanthan 2007). Tanzania National Voucher Scheme (CHMI 2013g) is an example of a program using vouchers to decrease financial barriers to their social marketing of ITNs. Vouchers are distributed to a targeted group and can be presented at a participating retailer to purchase an ITN at a reduced price (Sexton 2011). The combination of vouchers and social marketing of ITNs has most notably occurred in Tanzania and Ghana, with Tanzania expanding this approach on a national scale (de Savigny et al. 2012). Thirteen of CHMI's malaria programs use social marketing to encourage uptake of health products, while five use voucher schemes. One program, the Tanzania National Voucher Scheme, uses both.

Evidence from Tanzania shows that voucher-subsidized, socially marketed ITNs sold through commercial retailers can be combined with free ITN distribution and commercial markets to achieve rapid and sustainable ITN coverage in a poor rural African community (Khatib et al. 2008). This approach has resulted in impressive increases in ITN coverage (Hanson et al. 2009), and can successfully target vulnerable populations with long-term cost-effective distribution of ITNs (Khatib et al. 2008; Mulligan, Yukich, & Hanson 2008). Similar programs have high voucher redemption rates (Mushi 2003; Kweku, Webster, Taylor, Burns, & Dedzo 2007). In one study, 100 per cent of those receiving vouchers used them to purchase nets, and the target population, children under five, had a high ITN usage rate (80 per cent) (Tami et al. 2006). However, there are concerns about relatively low awareness and uptake of voucher schemes, which may miss the poorest households (Tami et al. 2006). In addition, proper supervision to prevent misuse is needed (Sexton 2011).

Example of a Program Reporting Results: Living Goods. This program is a network of franchised community health providers who provide health education and sell health products at affordable prices in Uganda and Kenya. Community health agents are trained to provide basic health counselling on the causes of malaria while encouraging clients to call an agent at the first sign of symptoms. The program also piloted voucher programs to jump-start client demand for priority interventions like mosquito nets. The program reports that its prices are 10–30 per cent below market as a result of its buying power prior to voucher use, resulting in more affordable products to target populations. Living Goods is also currently undergoing a randomized control trial (RCT) to measure the impact of its program on under-five child mortality and morbidity (CHMI 2013b).

INCREASING ACCESS TO MALARIA DIAGNOSIS IN REMOTE REGIONS USING POINT-OF-CARE RAPID DIAGNOSTIC TESTS (RDTS)

Inaccurate diagnosis of malaria can result in presumptive treatment, leading to wasted resources on antimalarials and acceleration of drug resistance (Msellem et al. 2009). As a result, the WHO now recommends parasitological confirmation of malaria through a blood test before treatment (WHO). However, while testing among suspected malaria cases in public facilities has increased from 20 per cent in 2005 to 47 per cent in 2011, a significant portion of those seeking care still do not receive a blood test for malaria (WHO 2012). Expert microscopy is the gold standard for diagnosis, yet many health facilities in poor regions lack microscopes as well as experienced and well-trained microscopists (Tahar et al. 2013). In order to overcome this challenge in remote and resource-constrained areas, some programs are providing malaria diagnosis though the use of rapid diagnostic tests (RDTs), which quickly display results after patients provide a prick of blood on the one-time-use devices. In remote areas where microscopy is unavailable or of poor quality, RDTs can be used as a cost-effective, mobile, and quick approach to diagnosing malaria (Tahar et al. 2013). Five of

CHMI's malaria programs use point-of-care RDTs to quickly diagnose patients in remote settings.

According to the WHO, 155 million malaria RDTs were supplied in 2011, up from 88 million in 2010 (World Health Organization 2012). The RDT market has varying ability to detect different malaria parasites and deliver accurate results. Some RDTs perform well while others can only detect some malaria parasites or are less accurate when samples have low parasite density (Tahar et al. 2013; WHO 2009). A randomized control trial (RCT) conducted in Ghana suggests that in areas where microscopy is not available and patients are diagnosed with malaria based on clinical symptoms, using RDTs leads to a significant reduction of inappropriate prescription of antimalarial medication (Ansah et al. 2010). RDT equipment correctly identifies cases of malaria (high specificity) and while it is more accurate when used by laboratory technicians (Chinkhumba et al. 2010), it can be used safely and effectively by community health workers (Mubi et al. 2011). One-day training for providers can improve testing accuracy and appropriateness of antimalarial drug prescribing (Kyabayinze et al. 2012). Moreover, some research suggests that retail outlets can successfully use RDTs. An intervention study of distributing RDTs to drug stores in a mostly rural area of Uganda found that drug stores wanted to stock RDTs, used and disposed of them properly, and charged a reasonable markup, which led to more appropriate malaria treatment (Cohen et al. 2012).

Example of a Program Reporting Results: Malaria Control in Cambodia (MCC). MCC is a community-based control and prevention project that aims to reduce malaria-related impacts in the western part of Cambodia. It supports and facilitates the training of community health workers on malaria case management including early diagnosis, appropriate treatment, and timely patient referral. In 2011, over 500 health workers in the target areas received training on malaria diagnosis and treatment, and were regularly provided RDTs and drugs from their health centres. Four years after its launch in 2007, the incidence of confirmed malaria cases decreased from 21.6 to 2.5 per 1,000 members of the population in project-supported provinces (CHMI 2013c).

SUBSIDIZING THE SUPPLY OF ACTS: INCREASING ACCESS AND AFFORDABILITY OF NECESSARY MEDICATION

Traditional inexpensive treatments for malaria have become less effective because of growing drug resistance. ACT is now the first-line treatment but it can be up to twenty times more costly than older drugs, so subsidies are needed to reach the poor (Kamat & Nyato 2010). To make the recommended treatment accessible to the poor, malaria programs have pursued efforts to subsidize ACTs and distribute them at a lower cost to the consumer. The Global Fund has established the Affordable Medicines Facility – Malaria (AMFm) (CHMI 2013a), an innovative financing program to expand access to affordable ACTs through price negotiation and subsidy (Adeyi & Atun 2010). This CHMI program has been piloted in eight countries (Cambodia, Ghana, Kenya, Madagascar, Niger, Nigeria, Tanzania, and Uganda). Three other CHMI malaria programs also distribute subsidized ACTs.

The pilot evaluation of the AMFm (Yamey, Schaferho, & Montagu 2012) indicated that ACT availability increased by 20 per cent in six of the eight countries and the price of ACTs was less than three times the price of the most common antimalarial in six of eight countries (AMFm Independent Evaluation Team 2012). In rural Tanzania, the program increased ACT use from 1 per cent to 44 per cent in one year, and ACT costs decreased significantly, to about the level of the previously most popular antimalarial (Sabot, Mwita, Cohen, Ipuge, & Gordon 2009). In Uganda, after one year, ACT use for children under five increased from 10 per cent to 55 per cent and ACT retail markup by the private drug stores was reasonable (Talisuna et al. 2009). Although it is advised that rigorous distribution chain analysis and regulation occur to ensure savings are passed on to consumers (Patouillard, Hanson, & Goodman 2010), this is a promising initiative for reducing mortality and morbidity associated with malaria and decelerating the development of artemisinin resistance.

Example of a Program Reporting Results: PSI South Sudan. This program provides a number of services to address malaria, HIV/AIDS, and child health in the country. This includes the distribution of ITNs and subsidized ACTs in conjunction with local ministries of health, as well as capacity training and support for health workers. In 2010, it provided clinical malaria training to 703 health workers in 107 facilities. Through these efforts, it contributed to 309,794 malaria control disability-adjusted life years in 2010 (CHMI 2013d).

Approaches with Less Evidence: Emerging Models with the Potential for Impact

There are a number of emerging approaches in the delivery of malaria care that show promise, based on limited initial research.

TARGETING WORKERS THROUGH EMPLOYEE MALARIA PROGRAMS

In malaria-endemic areas, some employers are working with health care providers to target workers to reduce malaria incidence and prevalence. Malaria can be costly to employers due to the loss of employee-hours related to illness

(Clinton Health Access Initiative, Rwandan Ministry of Health, African Leaders Malaria Alliance, & Evidence to Policy Initiative 2011), and certain occupations, such as plantation work, tend to put workers at risk for contracting malaria (Satatvipawee, Wongkhang, Pattanasin, Hoithong, & Bhumiratana 2012). Many companies have launched malaria control programs to reap health and economic benefits. Companies such as ExxonMobil, Konkola, and Anglo-Gold Ashanti have implemented ambitious programs to combat malaria, primarily in African countries such as Ghana, Nigeria, Chad, Cameroon, Senegal, and Angola (Ashanti 2009; Kinross 2012). Three of CHMI's malaria programs describe providing malaria prevention, diagnosis, and treatment services for workers.

There is limited academic literature on malaria control programs for employees. One study found that employer-based ITN programs in Kenya are more successful than community-based ITN programs at ITN coverage and retreatment rates (Wacira, Hill, McCall, & Kroger 2007). While available reports from programs in Mozambique, Cameroon, and Ghana show a decrease in malaria cases among workers (Kinross 2012; World Economic Forum 2002) there is a need for more rigorous academic evidence on the health impact of worker-targeted programs on the worker population and the broader community.

Example of a Program Reporting Results: Public Health and Malaria Control (PHMC) Integrated Control Program. This program was launched by PT Freeport Indonesia, a mining company, and LPMAK, a community-based organization, to provide an integrated malaria control program for neighbourhoods where employees reside. All confirmed malaria cases from the workforce and their dependents are treated with ACT drugs at clinics on site. An indoor residual spraying program, targeting all households in the concession, is conducted twice a year. More than 43,000 households were covered in the program during 2011. The same year, approximately 11,700 community-member cases and 3,000 employee cases were detected and treated at company-operated employee and community medical facilities (CHMI 2013e).

DATA COLLECTION AND SURVEILLANCE USING MOBILE DEVICES

Mobile technologies such as mobile phones and tablets are tools that can be used to inexpensively and effectively collect data on patients and malaria incidence. Targeting malaria prevention and treatment interventions requires information on the incidence and prevalence of malaria, which is also necessary for tracking the effectiveness of these interventions (World Health

Organization 2012). On average, national malaria surveillance systems collect data from about 20–5 per cent of private health care facilities, even though in many malaria-endemic areas, people are more likely to seek treatment for malaria from a private sector facility (World Health Organization 2012). Data collection with mobile phones can help private sector programs track this information and contribute to the national malaria surveillance system. Data collection, as a market-based solution to combating malaria, is growing rapidly, and nine CHMI malaria programs collect patient data using mobile devices.

There is little high-quality data on the effectiveness of data collection, which leaders in the field are concerned might inhibit future growth (Schellenberg 2010; Seidel et al. 2012). One study found that a wireless malaria communication system in Uganda required minimal setup and on-going costs, and promoted timely malaria surveillance data (Asiimwe et al. 2011). In addition, some project evaluation suggests that cell phone-based data management systems for malaria can increase reporting timeliness and improve malaria surveillance and epidemic detection (The President's Malaria Initiative 2012). The field requires additional research that elucidates not just whether these programs work, but how they work and their key factors for success.

Example of a Program Reporting Results: Mozambique Health Information System. This pilot program focused on supporting the Ministry of Health in equipping health practitioners with data collection and communication tools. This includes introducing handheld computers with GPS to collect health management information data and map malaria control activities to enhance resource allocation. A cost-effectiveness study found that this model provided a 20 per cent cost saving compared to paper-based epidemiological surveillance data gathering and reporting through the elimination of supply, printing, storage, and transportation costs.

TRACKING THE SUPPLY CHAIN AND DISTRIBUTION OF MALARIA HEALTH
PRODUCTS WITH MOBILE DEVICES

Stock-outs of needed diagnostic tools and medications compromise patient access (Githinji, Kigen, Memusi, Nyandigisi, & Mbithi 2013). Mobile phones can track inventory levels of these medicines and RDTs to decrease the likelihood of stock-outs, which leave health workers without the tools to diagnose malaria and patients without immediate access to treatment. These programs rely on mobile communications to track supply chain inventory levels, normally via SMS. Health workers periodically SMS their stock details to those responsible for managing their supply, allowing for replenishment of depleted items before a stock-out (Barrington, Wereko-Brobby, Ward, Mwafongo, & Kungulwe 2010). Mobile technology can also be used to track bed net distribution efforts, allowing health workers to electronically record the status and location of bed nets during surveys following their distribution. Three CHMI malaria programs use mobile phones to track malaria medications and supplies.

There is some evidence for this approach, which mostly focuses on the SMS for Life program in Tanzania. This program has been successful at reducing stock-outs by using mobile phones to track inventory levels. They reduced stock-outs of one or more weight-specific malarial medication packages by 28 per cent over 26 weeks, and RDT stock-outs fell from 43 per cent to 20 per cent over the same period (Githinji et al. 2013). The program provides an example of efficient and accurate stock management through mobile technologies (Barrington et al. 2010). This approach is promising, and more research is needed to understand how it operates in other contexts and the feasibility of scaling up this activity in resource-constrained settings.

Example of a Program Reporting Results: SMS for Life. This public-private partnership tracked malaria and TB medicines, antibiotics, bed nets, blood supplies, and rapid diagnostic tests in Tanzania. The pilot program worked by sending an SMS to health workers once a week requesting stock information, and sending a reminder SMS the next day if necessary. The system sent this information to the district medical officer, who could re-corder or redistribute stock as needed (Interactive Research and Development & Stop TB Partnership 2012). At the start of the pilot project in 2009, 25 per cent of all health facilities did not have any ACTs in stock, but by the end in 2009, 95 per cent had at least one ACT dosage form in stock (CHMI 2013f).

Evidence Gaps and Research Opportunities in Malaria Health Care

There are many private sector innovations designed to improve malaria health care, including both approaches with evidence and those that still require much more research. Innovative activities may have even more potential when combined in mutually beneficial ways to increase efficiency, quality, and scale. One such example of integration in malaria involves combining supply chain enhancements, provider training, and social marketing. Supply chain enhancements can increase efficiency by reducing costs and speeding up delivery of necessary medical products such as ITNs, RDTs, and ACTs from suppliers to health clinics and retailers. These enhancements can also help to scale up projects by expanding supply chains for wider geographic access. Provider training can increase quality by ensuring providers accurately and appropriately diagnose malaria patients and provide appropriate antimalarial medications. Social marketing can help to create demand for products and services, which is important for scaling up projects, and also improves quality in terms of educating the population about appropriate use of products such as ITNs.

The most frequent innovative activities of antimalarial programs are consumer education, provider training, ICT, social marketing, franchising, and supply chain enhancements. Innovative approaches with some evidence of impact include targeted free distribution of LLINs to pregnant women and children under five, using social marketing and vouchers to increase coverage of ITNs, subsidizing the supply of ACTs, and use of RDTs to diagnose malaria in remote regions. Innovative approaches that are promising but with less evidence include data collection and surveillance with mobile devices, malaria programs targeting workers, and using mobile devices to track the supply chain and distribution of health products. Combining innovative activities like supply chain enhancements, provider training, and social marketing could increase program health impact, but further study is needed to understand what combinations might help control and eventually eliminate malaria on a large scale.

Appendix

Geographic Regions of Malaria Programs

There are 63 malaria programs in the CHMI database operating in eight regions, namely East Africa.

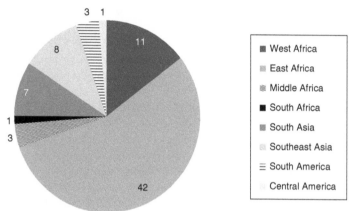

- West Africa
- East Africa
- Middle Africa
- South Africa
- South Asia
- Southeast Asia
- South America
- Central America

Figure 10.A1 Malaria programs by region

Legal Status of Malaria Programs

The largest area of operation for malaria programs in the CHMI database is in the private, not-for-profit sector (40; 63 per cent), followed by public-private partnerships (16; 25 per cent).

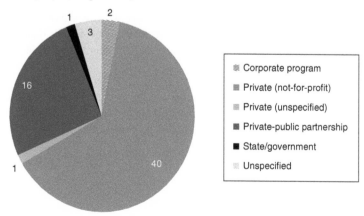

- Corporate program
- Private (not-for-profit)
- Private (unspecified)
- Private-public partnership
- State/government
- Unspecified

Figure 10.A2 Legal status of malaria programs

NOTE

1 This data is drawn from the CHMI database, downloaded on 21 January 2013, from http://healthmarketinnovations.org.

REFERENCES

Adeyi, O., & Atun, R. 2010. "Universal Access to Malaria Medicines: Innovation in Financing and Delivery." *The Lancet* 376(9755): 1869–71. https://doi.org/10.1016/S0140-6736(10)61189-0.

Agha, S., Van Rossem, R., Stallworthy, G., & Kusanthan, T. 2007. "The Impact of a Hybrid Social Marketing Intervention on Inequities in Access, Ownership, and Use of Insecticide-Treated Nets." *Malaria Journal* 6(13). https://doi.org/10.1186/1475-2875-6-13.

AMFm Independent Evaluation Team. 2012. "Independent Evaluation of Phase 1 of the Affordable Medicines Facility-Malaria (AMFm), Multi-Country Independent Evaluation Report: Final Report, September 28, 2012." London.

Ansah, E.K., Narh-Bana, S., Epokor, M., Akanpigbiam, S., Quartey, A.A., Gyapong, J., & Whitty, C.J.M. 2010. "Rapid Testing for Malaria in Settings Where Microscopy Is Available and Peripheral Clinics Where Only Presumptive Treatment Is Available: A Randomised Controlled Trial in Ghana." *BMJ* 340: c930. https://doi.org/10.1136/bmj.c930.

Ashanti, A. 2009. *A National Model for Malaria Control in Ghana. AngloGold Sustainability Review.* Johannesburg.

Asiimwe, C., Gelvin, D., Lee, E., Ben Amor, Y., Quinto, E., Katureebe, C., ... Berg, M. 2011. "Use of an Innovative, Affordable, and Open-Source Short Message Service-Based Tool to Monitor Malaria in Remote Areas of Uganda." *The American Journal of Tropical Medicine and Hygiene* 85(1): 26–33. https://doi.org/10.4269/ajtmh.2011.10-0528.

Barrington, J., Wereko-Brobby, O., Ward, P., Mwafongo, W., & Kungulwe, S. 2010. "SMS for Life: A Pilot Project to Improve Anti-malarial Drug Supply Management in Rural Tanzania Using Standard Technology." *Malaria Journal* 9(298). https://doi.org/10.1186/1475-2875-9-298.

Chinkhumba, J., Skarbinski, J., Chilima, B., Campbell, C., Ewing, V., San Joaquin, M., ... Mathanga, D. 2010. "Comparative Field Performance and Adherence to Test Results of Four Malaria Rapid Diagnostic Tests among Febrile Patients More Than Five Years of Age in Blantyre, Malawi." *Malaria Journal* 9: 209. https://doi.org/10.1186/1475-2875-9-209.

CHMI. 2013a. "Affordable Medicines Facility – Malaria." http://healthmarketinnovations .org/.

CHMI. 2013b. "Living Goods." Retrieved 6 August 2013. http://healthmarketinnovations.org/.

CHMI. 2013c. "Malaria Control in Cambodia." Retrieved 13 February 2013. http:// healthmarketinnovations.org/.

CHMI. 2013d. "PSI South Sudan." http://healthmarketinnovations.org/.

CHMI. 2013e. "Public Health and Malaria Control (PHMC) Integrated Program." http://healthmarketinnovations.org/.

CHMI. 2013f. "SMS for Life." http://healthmarketinnovations.org/.

CHMI. 2013g. "Tanzania National Voucher Scheme." http://healthmarketinnovations .org/.

Clinton Health Access Initiative, Rwandan Ministry of Health, African Leaders Malaria Alliance, & Evidence to Policy Initiative. 2011. "Maintaining the Gains in Global Malaria Control." New York.

Cohen, J., Fink, G., Berg, K., Aber, F., Jordan, M., Maloney, K., & Dickens, W. 2012. "Feasibility of Distributing Rapid Diagnostic Tests for Malaria in the Retail Sector: Evidence from an Implementation Study in Uganda." *PloS One* 7(11): e48296. https://doi.org/10.1371/journal.pone.0048296.

de Savigny, D., Webster, J., Agyepong, I.A., Mwita, A., Bart-Plange, C., Baffoe-Wilmot, A., ... Lengeler, C. 2012. "Introducing Vouchers for Malaria Prevention in Ghana and Tanzania: Context and Adoption of Innovation in Health Systems." *Health Policy and Planning* 27(Suppl 4): 32–43. https://doi.org/10.1093/heapol/czs087.

Denis, M.B. 1996. "Improving Compliance with Quinine and Tetracycline for Treatment of Malaria: Evaluation of Health Education Interventions in Cambodian Villages." *Bulletin of the World Health Organization* 76(Suppl 1): 43–9.

Githinji, S., Kigen, S., Memusi, D., Nyandigisi, A., & Mbithi, A.M. 2013. "Reducing Stock-outs of Life-Saving Malaria Commodities Using Mobile Phone Text Messaging: SMS for Life Study in Kenya." *PLoS One* 8(1): e54066. https://doi.org/ 10.1371/journal.pone.0054066.

Goodman, C., Kachur, S.P., Abdulla, S., Bloland, P., & Mills, A. 2009. "Concentration and Drug Prices in the Retail Market for Malaria Treatment in Rural Tanzania." *Health Economics* 18(6): 727–42. https://doi.org/10.1002/hec.1473.

Hanson, K., Marchant, T., Nathan, R., Mponda, H., Jones, C., Bruce, J., ... Schellenberg, J. a. 2009. "Household Ownership and Use of Insecticide-treated Nets among Target Groups after Implementation of a National Voucher Program in the United Republic of Tanzania: Plausibility Study Using Three Annual Cross-Sectional Household Surveys." *BMJ* 339: b2434. https://doi.org/10.1136/bmj.b2434.

Heierli, U., & Lengeler, C. 2008. *Should Bednets Be Sold or Given Free? The Role of the Private Sector in Malaria Control. Poverty Allieviation as a Business Series.* Berne: Swiss Agency for Development and Cooperation.

Interactive Research and Development, & Stop TB Partnership. 2012. *mHealth to Improve TB Care.* Geneva.

Kamat, V.R., & Nyato, D.J. 2010. "Soft Targets or Partners in Health? Retail Pharmacies and Their Role in Tanzania's Malaria Control Program." *Social Science and Medicine* 71(3): 626–33. https://doi.org/10.1016/j.socscimed.2010.04.016.

Khatib, R.A., Killeen, G.F., Abdulla, S.M.K., Kahigwa, E., McElroy, P.D., Gerrets, R.P.M., ... Kachur, S.P. 2008. "Markets, Voucher Subsidies, and Free Nets Combine to Achieve High Bed Net Coverage in Rural Tanzania." *Malaria Journal* 7(98). https://doi.org/10.1186/1475-2875-7-98.

Kinross. 2012. "Case Study 06: The Chirano Malaria Control Program." http://takingresponsibility2011.kinross.com/health-and-safety/case-study-06-the-chirano-malaria-control-program.

Kweku, M., Webster, J., Taylor, I., Burns, S., & Dedzo, M. 2007. "Public-Private Delivery of Insecticide Treated Nets: A Voucher Scheme in Volta Region, Ghana." *Malaria Journal* 6(14). https://doi.org/10.1186/1475-2875-6-14.

Kyabayinze, D.J., Asiimwe, C., Nakanjako, D., Nabakooza, J., Bajabaite, M., Strachan, C., ... Van Geetruyden, J.P. 2012. "Program-Level Implementation of Malaria Rapid Diagnostic Tests (RDTs) Use: Outcomes and Cost of Training Health Workers at Lower Level Health Care Facilities in Uganda." *BMC Public Health* 12(1): 291. https://doi.org/10.1186/1471-2458-12-291.

Msellem, M.I., Mårtensson, A., Rotllant, G., Bhattarai, A., Strömberg, J., Kahigwa, E., ... Björkman, A. 2009. "Influence of Rapid Malaria Diagnostic Tests on Treatment and Health Outcome in Fever Patients, Zanzibar: A Crossover Validation Study." *PLoS Medicine* 6(4): e1000070. https://doi.org/10.1371/journal.pmed.1000070.

Mubi, M., Janson, A., Warsame, M., Martensson, A., Kallender, K., Petzold, M.G., ... Bjorkman, A. 2011. "Malaria Rapid Testing by Community Health Workers Is Effective and Safe for Targeting Malaria Treatment: Randomised Cross-over Trial in Tanzania." *PLoS One* 6(7): e19753. https://doi.org/10.1371/journal.pone.0019753.

Mulligan, J.-A., Yukich, J., & Hanson, K. 2008. "Costs and Effects of the Tanzanian National Voucher Scheme for Insecticide-treated Nets." *Malaria Journal* 7: 32. https://doi.org/10.1186/1475-2875-7-32.

Mushi, A.K. 2003. "Targeted Subsidy for Malaria Control with Treated Nets Using a Distant Voucher System in Tanzania." *Health Policy and Planning* 18(2): 163–71. https://doi.org/10.1093/heapol/czg021.

Noor, A.M., Omumbo, J.A., Amin, A.A., Zurovac, D., & Snow, R.W. 2006. "Wealth, Mother's Education, and Physical Access as Determinants of Retail Sector Net Use in Rural Kenya." *Malaria Journal* 5(5). https://doi.org/10.1186/1475-2875-5-5.

Patouillard, E., Hanson, K.G., & Goodman, C.A. 2010. "Retail Sector Distribution Chains for Malaria Treatment in the Developing World: A Review of the Literature." *Malaria Journal* 9(50). https://doi.org/10.1186/1475-2875-9-50.

Sabot, O.J., Mwita, A., Cohen, J.M., Ipuge, Y., & Gordon, M. 2009. "Piloting the Global Subsidy: The Impact of Subsidized Artemisinin-Based Combination Therapies Distributed through Private Drug Shops in Rural Tanzania." *PLoS One* 4(9): e6857. https://doi.org/10.1371/journal.pone.0006857.

Satatvipawee, P., Wongkhang, W., Pattanasin, S., Hoithong, P., & Bhumiratana, A. 2012. "Predictors of Malaria-Association with Rubber-Plantations in Thailand." *BMC Public Health* 12(1): 1115. https://doi.org/10.1186/1471-2458-12-1115.

Schellenberg, D. 2010. *The Control of Malaria 2005–15: Progress and Priorities towards Eradication.* London: The All Party Parliamentary Group on Malaria and Neglected Tropical Diseases.

Seidel, R., Pennas, T., Kovach, T., Kim, P., Divine, B., Alilio, M., ... Choi, P. 2012. *The Strategic Framework for Malaria Communication at the Country Level.* 2012–17. Geneva: World Health Organization.

Sexton, A.R. 2011. "Best Practices for an Insecticide-treated Bed Net Distribution Program in Sub-Saharan Eastern Africa." *Malaria Journal* 10(1): 157. https://doi.org/10.1186/1475-2875-10-157.

Tahar, R., Sayang, C., Ngane Foumane, V., Soula, G., Moyou-Somo, R., Delmont, J., & Basco, L.K. 2013. "Field Evaluation of Rapid Diagnostic Tests for Malaria in Yaounde, Cameroon." *Acta Tropica* 125(2): 214–19. https://doi.org/10.1016/j.actatropica.2012.10.002.

Talisuna, A., Grewal, P., Rwakimari, J.B., Mukasa, S., Jagoe, G., & Benerji, J. 2009. "Cost Is Killing Patients: Subsidizing Effective Antimalarials." *The Lancet* 374(9697): 1224–6. https://doi.org/10.1016/S0140-6736(09)61767-0.

Tami, A., Mbati, J., Nathan, R., Mponda, H., Lengeler, C., & Schellenberg, J.R.M.A. 2006. "Use and Misuse of a Discount Voucher Scheme as a Subsidy for Insecticide-treated Nets for Malaria Control in Southern Tanzania." *Health Policy and Planning* 21(1): 1–9. https://doi.org/10.1093/heapol/czj005.

The President's Malaria Initiative. 2012. "The President's Malaria Initiative: Sixth Annual Report to Congress, April 2012." Washington, DC.

Wacira, D.G., Hill, J., McCall, P.J., & Kroger, A. 2007. "Delivery of Insecticide-Treated Net Services through Employer and Community-Based Approaches in Kenya." *Tropical Medicine and International Health* 12(1): 140–9. https://doi.org/10.1111/j.1365-3156.2006.01759.x.

Weberg, D. 2009. "Innovation in Healthcare: A Concept Analysis." *Nursing Administration Quarterly* 33(3): 227–37. https://doi.org/10.1097/NAQ.0b013e3181accaf5.

World Economic Forum. 2002. *Global Health Initiative, Exxon Mobil Malaria Private Sector Intervention Case Example.* Geneva.

World Health Organization (WHO). 2009. "Malaria: Evaluation of Rapid Diagnostic Tests." *WHO Drug Information* 23(3): 227–8. apps.who.int/medicinedocs/documents/s17560en/s17560en.pdf.
– 2012. *World Malaria Report 2012.* Geneva: World Heath Organization. https://doi.org/10.1071/EC12504.
Yamey, G., Schaferho, M., & Montagu, D. 2012. "Piloting the Affordable Medicines Facility Malaria: What Will Success Look Like?" *Bulletin of the World Health Organization* 90(6): 452–60.
Yeung, S., Damme, W.V., Socheat, D., White, N.J., & Mills, A. 2008. "Access to Artemisinin Combination Therapy for Malaria in Remote Areas of Cambodia." *Malaria Journal* 7(96). https://doi.org/10.1186/1475-2875-7-96.

11 Innovative Practices in Global Health to Manage Diabetes Mellitus

HIMANSHU PARIKH, ONIL BHATTACHARYYA,
ANITA MCGAHAN, WILL MITCHELL, KATHRYN MOSSMAN,
LEIGH HAYDEN, JOHN A. MACDONALD, ILAN SHAHIN,
JOHN GINTHER, AND RAMAN SOHAL

Introduction

Diabetes has traditionally been viewed as a disease of rich countries, but prevalence estimates show that four out of five people with diabetes live in low- and middle-income countries (LMICs). Of the 3.6 billion adults living in LMICs in 2011, 291 million have diabetes compared to 75 million in high-income countries (HICs) (The World Bank 2011). People with diabetes require at least two to three times the health care resources compared to people who do not have diabetes, and diabetes care may account for up to 15 per cent of national health care budgets (Zhang et al. 2010). We need novel approaches to manage the high prevalence of chronic disease, including diabetes (WHO, 2010), in low-resource settings, especially if we were to achieve the World Health Assembly's goal of reducing avoidable mortality from non-communicable diseases (NCDs) by 25 per cent by 2025 (the 25 by 25 goal; Horton 2013).

There is significant private provision of health care in LMICs, and novel approaches to overcome barriers to care are being developed by a range of organizations to provide affordable and high-quality services in a sustainable fashion (Berelowitz, Horn, Thorton, Leeds, & Wong 2013; World health statistics 2012). These organizations have generated great interest among governments, donors, and private investors as well. One area where the private sector may contribute is as a source of disruptive innovations, which are simpler and cheaper services or programs that enable the participation of new sets of consumers previously excluded from conventional markets (Hwang & Christensen 2008). It is hypothesized that such local-context-led innovative practices from LMICs are more likely to be replicable and scalable in low-resource settings (Berelowitz et al. 2013; CHMI 2012; Richman, Udayakumar, Mitchell, & Schulman 2008).

This study aims to identify practices employed by innovative LMIC programs to address the rise of diabetes in low-resource settings. It further maps them onto the Chronic Care Model (CCM), an approach developed in the US to redesign health care organizations and practice to improve the quality of care (Wagner 1998), and which has been shown to improve the management of chronic disease (Tsai, Morton, Mangione, & Keeler 2005). It is unclear whether this model has been adapted to address and prevent the future burden of diabetes complications in low-resource settings.

Methods

This study uses a case series methodology to systematically identify innovative health care programs from LMICs. The Center for Health Market Innovations (CHMI), managed by the Results for Development Institute, is a collaborative project to catalogue innovative organizations in LMICs. CHMI maintains a programs database in which they identify programs and policies, analyse promising new models, and connect program managers with potential funders and other partners (CHMI 2012). CHMI's partner organizations in 16 LMICs help to identify innovative programs for the database, and programs can also be suggested by program managers or members of the public, which will then be reviewed by these regional partners. The CHMI database is the largest source of information about health market innovations from over 120 countries, and it provides an initial base for assessing the effectiveness of programs operating in LMICs (Thorton 2013).

Using the CHMI database, information on innovative diabetes programs was extracted and matched to identifier fields in an existing performance-measurement tool known as the Toronto Health Organization Performance Evaluation (T-HOPE) framework (Bhattacharyya et al. 2015). The T-HOPE framework was synthesized using the CHMI's reported-results framework and incorporates elements from other performance measurement frameworks in health services and management literature (Bhattacharyya et al. 2015). It includes 14 performance categories and seven descriptive categories that are useful for building profiles of programs and understanding the contexts in which they operate. The indicators are grouped into the domains of Health Status (including health output and outcome), Health Access (affordability, availability, and pro-poor targeting), and Operations/Delivery (including efficiency and quality indicators) (Bhattacharyya et al. 2015). The program profile and information available in the database was further supplemented with data from other publicly available sources, including program websites and reports, journal articles, and news websites. This additional data was likewise classified and entered into the respective fields of the T-HOPE framework. Next, the innovative practices employed by these programs were identified and then catalogued using the Innovative Practices Framework developed by the T-HOPE team (table 11.1) (Bhattacharyya, McGahan, & Mitchell 2012). This framework was created by combining elements of existing frameworks on business process innovations in LMIC health care (Bhattacharyya et al. 2010), the Monitor Group's 17 business models (Kubzansky, Cooper, & Barbary 2011), and health market innovations identified by CHMI (2012). Definitions for each of the innovative practices were then tested on 80 different organizations from the CHMI database in order to revise categories and definitions to ensure they reflected a wide range of activities from organizations working in various health sectors in LMICs.

Later, their frequency of use across programs was analysed, followed by their evaluation using the CCM. The CCM identifies a cluster of practice and system changes. These elements are personal skills and self-management support, delivery system design, provider decision support, information systems, community partnerships, and health care organization and leadership (Wagner 1998). This was followed by a review of the reported performance of the identified programs, which was then correlated with their use of innovative practices.

Results

The CHMI database consisted of 1155 reported programs when it was downloaded on 5 September 2012. From the subset of 46 programs identified as having a focus on chronic disease, 20 programs specifically described managing diabetes mellitus. From these 20 programs, one program (Dream Trust)

Table 11.1 Innovative practices framework

Innovative Practices	
1. Social Marketing	16. mHealth (Mobile Health)
2. Tailoring Services to the Poor	17. Health Outreach
3. Vouchers	18. Distribution through Direct Sales Force
4. Mobile Money	19. Distribution through Informal Shops
5. Microinsurance	20. Distribution through Shared Channels
6. Microcredit	21. Network
7. Franchising	22. Supply Chain Enhancements
8. High-Volume Low-Unit Cost	23. Policy Development
9. Specialization	24. Chain
10. Cross-Subsidization	25. Integrated Delivery System
11. Capital Funding	26. Government Health Insurance
12. Generating Revenue	27. Contracting
13. Provider Training	28. Monitoring Standards
14. Process and Product Re-engineering	29. Pay for Performance
15. Paraskilling	30. Health Awareness/Education

was excluded as it reported using donations to provide free insulin to children with Type 1 diabetes, and did not describe using any other innovative practices. Organization-wide uses of innovative practices are depicted in table 11.2.

The innovative practices employed by the programs spanned a broad spectrum of clinical and screening activities, patient education, day-to-day management, and interventions to address diabetic complications. For example, Dr Mohan's Diabetes Specialities Centre offers services across the clinical spectrum. Specific innovative practices used by these programs (table 11.2), catalogued according to the list of 30 innovations (table 11.1), are represented in table 11.3.

Table 11.2 Innovative practices employed by the programs

Program/ Organization	Country	Innovative Practices
GlicOnline	Brazil	Online insulin dose calculation (provides caloric content of locally available foods) and use of mobile technology for patient monitoring and follow-up by physicians
Afya Njema	Kenya	Use of tourists (Kenyans and other nationals) to assist with diabetes screening
Amcare	Bangladesh	Call centres staffed with physicians and nurses to respond to patient queries; patients, providers, and partners linked by a common communication platform; standardized treatment protocols/algorithms
Chinese Aged Diabetic Assistant (CADA)	China	Online games for educational purposes and use of interactive games on mobile devices for consistent self-monitoring and reporting
Diabetes care in Nairobi slums	Kenya	Use of existing facilities to provide outreach care in slums
Diabetic foot care Kenya	Kenya	Use of existing clinic and mobile units to screen patients and train other health professionals; use of standardized treatment protocols/algorithms
Mobile phones for health monitoring	India	Miniaturizing sensors for remote monitoring of ECG, blood pressure, and blood glucose relayed over mobile devices
Peer education network	Cambodia	Use of peer groups to educate patients
Text Messaging for Health	South Africa	Text messaging by peers to build healthy lifestyles

(Continued)

Table 11.2 Concluded

Program/ Organization	Country	Innovative Practices
Arogya World Diabetes SMS services	India	Text messages that educate consumers, initially provided free for six months
Clinicas Del Azucar	Mexico	Low-cost screening followed by fixed-cost monthly subscription for unlimited access to diagnostic and consultative services; use of mobile technology for physician monitoring and follow-up; standardized treatment protocols/algorithms
Project Oral Health for Juvenile Diabetics	Philippines	Standardized treatment protocols/ algorithms; use of post-graduate paediatric dentistry students to screen and educate children with diabetes mellitus
Dr Mohan's Diabetes Specialities Centre	India	Use of standardized treatment protocols, mobile telemedicine for rural outreach, community health workers, a clinical team approach, and a common communication platform linking providers and patients
M-Afya Kiosks	Kenya	Rural health kiosks equipped with Android phones for consulting with specialists and to relay patient data
D-Tree International	India, Malawi, South Africa, Tanzania	Mobile devices operated by community health workers with eAlgorithms linked to centralized patient records, which also track longitudinal data; standardized treatment protocols/algorithms
MediNet	Trinidad, Tobago	Centralized database with reasoning engines that flag for follow-up visits or phone calls to patients
MiDoctor	Chile	Automated monitoring and promotion of self-care by providing a timely diagnosis, centralized patient records, automated calls, and reminders via text messaging (SMS); standardized treatment protocols/algorithms
UHAI	Kenya	Combined screening for diabetes, hypertension, and cervical cancer
ClinEval – Chronic Disease Evaluation and Management	Egypt	Use of proprietary algorithms to risk stratify patients for diabetes/cardiovascular disease and offer patient-specific, holistic solutions

Table 11.3 Profiles of innovative practices employed by organizations

Programs	Innovative Practices (Strategy Codes)																													
	1	2	3	4	5	6	7	8	9	10	11	12	13	14	15	16	17	18	19	20	21	22	23	24	25	26	27	28	29	30
GlicOnline																														
Afya Njema													■	■		■	■													■
Amcare														■		■														■
CADA																														
Diabetes care Nairobi														■			■			■										■
Diabetic foot care																■									■					
Mobile phones																■														■
Peer educators					■							■									■									■
Text messaging																■														■
Arogya World SMS									■							■														■
Clinicas Del Azucar		■																				■	■		■			■		■
Project Oral Health														■		■									■					■
Dr Mohan's		■					■	■			■	■		■	■															■
M-Afya Kiosks				■															■											■
D-Tree International														■										■						■
MediNet														■																■
MiDoctor																■														■
UHAI																				■										■
ClinEval	■																													

Individual programs reported between one to ten innovations from the list. Two of the programs (Dr Mohan's and Clinicas Del Azucar) use 10 distinct innovations to re-engineer their business processes. Furthermore, almost all the programs had health awareness/education as one of their practices.

Figure 11.1 depicts the frequency of use of particular innovative practices in the group of 19 organizations (only if utilized by > 20 per cent of reporting programs). Health awareness/education (16), Process and product re-engineering (13) and mobile health (mHealth) (10) are the most commonly employed innovative practices; seven out of 19 organizations reported the combined use of these three innovative practices.

The uses of specific innovations were also extracted from the reported list of innovative practices in table 11.2 and mapped onto the CCM across the domains of Self-management support (SMS), Delivery system design (DSD), Clinical decision support system (CDSS) and Clinical information system (CIS). The results of this mapping are shown in table 11.4.

The CCM domains used by programs were analysed to better understand the distribution of their use. As shown in table 11.5, eight out of 19 programs reported the use of more than one of the CCM domains. DSD (13) was the most frequently reported, and CIS (3) the least. Five programs incorporated two domains and the remaining three have incorporated three or four CCM domains.

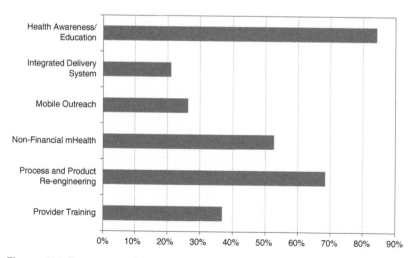

Figure 11.1 Frequency of innovative practices employed by programs targeting diabetes care in the CHMI database

Table 11.4 Innovative practices classified across the CCM model

CCM Model Domains	Sub-domains	Innovation	CHMI Organizations
Self-management support	Non-interactive	Text messaging	Arogya World Text Messaging for Health
		Online caloric content of foods	GlicOnline
		Automated phone calls	MiDoctor
	Interactive	Online games for education	CADA
		Use of peers	Peer education network – Cambodia
		Food intake and insulin dose calculations	GlicOnline
		Call centres staffed with physicians	Amcare
Delivery system design	Task-shifting	Use of community health workers	D-Tree International
		Use of tourists for screening	Dr Mohan's
	Innovative patient interactions	Using interactive games for monitoring and reporting	Afya Njema CADA
		Monitoring and follow-up by using mobile technology	GlicOnline Clinicas Del Azucar
	Integrating services at the point of delivery	For diabetes, hypertension, and cervical cancer	UHAI
		Use of existing clinics to enhance access	Diabetic foot care Kenya Diabetes care – Nairobi slums
	Remote monitoring	Use of microsensors to monitor blood glucose, ECG, blood pressure	Mobile phones for health monitoring

(Continued)

Table 11.4 Concluded

CCM Model Domains	Sub-domains	Innovation	CHMI Organizations
	Rural outreach	Rural kiosks with Android phones	M-Afya kiosks
	Fixed cost subscription	Diagnostic and consultative services	Clinicas Del Azucar
	Networking and integration of care	Patients, providers, partners linked on common communication platform	Amcare Dr Mohan's
		Use of mobile devices linked with centralized patient records	D-Tree International MiDoctor
Clinical decision support system	Use of treatment algorithms/ protocols	Management and prevention of complications	Diabetic foot care Kenya Amcare Project Oral Health Dr Mohan's
		Day-to-day management	D-Tree International ClinEval MiDoctor Clinicas Del Azucar
Clinical information system		Central database with capacity to identify specific patients in need of care	MediNet MiDoctor D-Tree International

Using the T-HOPE framework, performance reporting by the 19 programs was also analysed to explore their impact in terms of efficiency, quality, utilization, and access. Table 11.6 displays these results.

Given the limited performance data on programs, it is difficult to arrive at robust conclusions on program impact or provide performance comparisons across programs or other settings (table 11.6). Out of the six programs that reported performance data, only three (Amcare, GlicOnline, and Diabetic foot

Table 11.5 Innovative practices profiled across the CCM model by program

Program	Number of CCM domains	SMS	DSD	CDSS	CIS
GlicOnline	2	■	■		
Afya Njema	1		■		
Amcare	3	■	■	■	
CADA	2	■	■		
Diabetes care in Nairobi	1		■		
Diabetic foot care	2		■	■	
Mobile phones	1		■		
Peer educators	1	■			
Text Messaging	1	■			
Arogya World SMS	1	■			
Clinicas Del Azucar	2			■	■
Project Oral Health	1			■	
Dr Mohan's	2		■	■	
M-Afya Kiosks	1		■		
D-Tree International	3		■	■	■
MediNet	1		■		
MiDoctor	4	■	■	■	■
UHAI	1		■		
ClinEval	1			■	
Total		7	13	8	3

care) reported their health outcomes, but none used standard measures of diabetes quality of care or outcomes. Another organization (Clinicas Del Azucar) has reported improvements in access to diabetes care and achieved 60 per cent reduction in the cost to their patients, making its services more affordable.

Discussion

Impact of CCM Components

This study describes 19 innovative health programs managing diabetes in LMICs and profiles their innovative practices. Some mature programs use up to 10 different practices with the aim of re-engineering their processes to add value for the patients they treat. The programs use a range of innovative practices, which can be mapped to the CCM domains, but there is very little data on their impact. Further, they have incorporated the components of the CCM in

Table 11.6 Performance reporting by diabetes-focused organizations

Program	Performance Reported
	Efficiencies
GlicOnline	Time required to adjust insulin dose reduced from 6 months to 1 month
Peer educators	Patients as diabetes educators led to their own enhanced diabetic control
	Quality – Health Outcome
GlicOnline	94% patients reported improvement in lifestyle 68% felt happier and 84% reported more flexibility in their diet Treatment success rate – 9.6/10
Amcare	62% of irregular patients had improved compliance following education and home monitoring 61.2% had reduced hospital/doctor visits (from 5–6 per to 1–2 per year)
Diabetic foot clinic	1835 feet were saved
	Quality – Clinical Quality
Dr Mohan's Diabetes Centre	Use of standardized clinical protocols, and training and performance monitoring of clinical staff
	Access
Clinicas del Azucar	Reduction in annual treatment costs by 60% from US$750 to US$250 Increased availability – 95% of patients treated in 2 months received treatment for the first time

various combinations. Most have incorporated only one of the CCM domains into their programs, while others have incorporated them in various combinations, with DSD being the most common domain.

As most of the programs in the data set have not reported their performance accurately, it is difficult to comment on the relationship between the use of innovative practices across various CCM components and the impact on quality of care and patient outcomes. Previous studies have yielded mixed results on this topic. For example, Si and colleagues (2005), studying Aboriginal health centres in Australia, found that DSD and CIS were independently associated with the quality of diabetes care. Sperl-Hillen and colleagues (2004) found that only DSD was significantly correlated with better diabetes outcomes in clinics that were part of a large health care system. In the present study it was the most frequently used CCM domain. Thirteen programs in the data set reported using DSD either in isolation or in combinations with other CCM domains. An example of a delivery system includes specialist outreach clinics that are used by programs such as M-Afya kiosks and Dr Mohan's Diabetes Centre to reach a wider patient population.

Two others domains, SMS and CIS, have elsewhere "demonstrated associations that may have substantive significance" (Sperl-Hillen et al. 2004). However, only three programs out of 19 reported using CIS, and this mirrors the findings of a recent report on replicable delivery models from LMICs, which concluded that "delivery models based on Information and Communication Technology (ICT) are the last mature of all the models examined" (Berelowitz et al. 2013). The literature also shows mixed results on the CDSS component, used by eight out of 19 evaluated programs. In a recent systematic review and meta-analysis, Jeffery, Iserman and Haynes (2012) concluded that all trials favoured the CDSS over the control, although none were statistically significant. CDSS may marginally improve clinical outcomes, however this evidence may carry the risk of bias, inconsistency, and imprecision. In another systemic review by Roshanov et al. (2011) investigating the decision-maker/researcher partnership, the authors discovered that while the CDSS impacted the process and surrogate patient outcomes, factors of interest to decision-makers (e.g., cost, user satisfaction, system interface and feature sets, unique design and deployment characteristics, and effects on user workflow) were rarely investigated or reported. There remains an ongoing need for well-designed investigations evaluating the role and feasibility of technological interventions (customized to each LMIC's locality) in clinical decision-making for diabetes care (Ali, Shah, & Tandon 2011). On the basis of this evidence, it may be concluded that at present there's no sufficient data to recommend CDSS technologies for replication or scale up in other settings.

Still, much of the literature in this area reports that composite measures of CCM implementations are significantly associated with either improvements in or higher levels of quality of care as measured by process or outcome measures. For example, Parchman, Zeber, Romero, and Pugh (2007) found that glycated haemoglobin (HbA1c) scores and ten-year risk of heart disease were lowest in patients with diabetes whose primary care conformed most to the CCM. In a Cochrane review investigating interventions to improve the management of diabetes mellitus in primary care, outpatient, and community settings, the reviewers noted that a combination of professional interventions improved process outcomes (Renders et al. 2001). However, the effect on patient outcomes remained less clear as these were rarely assessed. They concluded that multifaceted professional interventions have the potential to enhance the performance of health professionals in managing patients with diabetes. Organizational interventions that improve regular prompted recall and review of patients (patients contacted through central computerized tracking systems or nurses) may also improve diabetes management (Renders et al. 2001).

Impact of Innovative Health Care Practices

To our knowledge, this study is the first case series analysing diabetes programs in the largest publicly available data set of innovative health programs operating in LMICs. It provides a broad perspective on the innovative activities of these programs and how they are performing, whereas previous reports focus on isolated organizations as individual case studies (CHMI 2012). Furthermore, the current study uses an a priori defined comprehensive and practical Innovative Practices Framework to catalogue the reported innovations from these programs.

This study highlights several interesting innovations employed by health care programs in LMIC's. This includes the use of interactive games and text messaging to create patient engagement, the use of standard algorithms and clinical decision support systems to promote adherence to guidelines, and the employment of remote consultations and specialist outreach clinics for specific populations. The evidence on effectiveness of these innovations tends to be limited. For example, interactive games have been used by programs such as Chinese Aged Diabetic Assistant (CADA) to enhance self-management support and for diabetes educational purposes (Talbot 2011). One study compared a control group to diabetes education using interactive multimedia to improve knowledge, control, and self-care among people in Taiwan with diabetes and concluded that the use of an interactive multimedia device was effective only in raising the subjects' knowledge about the disease, but it did not impact the blood sugar level at the end of three months (Huang, Chen, & Yeh 2009). Interventions show promise of increasing adherence; however, there is a lack of sufficient data to recommend this innovative practice for replication or scale up in other settings. In our data set, Chinese Aged Diabetic Assistant (CADA) was the only program to use interactive games to engage patients to enhance self-management support.

Remote consultations may also be promising, but more evidence is needed. The Cochrane Effective Practice and Organisation of Care (EPOC) review assessed the effects of telephone consultation on safety, service usage, and patient satisfaction. It discovered that three of five studies found a decrease in visits to general practitioners while two studies found a significant increase in return consultations. The authors concluded that telephone consultations reduce the number of surgery contacts and off-hours visits by general practitioners;

however, questions remain about its effect on service use. Three programs (Amcare, Dr Mohan's Diabetes Centre, and Clinicas del Azucar) in the current study have utilized remote consultations to enhance patient interactions.

The use of specialist outreach clinics can be particularly useful in providing access to a wider patient population. A review was undertaken to assess the effectiveness of specialist outreach clinics on access, quality, health outcomes, patient satisfaction, use of services, and costs (Gruen, Weeramanthri, Knight, & Bailie 2004). Simple shifted outpatients styles of specialist outreach were shown to improve access, but without any evidence of impact on health outcomes. In contrast, specialist outreach alongside collaboration with primary care, education, or other services was associated with improved health outcomes, more efficient and guideline-consistent care, and less use of inpatient services. Due to the fact that most comparative studies used urban non-disadvantaged populations in developed countries, there remains a need for good comparative studies of outreach in rural and disadvantaged settings where outreach may confer most benefit to access and health outcomes. Two programs (M-Afya kiosks and Dr Mohan's Diabetes Centre) in the current study have made use of outreach clinics to provide access to a wider patient population.

The use of text messaging has also been found to have the potential to create health impacts, and two programs (Arogya World Diabetes SMS Service and Text Messaging for Health) in the current study have used text messaging for enhancing self-managing support. In a pilot study to evaluate the effect of text messaging in Diabetes Buddies, a peer support group, mobile phones were considered an easy and reliable method of peer support and a mean of disseminating health messages. However, while members' attendance at meetings increased and the level of positive action and social support coping increased, their blood glucose levels increased by 3.3 points (Rotheram-Borus et al. 2012). In another study evaluating the impact of text messaging, participants reported increased social support, feelings that the program "made them accountable [for their health]," and increased awareness of health information. Furthermore, they demonstrated increased compliance to provide glucose readings when prompted (Fischer et al. 2012). In a study evaluating a mobile health intervention for inner-city patients with poorly controlled diabetes (TExT-MED program), Arora, Peters, Agy, and Menchie (2012) concluded that the program demonstrated increased healthy behaviours, improved self-efficacy and medication adherence, and received excellent satisfaction scores in resource-poor, inner-city patients with diabetes, but made no reference to impact on glycemic control. Further, in a meta-analysis studying the effect of mobile phone intervention for diabetes on glycemic control, Liang et al. (2011) concluded that mobile phone interventions for diabetes self-management reduced HbA1c values by a mean of 0.5 per cent over a median of six months of follow-up, although this did not differ significantly from other intervention strategies. While these studies are informative, to date there has been no formal study to evaluate the efficiency of this intervention in low-resource settings, and important contextual factors such as language, length, and frequency of messages may need consideration while designing such programs. Two programs (Arogya World Diabetes SMS Service and Text Messaging for Health) in the data set have used text messaging for enhancing self-management support.

Limitations and Recommendations

While the evidence on the effectiveness, efficiency, and scalability or replicability of these innovations has not been conclusive, there is some evidence that these innovations can improve diabetes management, and it may be worthwhile to replicate or scale up in specific populations. Many of the innovative practices identified in this study have the potential for scale up across different contexts in LMICs and perhaps even in high-income settings. There are very high rates of diabetes among aboriginal populations in the United States, Canada, Australia, and New Zealand (United Nations 2009). These groups often live in remote areas with limited resources and may benefit from reverse innovations where LMIC practices are introduced in high-income settings. Before these innovations are further replicated or scaled up, it is important to critically evaluate them to identify nuances and contextual dependencies that may be critical to their effectiveness.

However, with a high prevalence of diabetes, it may be quite feasible to undertake structured research in LMIC settings, the findings of which may then be applied to HIC settings. One way in which reverse innovations are being explored is through the Colour Outside the Line: Reverse Innovation challenge encouraging Canadian students to submit proposals for reverse innovations that are applicable to Canadian settings (Snowdon, Bassi, Scarffe, & Smith 2015). In addition, social impact investments are projected to grow to $500 billion in the next decade, with the potential to fund novel approaches by private sector organizations (Freireich & Fulton 2009).

While these novel activities are promising, due to the low number of programs focused specifically on diabetes mellitus, coupled with incomplete performance reporting by these organizations, sufficient data was not available to make broad generalizations about the impact of these innovative practices on performance. A limitation of the CHMI database is that it yields a higher concentration of data from programs in countries landscaped by CHMI partner organizations, and the distribution of programs in the CHMI database does not necessarily represent a global distribution of programs.

In particular, the lack of performance data on diabetes programs in LMICs may be due to the lack of awareness of key performance measures or insufficient resources or training to collect this information. Funders, like donors and social impact investors, have an interest in measuring impact and managers have an interest in attracting funding. Future work could be directed towards training the program managers and staff on the importance of recording patient- and program-specific information. They should further be provided with specific, user-friendly data collection tools to record such information. Structured research is also required towards developing practical evaluation tools that can be implemented in LMIC settings. Such tools will not only help local program managers better understand their overall performance, but will also help identify high-performing practices, along with a thorough analysis of various contextual factors. This could increase the potential to identify inexpensive, accessible, and effective practices from low-income settings that could be used in high-income settings, where the growing burden of chronic disease in their aging populations is pushing governments to identify innovative solutions to control rising costs while addressing the population's needs.

Conclusion

This study is the first case series identifying innovative practices employed by diabetes-focused organizations and programs in LMICs using the publicly available CHMI database. The programs identified are using different combinations of the primary CCM domains, and while the result of this analysis is inconclusive, it does provide some evidence that these innovations create impact for the populations they serve. The most frequently used innovations identified involved delivery system design, which has earlier been shown to have the most potential to impact health outcomes.

REFERENCES

Ali, M., Shah, S., & Tandon, N. 2011. "Review of Electronic Decision-Support Tools for Diabetes Care: A Viable Option for Low and Middle Income Countries?" *Diabetes Science and Technology* 5(3): 553–70. https://doi.org/10.1177/193229681100500310.

Arora, S., Peters, A.L., Agy, C., & Menchine, M. 2012. "A Mobile Health Intervention for Inner City Patients with Poorly Controlled Diabetes: Proof-of-Concept of the

TExT-MED Program." *Diabetes Technology and Therapeutics* 14(6): 492–6. https:// doi.org/10.1089/dia.2011.0252.

Berelowitz, D., Horn, J., Thorton, A., Leeds, E., & Wong, D. 2013. "Identifying Replicable Healthcare Delivery Models with Significant Social Benefit." London: The International Centre for Social Franchising.

Bhattacharyya, O., Khor, S., McGahan, A., Dunne, D., Daar, A.S., & Singer, P.A. 2010. "Innovative Health Service Delivery Models in Low and Middle Income Countries – What Can We Learn from the Private Sector?" *Health Research Policy and Systems/BioMed Central* 8(24). https://doi.org/10.1186/1478-4505-8-24.

Bhattacharyya, O., McGahan, A., & Mitchell, W. 2012. "Describing Practices of Innovative Health Care Programs in Low- and Middle-Income Countries." Report prepared for Results for Development (R4D).

Bhattacharyya, O., Mossman, K., Ginther, J., Hayden, L., Sohal, R., Cha, J., Bopardikar, A., MacDonald, J.A., Parikh, H., Shahin, I., McGahan, A., Mitchell, W. 2015. "Assessing Health Program Performance in Low and Middle Income Countries: Building a Feasible, Credible, and Comprehensive Framework." *Globalization and Health* 11(51). https://doi.org/10.1186/s12992-015-0137-5.

CHMI. 2012. "Center for Health Market Innovations." http://healthmarketinnovations.org.

Fischer, H.H., Moore, S.L., Ginosar, D., Davidson, A.J., Rice-Peterson, C., ... Steele, A.W. 2012. "Care by Cell Phone: Text Messaging for Chronic Disease Management." *The American Journal of Managed Care* 18: 42.

Freireich, J., & Fulton, K. 2009. "Investing for Social and Environmental Impact: A Design for Catalyzing an Emerging Industry." Cambridge, MA: Monitor Institute. https://www2.deloitte.com/content/dam/Deloitte/global/Documents/Financial -Services/gx-fsi-monitor-Investing-for-Social-and-Environmental-Impact-2009.pdf.

Gruen, R.L., Weeramanthri, T.S., Knight, S.E., & Bailie, R.S. 2004. "Specialist Outreach Clinics in Primary Care and Rural Hospital Settings." *Cochrane Database of Systematic Reviews* 1(4). https://doi.org/10.1002/14651858.CD003798.pub2.

Horton, R. 2013. "Non-communicable Diseases: 2015 to 2025." *The Lancet* 381(9866): 509–10. https://doi.org/10.1016/S0140-6736(13)60100-2.

Huang, J.P., Chen, H.H., & Yeh, M.L. 2009. "A Comparison of Diabetes Learning with and without Interactive Multimedia to Improve Knowledge, Control, and Self-care among People with Diabetes in Taiwan." *Public Health Nurse* 26(4): 317–28. https://doi.org/10.1111/j.1525-1446.2009.00786.x.

Hwang, J., & Christensen, C. 2008. "Disruptive Innovation in Health Care Delivery: A Framework for Business Model Innovation." *Health Affairs* 27(5): 1329–35. https://doi.org/10.1377/hlthaff.27.5.1329.

Jeffery, R., Iserman, E., & Haynes, R. 2012. "Can Computerized Clinical Decision Support Systems Improve Diabetes Management? A Systematic Review and Meta-analysis." *Diabetic Medicine* 30(6): 739–45. https://doi.org/10.1111/dme.12087.

Kubzansky, M., Cooper, A., & Barbary, V. 2011. "Promise and Progress: Market-Based Solutions to Poverty in Africa." Cambridge, MA: Monitor Group. http://web.mit.edu/idi/idi/Africa-%20PromiseAndProgress-MIM.pdf.

Liang, X., Wang, Q., Yang, X., Cao, J., Chen, J., ... Cu, D. 2011. "Effect of Mobile Phone Intervention for Diabetes on Glycaemic Control: A Meta-analysis." *Diabetic Medicine* 28(4): 455–63. https://doi.org/10.1111/j.1464-5491.2010.03180.x.

Parchman, M. Zeber, J.E., Romero, R.R., & Pugh, J.A. 2007. "Risk of Coronary Artery Disease in Type 2 Diabetes and the Delivery of Care Consistent with the Chronic Care Model in Primary Care Settings: A STARNet Study." *Medical Care* 45(12): 1129–34. https://doi.org/10.1097/mlr.0b013e318148431e.

Renders, C.M., Valk, G.D., Griffin, S., Wagner, E.H., Eijk, J.T., & Assendelft, W.J. 2001. "Interventions to Improve the Management of Diabetes Mellitus in Primary Care, Outpatient, and Community Settings." *Cochrane Database of Systematic Reviews* 1(4): 1481. https://doi.org/10.1002/14651858.CD001481.

Richman, B.D., Udayakumar, K., Mitchell, W., & Schulman, K.A. 2008. "Lessons from India in Organizational Innovation: A Tale of Two Heart Hospitals." *Health Affairs* 27(5): 1260–70. https://doi.org/10.1377/hlthaff.27.5.1260.

Roshanov, P., Misra, S., Gerstein, H., Garg, A., Sebaldt, R., Mackay, J., Weise-Kelly, L., Navarro, T., Wilczynski, N.L., Haynes, R.B. 2011. "Computerized Clinical Decision Support Systems for Chronic Disease Management: A Decision Maker-Researcher Partnership Systematic Review." *Implementation Science* 6(1). https://doi.org/10.1186/1748-5908-6-92.

Rotheram-Borus, M., Tomlinson, M., Gwegwe, M., Comulada, W.S., Kaufman, N., & Keim, M. 2012. "Diabetes Buddies: Peer Support through a Mobile Phone Buddy System." *Diabetic Education* 38(3): 357–65. https://doi.org/10.1177/0145721712444617.

Si, D., Bailie, R., Connors, C., Dowden, M., Stewart, A., Robinson, G., Cunningham, J., & Weeramanthri, T. 2005. "Assessing Health Centre Systems for Guiding Improvement in Diabetes Care." *BMC Health Services Research* 5(56). https://doi.org/10.1186/1472-6963-5-56.

Snowdon, A.W., Bassi, H., Scarffe, A.D., & Smith, A.D. 2015. "Reverse Innovation: An Opportunity for Strengthening Health Systems." *Globalization and Health* 11(2). https://doi.org/10.1186/s12992-015-0088-x.

Sperl-Hillen, J., Solberg, L., Hroscikoski, M., Crain, A., Engebretson, K., & O'Connor, P. 2004. "Do All Components of the Chronic Care Model Contribute Equally to Quality Improvement?" *Joint Commission Journal on Quality and Safety* 30(6): 303–9. https://doi.org/10.1016/s1549-3741(04)30034-1.

Talbot, T. 2011. "Virtual Reality and Interactive Gaming Technology for Obese and Diabetic Children: Is Military Medical Technology Applicable?" *Journal of Diabetes Science and Technology* 5(2): 234–8. https://doi.org/10.1177/193229681100500205.

The World Bank. 2011. "Country and Lending Groups 2011." http://data.worldbank.org/about/country-classifications/country-and-lending-groups.

Thorton, A. 2013. "Big Business and Healthcare: It's Not about the Money." https://ssir.org/articles/entry/big_business_and_healthcare_its_not_about_the_money.

Tsai, A., Morton, S., Mangione, C., & Keeler, E. 2005. "A Meta-analysis of Interventions to Improve Care for Chronic Illnesses." *The American Journal of Managed Care* 11: 478–88.

United Nations. 2009. *State of the World's Indigenous Peoples.* New York. www.un.org/esa/socdev/unpfii/documents/SOWIP/en/SOWIP_web.pdf.

Wagner, E. 1998. "Chronic Disease Management: What Will It Take to Improve Care for Chronic Illness?" *Effective Clinical Practice* 1: 2–4.

WHO. 2010. *Global Status Report on Noncommunicable Diseases.* www.who.int/nmh/publications/ncd_report2010/en/.

WHO. (2011). *Global Status Report on Noncommunicable Diseases 2010: Description of the Global Burden of NCDs, Their Risk Factors, and Determinants.* 1–176. Geneva: World Health Organization. http://www.who.int/nmh/publications/ncd_report2010/en/.

World Health Statistics. 2012. www.who.int/gho/publications/world_health_statistics2012/en/.

Zhang, P., Zhang, X., Brown, J., Vistisen, D., Sicree, R., Shaw, J., & Nichols, G. 2010. "Global Healthcare Expenditure on Diabetes for 2010 and 2030." *Diabetes Research and Clinical Practice* 87(3): 293–301. https://doi.org/10.1016/j.diabres.2010.01.026.

12 Innovations in Global Mental Health Practice

ILAN SHAHIN, JOHN A. MACDONALD, JOHN GINTHER,
LEIGH HAYDEN, KATHRYN MOSSMAN, HIMANSHU PARIKH,
RAMAN SOHAL, ANITA MCGAHAN, WILL MITCHELL,
AND ONIL BHATTACHARYYA

Introduction

The importance of mental health services is rising around the world as the prevalence of infectious disease and other conditions declines. It is estimated that 7.4 per cent of the disability-adjusted life-years (DALYs) lost in the early 2000s is accounted for by mental and behavioral disorders, compared with 5.4 per cent 20 years earlier (Murray et al. 2012). Unipolar depression, which has seen a 37 per cent increase in burden over 20 years, will be the second-leading cause of DALYs lost in low- and middle-income countries (LMICs) by 2030 (Mathers & Loncar 2006). Moreover, measures such as DALYs do not fully capture the burden since much of it falls on family members, causing loss of productive time and stress on caregivers.

Addressing mental health must be part of a strategy to address health and well-being because it figures prominently in prioritized health areas such as perinatal health and non-communicable disease. More generally, mental health interventions can improve patients' economic status, thereby contributing to community development.

Despite the existence of effective and affordable treatments, delivery of services is extremely limited in most LMICs. For example, 76 per cent to 99 per cent of patients with serious mental disorders in Africa are inadequately treated (Faydi et al. 2011). The World Health Organization (2011) report on Human Resources in Global Mental Health estimates treatment rates of mental health disorders in LMICs to be only 30 per cent to 50 per cent due in part to a shortage of 1.18 million health workers.

This article describes innovative efforts among private sector, non-profit, philanthropic, and public-private partnerships (hereafter "private providers") engaged in providing mental health services in the resource-limited settings of

LMICs. We identified striking examples of private providers in several countries that offer initial evidence of opportunities for private models of mental health services to operate as complements to public services.

The Health[E] Foundation, for instance, uses computer-based courses blended with in-person sessions to provide mental health services in more than a dozen countries in Asia, Africa, South America, and Eastern Europe.

The Anjali non-profit, meanwhile, partners with the public health system in West Bengal, India, to offer psychiatric and therapeutic services along with programs to economically empower and reintegrate patients back into their communities.

We used a database of innovative efforts that address barriers and challenges in mental health services delivery for the basis of this study. The Center for Health Market Innovations (CHMI), managed by the Results for Development Institute, curates an open-access online database of over 1,000 organizations in LMICs that catalogues novel approaches to improve health services for the poor (CHMI 2016). The study draws on this data set to map the landscape of innovation in mental health services, find evidence in practice at meaningful scale, and review the activities of the organizations in the database that describe a focus on mental health. We identify approaches to the delivery of mental health services that carry the potential to improve patient wellness, have capacity for scalability, and address barriers such as stigma and politicization to sustainability.

We identified 13 mental health organizations for the study. Nine are private non-profits, three are public-private partnerships, and one is a for-profit organization. All 13 receive donor funding, while four are also financially supported by government sources; the for-profit venture also receives out-of-pocket payments from its clients.

Study Results

We clustered the organizations based on the activity domains they reported for their mental health services. Four domains of activity emerged from a qualitative analysis of the activities (table 12.1): (1) education programs, (2) advocacy and research, (3) novel platforms for patient contact, and (4) comprehensive care.

The clustering procedure assessed the information that the organizations reported about their activities in the CHMI database, along with information that they reported on their websites. We then aggregated the information into four categories that reflected both discussions in the literature and emergent patterns in the data.

Table 12.1 Summary of organizations with descriptions and activity areas

Organization	Country	Description	Education	Advocacy	Comprehensive	Platform
APAE São Paulo	Brazil	Breadth of services for those with developmental disabilities; advocates for patient rights, including providing legal services	X	X		
Anjali	India	General psychiatry services operate within current health system; advocates for patient rights addressing stigma	X	X		
ARDSI	India	Day programs and home for those with dementia; promotes awareness of dementia through seminars and workshops	X	X		
The Banyan	India	Clinical focus on women and community re-integration; program to educate health care workers in mental health; awareness efforts to increase referrals and address stigma	X	X	X	
BasicNeeds	10 countries	Mobile mental health camps to provide access in rural areas; works with traditional healers and educate on appropriate referrals	X		X	X
PULIH	Indonesia	Support groups for disaster victims; SMS, hotline, and web-based counselling after terrorist attacks				X
Health[e] Foundation	10 countries	Curriculum for health care workers on mental health, TB, HIV; combines web-based materials and in-person sessions	X			X
Instituto PROVE	Brazil	Psychiatric service tailored to victims of violence in São Paulo			X	
Linktam	Vietnam	Phone-based counselling in areas related to stress, sexual health, and domestic violence				X

(Continued)

Table 12.1 Concluded

Organization	Country	Description	Education	Advocacy	Comprehensive	Platform
Rebuilding Health in Rwanda	Rwanda	Providing training in mental health for nurses in Rwandan health system co-developed with Canadian universities	X			
Sangath	India	Comprehensive mental health services; research focus on effectiveness of delivery strategies			X	X
Strengthening Community-Based MH	Vietnam	Psychiatric visit community primary care facilities for clinical support; trains primary care health care providers	X			X
Teen SMS Health Line to Stop Suicide	South Africa	SMS suicide crisis line run by the South African Depression and Anxiety Group				X

Each of the four activity domains addresses a challenge to the access and availability of mental health services:

1. **Education Programs for Health Care Providers**. Several programs offer education on mental health to a variety of provider types, reflecting the point that a lack of trained workers constrains the availability and quality of mental health services.
2. **Advocacy and Research**. Several organizations have established formal advocacy efforts and research programs relevant to the clinical context they work in. Some cover a wide range of mental health needs, while others target specific issues such as Alzheimer's disease or women's health.
3. **Novel Platforms for Patient Contact**. The availability and accessibility of mental health services can be improved through decentralization from large institutions in urban centres. Several programs have addressed this problem with low- and high-tech platforms.
4. **Comprehensive Care**. Current mental health services have left large treatment gaps for some populations. Private sector organizations are seeking

to address these inadequacies through comprehensive whole-person care, often designed for a particular condition.

Most of the 13 organizations engage in more than one of the four activity domains, with average coverage of two domains, but no organization participated in all four domains. Thus, no matter how important the four domains are for addressing mental health needs, no organization appears to have the resources – whether financial or organizational – to attempt to take on the full suite of demands. Instead, they have focused their efforts where they believe they can achieve impact given their resources and missions.

Discussion

Examples of programs in each of the four activity domains help illustrate opportunities for success.

Education Programs for Health Care Providers

Lack of trained workers is a major barrier to improving mental health care. Integration of mental health care into primary care services can improve care delivery, so that education can be clinically effective. In addition, education that provides worker empowerment and experience of increased effectiveness can improve motivation.

Several of the organizations in the study educate health care workers. For instance, among its activities across 10 countries in Asia and Africa, BasicNeeds, founded in 1999, engages traditional healers in countries such as Ghana. The approach respects the prominence of these healers in the communities they serve, while addressing the delays in receiving appropriate care. Traditional healers are trained in how to recognize mental illness and to refer to psychiatric services when their own treatments have proved inadequate. Traditional healers also distribute basic household items to patients and their families.

Two other examples stand out. In partnership with the nursing faculties at Canadian universities, Rebuilding Health in Rwanda, founded in 2005, has developed a mental health curriculum that has been integrated into a general nursing training program. Strengthening Community-Based Mental Health, an organization in Vietnam and Angola founded in 2011, uses a similar educational approach while focusing on primary health care workers. Psychiatrists in the Strengthening Community-Based Mental Health program provide clinical support to primary care providers, seeking to strengthen the ability of the primary care system to manage mental illness.

These examples show how a community's capacity to address mental health can be increased by working with both non-medical and medical stakeholders. The approaches aim to engage patients where they come to seek care, rather than attempt to change existing entrenched health-seeking behaviours.

Ideally, the curriculum of national health education programs would include more training in the issues that these private organizations are addressing. However, all formal educational programs face limits in both time allocation and institutional constraints in curriculum contents. Hence, there is a meaningful educational role for private sector organizations.

Advocacy and Research

Many barriers to improved care in mental health can be overcome by political will, especially insufficient funding of services. Challenges to improving funding include fragmented advocacy efforts, the perception that mental health care is not cost-effective, and stigma. These challenges undermine the success of programs.

Advocacy must address policy, resource distribution, and funding priorities at the health systems level. One example of this is Anjali (see the Extended Examples section) in India, an organization that works closely with the public health system in three mental health hospitals in West Bengal. Anjali has positioned itself with a broader clinical mandate within the health system, seeking to drive policy and resource allocation and carry out focused research on epidemiology. The partnership relationships allow Anjali to deliver many services at significantly reduced cost, while also allowing them to participate in health policy development through advocacy rooted in a rights-based framework.

Other examples of advocacy stand out. APOE São Paulo has engaged in advocacy efforts at the legislative level in Brazil since 1961. In 2010, there were 30 legislative proposals at the state level and 24 at the municipal level pertaining to the rights of those living with disabilities. These are the results of collaborative efforts with other concerned organizations. In India, meanwhile, the Alzheimer's and Related Disorders Society of India (ARDSI), founded in 1993, promotes improvement of programs directed at Alzheimer's disease.

Some organizations also contribute to the systematic research base on mental health. Only 3 per cent to 6 per cent of articles on mental health in high-impact journals are from LMICs (Eaton et al. 2011; Razzouk et al. 2010). Hence, we need substantially more knowledge of challenges and practices in multiple LMIC contexts.

Sangath, founded in India in 1996, delivers a broad slate of mental health services through traditional and non-traditional workers while also linking services with research on epidemiology and the testing of delivery models. The organization has over 23 peer-reviewed publications. Sangath tests interventions such as using lay health workers through rigorous designs, describing the patient experience in LMICs with qualitative studies, describing outcomes for patients using observational designs, and making the case for addressing mental health internationally in journals such as *The Lancet*.

Sangath's research efforts capture knowledge gained from extensive experience in delivering care and translate it effectively to other care providers through a credible process. This experience shows how rigorous research on models of care can be carried out in low-resource settings, elucidating key mechanisms and highlighting effective ways of improving clinical practice in mental health.

The Banyan, which is an Indian organization founded in 1993 that cares for wandering women in Chennai, offers an example of advocacy and research, seeking to engage the community in order to increase awareness and reduce stigma. The Banyan's range of services now includes outpatient psychiatric care for 470 patients per month, as well as providing homes to help with the rehabilitation and community reintegration of 180 patients at any given time.

Recognizing the need for advocacy and research to identify best practices and barriers to improve care, the organization founded the Banyan Academy for Leadership in Mental Health. Its research is focused on the effect of social determinants of health on those with mental illness and its activities help empower various stakeholders to affect policy and promote access to care. Training seminars and courses address grassroots awareness of mental health issues and demand for mental health care.

The key point is that organizations like these that have been successful in delivering care have the potential to disseminate their knowledge in a formal, rigorous manner to improve services beyond the scale and clinical reach of the focal organization. These advocacy and research activities help to develop effective policy and health planning, and improve access to mental health services for those in need.

Online Platforms

Online platforms based on phones, SMS, and the web offer substantial potential benefits for mental health services. Immediate counselling is an obvious target. For instance, e-Counselling PULIH (Indonesia), LinkTam (Vietnam), and Teen SMS Help Line to Stop Suicide (South Africa) use the web, phone, and SMS to provide counselling services. Online platforms such as those in the above examples offer desirable options when confidentiality, geography, or cost are barriers to client access.

Some platform innovations also support educational and training activity. Health[e] Foundation (see the Extended Examples section) is an innovative education program that trains health care workers in multiple countries in Asia, Africa, and South America via an online platform, in conjunction with face-to-face training sessions. BasicNeeds, meanwhile, uses mobile mental health camps to provide access to psychiatrists, therapists, and medications to rural communities in multiple countries.

Comprehensive Care of Mental Health Needs

Several programs illustrate approaches to providing comprehensive care that addresses ongoing mental health needs, rather than attempting to deal with individual incidents that flare up into long-term problems.

Instituto Prove, for instance, was founded in 2008 by a psychiatrist and professor at the School of Medicine of the Federal University of São Paulo and offers free psychiatric treatment to victims of violence in São Paulo, Brazil. The Brazilian public health care system does not specifically target violence victims. The institute treats people who witnessed or were victims of violence. Treatment includes targeted and specific psychotherapy sessions, as well as antidepressant and antianxiety medicines. The institute is supported by the university and also receives funding from Instituto Rukha in Brazil and private donors.

Comprehensive care programs work both independently and in partnership with public facilities. Instituto Prove and The Banyan, which we described above, are examples of specialized facilities. The Anjali example that we described earlier, by contrast, operates within state hospitals, seeking to leverage available resources and encourage the state to engage with its responsibility towards mental health.

No one of the comprehensive care programs is a full solution. Nonetheless, they offer models for expanding the availability of care. Indeed, eight of the 46 organizations in the study address elements of comprehensive care, typically in combination with activities in other activity domains. Moreover, the gains from the other three domains – education, advocacy, and online platforms – can help generate systemic changes that provide the basis for additional longer-term advances in comprehensive care.

Extended Examples

Health[e] Foundation

The Health[e] Foundation demonstrates how online platforms can be used to educate health care workers at an unprecedented scale across multiple clinical areas and in many countries.

Health[e] Foundation was launched in 2006 as a not-for-profit dedicated to supporting nascent health care systems through the education of its health care workers. Initially developed as an HIV curriculum, the organization has expanded to include dozens of modules spanning areas such as mental health, child health and communicable diseases. The organization now operates in more than a dozen countries in Asia, Africa, South America, and Eastern Europe.

Courses are designed to bring knowledge of best practices in care to resource poor settings using computer-based courses blended with in-person sessions. Using this platform allows for easy implementation and uptake in new settings but also allows for expansion to cover other health areas as they have so successfully done thus far. By 2014, 4,600 health care workers had been trained since inception. In 2011, 10 courses were given to 867 trainees in nine countries. The budget for 2012 was under €700,000.

Anjali

Anjali demonstrates that private partnerships with resource-challenged public health systems in LMICs can improve access to services, reduce costs, and affect policy through effective, collaborative advocacy efforts.

Anjali is a not-for-profit based in West Bengal, founded in 2008, with a strong dedication to advocacy. It offers a breadth of psychiatric and therapeutic services as well as programs to economically empower and socially reintegrate patients back into their communities.

Anjali operates within the public health system at three mental hospitals. This relationship increases access and also reduces costs. For instance, Anjali is able to offer rehabilitation in halfway homes at a cost of US$870 per year, less than half the community average.

In India, less than 1 per cent of health expenditures are earmarked for mental health, so the organization uses its relationship with the government to advocate for the mentally ill and put their priorities and rights on the policy agenda. They have described their relationship with the government as "a fine balance of confrontation and support" (Anjali 2018).

Conclusion

Near-term benefits in achieving impact in mental health services in LMICs can arise in each of the four activity domains. Education and advocacy both have potential for high impact beyond the life or reach of a single organization, helping to raise all boats. Online platforms based on phone or web technology, whether to provide client services or in support of education programs, meanwhile, have substantial potential for immediate impact. Comprehensive care has immediate impact for the target clients, while providing models for similar programs.

Activities in the four domains also interact to contribute to longer-term gains. The organizations we studied commonly have found ways to engage education and advocacy within existing channels of care to deliver mental health services. This is being done with both traditional healers and primary care providers. Education can also be carried out using online platforms, leading to rapid expansion to train thousands of health care workers in multiple countries. Advocacy can be done either embedded within or outside the public health system, such as through community awareness programs aimed at reducing stigma or through legislation in pursuit of recognizing the rights of those with mental illness. Ongoing research can support advocacy, strengthening the case for making mental health a priority in development policy at local and global levels, all the while improving clinical care through thoughtful knowledge translation. Moreover, advances in health systems and related infrastructure that stem from education, advocacy, and platform innovation are likely to improve the long-term landscape for comprehensive care.

A key issue in any of the activity domains is program sustainability. All initiatives included in the study received at least part of their revenue from donor funding, which creates challenges for ongoing renewal. Nonetheless, most of the organizations in the study have operated for many years, with the oldest being founded in 1961 and a median founding year of 2000. Hence, these organizations, at least, have succeeded in meeting the pressure to maintain donor support.

One limit to the study concerns assessing the impact that the organizations have achieved. It is difficult to determine systematic outcomes of interventions of this nature because they are upstream, making measurement of relevant indictors challenging and forcing the attribution of downstream causality to be less direct. There is some evidence of programs achieving notable outputs, but a lack of evidence quantifying health impact. T-HOPE (2015) suggests a set of metrics that provides a feasible, credible, and comparable approach to measuring impact.

In addition, we must improve our understanding of the organizational characteristics and activities that are associated with scale. The organizations in the CHMI-derived subset are all private, with some working in close partnership with government sources. Further work should determine patients' health-seeking behaviours, attitudes towards private providers, and to what extent this overcomes traditional barriers to accessing psychiatric care such as stigma.

This article has identified potentially promising programs that could serve as templates for addressing mental health services in LMICs. Rigorous measurement of these activities focusing on efficiency, quality, and scale will help identify the most promising approaches for support or replication by governments, donors or others.

REFERENCES

Anjali. 2018. "Anjali's Approach." http://www.anjalimentalhealth.org/approach.php.

Center for Health Market Innovations. 2016. "CHMI Programs." http://healthmarketinnovations.org/.

Eaton, J., McCay, L., Semrau, M., Chatterjee, S., Baingana, F., Araya, R., Ntulo, C., Thornicroft, G., & Saxena, S. 2011. "Scale Up of Services for Mental Health in Low Income and Middle Income Countries." *The Lancet* 378(9802): 1592–603. https://doi.org/10.1016/s0140-6736(11)60891-x.

Faydi, E., Funk, M., Kleintjes, S., Ofori-Atta, A., Ssbunnya, J., Mwanza, J., Kim, C., & Flisher, A. 2011. "An Assessment of Mental Health Policy in Ghana, South Africa, Uganda, and Zambia."*Health Research Policy and Systems* 9(17). https://doi.org/10.1186/1478-4505-9-17.

Mathers, C.D., & Loncar, D. 2006. "Projections of Global Mortality and Burden of Disease from 2002 to 2030." *PLoS Med* 3(11):e442. https://doi.org/10.1371/journal.pmed.0030442.

Murray, C.J.L., Vos, T., Lozano, R., Naghavi, M., Flaxman, A.D., Michaud, C., ... Lopez, A.D. 2012. "Disability-adjusted Life Years (DALYs) for 291 Diseases and Injuries in 21 Regions, 1990–2010: A Systematic Analysis for the Global Burden of Disease Study 2010." *The Lancet* 380(9859): 2197–223. https://doi.org/10.1016/s0140-6736(12)61689-4.

Razzouk, D., Sharan, P., Gallo, C., Gureje, O., Lamberte, E.E., de Jesus Mari, J., ... Saxena S. 2010. "Scarcity and Inequality of Mental Health Research Resources in Low and Middle Income Countries: A Global Survey." *Health Policy* 94(3): 211–20. https://doi.org/10.1016/j.healthpol.2009.09.009.

T-HOPE. 2015. "Assessing Health Program Performance in Low and Middle Income Countries: Building a Feasible, Credible, and Comprehensive Framework." *Globalization and Health* 11(51). https://doi.org/10.1186/s12992-015-0137-5.

World Health Organization. 2011. "Human Resources for Mental Health: Workforce Shortages in Low and Middle Income Countries." http://whqlibdoc.who.int/publications/2011/9789241501019_eng.pdf.

SECTION D

Horizontal Cases – The Role of the Private Sector in Generating Integrated Solutions

This section explores the innovations of private sector organizations that provide horizontal or general health care services that target prevention and prevailing health problems. This includes a focus on maternal, newborn, and child health (MNCH), primary care, and integrated primary and MNCH care. Integrating services, which involves improved service coordination to increase continuity of patient care, has many benefits, including often being able to run at lower costs while offering superior patient experience and outcomes. Horizontal care provision and the integration of programs, while sometimes difficult to attain, can offer broader solutions for pressing health challenges, and there is a great need to scale up such approaches. We explore private sector innovations in MNCH, primary care, and integrated care, and identify some of the key activities supporting successful scale up in this area.

Chapter 13 ("Innovations in Privately Delivered Maternal, Newborn, and Child Health: Exploring the Evidence behind Emerging Practices") discusses MNCH programs that engage in operational, financial, marketing, and ICT innovations to improve delivery of care. Activities targeted by organizations such as Mahila Swhastha Sewa in Nepal, Chiranjeevi Yojana in India, and Childcount+ in Sub-Saharan Africa include social franchising, vouchers, and the use of mobile phones.

Chapter 14 ("Scaling Up Primary Care in Low- and Middle-Income Countries by Using Strategic Management Skills") explores the operations of 37 innovative primary care programs to identify strategic management skills contributing to their base operations that allow them to achieve their basic goals, as well as the focused set of skills or differentiators that facilitate scale up.

Chapter 15 ("Integrating Primary Care and MNCH in Low- and Middle-Income Countries") identifies incentives, barriers, and strategies for integration of MNCH and primary care services by examining 20 LMIC programs engaged in MNCH, primary, or integrated care.

Our research finds that some private sector health care organizations are able to offer integrated solutions at scale. Integration of services is important but challenging. Scaling up is key to providing basic and essential services to LMIC populations, but is exceedingly difficult. These organizations meet both of these challenges in a variety of innovative ways, including building relationships with clients via customer service and marketing, skilled internal operations including HR and logistics, innovative financial models, and building alliances, including private public partnerships. Improving and expanding access to primary care and MNCH services is vital to closing the gaps in the pursuit of universal health care, and these chapters identify innovative activities and strategies to support increased access to basic care.

13 Innovations in Privately Delivered Maternal, Newborn, and Child Health: Exploring the Evidence behind Emerging Practices

ONIL BHATTACHARYYA, KATHRYN MOSSMAN,
ANITA MCGAHAN, WILL MITCHELL, LEIGH HAYDEN,
JOHN GINTHER, RAMAN SOHAL, JOHN A. MACDONALD,
HIMANSHU PARIKH, AND ILAN SHAHIN

Introduction

Every year, 287,000 mothers and 7.6 million children under the age of five die from largely preventable causes (World Health Organization 2010b; You, Jones, & Wardlaw 2011; PMNCH 2012a). This has resulted in many international efforts focused on maternal, newborn, and child health (MNCH), which refers to "the integrated continuum of care that delivers tools and treatments to mothers and their infants at critical points, and to children in their first five years of life" (Bill and Melinda Gates Foundation 2012).[1] The Global Campaign for the Health Millennium Development Goals has identified several priority areas as necessary in reducing high maternal and child mortality rates. These include providing high-quality interventions during and after pregnancy and childbirth; ensuring skilled health workers are available where and when needed with the necessary medications, equipment, infrastructure, and regulations; and removing financial, cultural, and social barriers to access (Altman, Fogstad, Gronseth, & Kristensen 2011). The private sector is engaging in a variety of innovative approaches to address these priority areas and meet the pressing health care needs of women and children in low- and middle-income countries (LMICs). What role does the private sector play in MNCH, and what innovative approaches are emerging in this field? In this chapter, we explore the current role of the private sector in the field of MNCH and describe the innovative approaches they use. This includes a discussion of approaches with evidence as well as emerging approaches. They were identified through a review of MNCH programs in the CHMI database along with academic and grey literature on MNCH. We conclude with a discussion of how combining innovative activities can increase the potential for programs to achieve health impact and organizational sustainability, while pointing to areas for future research.

Background

The Role of the Private Sector in MNCH

The private sector includes for-profit and non-profit, formal and non-formal entities (Hanson & Berman 1998), such as private companies, NGOs, clinics, hospitals, physicians, midwives, community health workers, and traditional birth attendants (Mills, Chowdhury, Miranda, Seshadri, & Axemo 2009; Madhavan, Bishai, Stanton, & Harding 2010). This sector plays a vital role in the delivery of care to women and children in LMICs in many countries today (McCoy et al. 2010). Indeed, in developing countries, an average of 8.2 per cent of deliveries take place in a private facility, while 47.4 per cent of deliveries take place at home (Gwatkin et al. 2007). Meanwhile, in Sub-Saharan Africa, 77.7 per cent of the poorest women reported giving birth at home; 41 per cent of these home births were attended by a traditional birth assistant (Montagu, Yamey, Visconti, Harding, & Yoong 2011). Private sector providers are frequently consulted for child illnesses in many developing countries (Waters, Hatt, & Peters 2002), and where medical treatment was sought, an average of 28 per cent of cases of fever, 27 per cent of acute respiratory infection, and 28 per cent of diarrhoea were treated in private facilities (Gwatkin et al. 2007). Furthermore, an average of one in five children with acute respiratory illness symptoms in Sub-Saharan Africa is treated at a private health facility (Yoong, Burger, Spreng, & Sood 2010). Thus, many are seeking and receiving MNCH care from private providers in LMICs.

MNCH at a Glance: Exploring MNCH Program Activities in the CHMI Database

Many MNCH private providers are innovating, or engaging in new activities that have the potential to drive change and redefine health care (Weberg 2009). There are 230 MNCH programs in the CHMI database,[2] and they operate in eleven regions, most notably South Asia (83; 36 per cent) and East Africa (92; 40 per cent). Most of these programs are private, not-for-profit (134; 58 per cent), and tend to be local or international NGOs (see the appendix to this chapter). Among the 230 MNCH programs, the most frequently reported health market innovations are: information technology (61; 27 per cent); consumer education (59; 26 per cent); provider training (49; 21 per cent); micro/community health insurance (26; 11 per cent); and franchising (24; 10 per cent).

Overcoming financial, social, and cultural barriers to improve access to care and ensuring skilled providers are available when and where needed are key issues for this health area. Innovations in information technology and social franchising can help to remove geographic barriers, while microinsurance can help to overcome financial barriers to seeking care. Consumer education can encourage groups to engage in healthy behaviours and remove social and cultural barriers to accessing needed services, and provider training can help to increase the number of skilled health care workers, expanding geographic access to quality care. Programs that aim to improve MNCH health care delivery frequently engage in these innovative activities, and how such activities are actually practised and the evidence for them will be described in the following section.

Exploring the Evidence on Innovative MNCH Models

Approaches with Evidence: Exploring the Impact of Innovative Models in MNCH

A number of novel approaches are being used to reduce high mortality rates and ensure the delivery of accessible, quality care for mothers and children. Some approaches are becoming more widespread and have been evaluated for their effectiveness in terms of providing accessible, quality care that improves the health of poor populations.

SOCIAL FRANCHISING: ORGANIZING PROVIDERS TO INCREASE MNCH CARE FOR THE POOR
Social franchising involves a network of private providers contracted to provide services that are considered socially beneficial under a common brand (Schlein & Montagu 2012). Practitioners of social franchises often receive benefits such as training, advertising, and business loans (Prata, Montagu, & Jefferys 2005). In a review of 52 social franchises, the Global Health Group found that almost half offer MNCH services, and that the number providing MNCH services has almost doubled in the last four years (Schlein & Montagu 2012). Twenty-four of CHMI's MNCH programs use social franchising.

Some evidence suggests that this model can slightly increase the likelihood of delivery in a health facility, the overall number of prenatal visits pregnant women receive (Kozhimannil, Valera, Adams, & Ross-Degnan 2009), and service utilization by the poor (Madhavan & Bishai 2010). However, the impact on client satisfaction has been variable (Stephenson et al. 2004). Concerns have also been raised about the affordability and accessibility of services for very poor women and those in rural areas (Stephenson et al. 2004; Ravindran 2011; Ravindran 2010). In addition, the quality of care is variable, and not always of an acceptable standard (Ravindran 2010).

Example of a Program Reporting Results: Mahila Swahsta Sewa. This program is a franchise model in Nepal that provides family planning, reproductive health, and MNCH services. In 2010, the program reported that they charged US$2.81 for an intrauterine device, whereas the average cost of this service in Nepal's private sector was US$7. The program also reports an improvement in quality ratings from 80 per cent in 2010 to 86 per cent in 2011, based on internal quality assurance visits using the Lot Quality Assurance Sampling method (CHMI 2013f).

MICROINSURANCE AND COMMUNITY-BASED HEALTH INSURANCE: FINANCIAL PROTECTION AND ACCESS TO NECESSARY MNCH SERVICES[3]

The private sector can increase access to MNCH care by providing customized financial services such as microinsurance schemes that covers women and children's health needs (e.g., antenatal visits, delivery, vaccinations, emergency procedures, etc.) (PMNCH 2012a). Members pay fixed premiums for partial or complete coverage of services that could lead to potentially catastrophic health expenditures, improving access by reducing the financial burden when care is needed (Borghi, Ensor, Somanathan, Lissner, & Mills 2006). While microinsurance covers a small proportion of the population (Smith & Sulzbach 2008), it is growing fast, particularly in West and Central Africa (Roth, McCord, & Liber 2007). Many of these schemes cover routine maternal care, and a small but growing number cover emergency obstetric care (Soors, Waelkens, & Criel 2008). Twenty-six of CHMI's MNCH programs provide microinsurance schemes for their clients.

There is evidence that microinsurance schemes that include maternal health care in the benefits package can increase utilization of maternal health services (Smith & Sulzbach 2008), including greater use of antenatal care by poor women (Islam, Igarashi, & Kawabuchi 2012); Criel, Van der Stuyft, & Van Lerberghe 1999). By reducing out-of-pocket spending, microfinance or community health insurance can provide financial protection and greatly improve access to health care for members (Ekman 2004), including hospital care for maternal health issues (Soors et al. 2008). However, some researchers have raised concerns about the ability for schemes to include the poorest (Borghi et al. 2006), and the feasibility of microinsurance varies by context (Ekman 2004).

Example of a Program Reporting Results: Hygeia Community Health Plan. Hygeia offers microinsurance in Lagos and Kwara State, Nigeria, including 40,000 female members of local market associations. The program reports that the microinsurance plan has resulted in decreased costs for the poor in its target market. Participating individuals in the poorest income quintile are paying nearly 300 naira less compared to average out-of-pocket costs; those in the second quintile pay 1,500 naira less. This seems to be linked to a compound annual growth rate in normal delivery services by 56 per cent from 2007 to 2010 (CHMI 2013e).

VOUCHERS: INCREASING FINANCIAL ACCESS TO SAFE MNCH CARE
Voucher schemes involve distributing vouchers to designated recipients, which allows them to receive free or subsidized health services from private or public providers (Madhavan & Bishai 2010). Private providers may be hired under contract by the government to provide these services (Madhavan & Bishai 2010). In MNCH, voucher programs often include services such as delivery services by skilled providers, antenatal and postnatal care, and sometimes child immunizations and nutrition services. These voucher schemes usually target poor women (Mavalankar, Singh, Patel, Desai, & Singh 2009), often using an instrument to measure a woman's poverty level to determine her eligibility (CHMI n.d.). MNCH voucher programs are operational throughout many LMICs, including Uganda, Kenya, Myanmar, Ethiopia, Bangladesh, Cambodia, India, Pakistan, and Indonesia. Voucher schemes have grown significantly in recent years. For example, in Uganda, vouchers for safe motherhood were first distributed in February 2009, and by June 2010 over 8,000 vouchers were being distributed per month (Bellows 2012). Thirteen of CHMI's MNCH programs use vouchers to target the delivery MNCH services to poor women.

There is evidence that voucher systems increase the utilization of skilled service providers (Janisch, Albrecht, Wolfschuetz, Kundu, & Klein 2010; Ir, Horemans, Souk, & Van Damme 2010) and institutional deliveries (PMNCH 2012b). There is less data on whether voucher schemes reduce maternal mortality, but the evaluators of the Chiranjeevi Yojana voucher program in India estimate that theirs has reduced maternal mortality by 90 per cent (Mavalankar et al. 2009). This program saved women an average of US$75 in out-of-pocket expenditures (Bhat, Mavalankar, Singh, & Singh 2009). Voucher schemes are more successful if they are distributed appropriately and there is strong site oversight and management; they can achieve large-scale coverage (Madhavan & Bishai 2010). Even though voucher schemes can improve equity of MNCH care, health inequities between rich and poor in areas with voucher schemes continue to exist, implying that demand-side financing, like voucher schemes, should be included in a comprehensive approach that incorporates initiatives to address social barriers and supply-side concerns (Ahmed & Khan 2011).

Example of a Program Reporting Results: Bangladesh Demand Side Financing (DSF) Pilot Program. This maternal health voucher program was developed to increase utilization of maternal health care services by poor women. The program reports an unprecedented positive effect on the utilization of maternal health services since initiation – the rate of institutional deliveries is now twice as high in program sub-districts (38 per cent) compared to control sub-districts (19 per cent); and the likelihood of three ANC visits is 55 per cent in program sub-districts as compared to 34 per cent in control sub-districts. However, the program is finding that while women from poorer quintiles are significantly more likely to receive vouchers than from wealthier quintiles, there is substantial leakage to women who do not meet land ownership criteria, asset ownership criteria, and income criteria (CHMI 2013a).

Approaches with Less Evidence: Emerging Models with the Potential for Impact

There are a number of emerging areas of innovation in MNCH, with most activity and experimentation taking place in the field of information and communication technology (ICT). ICT is being used by a growing number of private sector organizations in novel ways that may improve the delivery of MNCH care, but for which there is less evidence (Noordam, Kuepper, Stekelenburg, & Milen 2011). They are addressing the most salient barriers: timely access to urgent care, low health provider capacity in many areas, and low health literacy and savings. When ICT is used in combination with other innovations in care – such as improved delivery mechanisms and novel financial arrangements – it shows the greatest promise (Howitt, Darzi, Yang, Ashrafian, & Atun 2012).

CONNECTING MNCH PROVIDERS BY MOBILE PHONE OR INTERNET
Delay in receiving timely, appropriate care is a significant factor in maternal deaths (Thaddeus & Maine 1994). New communication technologies can help providers make more appropriate decisions about care provision and timing (Ratzan & Gilhooley 2010). Indeed, mHealth, which involves using mobile phone technologies for health care (WHO 2011), and internet applications, can improve the capacity of lesser-trained health workers by connecting them to better-trained medical staff. By giving mobile phones to community health workers (CHWs) to consult with more highly skilled providers, programs aim to reduce the delay in patients receiving appropriate

care (Noordam et al. 2011). Mobile technologies can improve coordination of care through more rapid communication and data exchange between CHWs, health centres, and hospitals. Twelve of CHMI's MNCH programs use mobile technologies to help practitioners connect and coordinate in the provision of MNCH care.

One study suggests that mobile technologies improve access to more highly trained medical staff, increase the capacity of less-trained health workers such as midwives, and reduce response time (Chib 2010). Other programs are currently being tested, and new data on program and model performance should be available in the near future (USAID 2011). Some program assessment data suggests that telemedicine programs that provide isolated health facilities with MNCH services, such as high-risk pregnancy consultations, reduce neonatal mortality by providing timely expertise and lower health care spending by reducing unnecessary transport (WHO 2010a). More research is needed regarding the feasibility of adopting such technologies, and their ability to increase access to remote communities.

Example of a Program Reporting Results: ChildCount+. This mHealth platform enables SMS coordination of the activities of community health workers, bringing real-time decision support and monitoring for MNCH services across ten Sub-Saharan African countries. While the program is currently undergoing a third-party evaluation of the project, it has reported on user satisfaction data from its community health workers with mixed results. Three of the four sites report a high level of improved efficiencies as a result of the mHealth product, citing decreases in working hours and improved ability to set care priorities. However, results were mixed in other areas evaluated, including ease of learning and data entry (CHMI 2013c).

SUPPORTING HEALTH WORKERS WITH CLINICAL DECISION SUPPORT SOFTWARE
Given the shortage of highly trained providers in LMICs, there is growing interest in task shifting, or delegating routine tasks to lesser-trained categories of health workers. To maintain high standards of care, lesser-trained health workers can follow clinical protocols using clinical decision support software (CHMI 2013f). This software is often available on mobile phones, and it guides health workers through the screening, examination, and treatment process, helping them make appropriate decisions regarding care. It can also provide useful knowledge and incentives for performance, which can increase efficiency and improve health outcomes (Altman et al. 2011). Three of CHMI's MNCH programs use clinical decision support software in the provision of MNCH services.

There is some evidence that these programs work (Svoronos et al. 2010). Qualitative data from a pilot study testing the impact of clinical decision support software for CHWs suggest that the program has improved the quality and comprehensiveness of care and patient monitoring. However, the data also suggest that these programs require supervision to support the CHWs, and more comparative, quantitative research is required on the quality and feasibility of this approach.

Example of a Program Reporting Results: D-Tree International. This program provides clinical decision support software that can be used on mobile phones by community health workers. This software is based on clinical protocols for child health, antenatal, neonatal and postnatal care, reproductive health, HIV/AIDS, malaria, tuberculosis and diabetes. The platform guides health workers through a series of health questions, and indicates whether the patient requires referral to a physician. Helping health workers make appropriate decisions regarding care facilitates task shifting. In 2012, 43 front line health workers in Tanzania were trained in the severe acute malnutrition application in Zanzibar, and 24 traditional birth attendants also received training. In 2013, 71 per cent of births in the target area of Tanzania occurred in a health facility compared to 33.6 per cent in 2011 (CHMI 2013d).

SMS REMINDERS AND HEALTH UPDATES FOR PATIENTS

Interventions for mothers and children often fail due to a lack of focus on changing care-seeking behaviour (Bhutta et al. 2008). Low-cost tools are needed to build awareness and prompt healthy behaviours, such as attending antenatal visits and childhood vaccinations (Altman et al. 2011). New communication technologies can enhance clients' skills and knowledge while reducing complexity, helping them to make informed decisions about their health (Ratzan & Gilhooley 2010). Programs using communication technologies can disseminate engaging and personalized health messages through mobile phones and also remind patients about the need to attend appointments and take medications. This can improve health literacy and encourage adherence with treatment regimens (Ratzan & Gilhooley 2010). Eight of CHMI's MNCH programs provide SMS reminders and health updates for patients regarding MNCH services.

There is limited evidence on programs that use SMS reminders and health updates to encourage healthy and health-seeking behaviour in women (Noordam et al. 2011). However, studies from other health areas, such as smoking cessation (Free et al. 2011), suggest that these approaches can be successful. Furthermore, there seems to be a significant demand for women's health-related information using SMS technology in areas where reproductive health information is difficult to obtain (PMNCH 2012a). Key areas for future research include whether this approach can effectively impact care-seeking behaviour and the utilization of MNCH services.

Example of a Program Reporting Results: Mobile Technology for Community Health (MoTeCH). This program uses mobile technologies in Ghana to bridge the gap between patients and community health workers. Pregnant women register by providing their phone number, geographic area, estimated due date, and language preferences. They are then sent SMS and/or pre-recorded voice messages with time-specific information about their pregnancy, treatments they should be receiving, and the location of the closest health facility. After delivery, women receive health messages and information regarding necessary childhood vaccines and care for critical childhood illnesses. This program is linked to data collected by health workers, and expectant mothers are sent reminders and notifications if they miss critical prenatal care. Launched in 2010, by June 2013, the MoTeCH had trained 266 community health workers, uploaded close to 150,000 medical records, reached more than 20,000 enrolees, and delivered close to 60,000 messages (CHMI 2013g).

SAVING SCHEMES USING MOBILE TECHNOLOGY

Mobile phone-based savings and payment schemes have emerged as tools to overcome financial barriers to care for the poor (Innovation Working Group Task Force on Sustainable Business Models 2012). This includes financial-planning applications, which help budget health expenditures, and applications to pay for health care, which speeds transactions and may increase access to health services for the poor (PMNCH 2012a). Four of CHMI's MNCH programs provide saving schemes for MNCH services using mobile technology.

Preliminary results from a pragmatic case-controlled study showed that expectant mothers using the savings program were more likely to attend at least four prenatal clinics. The program seemed to be more convenient and secure than carrying cash, but did not seem to provide significant savings benefit (Long, van Bastelaer, & Woodman 2012). Overall, there is little data on the impacts of savings programs and more evidence is needed to understand their effect on care-seeking behaviour and savings.

Example of a Program Reporting Results: Mobile Technology for Community Health Changamka Microhealth Limited. Changamka utilizes technology to facilitate the financing of health care services to provide access for the poor to health facilities in Kenya. This includes a maternity smartcard that provides mothers with a dedicated savings mechanism to access antenatal, maternity, and post-natal services at participating facilities. Launched in 2008, the program has reported a 30 per cent increase in the number of women regularly visiting hospitals since they have started accepting the Changamka cards (CHMI 2013b).

Evidence Gaps and Research Opportunities in MNCH

A variety of innovative activities have emerged as promising approaches in MNCH. Some approaches have been studied for their impact, while other emerging areas require further research. These activities may hold more potential when combined in complementary ways that enhance program quality, efficiency, and scale. One such approach involves combining consumer education, provider training, and mobile clinics. Consumer education can help to encourage demand for health services, which is important for increasing scale, but also can increase efficiency by ensuring that existing facilities are well used. Provider training is important for ensuring that health practitioners are skilled in providing care, which helps to enhance quality. Consumer education and health services offered by trained providers can be delivered through mobile clinics, which are useful in targeting difficult to reach populations. This can help to expand the scale of operations while also increasing efficiency and quality through providing more timely care. As the private sector works to improve health services for women and children in LMICs, innovation will involve not only novel activities, but also innovative combinations of these activities in mutually reinforcing ways that increase quality, efficiency, and scale, which are key components for achieving health impact.

The area of MNCH has a large number of innovative organizations, and among CHMI MNCH programs, the most frequently practised activities include information technology, consumer education, provider training, micro/community health insurance, and franchising. Social franchising, microinsurance, and vouchers have some evidence to support their impact, while approaches using IT are promising, but not as well studied. Many organizations are combining different activities in ways that are often complementary, but these clusters are just emerging and have not been adequately studied. The area of maternal and child health has a large number of innovative organizations, but future research is needed to understand and document the impact of their activities in terms of their ability to provide high-quality services in an efficient manner on a large scale.

Appendix

Geographic Region

There are 230 programs engaged in maternal, newborn, and/or child health in the CHMI database. These programs operate in 11 regions,[4] most notably South Asia and East Africa.

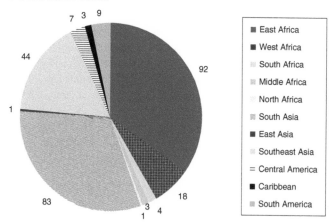

Figure 13.A1 MNCH programs by region

Legal Status

The largest area of operation for MNCH programs in the CHMI database is the not-for-profit private sector (134/230; 58 per cent), which largely consists of local and international NGOs.

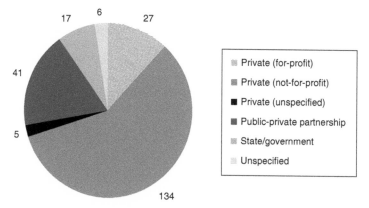

Figure 13.A2 Legal status of MNCH programs

NOTES

1 We have followed the lead taken by the Gates Foundation, Partnership for Maternal, Newborn and Child Health (PMNCH), and the Global Campaign for the Health Millennium Development Goals by considering the spectrum of care for mothers, newborns, and children for this chapter, rather than separating this field into its constituent groups. This decision is also based on the approach taken by MNCH programs in the CHMI database, the majority of which (168/230 or 73 per cent) describe engaging in activities for more than one of these groups.

2 This data is drawn from the CHMI database, downloaded on 1 December 2012, from http://healthmarketinnovations.org.

3 Microinsurance and community-based health insurance are often used synonymously in the literature (see Smith, K.V. and Sulzbach, S. 2008. "Community-Based Health Insurance and Access to Maternal Health Services: Evidence from Three West African Countries." *Social Science & Medicine* 66(12): 2460–73).

4 Regions are based on the UN categorization of geographical regions: http://unstats.un.org/unsd/methods/m49/m49regin.htm.

REFERENCES

Ahmed, S., & Khan, M. 2011. "Is Demand-side Financing Equity Enhancing? Lessons from a Maternal Health Voucher Scheme in Bangladesh." *Social Science and Medicine* 72(10): 1704–10. https://doi.org/10.1016/j.socscimed.2011.03.031.

Altman, D., Fogstad, H., Gronseth, L., & Kristensen, F. 2011. *Innovating for Every Woman, Every Child: The Global Campaign for the Health Millennium Development Goals*. Oslo: Ministry of Foreign Affairs.

Bellows, N.M. 2012. *Vouchers for Reproductive Health Care Services in Kenya and Uganda: Approaches Supported by Financial Cooperation*. Frankfurt: KfW Entwicklungsbank.

Bhat, R., Mavalankar, D.V., Singh, P.V., & Singh, N. 2009. "Maternal Healthcare Financing: Gujarat's Chiranjeevi Scheme and Its Beneficiaries." *Journal of Health, Population, and Nutrition* 27(2): 249–58. https://doi.org/10.3329/jhpn.v27i2.3367.

Bhutta, Z.A., Ali, S., Cousens, S., Ali, T.M., Haider, B.A., Rizvi, A., ... Black, R.E. 2008. "Interventions to Addresss Maternal, Newborn, and Child Survival: What Difference Can Integrated Primary Health Care Strategies Make?" *The Lancet* 372(9642): 972–89. https://doi.org/10.1016/s0140-6736(08)61407-5.

Bill and Melinda Gates Foundation. 2012. "Maternal, Newborn, and Child Health: Overview." http://www.gatesfoundation.org/maternalnewbornandchildhealth/Pages/overview.aspx.

Borghi, J., Ensor, T., Somanathan, A., Lissner, C., & Mills, A. 2006. "Mobilising Financial Resources for Maternal Health." *The Lancet* 368(9545): 1457–65. https:// doi.org/10.1016/s0140-6736(06)69383-5.

Chib, A. 2010. "The Aceh Besar Midwives with Mobile Phones Project: Design and Evaluation Perspectives Using the Information and Communication Technologies for Healthcare Development Models." *Journal of Computer-Mediated Communication* 15(3): 500–25. https://doi.org/10.1111/j.1083-6101.2010.01515.x.

CHMI. (n.d.). "Mobile Health Clinic." http://healthmarketinnovations.org/.

– (2013a). "Bangladesh Demand Side Financing (DSF) Pilot Program." http:// healthmarketinnovations.org/.

– (2013b). "Changamka Microhealth." http://healthmarketinnovations.org/.

– (2013c). "ChildCount+." Accessed 27 March 2013. http://healthmarketinnovations .org/.

– (2013d). "D-Tree International." http://healthmarketinnovations.org/.

– (2013e). "Hygeia Community Health Plan (HCHP)." http://healthmarketinnovations .org/.

– (2013f). "Mahila Swahsta Sewa." Accessed 27 March 2013. http:// healthmarketinnovations.org/.

– (2013g). "Mobile Technology for Community Health (MOTECH)." http:// healthmarketinnovations.org/.

Criel, B., Van der Stuyft, P., & Van Lerberghe, W. 1999. "The Bwamanda Hospital Insurance Scheme: Effective for Whom? A Study of Its Impact on Hospital Utilization Patterns." *Social Science & Medicine* 48(7): 897–911. https://doi .org/10.1016/s0277-9536(98)00391-8.

Ekman, B. 2004. "Community-Based Health Insurance in Low Income Countries: A Systematic Review of the Evidence." *Health Policy and Planning* 19(5): 249–70. https://doi.org/10.1093/heapol/czh031.

Free, C., Knight, R., Robertson, S., Whittaker, R., Edwards, P., & Zhou, W. 2011. "Smoking Cessation Support Delivered via Mobile Phone Text Messaging (txt2stop): A Single, Blind, Randomized Trial." *The Lancet* 378(9785): 49–55. https://doi.org/10.1016/s0140-6736(11)60701-0.

Gwatkin, D.R., Rutstein, S., Johnson, K., Suliman, E., Wagstaff, A., & Amouzou, A. 2007. *Social-Economic Differences in Health, Nutrition, and Population within Developing Countries: An Overview. Country Reports on HNP and Poverty.* Washington, DC: World Bank Group

Hanson, K., & Berman, P. 1998. "Private Health Care Provision in Developing Countries: A Preliminary Analysis of Levels and Composition." *Health Policy and Planning* 13(3): 195–211. https://doi.org/10.1093/heapol/13.3.195.

Howitt, P., Darzi, G., Yang, G., Ashrafian, H., & Atun, R. 2012. "Technologies for Global Health." *The Lancet* 380: 507–35. https://doi.org/10.1016/ S0140-6736(12)61273-2.

The Every Woman, Every Child Innovation Working Group Task Force on Sustainable Business Models, NORAD, and Merck for Mothers. 2012. *Fostering Healthy Businesses: Delivering Innovations in Maternal and Children's Health.* Geneva.

Ir, P., Horemans, D., Souk, N., & Van Damme, W. 2010. "Using Targeted Vouchers and Health Equity Funds to Improve Access to Skilled Birth Attendants for Poor Women: A Case Study in Three Rural Health Districts in Cambodia." *BMC Pregnancy and Childbirth* 10(1). https://doi.org/10.1186/1471-2393-10-1.

Islam, M.T., Igarashi, I., & Kawabuchi, K. 2012. "The Impact of Gonoshasthaya Kendra's Micro Health Insurance Plan on Antenatal Care among Poor Women in Rural Bangladesh." *BioScience Trends* 6(4): 165–75. https://doi.org/10.5582/bst.2012 .v6.4.165.

Janisch, C.P., Albrecht, M., Wolfschuetz, A., Kundu, F., & Klein, S. 2010. "Vouchers for Health: A Demand Side Output-based Aid Approach to Reproductive Health Services in Kenya." *Global Public Health* 5(6): 578–94. https://doi .org/10.1080/17441690903436573.

Kozhimannil, K.B., Valera, M.R., Adams, A.S., & Ross-Degnan, D. 2009. "The Population Level Impacts of a National Health Insurance Program and Franchise Midwife Clinics on Achievement of Prenatal and Delivery Care Standards in the Philippines." *Health Policy* 92(1): 55–64. https://doi.org/10.1016/j .healthpol.2009.02.009.

Long, D., van Bastelaer, T., & Woodman, B. 2012. *Study of Changamka's Maternity Savings Card: Preliminary Evaluation Results.* Second Global Symposium on Health Systems Research, November 1, 2012. Beijing.

Madhavan, S., & Bishai, D. 2010. *Private Sector Engagement in Sexual and Reproductive Health and Maternal and Neonatal Health: A Review of the Evidence.* Baltimore: Johns Hopkins School of Public Health.

Madhavan, S., Bishai, D., Stanton, C., & Harding, A. 2010. *Engaging the Private Sector in Maternal and Neonatal Health in Low and Middle Income Countries.* Baltimore: Future Health Systems.

Mavalankar, D., Singh, A., Patel, S.R., Desai, A., & Singh, P.V. 2009. "Saving Mothers and Newborns through an Innovative Partnership with Private Sector Obstetricians: Chiranjeevi Scheme of Gujarat, India." *International Journal of Gynecology & Obstetrics* 107(3): 271–6. https://doi.org/10.1016/j.ijgo.2009.09.008.

McCoy, D., Storeng, K., Filippi, V., Ronsmans, C., Osrin, D., Borchert, M., ... Hill, Z. 2010. "Maternal, Neonatal and Child Health Interventions and Services: Moving from Knowledge of What Works to Systems That Deliver." *Journal of International Health* 2(2): 87–98. https://doi.org/10.1016/j.inhe.2010.03.005.

Mills, S., Chowdhury, S., Miranda, E., Seshadri, S.R., & Axemo, P. 2009. *Reducing Maternal Mortality: Strengthening the World Bank Response.* Washington, DC: The World Bank.

Montagu, D., Yamey, G., Visconti, A., Harding, A., & Yoong, J. 2011. "Where Do Poor Women in Developing Countries Give Birth? A Multi-country Analysis of Demographic and Health Survey Data." *PloS One* 6(2): e17155. https://doi.org/ 10.1371/journal.pone.0017155.

Noordam, A.C., Kuepper, B.M., Stekelenburg, J., & Milen, A. 2011. "Improvement of Maternal Health Services through the Use of Mobile Phones." *Tropical Medicine & International Health* 16(5): 622–6. https://doi.org/10.1111/j.1365 -3156.2011.02747.x.

PMNCH. 2012a. *Private Enterprise for Public Health. Opportunities for Business to Improve Women's and Children's Health: A Short Guide for Companies.* Geneva: PMNCH.

– 2012b. *The PMNCH 2012 Report: Analysing Progress on Commitments to the Global Strategy for Women's and Children's Health.* Geneva: PMNCH.

Prata, N., Montagu, D., & Jefferys, E. 2005. "Private Sector, Human Resources, and Health Franchising in Africa." *Bulletin of the World Health Organization* 83(4): 274–9.

Ratzan, S.C., & Gilhooley, D. 2010. "Innovative Use of Mobile Phones and Related Information and Communication Technologies." In *Every Woman, Every Child: Investing in Our Common Future. Global Strategy for Women's and Children's Health.* Geneva: World Health Organization. https://www.who.int/pmnch/activities/ jointactionplan/100922_2_investing.pdf.

Ravindran, T.K.S. 2010. "Privatisation in Reproductive Health Services in Pakistan: Three Case Studies." *Reproductive Health Matters* 18(36): 13–24. https://doi.org/ 10.1016/S0968-8080(10)36536-0.

– 2011. "Public-Private Partnerships in Maternal Health Services." *Economic and Political Weekly* XLVI(48): 43–52. www.jstor.org/stable/41319433.

Roth, J., McCord, M.J., & Liber, D. 2007. *The Landscape of Microinsurance in the World's 100 Poorest Countries.* The Microinsurance Centre, LLC. www .microinsurancecentre.org.

Schlein, K., & Montagu, D. 2012. *Clinical Social Franchising Compendium: An Annual Survey of Programs, 2012.* San Francisco, CA: The Global Health Group.

Smith, K.V., & Sulzbach, S. 2008. "Community-based Health Insurance and Access to Maternal Health Services: Evidence from Three West African Countries." *Social Science and Medicine* 66(12): 2460–73. https://doi.org/10.1016/j.socscimed .2008.01.044.

Soors, W., Waelkens, M., & Criel, B. 2008. "Community Health Insurance in Sub-Saharan Africa: Opportunities for Improving Access to Emergency Obstetric Care?" *Studies in Health Services Organization and Policy* 24: 149–64.

Stephenson, R., Tsui, A.O., Sulzbach, S., Bardsley, P., Bekele, G., Giday, T., ... Feyesitan, B. 2004. "Reproductive Health in Today's World: Franchising

Reproductive Health Services." *Health Services Research* 39(6): 2053–80. https://doi.org/10.1111/j.1475-6773.2004.00332.x.

Svoronos, T., Mjungu, D., Dhadialla, P., Luk, R., Zue, C., Jackson, J., & Lesh, N. 2010. *CommCare: Automated Quality Improvement To Strengthen Community-Based Health.* Weston: D-Tree International.

Thaddeus, S., & Maine, D. 1994. "Too Far to Walk: Maternal Mortality in Context." *Social Science and Medicine* 38(8): 1091–110. https://doi.org/10.1016/0277 -9536(94)90226-7.

USAID. 2011. *Testing Innovative Maternal, Newborn, and Child Health Approaches to Serve Vulnerable Communities: USAID's Partnerships with 14 International Non-Governmental Organizations (INGOs) through the Child Survival & Health Grants Programs in 16 Countries.* Washington, DC: USAID.

Waters, H., Hatt, L., & Peters, D. 2002. "Working with the Private Sector for Child Health. HNP Discussion Paper." *Health Policy and Planning* 18. Washington, DC: The World Bank.

Weberg, D. 2009. "Innovation in Healthcare: A Concept Analysis." *Nursing Administration Quarterly* 33(3): 227–37. https://doi.org/10.1097/NAQ .0b013e3181accaf5.

World Health Organization (WHO). 2010a. *Telemedicine: Opportunities and Developments in Member States.* Geneva: World Health Organization.

– 2010b. *Trends in Maternal Mortality: 1990 to 2008 Estimates Developed by WHO, UNICEF, UNFPA, and the World Bank.* G. Hamel & A. Heene, eds. 32. Geneva: World Health Organization.

– 2011. *mHealth: New Horizons for Health through Mobile Technologies: Global Observatory for eHealth Series* 3. Geneva: World Health Organization.

Yoong, J., Burger, N., Spreng, C., & Sood, N. 2010. "Private Sector Participation and Health System Performance in Sub-Saharan Africa." *PLoS One* 5(10): e13243. https://doi.org/10.1371/journal.pone.0013243.

You, D., Jones, G., & Wardlaw, T. 2011. *Levels and Trends in Child Mortality. Report 2011: Estimates Developed by the UN Inter-Agency Group for Child Mortality Estimation.* New York: UNICEF.

14 Scaling Up Primary Care in Low- and Middle-Income Countries by Using Strategic Management Skills

KATHRYN MOSSMAN, LEIGH HAYDEN, DAVID LEUNG,
ILAN SHAHIN, RAMAN SOHAL, JASON SUKHRAM,
ONIL BHATTACHARYYA, ANITA MCGAHAN,
AND WILL MITCHELL

The Importance of Scaling Up Primary Health Care

Better access to primary care underpins improvements in health around the world. By providing ready access to basic health services and, when necessary, referring patients to more specialized services, primary care helps deliver fewer hospitalizations, lower mortality rates, and better overall health (Beasley, Starfield, van Weel, Rosser, & Haq 2007; Beckman & Katz 2000; Kepp 2008; Starfield, Shi, & Macinko 2005). Our research suggests that a key factor in scaling up primary health care services in low- and middle-income countries (LMICs) is the ability to complement medical expertise with effective management skills.

A 2003 *Lancet* study reported that 63 per cent of child deaths in the 42 countries that account for 90 per cent of global child mortality could be prevented each year through more effective primary care interventions (Jones, Steketee, Black, Bhutta, & Morris 2003). That is 6 million lives – 100 football stadiums of children – that could be saved each year. Improvements in child health over the past 10 years have led to considerable advances – including a better accounting of just how many children are dying of preventable conditions. Quite simply, there is still a long way to go.

Scaling up refers to the process of providing services to more people and/ or increasing the range of health care services that programs provide, with the aim of increasing health impact (Bhattacharyya et al. 2015; Simmons, Fajans, & Ghiron 2007).Scaling up primary care services is essential for improving the health of many millions of people in developing countries who lack access to effective health services (Lewin et al. 2008).While multiple experiments with small-scale pilot projects have demonstrated potentially successful outcomes, relatively few have achieved broader coverage in a country or region (Myers 1984). Nonetheless, while delivering quality primary care in LMICs faces many challenges, some organizations are not only creating successful models of primary care services, they are doing so with substantial scale.

Consider North Star Alliance in Africa. Founded in Malawi in 2005, North Star is now a non-profit chain of 35 roadside health centres, operating along major transportation corridors across 33 African countries. North Star plans to expand to at least 100 centres. North Star primarily serves truck drivers and sex workers, operating in the afternoons and evenings to fit their clients' schedules. The centres hire peer educators to teach these populations about the program's services and gain trust. To encourage clients to seek curative and preventative services, North Star provides services free of charge. To minimize costs and build their brand, they operate clinics from converted shipping containers, which are mobile and standardized. North Star uses IT systems that support real-time transmission of patient data to the different clinics and uses biometrics to track patients and ensure they do not duplicate files and treatments. This helps the centres gain efficiency and maintain quality standards. The IT systems also help track trends in disease and collect demographic information, which helps determine optimal locations for new centres. North Star has a wide range of partnerships: it works with regional governing bodies to influence health policy, partners with global companies to help build new clinics, and has close relationships with nearby hospitals to ensure continuity of patient care.

In addition to North Star, other examples of success in scaling up primary care services in low- and middle-income countries offer insights. Healthspring and Ross Clinics in India, LifeNet International in Burundi and Uganda, Living Goods and Amref in Sub-Saharan Africa, and Viva Africa in Kenya, among others, are striking cases.

The key question is what we can learn from organizations such as these, so that others can build from their success while avoiding wasted effort and dead ends. The emerging answers have elements of common sense – and some important surprises, with strong implications for people involved in management practice and education.

Rapid Routes to Scale: Study

The Rapid Routes to Scale project is seeking to learn how successful primary care models can be replicated and scaled. In research conducted by the University of Toronto's Toronto Health Organization Performance Evaluation (T-HOPE) team, in collaboration with the International Centre for

Social Franchising (ICSF), the International Partnership for Innovative Health Delivery (IPIHD), and Results for Development, we are evaluating scalable primary care models through a mixed methods study approach. This approach, involving reviewing the relevant literature, database assessment, and in-depth interviews with program implementers and experts in this field, allowed for an integrated view and a rich variety of data for analysis (Tritter 2012).

Literature and Database Review

As a first step, we reviewed more than 100 publications on the scale up of health services in LMICs, with a focus on primary care (list offered per request). This literature has measured scaling up in several ways, including measuring inputs, such as adding staff, funds, and supplies; health impact, such as improving health outcomes; and outputs, such as serving larger numbers of patients and delivering more health products (Braitstein, Einterz, Sidle, Kimaiyo, & Tierney 2009; Coffman 2010). For this study, we focus on scaling up in terms of outputs: serving a substantial number of people, while operating without major setbacks in terms of range of services provided and number of clients served.

Scaling up health services to larger numbers of clients can be beneficial in terms of increasing access to health care and in building experience that provides higher quality care. As a well-known example, Narayana Hrudayalaya is one of the largest paediatric heart hospitals in the world. Located in south India, with headquarters in Bengaluru, Narayana performs 32 heart surgeries a day, eight times more volume than average Indian hospitals. In this model, individual doctors gain expertise in one or two types of surgeries that they perform at high volume. This high-volume repetition and specialization contributes to high-quality care: Narayana's thirty-day mortality rate after coronary artery bypass graft surgery is 1.4 per cent, compared to 1.9 per cent in the US (Bhattacharyya et al. 2010). For primary care programs, up to at least some upper bound of organizational size, scaling also can contribute to cost-effectiveness. Learning economies that arise through greater experience can help reduce the variable costs of services while distributing fixed costs over a greater number of patients and services can reduce average fixed costs (Adam, Ebener, Johns, & Evans 2008). Methods for scaling pilot projects in LMICs include expanding initial internal activities as well as collaboration through networks, formal partnerships, and strategic alliances (Cooley & Kohl 2006).

Certainly, there are potential limits to the benefits of scale for health care access, quality, and cost. However, few primary care organizations in LMICs appear to even approach such limits. LMICs are home to the vast majority of base of the pyramid populations, consisting of four billion people with incomes below US$3000 per year in local purchasing power (Hammond, Kramer, Katz, Tran, & Walker 2007). Most of the populations in Asia, Africa, Eastern Europe, and Latin America and the Caribbean are in this segment, where they are often rural, poorly served by established organizations, and dominated by an informal economy. They commonly lack access to basic health care and tend to pay higher prices for basic goods and services, which are also often lower in quality (Hammond et al. 2007). While the need for accessible, quality health services in these contexts is great, there are immense challenges to reaching such LMIC populations. Resource constraints, weak health systems, poor infrastructure, and a severe lack of skilled health workers create significant barriers to effectively and efficiently delivering and expanding access to health services (Bustreo, Okwo-Belle, & Kamara 2015; Ranson, Hanson, Oliveira-Cruz, & Mills 2003; World Health Organization 2014). Accessing the financial resources needed to scale up can be a barrier for organizations serving low-income groups, particularly in LMIC contexts with substantial infrastructure challenges (Yamey 2012).

Primary health care delivery faces additional management challenges for scaling up because it is often not highly valued by patients, operates on thin margins, and is not seen as prestigious by trained health care providers (The Center for Health Market Innovations 2015; Kumar 2012). In LMICs, there are numerous barriers to providing quality primary care, including difficulty attracting, motivating, and retaining primary care staff, (Chimwaza et al. 2014; Dussault & Franceschini 2006) particularly in rural areas (Van Dormael et al. 2008); a lack of adequately trained physicians and nurses (Chen et al. 2012; Kober & Van Damme 2006);high rates of doctor absenteeism (Chaudhury 2004); and a lack of sufficient health worker management and supervision. These challenges contribute to low motivation, lack of accountability, and poor clinical practices (Lindelow & Serneels 2006; Rowe, de Savigny, Lanata, & Victora 2005).

In addition, the management skills needed to address these difficulties and plan and implement the scale up of health service coverage and impact are often scarce in LMICs. The capacity to prioritize both clinical skills and relevant management skills, such as expertise in human resources, finance, strategic planning, marketing, and operations in developing and scaling up programs is often lacking for organizations that already face staffing and resource shortages. While some of these operational challenges for health care services are documented, we found that much of the literature on scaling up health services focuses on vertical interventions for HIV/AIDS and reproductive health, with comparatively little guidance for primary care services (Mangham & Hanson 2010).

Still, our review revealed an intriguing suggestion. Although evidence is still limited, several studies and reports suggest that scaling up high-quality health care may not depend solely on effective clinical skills, but also on thoughtful use of strategic management skills that are common in high-performing companies but unfortunately less common in primary health care organizations (Cooley & Kohl 2006).

Following our literature review, we scanned 465 general primary care programs listed in the Center for Health Market Innovation's (CHMI) database developed by Results for Development. These programs provide a range of primary care services, ranging from comprehensive primary care services at integrated health centres and services that support primary care provision, such as training health workers, developing technologies for primary care programs, developing infrastructure and supply chains, engaging in advocacy and policy around primary care, developing and disseminating health information, or developing financial mechanisms that help patients pay for primary care services (the full database contains information on over 1,400 innovative health programs in LMICs). In our review, we examined primary care programs for information on their activities and evidence of scaling, such as increases in impact, output, or coverage over time. We found that India and Kenya were the top two countries of operation for general primary care programs and that these programs were engaging in a variety of innovative activities including using information technologies; providing consumer education and provider training; and setting up networks, franchises, and mobile clinics. However, the database lacked the detailed information needed to understand which programs were successfully scaling and the factors shaping program scale up.

Site Visits and Interviews

To better understand the routes to scale, we followed up the literature and database review by undertaking a series of site visits and interviews with providers of primary health care services in multiple LMICs in Africa, Latin America, and Asia. The goal of the hands-on discussions was to delve into learning more about the importance of clinical and management skills for successful scaling.

In July 2014, we completed this review, involving on-site and telephone interviews with 37 private for-profit and non-profit health care programs operating in over 25 countries in Asia, Africa, and South America. We placed particular emphasis on programs operating in Kenya and India, which have differing health system structures yet with substantial numbers of documented programs in international databases. We gathered information about these programs from publicly available sources and from the programs themselves. We complemented the interviews with primary care programs with 12 in-depth interviews with experts in primary care and health care scale up, including donors, investors, and academics. This comprehensive and in-depth approach had provided a rich and varied amount of data on how innovative primary care programs in LMICs achieve scale. Interviews and site visits allowed for greater detail and insight into the activities of primary care programs that facilitate scaling. Table 14.A1 in the appendix to this chapter lists the 37 programs in the study.

Analytical Approach

We conducted qualitative analysis of the interview data and field notes. This involved coding for key themes identified by the research team. We tested coder reliability halfway through the coding process, finding 81 per cent intercoder reliability; we coded the remainder of the interviews with a high level of confidence (Miles & Huberman 1994).Through the coding process, we identified key activities described as facilitating scaling up of primary care programs.

For the study, we based the criteria for scaling by determining whether a program had passed a pilot stage, served at least several tens of thousands of people, and had been operating without major setbacks in terms of range of services provided or number of clients served. In practice, the successfully scaled programs in our study each had reached at least 40,000 people, while the less successful programs reached many fewer people and/or encountered substantial operating difficulties.

Based on these criteria, we categorized the 37 programs into three groups. Seven were still in the testing or pilot phase, where they were developing, adapting, and refining their core models without yet attempting to achieve a larger scale (Korten 1980). Twenty programs had successfully scaled up. Ten had been less successful in scaling (two were no longer active and eight had recent setbacks such as substantial decreases in core operations or number of clients served). We were particularly interested in comparing activities of the 10 programs that had struggled to achieve scale with activities of the 20 programs that had scaled successfully.

The literature review and interviews suggested several activities that may facilitate scale up. We used the interview data to conduct statistical analysis to examine which of the factors were statistically associated with successful scaling. We carried out two focus groups to share and validate our findings with selected interview participants.

One of the powerful messages that emerged from assessing differences in the activities of scaled and non-scaled programs is the importance of several types of management skills. While clinical skills are essential for operating a primary health care service, programs that achieved scale commonly complemented their clinical skills with management expertise.

Results

Categories of Management Skills

We found four categories of management skills that helped drive basic operating effectiveness and, in some cases, contributed to the scaling success of primary care providers. The first category of skills is the key demand-side driver that is central to all effective strategic management – a focus on building strong consumer relationships. The other three skill sets involve supply-side management strength in building effective organizations that can deliver reliable value to consumers – fostering innovative financial mechanisms, developing strong administrative and leadership skills, and fostering effective partnerships. Together, these four categories encompass a range of functional and managerial capabilities that the literature on organizational skills highlights (Fortune & Mitchell 2012). What the existing literature does not make clear, though, is which skills are likely to contribute to scaling up of primary care services – our goal is to help identify such impact.

Within the four categories of demand- and supply-side management skills, we found multiple activities that facilitated the programs' ability to offer effective primary care services. Some of the activities arose in many programs. Others, while less common, were intriguing examples of outlier innovations that offer potential for wider spread adoption.

In turn, we investigated whether the activities appeared to provide benefits for scaling an organization's services, beyond simply helping a program operate at a base level. In this comparison, we found two classes of activities: base activities and scaling differentiators.

Base activities are equally common in programs that both do and do not achieve scale. These are activities that program leaders told us are important for facilitating scale up, yet statistically were no more common in programs that achieved scale than in programs that did not scale up. Hence, base activities contribute to the ability of a program to operate, but do not differentiate scaled and unscaled programs.

More intriguingly, some activities were scaling differentiators. If a program had one or more of what we refer to as differentiator features, it was more likely to achieve scale than a program that did not have these features. Statistical and qualitative analysis of the data from our interviews suggest that these differentiating features, sometimes alone and sometimes in combination, tend to distinguish among scaled and unscaled programs. Figure 14.1 reports the scaling differentiators.

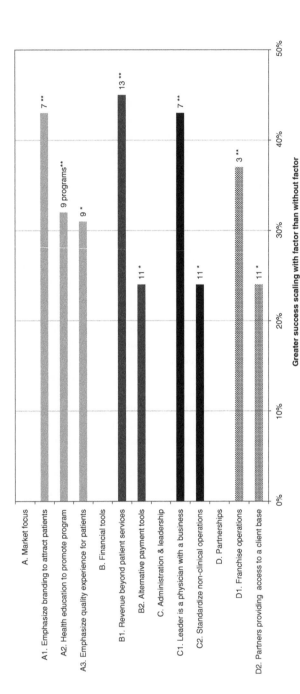

Figure 14.1 Differentiating factors that distinguish successfully scaled primary care programs: Comparison of 20 scaled versus 10 not scaled

Note: The bars report the difference in scaling success among programs with the differentiating factor compared to those without the differentiator, along with the number of the 30 programs in the study that had adopted the factor. For instance, the 13 programs that sought revenue sources beyond fee-for-service by patients were about 45 per cent more likely to scale than programs that relied primarily on fee-for-service payments (significant differences based on paired-sample t-tests; ** p <0.05; * p <0.10).

Two additional null results concerning financial status are intriguing. First, we used the CHMI data to determine whether the programs had for-profit status (57 per cent of the cases). We found no significant relationship between for-profit status and successful scaling; 65 per cent of the programs with for-profit status that had moved beyond pilot stage had scaled successfully, while 69 per cent of the other post-pilot programs had done so.

Second, we used the CHMI data to determine the types of funding that each of the programs relied on, based on six types of financial sources: donor (57 per cent of the programs), out-of-pocket payment (46 per cent), membership/subscriptions (32 per cent), investors (27 per cent), government (24 per cent), and in kind contributions (14 per cent). The shares add up to more than 100 per cent, because many programs used more than one financial source (mean of 2.0 sources, with range from 1 to 4). We found no significant differences for successful versus unsuccessful scaling based on six types of funding sources. We were not able to determine the level of funding that the programs obtained, which in any case would be as much a result of their scaling success as a contributor to scaling. Nonetheless, the fact that type of funding does not appear to drive scaling is important, because it indicates that scaling arises more from the activities of the program than from the type of support it is able to attract. As we note below, however, programs that developed more nuanced financial innovations did gain benefits for achieving scale.

The following discussion highlights the scaling differentiators in the four categories of management skills, while also listing the base activities (we provide examples of the base activities later in the article).

1. MARKET FOCUS: BUILD STRONG CONSUMER RELATIONSHIPS

Health care organizations often take a "supply side" view of their activities, expecting that if they make health services available, people will utilize them because of the organization's technical expertise. Yet, in multiple countries, many primary care facilities are underutilized, while specialist services are oversubscribed.

By contrast, a few primary care organizations in our study were working to develop a demand-side understanding of the market with a focus on attracting health consumers (O'Donnell 2007). Some programs focus on bringing their services to patients, such as with mobile clinics to reach rural areas, while others bring patients to their facilities for services. Health by Motorbike in Kenya, for instance, sends nurses on foot or motorbike to visit houses door to door to provide medications, health supplies, and services, and will also use the motorcycle for emergency transportation for pregnant women and those who cannot walk to bring them to health facilities.

The demand-side focus is important because, even though poor populations are price sensitive, they are willing to pay for health care if they consider it to provide value for their money (Berelowitz, Horn, Thornton, Leeds, & Wong 2013). Bottom-of-the-pyramid populations are unable to spend their limited funds on non-basic needs, but they may have more buying power for some necessary products and services than others, and this segment represents 50 per cent of the purchasing power in developing countries (Guesalaga & Marshall 2008). The market focus category included skills and activities emphasizing building strong relationships with patients, essentially treating them as customers whose systemic needs and desires needed to be addressed beyond their core medical needs.

We found two base activities in the market focus category: engaging with community mobilizers and adjusting offerings to meet patient demand. In the literature on scaling, fostering community engagement and adapting a program to the needs and interests of local populations are both often described as success factors for scaling up health interventions (World Health Organization and Expand Net 2009). However, in our study, we found that while these are important base activities for primary care programs, they are not scaling differentiators.

Beyond the base activities, we found three market-focus scaling differentiators that involve conveying the value and quality of services in order to attract clients to the program. The three scaling differentiators included patient experience, branding, and health education.

- *Patient experience.* Teach people throughout the organization to focus on the patient experience, making people feel welcome rather than sick. Even ill people – indeed, perhaps especially ill people – will avoid environments that do not feel welcoming. Examples of efforts to engage patients as clients in our cases included welcoming people to the clinics, creating comfortable waiting rooms, and taking time to explain treatment options.
- *Branding and marketing.* Develop active branding and marketing strategies. Marketing the benefits of health and health practices is particularly effective when it is designed to sell on the same kinds of criteria that often shape marketing over non-health products. Radio and online media, particularly accessible through mobile devices, are prevalent in resource-limited settings, and are important vehicles for conveying information about health care products and services. When the benefits of good health practices are sold to the public, their uptake tends to spread more quickly. Gilson and Schneider (2010) note that having clear messaging about the advantages of an intervention can be beneficial for scaling up.

Examples in our cases included local press campaigns, social marketing, and connecting one's brand with quality, comfortable services.

• *Health education.* Create health education campaigns to promote services. Simply offering services without helping people understand why the services are useful to promote health and/or address illness will not attract clients. Examples of health education in our cases included campaigns in small businesses, churches, schools, and markets.

2. FINANCIAL TOOLS: FOSTER INNOVATIVE FINANCIAL MECHANISMS

LMIC populations often need to make health decisions based on low daily incomes. Consider that in India, an estimated 22 per cent of the population lives below the poverty line, with 70 per cent of health care paid for out of pocket, impoverishing approximately 40 million people a year (Balarajan, Selvaraj, & Subramanian 2011; World Bank 2014). Primary health care patients in LMICs often cannot afford to or are unwilling to pay directly for services from formal primary care facilities, preferring to visit pharmacies or informal providers for medications and advice, (Kapoor, Raman, Sachdeva, & Satyanarayana 2012; Ross-Degnan et al. 1996; Sudhinaraset, Ingram, Lofthouse, & Montagu 2013) such that primary care providers struggle to generate sufficient revenue. Enabling access through alternative financial and payment models can be an important strategy for reaching poor market segments (Hammond et al. 2007), and developing mechanisms to ensure access to sustainable financial resources is essential to facilitate the scaling-up process (Cooley & Kohl 2006). Financial tools included the ability to generate revenue in innovative ways.

The financial tools category had no base activities, while providing two scaling differentiators. Strikingly, these financial scaling differentiators are more nuanced – and impactful – than simply relying on a broader range of funding sources, which we noted above did not differentiate programs that achieved or did not achieve scale.

• *Complementary revenue.* Develop a suite of other products and services that provide additional revenue, beyond patient payments for services. Examples of complementary revenue in our cases including selling personal care products, renting space and vehicles, selling evacuation insurance, and selling IT tools.

• *Alternative payment mechanisms.* Develop payment tools that do not rely on out-of-pocket payment at point of care when people need services. Examples of alternative payment mechanisms in our cases included microinsurance, health plans, and subscription or membership fees.

3. ADMINISTRATION AND LEADERSHIP: ENSURE OPERATING EFFECTIVENESS

As low-margin organizations, primary care programs need to keep their operations lean. Yet, while operating as efficiently as possible, programs need to ensure that they maintain quality and customer service. Many programs described lacking leadership and staff with knowledge and experience on operating and scaling a low-margin business. The administration and leadership category highlighted the need to run primary care services not simply as medical facilities, but as smoothly operating businesslike facilities, including the ability to develop efficient and standardized processes that support the scale up of health care services (UNICEF 2012; Waddington 2012). This skill set included both basic administrative skills and strong leadership. Indeed, several studies suggest that leadership, commitment, and competence from key actors are important drivers of change and innovation adoption in primary care organizations (Longo 2007).This is vital for succeeding in resource-constrained contexts where new processes and models are needed to overcome traditional health care barriers (Bhattacharyya et al. 2010).

We found that the administration and leadership category had several base activities: building strong supply chains, investing in relevant IT to increase efficiency and connect clients and providers, developing non-doctor staffing, attracting doctors from alternative demographics, developing selective hiring processes, emphasizing ongoing staff training, and creating staff incentives that align with goals. The administrative and leadership capacity to hire and motivate qualified staff is often described in the literature as one of the top enablers of scale up (De Maeseneer 2013; Mackinco, de Souza, Guanais, & Simoes 2007; Sibthorpe, Glasgow, & Wells 2005; Walley et al. 2008). Intriguingly, though, we found that innovative human resources management is a base activity that contributes to programs achieving their goals, but is not a differentiating feature that distinguishes successfully scaling programs.

We did find two administration and leadership scaling differentiators.

- *Dual medical and business skills.* Develop leaders who have both medical and business skills. Several strong clinicians in our cases described previous business experience or training as giving them the management tools and insights to design and scale up their primary care models. Some also hired management consultants while pursuing partnerships with organizations able to provide management and technical support. Indeed, consulting comprises an in-kind contribution that experienced business executives can provide to health care organizations, providing coaching and on-the-job training that may be easier for health care leaders than taking time off to take management courses.

- *Administrative standardization.* Standardize administrative practices. Standardization helps generate efficiency in base operations so that staff can focus on the needs of individual patients. Examples of standardization in our cases included IT, clinic layout, branding, and human resources models.

4. PARTNERSHIPS: FOSTER EFFECTIVE COLLABORATION

Primary health care operates within complex ecosystems, which require thoughtful engagement and coordination both to overcome barriers and to create opportunities for growth. Primary care programs collaborate with a wide range of institutions and organizations to implement their projects, including NGO collaborators, funders, financial institutions, and businesses (Burleigh n.d.: Innovations in Healthcare 2013). Unconventional partnerships among diverse partners can be a useful strategy for targeting hard-to-reach poor populations (Hammond et al. 2007). The partnership category included activities involved in building complementary relationships with external stakeholders. While partnerships are considered beneficial for scaling up, (Bradley et al. 2012) only certain types of partnerships appear to differentiate successfully scaling programs from those that are not.

The partnerships category had two base activities: aligning with government actors and partnering with organizations that provide technical support.

We found two partnership scaling differentiators.

- *Franchising.* Seek franchising opportunities, which help expand an existing business model. Franchising entails contracting a network of private providers to deliver services under a common brand (Schlein & Montagu 2012), regulating the services of this heterogeneous network that often receives access to advertising, training, and business loans (Prata, Montagu, & Jefferys 2005). Though relatively uncommon in our cases (three programs), franchising is an intriguing outlier innovation that facilitated expansion for some programs. Franchising includes elements of administrative standardization but goes beyond a standardization strategy by training personnel from multiple facilities while creating joint supply chains, branding, financial support, and other services for a wider span of organizations.
- *Partnerships for clients.* Create demand-side partnerships with organizations that provide access to a customer base. Client partnerships in

our cases included health care professionals, local non-profits and businesses, and government agencies. Such partnerships are often compatible with the incentives of both sets of stakeholders, whether for-profit, non-profit, or public actors, helping provide greater operating scale and, especially, linking complementary resources across different types of organizations.

Combinations of Differentiating Skills and Impact of Skills in Different Contexts

We investigated combinations of the differentiating factors to determine whether best practices for scaling tend to cluster. For the most part, we found few significant combinations. Instead, it appears that programs that scale successfully tend to link relevant approaches that make sense in their contexts, rather than attempt to follow a standard one-size-fits-all recipe.

Nonetheless, we did find one set of significant joint relationships, with a powerful message. Scaled programs with strong skills in the leadership and administration category correlated with the extent of activities in each of the three other categories – market focus, financials tools, and partnerships. (The correlations of the "administration and leadership" skills category with the market focus, financial tools, and partnerships categories ranged from $r=0.26$ to $r=0.43$). Among the leadership and administration activities that made up the category, the correlations were particularly strong with the "dual skills" combination of medical and business skills component.

The key implication here is that executives with strong leadership skills are best able to identify and implement the need for relevant complementary skills that underlie successful scale up. These include improvements of internal operating skills, as well as greater ability to identify and manage partnership relationships. We note that the link between leadership and execution will commonly arise as a sequential process, in which initial leadership expertise creates the base skill from which organizations are able to build effective operational activities. In turn, there is the potential for a virtuous cycle, in which organizations invest in improving their leadership capabilities in order to drive ongoing operational excellence. Table 14.1 highlights this linking relationship for business leadership.

In order to explore possible differences in contextual relevance, we investigated whether the base activities or scaling differentiators had differing impact across geographic and/or income segments. The programs operated in a mix of rural and urban settings, as well as in different income groups. Owing to the

Table 14.1 Related combinations of differentiating categories

	Market Focus	Financial Tools	Partnerships
Administration and leadership	Yes	Yes	Yes
Market focus		No	No
Financial tools			No

Note: Relationships based on correlations (r ≥ 0.25).

relatively small number of cases within each setting, we aggregated the base activity and scaling differentiator factors within each of the four categories of management skills, rather than attempting to assess the impact of each of the individual factors.

The results for the scaling differentiators were intriguing. We found that adopting the base activities had similar impact across the settings. By contrast, we found that adopting scaling differentiators had somewhat greater impact on scaling in urban settings and for income groups outside the bottom of the pyramid (bottom 20 per cent of the income distribution), possibly because both these settings are more competitive and more complex.

These differences across geography and income segments point to relevant contextual factors for choosing among scaling differentiators. Volume-driven models have less benefit in remote areas, for instance, while cross-subsidies will be less valuable when potential clients are uniformly poor. Nonetheless, despite some differences in relative impact, the scaling differentiators typically offered at least moderate benefits in all geographic and income segments.

Rapid Routes to Scale: Examples

We expand the discussion with a series of examples that illustrate the base activities and scaling differentiators. In addition, we outline three integrative examples of programs that have scaled successfully. Table 14.2 summarizes the base activities and scaling differentiators.

Examples of Scaling Differentiators

Here are some examples from our interview programs of differentiator activities that have facilitated scaling up. Programs in the study that developed differentiator skills were more likely to scale than programs that did not.

Table 14.2 Summary of program characteristics: Base activities and scaling differentiators

Category	Base Activities	Scaling Differentiators
1. Market focus: Build strong consumer relationships	• Community mobilizers • Adjusting offerings to meet patient demand	• Patient experience: Focus on patient experience • Branding: Branding and marketing • Health education: Health education campaigns to promote services
2. Financial tools: Foster innovative financial mechanisms		• Alternative payment tools: Develop payment tools that do not rely on out-of-pocket payment at point of care when people need services • Complementary revenue: Selling other products and services
3. Administration and leadership: Ensure operating effectiveness	• Supply-chain enhancements • Investing in new technologies, including remote technology to connect patients with clinicians • Non-doctor staffing models • Selective hiring processes • Ongoing staff training • Staff incentives • Attract doctors from alternative demographics	• Administrative standardization: Standardizing non-clinical practices • Dual medical and business skills: Combination of medical and business skills
4. Partnerships: Foster effective collaboration	• Alignment and partnership with government • Partnerships with organizations that provide technical support and/or build capabilities	• Partnerships for clients: Partnerships with organizations that provide access to a customer base • Franchising: Seek franchising opportunities

Note: Base activities contribute to the ability of a primary care program to achieve its basic operating goals, but do not differentiate scaled and unscaled programs. By contrast, if a program had one or more differentiator features, it was more likely to achieve scale than a program that did not have these features.

1. MARKET FOCUS: BUILD STRONG CONSUMER RELATIONSHIPS

Health Education (Eight Scaled Programs). Two examples illustrate health education.

- Lifebuoy Friendship Hospital is a non-profit in Bangladesh that provides primary and secondary health care to remote communities through floating hospitals developed from retired barges. Lifebuoy sponsors health education events in the communities that it serves, using its staff on its vessels and also via satellite clinics that it operates in the villages, highlighting the benefits of its services.
- Penda Health, a clinic chain in Kenya that is in its pilot stage while appearing to move towards successful scaling (Starfield et al. 2005), offers health education and awareness events with small businesses, churches, schools, and at markets. They focus on bringing the community together and offer education on health care while also letting people know where the clinic is. This has helped the clinic increase patient numbers and also motivates staff.

Patient Experience (Seven Scaled Programs). Several programs have active tactics for highlighting the patient experience. For instance, Healthspring, a clinic chain in Mumbai, describes customer experience as being critical – "the act of coming to the centre should make you feel better, not worse. We put the emphasis on people." Staff members at their clinics are expected to greet patients with a smile and make sure they are seen on time, make patients feel important and answer their questions, and thoroughly explain treatment options. Their doctors are restricted to four appointments per hour – this restriction may appear to limit scale, but helps the clinic get the right mix of quality and throughput that drive demand. As well, their waiting area is tidy and clean with calming colours, comfortable sofas, and free reading material – an environment that may appear standard in many developed market contexts, but contrasts strikingly with many of Healthspring's competitors.

Branding (Seven Scaled Programs). Two examples demonstrate the benefits of active branding.

- LifeNet is a non-profit organization in Burundi that franchises clinics owned by local entrepreneurs and churches. Patients recognize the LifeNet clinic brand as being high-quality care – this is a point of pride for franchisees, who gain clients because of the branding.
- MeraDoctor is a health hotline and medical discount service operating in over 19 states in India. It positions its brand as providing honest,

patient-focused, compassionate care. MeraDoctor promotes its brand and markets its services using seminars, health camps, radio, and a sales force that shares testimonies from existing patients.

2. FINANCIAL TOOLS: FOSTER INNOVATIVE FINANCIAL MECHANISMS

Complementary Revenue (13 Scaled Programs). Several programs have initiated innovative ways of increasing revenue sources.

- *Evacuation insurance.* Amref Health Africa is an international NGO that provides health services and capacity building in seven African countries. Amref often works in remote areas and provides evacuation insurance through its wholly owned AMREF Flying Doctors, which helps to generate revenue for the organization with its international air ambulance services.
- *Vehicle rental.* Health by Motorbike uses motorcycles to transport health professionals to rural areas in Kenya. When a motorbike is not in use by the program, they rent it out to women to use for non-medical purposes.
- *IT tools.* Several primary care programs in India, including Swasth Health Centres, have developed their own IT platforms with electronic medical records for primary care that are tailored to be user friendly for clinicians and staff to enter and review data. Swasth generates revenue by providing this software to other providers. Similarly, IT innovations such as Dimagi's mobile data collection platform, CommCare, and Neurosynaptics remote diagnostic tools are sold to primary care providers and generate income for these IT-enabled programs.
- *Subscriptions.* Several programs in India, such as Ross Clinics and Healthspring, sell organizational subscriptions to corporations, schools, and NGOs to provide health services for their members. The large clients provide a larger, more stable base of income for programs. Notably, both of these examples operate in middle-income segments, in which patients and their sponsors enjoy some income flexibility, rather than the bottom of the pyramid, where most patients lack cash flow needed for such subscriptions.

Alternative Payment Tools (10 Scaled Programs). Multiple programs have developed payment tools that do not rely on payment for individual services, including microinsurance, health plans, and subscription or membership fees.

- Mediphone is a health hotline in India that allows clients to speak to doctors and get a prescription. The program sells subscriptions so clients can pay for 100 calls in advance to get subsidized calls for the whole family.

- Sevamob provides mobile clinic services in periurban areas around Delhi, India. It provides health payment plans, and for around 600 INR (US$10 a year, a client can have four visits with one of their heath professionals and access to their health hotline. Health plans are tailored to the target group, such as orphanages or sex workers, and some plans included medical testing while others require an additional fee.
- Ross Clinics in India provides a family health plan. For 699 India rupees (around US$11) a year, enrollees receive a discount on medications, and there is no additional fee for consultation.
- Changamka Microhealth in Kenya offers microinsurance that can be paid for using mobile money through Safaricom's mPesa. Changamka offers family health insurance plans for annual cost of 6,000 to 12,000 Kenyan shillings (about US$60 to $120) that include outpatient and inpatient care, as well as funeral coverage.

3. ADMINISTRATION AND LEADERSHIP: ENSURE OPERATING EFFECTIVENESS

Administrative Standardization (Nine Scaled Programs). Programs gained scaling benefits when they created standardized operations.

- Swasth Health Centres in Mumbai has a standardized checklist for launching centres, which assists the complex process of launching clinics. They have the same branding and basic layout in their 150–200 square foot clinics, as well as the same staffing of each clinic – a doctor, a dentist, and a medical assistant, a dental assistant and a receptionist. They offer the same basic services at each clinic, and have a standardized IT system.
- Founded in 2011, Penda Health is a pilot-stage chain of for-profit primary care clinics operating in Kenya. By standardizing procedures for a limited set of high prevalence health issues, the chain provides most services through clinical officers rather than more scarce and costly physicians or nurse practitioners. This helps to decrease costs while ensuring high quality of care. The program is also using technology to improve inventory management through remote monitoring of sales and medical supplies. By focusing on keeping operating costs low through increased efficiency, Penda Health, while still in its pilot stage, was in the process of opening its third clinic at the time of the interviews and has ambitious plans to open 100 clinics across East Africa by 2020.

Dual Medical and Business Skills (Seven Scaled Programs). Our research found that while programs led by physicians were not necessarily more likely to scale up successfully, those with leaders that had a medical background and also had experience or training in business were more likely to be in the scaling group.

* The founder of Ross Clinics in India told us that when he first opened the clinics he thought that providing good quality care at a price they could afford would bring people in. He learned that was not the case, that people needed a reason to use the services that reflected their own understanding of needs. He had previously taken a management course on developing one's own business and, seeing that the underlying challenge to gaining clients was a business problem, used his management skills to experiment with methods of generating demand and creating client loyalty, and then focused on system optimization to reduce costs.
* The founder of Nationwide, another clinic chain in India, was trained as a physician, and realizing he lacked experience and skills in management, he pursued an MBA with a focus on strategy and leadership. He used the business training to help scale in two ways. First, strategically, he developed a method of retaining family physicians (which was initially difficult and risky) to reduce operational risk and staff turnover costs. He also recognized the importance of building a brand, and hired a branding and marketing expert. Second, he used the network he developed while training in the United States to attract and manage investors.

4. PARTNERSHIPS: FOSTER EFFECTIVE COLLABORATION

Partner for Clients (Nine Scaled Programs). Partnerships can provide scaling benefits when the relationships provide access to clients.

* *Local professionals.* Ross Clinics in India provides health camps and services for corporations in India, often partnering with local labs and doctors in areas where Ross Clinics does not yet have a presence.
* *Government.* Karuna Trust in India contracts to run government clinics. Starting with two primary health centres, the non-profit currently manages 68 centres in eight states through a public-private partnership model.
* *Local infrastructure.* Sevamob partners with NGOs, schools, and orphanages in India, providing health services to their clients. The program sometimes uses the existing infrastructure available through their local partners, such as sharing office space with Swasti, a non-profit resource centre in Karnataka. This helps to reduce start-up and overhead costs in new areas and provides ready access to a client base.

- *Franchising (three scaled programs).* Franchising involves efforts to standardize the operations of franchisees, as well as provide them with supplies, branding, and training. Living Goods is a micro-franchise in East Africa that recruits and trains community health workers to provide some basic curative and prevention services while also selling medical and other household products door to door. They provide business training and provide branding and a "business in a bag" with a uniform, record books, and consumer goods. They also monitor quality by having regular field visits and testing knowledge. This standardized approach recently has helped Living Goods to expand from Uganda to Kenya.

Examples of Base Activities

Programs that scale also may feature several base activities, as do many programs that do not achieve scale. Hence, base activities contribute to the ability of a program to operate, but do not differentiate scaled and unscaled programs.

1. MARKET FOCUS: BUILD STRONG CONSUMER RELATIONSHIPS

Base Activities. Adjust offerings to meet patient demand; engage with community mobilizers.

Adjust Offerings to Meet Patient Demand (Eight Programs). Access Afya is a pilot-stage clinic chain in the slums of Nairobi. They originally started with health kiosks on health prevention and sanitation. They then held a focus group with members of the community, who said they would not pay for information alone. They realized that to sell wellness and prevention, a provider must begin by selling sick care. Once they are there, then they can be informed about family planning or immunizations. Community feedback helped them see that they needed to look and feel more conventional for people to want their services. As a result, the program has been opening small clinics in slum areas with both preventative and curative services.

Engage with Community Mobilizers (Seven Programs). CHADIK (Kenya) provides a mobile clinic to rural areas of Kenya. Before the camps take place, community health workers go door to door to let community members know when the mobile clinic will arrive. They help to bring in patients, and communicate with CHADIK to prepare them for the type of services that will be required. These community mobilizers encourage patients to use their services.

2. FINANCIAL TOOLS: FOSTER INNOVATIVE FINANCIAL MECHANISMS

Both of the financial mechanisms (alternative payment tools and complementary revenue) that we identified provided differentiating benefits as we described above, rather than simply being base activities.

3. ADMINISTRATION AND LEADERSHIP: ENSURE OPERATING EFFECTIVENESS

Base Activities. Managing logistics and recruiting appropriately skilled staff is difficult in LMICs, especially in rural areas, while maintaining staff motivation is challenging in all settings. Base activities include investing in relevant local and distant IT, developing selective hiring processes, emphasizing ongoing staff training, creating staff incentives that align with goals, developing non-doctor staffing, attracting doctors from alternative demographics, and building strong supply chains.

Invest in Relevant Local and Distant IT (31 Programs). Information technology (IT) often provides a necessary base for operations in programs of any scale. Almost all of the programs in the study incorporate IT in their activities; hence, while providing a base for operations, IT investment did not differentiate scaled programs.

- North Star in Africa is using IT systems to allow for real-time transmission of patient data to their different clinics along transport routes in Africa. It also uses biometrics to track patients and ensure they do not duplicate files and treatments. This helps them to increase efficiency and maintain quality standards. It also assists in tracking trends in disease and collecting demographic information, which allows them to determine optimal locations for new centres.
- World Health Partners connects patients in rural areas visiting franchised informal providers using telemedicine. By providing a computer and internet connection, as well as using remote diagnostics designed by Neurosynaptics, patients can then be seen through a video link by doctors at the Central Medical Facility in Delhi.

Selective Hiring Processes (Five Programs). A few programs have active methods of identifying committed staff. Ross Clinics in Delhi, for instance, described having a vigorous hiring process for clinical managers, who are an integral part of the model because they help to run the clinics, manage patients, and assist the doctor. In their interview process, they look for applicants that are motivated, capable at multitasking, quick learners, and have good people skills. In a recent hiring process, they described going through 80 applicants to make sure they make the right choice.

Ongoing Staff Training (22 Programs). Providing training to program staff helps to promote quality clinical care, staff engagement, and adherence to program policies and practices. Penda Health in Kenya uses online programs to train staff on clinical practices, as well as in-person training on medical techniques such as IUD insertion. CHADIK also operates in Kenya and uses web conferencing to allow access to medical experts and trainers who provide training remotely to its health workers.

Staff Incentives (13 Programs). In addition to hiring motivated staff with the right skills, programs are offering incentives to retain staff. This includes providing manageable set working hours, comfortable working environments, and a salary at the market rate.

• Healthspring in Mumbai India provides pay for performance for its doctors based on customer satisfaction.
• Nationwide is a clinic chain in India that recruits medical school graduates who are unable to obtain limited specialist residency spots and instead provides them with family medicine training and an opportunity to write the UK examinations and obtain a UK recognized certification in family medicine. This training attracts new recruits and also helps to improve the quality of their staff. In turn, Nationwide pays its doctors a fixed salary and, as an incentive, provides performance bonuses based on protocol adherence, clinical outcomes, and patient satisfaction surveys.

Non-Doctor Staffing Models (19 Programs). Half the programs in the study have found ways to circumvent shortages of physicians by using other health care professionals to provide sophisticated health care services. This is another factor that helps provide a strong base but does not differentiate scaling.

• Health by Motorbike in Kenya uses nurses and locally trained and recruited health promoters to visit remote communities and engage in basic curative services and health promotion.
• Vaatsalya is a chain of primary and secondary care hospitals in India. 80 per cent of their staff are nurses, considered the backbone of the program. They focus on training and incentive programs to retain these health workers.
• Three clinic chains in Nairobi – Viva Afya, Penda Health, and Access Afya – hire non-physician clinical officers, who are mid-level health workers with a more restricted scope of practice.

Doctors from Alternative Demographics (Five Programs). A few programs are appealing to certain types of doctors that may be more interested in working in lower-cost primary care settings. Swasth Health Centres operates a clinic chain in Mumbai's slums; it hires retired government doctors who are motivated to help lower-income populations, and also appreciate having a fixed salary while not having to deal with administrative issues. At this point in their careers, they do not want to take the risk of setting up their own clinics or have to take night shifts at a government hospital, and the Swasth model appeals to them.

Build Strong Supply Chains (11 Programs). World Health Partners in rural India hires local people to use motorcycles to replenish supplies to their network of pharmacies. They have also developed a branded supply of medications, Sky Meds, made available to their own network and to outside pharmacies. The program decided to branch into this area due to the lack of local pharmaceutical supply, where previously there were either no medications available to communities or very small pharmacies with limited selection and high prices.

4. PARTNERSHIPS: FOSTER EFFECTIVE COLLABORATION

Base Activities. Align with government actors; partner with organizations that provide technical and management support.

Alignment with Government Priorities and Partnerships between Private Sector and Government Actors (24 Programs). Government agencies are often key providers of primary care and are responsible for legislating this area, where programs operate in complex health ecosystems. The role of primary care is to connect patients to the wider health infrastructure; being connected is crucial for this. In Rio de Janeiro, Brazil, the municipal government has decided to prioritize the scale up of primary care clinics. It encountered several bureaucratic barriers to scaling up rapidly and overcame this by contracting local NGOs to run the clinics. So far, this private public partnership, Clinicas da Familia, has scaled to over 200 clinics in the last six years. A majority of programs in the study have some form of government connections, again providing a base without differentiating.

Partner with Organizations That Provide Technical Support and/or Build Capabilities (18 Programs). Many programs have sought relationships with public, for-profit, and non-profit organizations that can provide technical support and build organizational capacity, while sometimes also providing financial support. Some relationships, such as those involving established partnerships with telecom providers, tend to provide ongoing support; in contrast, partnerships focused on management training and targeted consultancy may be shorter engagements. However, even short-term support can help build valuable networks that can be called upon in the future should further assistance with capacity building and technical support be needed.

- *Telecom providers.* Programs such as Changamka and Mediphone rely on partnerships with telecom companies to provide their services. Changamka provides microinsurance that can be paid for using mobile money through Safaricom's mPesa in Kenya. Mediphone is a health hotline and was developed through a partnership involving Medibank, Healthfore (a division of Religare Technologies), and AirTel (the largest telecom provider in India). The technical support and expertise support of the established firms can help primary health care programs develop their capacity to reach a client base; in addition, the larger companies also provide financial support that facilitates at least base operations.
- *Management training.* Community Health Africa Trust is a non-profit that provides primary care with a focus on reproductive health in remote parts of Kenya. The program has received management training on providing family planning from Marie Stopes International, as well as training on managing finances and monitoring results from CARE through the Global Fund. This support can be helpful because some programs lack experience in managing and expanding their operations.
- *Targeted consultancy.* Several programs have participated in collaborations with organizations such as Innovations in Healthcare (Innovations in Healthcare 2016) and CHMI (CHMI 2014) to gain insight, knowledge, and networks to scale their primary care and health care models.

Integrative Examples

Finally, here are three summaries of successfully scaled programs, in addition to the example of North Star Alliance that we described at the beginning of the article. The examples highlight different mixes of activities that underlie the success of the two programs.

ROSS CLINICS (INDIA)

Ross Clinics is a for-profit chain of eight primary care clinics in Gurgaon (a suburb of New Delhi). They are located in densely populated middle-class neighbourhoods, in areas with high visibility and accessibility. For customer convenience, they have a one-stop shop, providing primary care, dental, gynaecology, physiotherapy, a lab, and a pharmacy under one roof. They have also partnered with other organizations, providing corporate subscriptions involving the provision of medical services through corporate offices to make it easier for employees to receive preventive and curative care.

Ross Clinics sells individual services, including consultations, tests, and medications, and also provides annual plans for individuals and families to encourage timely care seeking and reduce unplanned health expenditures. For 1999 Indian rupees (about US$30), a plan for a family of four includes up to 24 free doctor and dental consultations and a discount on a number of services and medicines.

Ross Clinics is selective about who it hires. They depend heavily on good clinical managers who are organized, dedicated, creative, and compassionate. They work hard to attract and retain these managers, who are essential to clinic operations.

The clinic chain shares drug supply and staff supply information across clinics to streamline drug ordering and share resources. They also use electronic medical records to track patient information, fostering continuity and quality of care. They are developing partnerships with gated neighbourhoods to supply them with family doctors for home and clinic visits. They are partnering with pharmacies, providing them with a part-time family doctor to help them scale without building new brick-and-mortar clinics. Ross Clinics also receives technical assistance as a member of the CHMI Primary Care Learning Collaborative, a peer-learning network for sharing insight and knowledge on operating primary care models with other practitioners.

SWASTH HEALTH CENTRES (INDIA)

Swasth built its first health centre in the slums of Mumbai in 2011; they now have 15 clinics in the area. Swasth has ambitious scale-up plans; they have opened nine new clinics since January 2014 and want to open ten new clinics every quarter. They describe their model as 5 D services – doctor, drugs, dental, day care, and diagnostics – at 50 per cent of the market rate with 90 per cent user satisfaction.

Swasth is unusual in that they are a for-profit chain serving patients just above the poverty line, but for whom a health crisis could put them below the poverty line. They keep costs low by renting 150-square-foot spaces in slums, and focus on hiring retired doctors who they provide with a stable salary rather than fee for service. They also use clinical assistants rather than nurses. They have a charitable arm, Swasth Foundation, which allows them to raise money; donors can sponsor a clinic, which provides Swasth with the funds to set up and operate a clinic until it breaks even. They also have their own in-house electronic medical record and diagnostic service, which they allow other clinics and patients to use for a fee. In this way, Swasth focuses on being efficient and cost-effective, while also being creative in generating funds from other areas, which goes towards opening and operating clinics.

The executive members of Swasth have government, non-profit, and for-profit experience in health care and IT, and have focused on serving the poor and rapidly scaling programs. Swasth is a member of the CHMI Primary Care Learning Collaborative. The organization is also a member of the Social Entrepreneurship Accelerator at Duke (Duke University 2016) and the Innovations in Healthcare innovator network (Innovations in Healthcare 2016), for which selected programs receive technical assistance with scaling their models through business and strategy support, peer learning, and targeted connections with members of the investor community.

LIFENET INTERNATIONAL (BURUNDI AND UGANDA)

LifeNet International is a non-profit organization that franchises church-based clinics in both the public and private sectors. Its current franchise conversion model was implemented in 2012 and has grown to include 60 partner clinics.

The organization aims to improve population health by increasing the quality of patient care through providing its franchised clinics with supportive tools. It provides medical and management training for the largely nurse-run clinics, with training modules provided by local nurse trainers who then train clinic staff once a month. LifeNet tracks the progress of franchised clinics with medical and management quality scorecards, which are based on international health care standards and local Ministry of Health standards. The aim is to double the quality of care at partner clinics within 24 months of joining the network. Franchised clinics also receive professional LifeNet branding, which patients associate with high-quality care, resulting in increased patient volume as a result of this brand positioning.

Health centres charge patients for providing clinical services and dispensing medications, and LifeNet also assists with pharmaceutical supply. This includes linking rural partner clinics with wholesalers and having franchisees order medications in advance of a monthly training visit from LifeNet staff, who then bring the medication orders with them. This helps to project supply needs, reduce stock-outs, and avoid unnecessary long-distance travel by nurses to pick up medications.

In parallel, the organization provides access to growth financing for its franchises that have achieved at least 75 per cent of LifeNet's quality metric, providing loans of US$5,000 to US$30,000 to help clinics with construction projects and program implementation. LifeNet also provides a rent-to-own program for health centres to rent medical equipment for a small fee, gradually accumulating enough capital to purchase the item. This helps health centres to generate more revenue through expanded services, and also provides LifeNet with revenue from loan repayment.

As a non-profit organization, LifeNet is able to raise funds from donors, which allows it to support its almost US$920,000 in expenses in 2014. In addition, the organization benefits from technical support through its membership in both the CHMI Primary Care Learning Group Collaborative and the IPIHD innovator network.

Conclusion

Despite the challenges, some private for-profit and non-profit health care providers in LMICs are finding ways of scaling their initial success. Scale can involve providing more services to more people in more locations, with the goal of improving health care outcomes. Our research aims to identify key skills that both alone and in combination will help reduce the amount of time programs will need to spend on scale up experimentation so that they can identify customer needs, expand rapidly, and offer clinical services that improve health care throughout the world. Our current implications are tentative, because they are based on a moderate number of cases. Nonetheless, they are highly suggestive.

Our research suggests that the key differentiators to successful scaling are less about clinical skills – those are necessary for offering viable primary care services, but do not differentiate programs that scale from those that do not scale. Instead, rather than the high-tech investments that we often see celebrated – which are more likely to be base activities in our examples – scaling differentiators commonly involve high-touch on-the-ground contact with customers, staff, and stakeholders throughout the value chain. The differentiators help the primary care organizations focus on the market, foster innovative financial mechanisms, ensure operating effectiveness, and engage in robust partnerships.

The existing health care services literature at least hints at the point that management skills will contribute to successful scaling of primary care services in LMICs. However, work to date has largely focused on vertical interventions such as TB and HIV/AIDS treatment rather than more comprehensive, basic primary care services. Moreover, studies typically do not compare programs that have succeeded in scaling with those that have not been able to do so. As a result, discussions have identified a substantial list of potentially important skills, without determining which of these are simply necessary "table stakes" for being able to operate at any scale and which make a meaningful difference in expanding beyond an initially successful base. Hence, much of the discussion to date risks promoting deep investments in activities that do not make relevant differences. Our work highlights a more focused set of activities that provide differential advantages, including a small set of marketing, financial, leadership, and partnership skills.

The findings further suggest that programs combine different base activities and scale differentiators depending on the context; a one-size-fits-all model is not the solution for scaling up primary care. The targeted geography and income group shapes which approaches are most feasible, and programs serving populations in rural areas in the bottom 20 per cent will face more challenges in scaling up. However, we did find programs that are succeeding in serving these groups. Our research points to activities that can facilitate scale up across income groups and geographies.

Of particular note is the scale differentiator of leaders who have dual medical and business skills. This example highlights the need for programs to combine knowledge and insights from both disciplines to scale successfully. This includes the ability to provide quality medical care and have an intimate understanding of how the health system functions, as well as management tools and insights on how to attract patients, recruit, retain and motivate staff, devise innovative financing mechanisms, standardize operations, and build strategic partnerships.

Funding sources, funding levels, and ownership status remain important issues to investigate. We found no significant relationships with successful scaling relative to six types of funding sources (donors, out-of-pocket payments, membership andsubscriptions, investors, governments, in kind), either individually or in aggregate. Nonetheless, it is possible that tapping into more specific types of funding may facilitate scaling, along with the differentiating financial tools that we discussed earlier. Moreover, moving beyond reliance on donors is likely to be needed for long-term sustainability. Indeed, although a majority of the programs in the study used donor funding (57 per cent), an even larger majority (89 per cent) used at least one source other than donor funding. Hence, most programs seek to avoid sole reliance on donors.

Most generally, successful scaling of primary health care services appears to require two management mindsets as complements to traditional medical skills. Scaling requires deep attention on the demand side to the needs and lives of potential clients, together with equally deep attention on the supply side to building effective organizations that can deliver reliable goods and services that are relevant to the lives of those clients.

Appendix

Table 14.A1 Programs in the rapid routes to scale study

Program Name	Founded	Description
Academy of Family Physicians of India	2010	Non-profit organization (pilot stage) promoting family medicine and advocating for increased opportunities for primary care doctors in India.
Access Afya	2012	For-profit clinic chain (pilot stage) offering basic clinical and prevention services in Kenya.
Alchemist Clinics	2014	For-profit chain of primary health clinics and eye hospitals (pilot stage) being developed for rural areas in India.
Amref Health Africa	1957	International non-profit that provides health services and capacity building in seven African countries.
Bangladesh Second Urban Primary Care Project	1998	Public-private partnership developed between government and non-profit organizations to deliver primary health care services through clinics and health centres in Bangladesh.
Changamka MicroHealth Limited	2009	For-profit company that provides affordable microinsurance and allows for payment through the mobile platform mPesa in Kenya.
Children's Health and Development in Kenya (CHADIK)	2008	Non-profit providing outreach clinics to remote and poor areas with a focus on children and mothers in Kenya.
Clínicas da Família/ Rio Municipal Clinics	2008	Public-private partnership between the municipal government and local non-profits involving a clinic chain and family medicine residency program in Brazil.
Community Health Africa Trust (CHAT)	1999	Non-profit providing mobile clinics to remote and poor areas through backpack nurses, medical teams travelling by truck, and camel caravans in Kenya.

(Continued)

Table 14.A1 Continued

Program Name	Founded	Description
Dimagi	2002	For-profit social enterprise developing low-cost technologies such as CommCare, a configurable mobile data collection platform for community health workers in Asia, Africa, and Central America.
Health by Motorbike	2010	Non-profit health outreach program that sends a local health professional by motorbike to remote communities in Kenya and Tanzania.
Healthspring	2011	For-profit clinic chain with an emphasis on preventive medicine in India.
Institute of Health Management, Pachod and PUNE (IHMP)	1975	Non-profit organization providing health and development programs with village communities in India.
Karuna Trust	1986	Charitable trust serving poor populations through public-private partnerships in India.
Kriti Arogya Kendram	2011	For-profit clinic chain in India; no longer in operation.
Lifebuoy Friendship Hospital	2001	Non-profit providing primary and secondary health care to remote communities through floating hospitals developed from retired barges in Bangladesh.
LifeNet International	2009	Non-profit that franchises local clinics to improve population health in Burundi and East Africa.
Living Goods	2007	Non-profit franchise of entrepreneurial community health workers that sell health products and provide health information door to door in Kenya and Uganda.
mDhil	2009	For-profit that promotes health awareness through online and interactive digital content in India.
MediAngels	2011	For-profit providing primary and speciality care through integrating telemedicine, virtual health care, and patient diagnostic devices in Indi and globally.
Mediphone	2011	For-profit health hotline service in India.
MeraDoctor	2011	For-profit health hotline and medical discount service in India.
MicroClinic Technologies	2011	Technology company developing affordable technology for primary care health centres in Kenya.

(Continued)

Table 14.A1 Concluded

Program Name	Founded	Description
MicroEnsure	2002	For-profit insurance intermediary (pilot stage) that is developing affordable insurance protection for poor populations in South Asia and Africa.
NationWide Primary Healthcare Services	2010	For-profit clinic chain providing services through general practitioners, paediatricians, and gynaecologists in India.
Neurosynaptic Communications	2008	For-profit technology company developing tools to support health care for remote and rural populations in India.
North Star Alliance Roadside Wellness Centres	2006	Non-profit operating roadside clinics along transport routes in South, West, and East Africa.
Patan Academy of Health Sciences	2010	Non-profit medical training program (pilot stage) focused on rural medicine in Nepal.
Penda Health	2012	For-profit clinic chain (pilot stage) with a focus on serving women in Kenya.
Ross Clinics	2011	For-profit clinic chain providing services through family physicians, dentists, and physiotherapists in India.
Sevamob	2011	For-profit mobile clinic and primary care subscription service in India.
Swasth Health Centres	2011	For-profit clinic chain serving the slums in Mumbai, India.
Vaatsalya Healthcare	2004	For-profit hospital and clinic chain providing affordable health care to less-served areas in India.
Vishwas	2012	For-profit primary care program (pilot stage) focused on leadership training for family doctors in India.
Viva Afya	2009	For-profit chain of primary care clinics serving densely populated, low-income areas in Kenya.
World Health Partners	2008	Non-profit that franchises existing clinics in rural areas and uses technology to connect providers and patients in India and Kenya.
Anonymous program	2011	For-profit clinic chain in India; no longer in operation.

REFERENCES

Adam, T., Ebener, S., Johns, B., & Evans, D.B. 2008. "Capacity Utilization and the Cost of Primary Care Visits: Implications for the Costs of Scaling Up Health Interventions." *Effectiveness and Resource Allocation* 6: 22. https://doi .org/10.1186/1478-7547-6-22.

Balarajan Y., Selvaraj, S., & Subramanian, S.V. 2011. "Health Care and Equity in India." *The Lancet* 377(9764): 505–15. https://doi.org/10.1016/s0140 -6736(10)61894-6.

Beasley, J.W., Starfield, B., van Weel, C., Rosser, W.W., & Haq, C.L. 2007. "Global Health and Primary Care Research." *Journal of the American Board of Family Medicine* 20: 518–26. https://doi.org/10.3122/jabfm.2007.06.070172.

Beckman, S.L., & Katz, M.L., eds. 2000. "The Business of Health Care Concerns Us All: An Introduction." *California Management Review* 43(1): 9–12. https:// doi.org/10.2307/41166062.

Berelowitz, D., Horn, J., Thornton, A., Leeds, I., & Wong, D. 2013. "Identifying Replicable Healthcare Delivery Models with Significant Social Benefit." *The International Centre for Social Franchising*. www.springimpact.org/wp-content/ uploads/2016/05/Identifying-Replicable-Healthcare-Delivery-Models-with -Significant-Social-Benefit-1.pdf.

Bhattacharyya, O., Ginther, J., Hayden, L., MacDonald, J.A., Mossman, K., Parikh, H., McGahan, A., Mitchell, W., Shahin, I., Sohal, R. 2015. "Trans-national Scale-Up of Innovations in Global Health." *PLOS One* 9(11): e110465. https://doi.org/10.1371/ journal.pone.0110465.

Bhattacharyya, O., Khor, S., McGahan, A., Dunne, D., Daar, A.S., & Singer, P.A. 2010. "Innovative Health Service Delivery Models in Low and Middle Income Countries – What Can We Learn from the Private Sector?" *Health Research Policy and Systems* 8(1): 24. https://doi.org/10.1186/1478-4505-8-24.

Bradley, E.H., Curry, L.A., Taylor, L.A., Pallas, S.W., Talbert-Slagle, K., Yuan, C., ... Pérez-Escamilla, R. 2012. "A Model for Scale Up of Family Health Innovations in Low Income and Middle Income Settings: A Mixed Methods Study." *BMJ* 2: 1–13. https://doi.org/10.1136/bmjopen-2012-000987.

Braitstein, P., Einterz, R.M., Sidle, J.E., Kimaiyo, S., & Tierney, W. 2009. "'Talkin' about a Revolution': How Electronic Health Records Can Facilitate the Scale Up of HIV Care and Treatment and Catalyze Primary Care in Resource Constrained Settings." *Journal of Acquired Immune Deficiency Syndromes* 52: S54–S57. https:// doi.org/10.1097/qai.0b013e3181bbcb67.

Burleigh, E. (n.d.) *Best Practices in Scaling Up Case Study: Guatemala: Pro RedesSalud: Rapid Scale Up of Primary Health Care through NGOs*. John Snow, Inc.

Bustreo, F., Okwo-Bele, J.-M., & Kamara, L. 2015. "World Health Organization Perspectives on the Contribution of the Global Alliance for Vaccines and Immunization on Reducing Child Mortality." *Archives of Disease in Childhood* 100 (Suppl): S34–7. https://doi.org/10.1136/archdischild-2013-305693.

Chaudhury, N. 2004. "Ghost Doctors: Absenteeism in Rural Bangladeshi Health Facilities." *The World Bank Economic Review* 18(3): 423–41. https://doi.org/10.1093/wber/lhh047.

Chen, C., Buch, E., Wassermann, T., Frehywot, S., Mullan, F., Omaswa, F., & Olapade-Olaopa, E.O. 2012. "A Survey of Sub-Saharan African Medical Schools." *Human Resources for Health* 10: 4. https://doi.org/10.1186/1478-4491-10-4.

Chimwaza, W., Chipeta, E., Ngwira, A., Kamwendo, F., Taulo, F., Bradley, S., & McAuliffe, E. 2014. "What Makes Staff Consider Leaving the Health Service in Malawi?" *Human Resources for Health* 12: 17. https://doi.org/10.1186/1478-4491-12-17.

CHMI. 2014. "CHMI Primary Care Learning Collaborative Overview". http://healthmarketinnovations.org/document/chmi-primary-care-learning-collaborative-overview.

Coffman, J. 2010. *The Evaluation Exchange: Broadening the Perspective on Scale.* Harvard Family Research Project.

Cooley, L., & Kohl, R. 2006. *Scaling Up: From Vision to Large Scale Change – A Management Framework for Practitioners.* Management Systems International.

De Maeseneer, J. 2013. "Scaling Up Family Medicine and Primary Health Care in Africa: Statement of the Primafamed Network, Victoria Falls, Zimbabwe." *African Journal of Primary Health Care and Family Medicine* 5(1): a507. https://doi.org/10.4102/phcfm.v5i1.507.

Duke University. 2016. "Social Entrepreneurship Accelerator at Duke". http://www.dukesead.org/.

Dussault, G., & Franceschini, M.C. 2006. "Not Enough There, Too Many Here: Understanding Geographical Imbalances in the Distribution of the Health Workforce." *Human Resources for Health* 4: 12. https://doi.org/10.1186/1478-4491-4-12.

Fortune, A., & Mitchell, W. 2012. "Unpacking Firm Exit at the Firm and Industry Levels: The Adaptation and Selection of Firm Capabilities." *Strategic Management Journal* 33(7): 794–819. https://doi.org/10.1002/smj.972.

Gilson, L., & Schneider, H. 2010. "Managing Scaling Up: What Are the Key Issues?" *Health Policy and Planning* 25(2): 97–8. https://doi.org/10.1093/heapol/czp067.

Guesalaga, R., & Marshall, P. 2008. "Purchasing Power at the Bottom of the Pyramid: Differences across Geographic Regions and Income Tiers." *Journal of Consumer Marketing* 25(7): 413–18. https://doi.org/10.1108/07363760810915626.

Hammond, A.L., Kramer, W.J., Katz, R.S., Tran, J.T., & Walker, C. 2007. "The Next 4 Billion: Market Size and Business Strategy at the Base of the Pyramid."

World Resource Institute-International Finance Corporation, 1–164. http://www
.wri.org/publication/next-4-billion.

Innovations in Healthcare. 2013. "*Grand-Aides*." https://www.innovationsinhealthcare
.org/profile/grand-aides.

Innovations in Healthcare. 2016. "Scaling Healthcare Innovations Worldwide". https://
www.innovationsinhealthcare.org/.

Jones, G., Steketee, R.W., Black, R.E., Bhutta, Z.A., & Morris, S.S. 2003. "How
Many Child Deaths Can We Prevent this Year?" *The Lancet* 362(9377): 65–71.
https://doi.org/10.1016/S0140-6736(03)13811-1.

Kapoor, S.K., Raman, A.V., Sachdeva, K.S., & Satyanarayana, S. 2012. "How Did the
TB Patients Reach DOTS Services in Delhi? A Study of Patient Treatment Seeking
Behavior." *PLoS One* 7: e42458. https://doi.org/10.1371/journal.pone.0042458.

Kepp, M. 2008. "Cracks Appear in Brazil's Primary Health-Care Program." *The
Lancet* 372(9642): 877. https://doi.org/10.1016/s0140-6736(08)61379-3.

Kober, K., & Van Damme, W. 2006. "Public Sector Nurses in Swaziland: Can the
Downturn Be Reversed?" *Human Resources for Health* 4: 13. https://doi.org/
10.1186/1478-4491-4-13.

Korten, D.C. 1980. "Community Organization and Rural Development: A Learning
Process Approach." *Public Administration Review* 40(5): 480–511. https://doi.org/
10.2307/3110204.

Kumar, R. 2012. "Academic Institutionalization of Community Health Services: Way
Ahead in Medical Education Reforms." *Journal of Family Medicine and Primary
Care* 1: 10–19. https://doi.org/10.4103/2249-4863.94442.

Lewin, S., Lavis, J.N., Oxman, A.D., Bastias, G., Chopra, M., Ciapponi, A., ... Haines, A.
2008. "Supporting the Delivery of Cost Effective Interventions in Primary Health-
Care Systems in Low-Income and Middle-Income Countries: An Overview of
Systematic Reviews." *The Lancet* 372(9642): 928–39. https://doi.org/10.1016/
s0140-6736(08)61403-8.

The Center for Health Market Innovations. 2015. *The Primary Care Innovator's
Handbook*. Washington, DC: Results for Development Institute.

Lindelow, M., & Serneels, P. 2006. "The Performance of Health Workers in Ethiopia:
Results from Qualitative Research." *Social Science & Medicine* 62(9): 2225–35.
https://doi.org/10.1016/j.socscimed.2005.10.015.

Longo, F. 2007. "Implementing Managerial Innovations in Primary Care: Can We Rank
Change Drivers in Complex Adaptive Organizations?" *Health Care Management
Review* 32(3): 213–25. https://doi.org/10.1097/01.HMR.0000281620.13116.ce.

Mackinco, J., de Souza, M.F.M., Guanais, F.C., & Simoes, C.C.S. 2007. "Going to
Scale with Community-Based Primary Care: An Analysis of the Family Health
Program and Infant Mortality in Brazil, 1999–2004." *Social Science & Medicine*
65(10): 2070–80. https://doi.org/10.1016/j.socscimed.2007.06.028.

Mangham, L.J., & Hanson, K. 2010. "Scaling Up in International Health: What Are the Key Issues?" *Health Policy and Planning* 25(2): 85–96. https://doi.org/10.1093/heapol/czp066.

Miles, M.B., & Huberman, M. 1994. *Qualitative Data Analysis: A Sourcebook of New Methods.* Beverly Hills, CA: Sage Publications.

Myers, R.G. 1984. "Going to Scale: A Paper Prepared for UNICEFI for the Second Inter-agency Meeting on Community-Based Child Development." *The Consultative Group on Early Childhood Care and Development*, 1–20.

O'Donnell, O. 2007. "Access to Health Care in Developing Countries: Breaking Down Demand Side Barriers." *Cadernos de Saúde Pública* 23(12): 2820–34. https://doi.org/10.1590/S0102-311X2007001200003.

Prata, N., Montagu, D., & Jefferys. E. 2005. "Private Sector, Human Resource, and Health Franchising in Africa." *Bulletin of the World Health Organization* 83: 274–9.

Ranson, M.K., Hanson, K., Oliveira-Cruz, V., & Mills, A. 2003. "Constraints to Expanding Access to Health Interventions: An Empirical Analysis and Country Typology." *Journal of International Development* 15(1): 15–39. https://doi.org/10.1002/jid.964.

Ross-Degnan, D., Soumerai, S.B., Goel, P.K., Bates, J., Makhulo, J., Dondi, N., & Hogan, R. 1996. "The Impact of Face-to-Face Educational Outreach on Diarrhoea Treatment in Pharmacies." *Health Policy and Planning* 11(3): 308–18. https://doi.org/10.1093/heapol/11.3.308.

Rowe, A.K., de Savigny, D., Lanata, C.F., & Victora, C.G. 2005. "How Can We Achieve and Maintain High Quality Performance of Health Workers in Low-resource Settings?" *The Lancet* 366(9490): 1026–35. https://doi.org/10.1016/S0140-6736(05)67028-6.

Schlein, K. and Montagu, D. (2012). *Clinical Social Franchising Compendium: An Annual Survey of Programs, 2012.* San Francisco: The Global Health Group, Global Health Sciences, University of California, San Francisco.

Sibthorpe, B.M., Glasgow, N.J., & Wells, R.W. 2005. "Emergent Themes in the Sustainability of Primary Health Care Innovation." *The Medical Journal of Australia* 183: 77–80.

Simmons, R., Fajans, P., & Ghiron, L. 2007. "Introduction." In Simmons, R., Fajans, P., and Ghiron, L., eds, *Scaling Up Health Service Delivery: From Pilot Innovations to Policies and Programs.* Geneva: World Health Organization. vii–xvii.

Starfield, B., Shi, L., & Macinko, J. 2005. "Contribution of Primary Care to Health Systems and Health." *The Milbank Quarterly* 83: 457–502. https://doi.org/10.1111/j.1468-0009.2005.00409.x.

Sudhinaraset, M., Ingram, M., Lofthouse, H.K., & Montagu, D. 2013. "What Is the Role of Informal Healthcare Providers in Developing Countries? A Systematic Review." *PloS One* 8(9): e54978. https://doi.org/10.1371/journal.pone.0054978.

Tritter, J. 2012. "Mixed Methods and Multidisciplinary Research in Health Care."
In Saks, M. & Allsop, J., eds. *Researching Health: Qualitative, Quantitative, and Mixed Methods*, 2nd ed. 421–36. Thousand Oaks: Sage. https://research.aston .ac.uk/portal/en/researchoutput/mixed-methods-and-multidisciplinary-research -in-health-care%28b5f3c67f-9f14-48e8-8321-e0c51ec93994%29/export.html.

UNICEF. 2012. *Review of Systematic Challenges to the Scale Up of Integrated Community Case Management Emerging Lessons and Recommendations from the Catalytic Initiative (CI/IHSS)*. New York: UNICEF.

Van Dormael, M., Dugas, S., Kone, Y., Coulibaly, S., Sy, M., Marchal, B., & Desplats, D. 2008. "Appropriate Training and Retention of Community Doctors in Rural Areas: A Case Study from Mali." *Human Resources for Health* 6: 25. https://doi .org/10.1186/1478-4491-6-25.

Waddington, C. 2012. *Scaling Up Health Services: Challenges and Choices*. HLSP Institute.

Walley, J., Lawn, J.E., de Francisco, A., Chopra, M., Rudan, I., ... Lancet Alma-Ata Working Group. 2008. "Primary Health Care; Making Alma-Ata a Reality." *The Lancet* 372: 1001–7. https://doi.org/10.1016/S0140-6736(08)61409-9.

World Bank. 2014. "World Development Indicators: India." http://data.worldbank.org/ country/india.

World Health Organization. 2014. "World Health Statistics." 1–178. http://www.who. int/gho/publications/world_health_statistics/2014/en/.

World Health Organization and Expand Net. 2009. *Practical Guidance for Scaling Up Health Service Innovations*. World Health Organization.

Yamey, G. 2012. "What Are the Barriers to Scaling Up Health Interventions in Low and Middle Income Countries? A Qualitative Study of Academic Leaders in Implementation Science." *Globalization and Health* 8(1): 1–11. https://doi.org/ 10.1186/1744-8603-8-11.

15 Integrating Primary Care and Maternal, Newborn, and Child Health in Low- and Middle-Income Countries

RAMAN SOHAL, ONIL BHATTACHARYYA,
HIMANSHU PARIKH, KATHRYN MOSSMAN,
LEIGH HAYDEN, ANITA MCGAHAN,
AND WILL MITCHELL

Introduction

Integrating primary care with maternal, newborn, and child health (MNCH) delivery has increasingly been advocated as a strategy for advancing health care for the poor in low- and middle-income countries (LMICs) (Bhutta et al. 2008). Integrated care refers to organizing care delivery through better service coordination to improve patient care (Shaw, Rosen, & Rumbold 2011). There is no agreement, however, about what is meant by having integrated services, about which services should be integrated, or where integration should happen. While the concept of integrated care has been the focus of several studies internationally, confusion persists as to the overall nature and definition of the concept, and its relationship to improved patient outcomes (Kodner 2009; Strandberg-Larsen 2011). The term is commonly equated with managed care, continuity of care, interorganizational relationships, interprofessional teams, shared care, and disease or case management (Evans & Baker 2012; Kodner & Spreeuwenberg 2002). According to authoritative sources on integrated care delivery, fully integrated care consists of sustained coordination of clinical practices to deal with each patient's health problems in a comprehensive way (Provan 1997; Shortell et al. 1993; Brousselle et al. 2010; Kodner 2009). The WHO defines integration as "the management and delivery of health services so that clients receive a continuum of preventative and curative services, according to their needs over time and across different levels of the health system" (WHO 2008). For the purposes of this study, programs that provide integrated care are defined as those that expand their delivery platforms to offer a substantial range of primary care and MNCH services.

The impetus for integration stems in part from the underlying premise that improving public health demands less of a focus on specific diseases than on broad measures that affect populations' overall health (Garett 2007), and the realization that single-disease or population-specific programs can result in duplication and fragmented health service delivery. In high-income countries, primary care and MNCH services tend to be integrated, and MNCH is a constitutive component of primary care. In many LMICs, however, primary care and MNCH are often delivered separately.

To date, the literature on integrated care delivery in LMICs is confusing and contradictory (Dudley & Garner 2011). Some empirical examples from Pakistan and Uganda demonstrate that primary health care interventions can be used effectively with MNCH services (Bhutta et al. 2008). However, the broader literature on integrated care finds mixed results. The Global Health Council (2015) recently noted that while the current shift to integrated service delivery is laudable for high-capacity systems, there is a scarcity of evidence on the effectiveness and cost-effectiveness of integrated care approaches, especially in LMICs. LMICs are confronted with a high burden of disease in contexts characterized by weak health systems and emerging chronic diseases and comorbidities. A 2011 systematic review on the impact of integrating primary health care services in LMICs at the point of delivery finds that while adding services – such as diabetes screening and HIV treatment and care – improved the use of the added-on service, there is limited evidence that service integration improved health status. In addition, the review finds that in some instances, integration worsened service delivery (Dudley & Garner 2011). The systematic review further underscores the point that integration of services must be matched by capacity assessment and capacity building, and better quality of services (Global Health Council 2015; Dudley & Garner 2011). Many health systems in LMICs are characterized by a specialist-driven model of care (or a disease-driven model, also referred to as a vertical model). Consequently, some of the core principles underlying integrated care become more difficult to achieve.

The objectives of this chapter are four-fold: a) highlight programs' motivations to integrate primary care and MNCH, b) identify the challenges programs confront in integrating primary care and MNCH, c) identify the models health services programs use to integrate care, and d) highlight the lessons and insights emerging from the findings.

Study Data and Methods

This research conducted by the University of Toronto's Toronto Health Organization Performance Evaluation (T-HOPE) team, and Results for Development (R4D), evaluated 20 private for-profit and non-profit health care programs that provide primary care and MNCH. We examined programs providing primary care, MNCH, or primary care and MNCH. The integrated programs in this study evolved over time to either incorporate primary care with MNCH or MNCH with primary care. While some programs were offering multiple services from the outset, such as primary care, malaria, tuberculosis, and HIV/AIDS, none of the programs were offering both primary care and MNCH from the outset. Out of the 20 programs in the sample, 10 were primary care programs that evolved over time to include MNCH. Seven programs started with a MNCH platform and expanded over time to include primary care services. For comparative purposes, we also examined programs that delivered *either* primary care or MNCH services to understand whether these programs confronted the same types of challenges in expanding their scope of services and whether they used the same levers. Three of the 20 programs included in the study were primary care only or MNCH only programs. The programs, which span 22 countries, with particular emphasis on Bangladesh, Kenya and India, were identified using the Center for Health Market Innovations database. In-depth semi structured interviews were conducted with staff members from all 20 programs via Skype. Table 15.1 below describes the categories of programs comprising our sample.

We used content analysis and constant comparison to characterize program's strategies, focusing on the motivations, mechanisms, and challenges they encounter in integrating care. We propose that the capacity of a program to integrate primary care and MNCH is influenced by how effective the program has been at developing some combination of the following three levers: human resources, alliance-building, and financing.

Table 15.1 Categories of programs in study sample

Types of Programs	Total
Primary Care	1
MNCH	2
Primary care to integrated	10
MNCH to integrated	7

Results

Motivations for Integration

Programs' motivations for integration were framed around three key reasons: patient and community need and demand, financial availability, and desire to create a one-stop shop. The benefits of a one-stop shop include providing services in a consistent and coordinated way to improve operational efficiency, improve service coverage, and provide better patient experience. In understanding programs' motivations to integrate, it also important to consider that some programs do not have a mandate to integrate. Thrive Networks' Newborn Health program (formerly Breath of Life) for example, a Vietnam-based social enterprise that manufactures affordable medical devices for neonatal units and provides trainings on their use, has adopted a narrow focus and concentrates its efforts on decreasing neonatal morbidity and mortality in low-income countries.

PATIENT AND COMMUNITY NEED AND DEMAND
The burden of disease in the contexts in which programs were embedded, in part, determined the health foci of programs seeking to integrate primary care and MNCH. According to the Garhwal Community Development and Welfare Society (GCDWS) program in India, the high rates of stillbirths due to lack of antenatal care and the high rates of maternal and infant mortality were a major factor in the decision to incorporate primary care with MNCH services. Kollyani Clinics in Bangladesh, which provides integrated MNCH and primary care services, constructs health care facilities close to remote Bangladeshi villages in the Bandarban district as much of the area is only accessible by foot.

FINANCIAL AVAILABILITY
Government policies and financing mechanisms often drove programs to integrate specific services. One approach that programs adopt to expand their scope of services in low-resource settings is to align their priorities with the government or donor organizations in order to obtain funding. Possible Health, a program in Nepal that began by offering basic primary care, expanded its partnership with the Ministry of Health by aligning its priorities with the ministry to access resources to deliver MNCH services. A staff member from Possible Health observes, "We literally expand our MOU with them. It allows us to expand both in-kind and cash contribution to us. Whether it's chronic disease or MNCH resources we can access [them] if we expand in their system." The Ministry of Health in Burundi, in partnership with the Malawi College

of Medicine and Save the Children, sought to streamline health care service packages, which were delivered by community health care workers (CHWs). The Mwayi wa Moyo (Chance to Live) program in Malawi was established so that community health care workers could deliver a single coherent MNCH and family-planning package as part of the broader national primary care program. A senior advisor with Save the Children notes that this package includes "high-impact MNCH interventions to fill current gaps in the continuum of care and deliver more interventions at better quality and lower cost." The Ministry of Health in Malawi has decided to adopt this new package at scale, and it is also being used within USAID's bilateral project Support to Service Delivery Integration-Services in 15 districts. Prior to the Mwayi wa Moyo project, neither the Ministry of Health nor its partners had explored the potential savings or cumulative effects of an integrated community package that delivers interventions along the continuum of care from pregnancy to children less than five years old.

ONE-STOP SHOP

More coordinated care also offers value to patients through more comprehensive care that can include one-stop shopping whereby a medical clinic addresses a patient's multiple care needs under a common platform (Kodner 2009). By combining multiple services under one roof, integrated care reduces gaps in care delivery. Integrated care also drives system level efficiencies as health care organizations better use existing resources, resulting in less duplication and waste. Many programs in the study noted that too often, providers focus on single episodes of treatment, rather than the patient's overall wellbeing. By adopting a more comprehensive approach, integrated care offers patients higher quality, more efficient care that better meets their needs. In many cases, the increased efficiency also helps programs control costs. For example, the ability of programs, such as Possible Health and Village Health Works, to offer ultrasounds to pregnant women as opposed to sending them to a different ultrasound clinic not only enabled programs to generate revenue from ultrasound services, but also ensured that the patient had received the needed diagnostic.

Challenges and Constraints

Programs identified several constraints to integrating primary care and MNCH services. The main constraints include: human and financial resources constraints, regulatory frameworks, and community attitudes. We see potential barriers at three distinct but related levels: the program itself; the health care ecosystem of which the program is a part; and governmental laws, policies, and actions. Our research finds that integration barriers can lie within the program itself. Programs may lack the clinical and human resources skills needed to expand their scope of services as they grow over time. Some programs may simply not have enough financial capital and other internal resources required to advance integrated care delivery. Looking beyond the program, we find several barriers in health care ecosystem in which the program is embedded.

HUMAN RESOURCES CONSTRAINTS

Our research finds that program's efforts to bundle primary care services with MNCH was often curtailed by lack of qualified health care workers. Possible Health finds that "really the biggest step for us, is not resources or equipment, it's the care providers ... There are not a lot of incentives for trained care providers to come to work in rural Nepal. In terms of retention, it is always a struggle and it is quite far. Accham is about 200 kilometres from Kathmandu." Other programs raised concerns around overburdening staff as a result of expanding scope of services. An interview with Kheth'Impilo highlights the trade-offs that arise for programs attempting to expand their scope of services. A doctor at Kheth'Impilo observes, "integrated could mean one facility offers all those services or it could mean one person offers all those services ... One person offering all those services: antenatal care, plus TB, plus, plus ... might not be as efficient [as] if I had certain compartmentalizations for nurses."

Program examples: CFW Shops, Possible Health, Kheth'Impilo, Health One, Mwayi Wa Moyo.

FINANCIAL RESOURCES

Lack of financial resources was often a challenge to providing integrated primary care and MNCH services to low-income and hard-to-reach populations. Many programs were reliant on donor grants or government subsidies. A health care provider at Kollyani Clinics notes, "one big challenge is the sustainability, how to keep clinics functioning, this is the biggest challenge the community is facing." A discussion with RADDA Maternal Child Health and Family Planning Centre in Bangladesh highlights the challenge of obtaining the necessary resources and equipment to be able to offer multiple services under one roof. Similarly, Purple Source Healthcare notes that their program must also make investments in delivery equipment and a cold chain for pharmacies for immunizations. In some contexts, such as in Burundi and Nepal, governments offer performance-based funding for certain services, such as reproductive health and family planning.

Expansion of scope can also increase programs' revenue-generating capabilities from existing clients, new clients, or even attract new sources of funding (i.e., donor or government). A program, however, may have sufficient financial resources, but still be unable to expand its scope of services due to a shortage of qualified health care workers and regulatory barriers. The nature of integrated care often demands health care providers with a higher level of clinical skill. Consider Child and Family Wellness Shops and LifeNet International, which are two programs that shifted from using a CHW model to nurses and clinical offices due to the wider scope of clinical services of the latter cadre of health care providers. While cost-effectiveness analysis was outside the scope of this study, it would be important to determine whether the increased expenses resulting from recruiting higher qualified staff is offset by the increased revenue generation. Thus, while lack of access to financial services limits a program's ability to provide integrated care, our research finds that it is not the main determinant in a program's ability to expand scope of services. We argue, however, that access to financial resources is a baseline constraint that many programs experience when trying to provide affordable and quality services in resource-constrained settings.

Program examples: Tello Mobile Clinic, Kollyani Clinics, Garhwal Community Development and Welfare Society, Health One, World Health Partners.

REGULATORY FRAMEWORKS

Our research reveals that a program's ability to integrate care is shaped by regulatory guidelines. Regulatory restrictions on who (doctors, nurses, community health care workers, lay health workers, etc.) can provide certain health services, especially clinical ones such as vaccines and ultrasounds, limit models based on task-shifting and paraskilling. These limitations constrain the degree to which programs can deploy underutilized human resources, such as lay health workers. Purple Source Healthcare in Nigeria notes that from a regulatory perspective, their program must have a midwife or a registered nurse on staff for deliveries, and that the program must have a relationship with a gynaecologist and an obstetrician for when complications arise. Six out of the 20 programs interviewed specifically expressed concerns with the limited scope of practice of community health workers, which hindered their ability to offer a wider range of clinical services. Programs such as Thrive Networks' Newborn Health, Health One, LifeNet International, and Possible Health discussed how the availability of ultrasound services often attracted patients, but that such services had to be delivered by a trained radiologist or doctor. A discussion with Health One revealed that while such regulatory barriers are in place in Pakistan, there were many clinics that failed to comply with this regulation and thus attracted a higher flow of patients: "In one of the clinics, there is general practitioner, his wife operates the ultrasound. She is not even a doctor, but because the husband is a doctor she has convinced [patients] she is a doctor. She has become the neighbourhood gynaecologist. It's pretty sad on the ground reality."

Program examples: M-Afya Kiosks, LifeNet, Last Mile Health, Kollyani Clinics, Thrive Networks' Health Newborn Health, Health One.

COMMUNITY ATTITUDES

Our research finds that uptake of integrated primary care and MNCH services are dependent upon patient and community demand. Availability of services, however, is often not enough to increase utilization. Demand generation is critical in areas where health literacy is poor, and in contexts where ingrained cultural beliefs negatively impact health-seeking behaviours. We note, however, that community attitudes are a baseline constraint that impact health-seeking behaviour in general, as opposed to a specific constraint of integrated care. Tello Mobile Clinic's small medical team delivers medical care by boat to remote communities that lack access to health care services in the Rock Islands of South Nias, Indonesia. Tello Mobile Clinic has integrated MNCH services into its primary care platform; the program was only able to achieve integration after concerted efforts were made in communities to increase health awareness and education. An interview with a staff member from TMC revealed that cultural beliefs regarding the origins of illnesses prevent individuals or their families from seeking medical care: "Sometimes the family believes that the disease is not because of sickness but from [a] curse, or voodoo. To make the family believe that this family member needs to get further treatment is one of the most challenging [things]."

Possible Health, a not-for-profit program that operates a hospital and mobile clinic for the rural poor in Achham, Nepal, has adopted a model whereby community health workers are assigned a catchment area to provide primary care. Within their catchment area the CHWs also identify pregnant women and encourage them to attend an antenatal clinic once a month. A staff member at Possible Health notes: "One of our biggest challenges has been patient demand ... We thought if we provided services people would come. Unfortunately, the lack of health knowledge meant there was very little demand for Possible Health's MNCH services." As a result, Possible Health's Community Health Workers are responsible for increasing health awareness in their catchment areas.

Village Health Works' efforts to shift community attitudes reveal how health awareness and education can increase uptake of primary care and MNCH services. Village Health Works is a program that offers primary care and MNCH services in rural Burundi. In discussing the program's expansion of scope over time, a medical doctor with VHW observes, "As we add services, care-seeking behaviour shifts. A shift of a social explanation of illness to a biomedical one has happened. Before [a] child is sick you might think its a hex and now it's protein and malnutrition and you can treat that and all of that affects care-seeking behaviour."

Program examples: Possible Health, Tello Mobile Clinic, Village Health Works.

Mechanisms for Integrating Primary Care and MNCH

Programs predominantly use three levers to expand their scope of services when targeting health services delivery to the poor in low-resource settings: staffing, alliance building, and financing. (See table 15.A1 in the appendix to this chapter for an overview of the levers used by programs in our sample). Staffing refers to the effectiveness of a program in filling its health care labour needs with people with the requisite skills for the needed roles, including paid staff or volunteers. The capability of a program for alliance building refers to its effectiveness in forging partnerships to integrate primary care and MNCH services. The capability of programs for financing refers to the effectiveness with which the programs are able to secure financial resources to provide primary care and MNCH services such that the finances exceed their expenses (Bloom & Chatterji 2008).

Staffing

LEVERAGING COMMUNITY HEALTH CARE WORKERS

The strategic management literature has long emphasized the importance of having necessary human resources to support organizational growth (Huselid, Jackson, & Schuler 1997). When a program's labour needs are high, such as in the provision of integrated primary care and MNCH services, our research finds that staffing will be critical for successful integration. In several programs in our sample, CHWs were formal members of the health care model and played a pivotal role in developing structured linkages between the community and health care program. Nine out of the 20 programs used a community health worker model in delivering health care services to the poor. Community health workers were found to be effective in delivering minimum intervention packages (appropriate to their intervention level); identifying critical signs for malaria, diarrhoea, and acute respiratory infection; and maternal and neonatal care. Community health workers were also essential in conducting behaviour-change communication and health education, and in building linkages between communities and health care facilities. Programs using such a model further discovered that community-level use of MNCH services and preventative practices increased as a result of CHWs' outreach efforts. Programs found that CHWs can effectively manage protocolized medicine including diagnostics and treatment for narrow vertical interventions, such as tuberculosis and malaria. These findings are supported by the broader literature, which finds that where CHWs with minimal training were able to deliver clinical screening and interventions (Christopher, Le May, Lewin, & Ross 2011; Gilmore & McAuliffe 2013; Gaziano et al. 2015), especially in promoting mother performed strategies such as skin-to-skin care and exclusive breastfeeding. The ability to integrate scope of services relying on CHW model was restricted in areas requiring higher clinical capabilities, such as labour and delivery, especially complex or emergency deliveries (e.g., caesareans).

Program examples: Kheth'Impilo, LifeNet, Possible Health, Garhwal Community Development and Welfare Society.

Alliance Building: Partnerships and Referral Networks

LEVERAGING REFERRAL NETWORKS

Programs without in-house clinical capabilities to address high-risk pregnancies and complicated deliveries utilized referral networks to transfer women to quality government clinics or tertiary care hospitals. While referral networks do not enable programs to offer services under one roof, they offer a means to *manage* patients with complex and multiple care needs, which is an element of integrated care. Very few of the MNCH programs interviewed were able to offer procedures, such as caesareans. A health care provider at the Child in Need Institute of India, which trains Accredited Social Health Activists (ASHAs), government front-line health workers, observes, "there [are] only so many services that a community health worker can provide, very basic services, which means that a referral system must still be used."

GCDWS described how in the case of the high-risk patients, nurses from the patient's community manage referrals to the local district hospital where caesarean services are offered. The GCDWS hospital conducts approximately 250 to 300 surgeries and 200 deliveries annually. GCDWS nurses are selected from the communities in which they work so that they are able to follow-up on the referred patient's health status and liaise with the clinicians in the referral centre. Possible Health, which is able to handle vaginal deliveries in its hospital, also refers patients to its district hospital when complicated deliveries emerge, using its two ambulances for transportation. Several programs mentioned that the ability to carry out clinical handovers from one caregiver to another was difficult in contexts where infrastructure was poor, but crucial for ensuring patient case continuity and safety. M-Afya, Possible Health, and Village Health Works are programs that highlighted how in the case of maternal health and, in particular, labour and delivery, the consequences of ineffective handover led to incorrect treatment and life-threatening adverse events.

Communication, training, and sharing of expertise by partners with programs were essential components for building trust and developing integrated approaches. A doctor at Village Health Works states, "Every day we are faced with a barrage of individual patient needs and we are adjusting broader needs in terms of services. There is a lot that we don't do, fistula repair, we refer, and we don't do surgery. We developed a network with mostly domestic facilities and larger hospitals in the capital. We've developed partnerships with international organizations that do paediatric heart surgery and that will fund patients outside to get that." Village Health Works has formed a strong partnership with Partners in Health that allows them to transfer patients from Burundi to Rwanda for services outside of its scope. Village Health Works, for example, received philanthropic funding to create Women's Health Pavilion (WHP), a teaching hospital designed to meet the specific health needs of women and children. The pavilion, which is currently being developed, will provide safe delivery of babies, safe emergency obstetrical care, vital neonatal care, and the capacity to develop comprehensive surgical services. The ability of programs to form partnerships with recognized and trusted organizations, such as Partners in Health, enable them to obtain the institutional support needed to sustain the integration process.

Program examples: CFW Shops, Garhwal Community Development and Welfare Society, Possible Health, Tello Mobile Clinic, Kheth'Impilo.

PARTNERSHIPS

Our research found that programs' partnerships with different actors were critical in playing a supportive role in integrated health care delivery. Our findings align with the broader strategic management literature, which finds that programs able to formulate alliances with prominent partners are more likely to succeed due to the resources provided by partners and the status the relationship confers upon the program (Stuart, Hoang, & Hybels 1999). Partners provided different types of resources to programs that enabled them to deliver more coordinated and comprehensive care in low-resource settings. Partnerships with church-based organizations in Burundi and Uganda have enabled LifeNet's franchisees to deliver compassionate and quality care. LifeNet targets church-based clinics after discovering they provide patients with higher-quality care at lower cost than their counterparts. Through its piloting efforts, LifeNet learned that churches often operate networks of health centres, as well as educational and religious facilities, making them effective in providing health care services.

Program examples: LifeNet, World Health Partners, M-Afya Kiosks.

BUILDING CLINICAL CAPABILITIES VIA PARTNERSHIPS
Several programs in our study found that the capacity to integrate primary care and MNCH is not only dependent on factors such as availability of financial capital, but is also impacted by how programs are able to source capabilities, leverage various players and forces in their external ecosystems, and create alliances to acquire resources and political support. Our study finds that some interventions are especially suitable for delivery through community health workers, whereas others can only be delivered through effective use of partnerships or by linking community-based strategies to functional and quality referral facilities. Integrating primary care and MNCH for the poor in resource-constrained settings can be advanced by using a model that pairs the use of community health workers with skilled clinical health care providers, such as nurses or clinical officers. Last Mile Health's CHWs, for example, complete a rigorous training program over the course of twelve months, which includes mentorship from clinicians such as nurses, midwives, and physician assistants as well as training in four modules specially designed for the needs of Liberia's "last mile."

One means through which partnerships have enabled programs to develop clinical capabilities to integrate MNCH and primary care delivery to low-income populations is by sourcing existing capabilities. Village Health Works is partnering with international clinical partners to train its health care providers that will operate the new Women's Health Pavilion. The program's partnerships to build clinical capabilities are often temporary (typically 1–3 years) and project based, including short-term training and guidance, the development of infrastructure, and the setting up of equipment. Such alliances enable Village Health Works to address a core constraint around the need for building clinical capacity to provide integrated and more complex services.

Program examples: Last Mile Health, Village Health Works.

EXPANDING SCOPE OF SERVICES VIA PARTNERSHIPS

In many low-income countries, children needing medical attention and treatment are combating more than one health condition. In the Integrated Management of Childhood Illness (IMCI) model, community health workers are trained in diagnosis and treatment of key childhood illnesses, and also in identifying children in need of immediate referral. IMCI offers combined treatment of the major childhood illnesses with a focus on preventative and curative care (WHO 2005). The Mwayi wa Moyo program in Burundi forged a partnership with USAID through which its government-supported community health workers were trained in Integrated Management of Childhood Illness.

Program examples: Last Mile Health, LifeNet, Possible Health, Village Health Works.

Financing

SECURING FINANCIAL CAPITAL

The ability to secure financial capital was important for many programs seeking to expand scope of services. LifeNet International, for example, uses a conversion franchise platform model to improve primary care delivery for the poor in Sub-Saharan Africa. LifeNet International has a growth financing loan program that enables its franchisees to increase their scope of services and the revenue they generate. Health centres in the franchise can receive a financial loan up to US$30,000. If a health centre seeks to expand its clinic to include a labour and delivery room, they can access LifeNet's loan services. Alternatively, programs can benefit from LifeNet's rent-to-own program, which allows individual health centres to pay a small fraction of the market value of an item of medical equipment – such as an ultrasound machine or glucometer – to rent the item from LifeNet each month, gradually accumulating enough capital to purchase the equipment from LifeNet outright. LifeNet finds that equipment loans create several multiplier effects. LifeNet provides equipment placement with ongoing training and check-ins, ensuring no equipment goes unused. Our research reveals that health centres generate more revenue when they offer expanded services made possible by additional equipment, such as ultrasounds and lab testing.

Program examples: LifeNet, M-Afya Kiosks, World Health Partners.

FINANCIAL SOURCES

Programs' financing sources stemmed from donations, grants, membership fees, government subsidies, and revenue generation. Our research finds that for most programs, there is a reciprocal relationship between financing and the other two levers, staffing and alliance-building. The majority of programs in our study were non-profit programs relying on donor funding to sustain operations and expand their scope of services. Certain services such as lab testing and ultrasounds were commonly used revenue generators. While some programs such as the CFW Shops noted that many of their clinics sought such equipment, the decision to finance capital and equipment costs were based on surrounding competitors in the health care market. CFW Shops determines for example, how many other providers offer similar services. If the area was deemed to be saturated, CFW clinics were not provided the capital to purchase such equipment. In other cases, programs were limited to obtaining funding from donors, which often had a set of predefined priorities that did not always align with programs' needs. Programs benefited from the ability to source capital and equipment based on *their* operating and clinical needs.

While financing does have an impact on its own, lack of trained staff can thwart a program's ability to integrate services even if it is financially healthy. Similarly, absence of partnerships that enable programs to source capacity building and clinical support can also hinder integration of program's scope of services despite its financial status. The use of approaches such as the Integrated Management of Childhood Illness (IMCI) used by programs such as the Last Mile Health and the Mwayi wa Moyo program are designed and implemented using an integrated approach, which increases their effectiveness. A multicountry evaluation of the Integrated Management of Childhood Illness (IMCI) approach in Brazil, Bangladesh, Peru, Uganda, and the United Republic of Tanzania finds that IMCI is a cost-effective investment, as it costs up to six times less per child correctly managed than current care (Bryce et al. 2004). Moreover, the IMCI focuses on upgrading care in local clinics by training health workers in new methods to examine and treat children, and to effectively counsel parents (Bryce et al. 2004).

Program examples: CFW Shops, Purple Source Healthcare.

Conclusions and Recommendations

Despite its theoretical appeal, integrated primary care and MNCH remains a new frontier for many health services programs in LMICs. While primary care and MNCH are increasingly established concepts, their various manifestations in LMICs are so diverse, making comparisons difficult. How integration of primary care and MNCH services occurs depends heavily on the health system in place, as well as the health care market and ecosystem in each country. Effective integration requires coordination at multiple levels, from governments to international and local partner organizations, including policies and regulatory guidelines, funding, and human resources. Integration may also require service delivery by a multidisciplinary team, often supported by several partners and provided in a mutually reinforcing manner at the facility, community, and household levels.

Our qualitative research finds that the ability of health services programs in LMICs to integrate primary care and MNCH is achieved in part by simultaneously deploying several levers – staffing, alliance-building, and financing – and requires that programs pay particular attention to how the levers influence the effectiveness of one another. The ability of a program to use each lever is influenced by situational contingencies in the external environment, such as regulatory frameworks and availability of skilled health care providers. Our study highlights that in some situations, effective deployment of all three levers may be needed for successful integration. In other situations, strong effectiveness with only one or two levers can drive integration. Moreover, our research suggests that the interaction among the three levers was critical in integrating primary care and MNCH. Our research also implies that, where programs are unable to effectively address key integration barriers themselves, we need to consider how policy-makers and others might be able to help them do so.

Staffing

Our study reveals that securing human resources capabilities is a key lever that programs use and need to expand their scope of services. Programs attempting to expand their scope of services in the area of MNCH, however, were constrained in integrating complex and high-risk procedures (e.g., caesareans), which required skilled obstetricians and/or midwives. To integrate such services, programs need support in recruiting and retaining health care providers possessing greater clinical capabilities, such as clinical officers and nurses. One approach to consider for advancing integrated primary care and MNCH is supporting programs in adopting established treatment programs (e.g., IMCI) that bundle skills that logically group together in terms of content, needed training, and operational use. Thrive Networks' Newborn Health program trains doctors and nurses in hospitals to effectively use equipment.

The program provides hospitals additional clinical education on essential and advanced newborn care using a "train the trainers" approach, which leads to more sustainable capacity building within its network of 300 hospitals in 10 countries.

Alliance-Building

Partners able to offer sustainable approaches to training and clinical capacity building facilitated integration of primary care and MNCH. Programs that expanded their maternal health services, such as Village Health Works, benefited from capacity building support, which for example included clinical training in obstetrics and emergency deliveries. Programs that expanded from a primary care base to include MNCH, such as Last Mile Health, were able to do so by forging alliances with organizations with pre-existing maternal and child health services already in place. Last Mile Health, while unable to offer labour and delivery services on its own, has been able ensure its patients receive access to such services as a result of its alliance with a maternity home. Programs able to widen their scope benefited from alliances that offered them substantial training, supervision, and investment.

Financing

There has been relatively little work done on how different types and sources of financing impact the ability of health services programs to effectively integrate primary care and MNCH. Donors might consider how funding priorities affect integrated care delivery in LMICs. However, while donors are an important source of funds for advancing integrated care, the existence of donor funding was not critical to success in terms of integration. Our research suggests that donors can influence implementation practice in ways that were seen as both positive and negative. LifeNet's rent-to-own program offers a positive example of a program that is able to offer its franchises the ability to source capital based on their operating and clinical needs. Other cases present the negative side of donor influence. Select programs were able to obtain donor funding for certain vertical interventions, such as tuberculosis and family planning, even though programs did not consider them to be priority health concerns. Programs could potentially achieve greater integration if staffing was coupled with financing strategies, as attracting higher skilled health care workers requires adequate remuneration and incentives.

Appendix

Table 15.A1 Integration levers used by sample programs

Programs	Levers Used by Programs		
	Staffing	Alliance Building	Financing
MNCH-focused programs			
Child in Need Institute (India/1974)	CINI trains health service providers, such as government front-line community health ASHA workers, to act as effective health care agents as mandated by the National Health Mission. Women from communities are trained and organized in self-help groups who act as community-level workers, and interact with families to facilitate access to primary health care services for women and children residing in villages and slum areas.	CINI has a partnership with the state government in India. Through this partnership, CINI has implemented the Community Health through Community Management Initiative' (CHCMI) funded by the state government under the National Health Mission, through which the program delivers MNCH services.	CINI draws its financial resources from a variety of donors, primarily Government of India and state governments; UN agencies; international, national, and bilateral trusts and foundations; corporations; individuals; and CINI support groups.

Thrive Networks Newborn Health Program, formerly Breath of Life (Benin, Cambodia, East Timor, Ghana, Laos, Myanmar, Nepal, Philippines, Thailand, Uganda, Vietnam/2004)	In a public-private partnership with MTTS, a Vietnam-based social enterprise that manufactures affordable medical devices for neonatal units, Thrive provides appropriate medical devices and staff training. Thrive ensures these facilities can save the lives of infants suffering from jaundice and respiratory distress, common and easily treatable newborn conditions.	Thrive Networks receives its funding from a variety of foundations, government agencies, family and community foundations, and corporate foundations.

Primary care focused programs

HealthOne (Pakistan/2014)	HealthOne operates three clinics in Pakistan, each uniquely staffed with female doctors and male nurses. The program's clinics also provide primary care services in high-density, low-income areas. HealthOne targets diabetes patients at the primary care level through general practice doctors, not specialists. By using a primary care approach HealthOne is able to lower the burden on local government hospitals and offer patients lower cost health care.	HealthOne is a for-profit program that is self-funded.

(Continued)

Table 15.A1 Continued

Programs	Levers Used by Programs		
	Staffing	Alliance Building	Financing
MNCH to integrated			
Radda MCH FP Centre Bangladesh (Bangladesh/1974)		Radda provides preventive and curative health care services to mothers, children, and adolescents. The centre has a partnership with the government of Bangladesh, which offers capacity building and training support and logistics support and medical supplies to the centre.	Radda MCH FP Centre receives funding from various donors, and international and government agencies. The program also generates some revenue through out-of-pocket payments.
Last Mile Health (Liberia/2007)		Last Mile Health recruits, trains, equips, manages, and pays professionalized community health workers to provide primary health care in the last mile. The program operates a maternity home in partnership with a clinic that offers labour and delivery. The program has partnerships with Partners in Health, UNICEF, and IRC.	Last Mile Health operates based primarily on donor funding from various donors including: The Global Fund, Open Society Institute, Partners in Health (USA), and GE Foundation.

| M-Afya Kiosks (Kenya/2011) | M-Afya operates kiosks that carry basic medical supplies and operated by community health care workers. They are able to offer access to basic treatment, sexual and reproductive health services. The kiosks are stocked with basic medical supplies and operated by a community health care worker who can then diagnose and treat patients. Patients with more severe cases can then be referred to larger clinics and hospitals facilitating early treatment. This transaction is made even easier by M-Pesa, which allows the clients to pay the CHW via M-Pesa. | M-Afya has recived funding from the Health Enterprise Fund, which provides entrepreneurs with grants and technical assistance, and facilitates connections with investors, creating a base for entrepreneurs to scale their businesses and reach more people with affordable health services and products. |
| Sajida Foundation Health Program (Bangladesh/1999) | Community health workers named Sajida Bandhu provide doorstep services to mothers and children through a connection with doctors at a Sajida Hospital. Mobile and satellite clinics are also being operated in remote locations. Sajida's mobile health teams provide health care services, particularly eye care services, to people outside the reach of its hospitals. | Sajida sustains its operations through revenue generation. Sajida introduced a health card that provides access to care for low-income individuals. The health card offers yearly health care for an entire family for a fee of BDT 600 (about US$8). Individual health cards have also been introduced for BDT 150 (US$2). Health card holders can access general treatment |

(Continued)

Table 15.A1 Continued

Programs	Levers Used by Programs		
	Staffing	Alliance Building	Financing
			free of charge for their entire family, as well as receive a 30% discount on all pathological tests. Cardholders are given significant discounts on various other services, including operations.
Safe Water and AIDS Project (Kenya/2005)	The Safe Water and AIDS Project (SWAP) trains community health promoters who undertake door-to-door sales of health and hygiene products and provide health information.	SWAP partners with local and international organizations including the Center for Disease Control and Prevention (CDC), CARE Kenya, the government of Kenya, WHO, World Bank, Ministry of Health, USAID, UNICEF, Gates Foundation, and Population Services International Kenya for the implementation of various projects.	SWAP relies on donor funding and revenue generation to run its operations and expand its scope of services. The program has established business centres called Jamii Centers, where trained female community health promoters sell health products. These products are also sold door to door, with the Jamii Center acting as a central distribution hub. Community health promoters sell products such as WaterGuard, PUR, modified clay pots, insecticide-treated bed nets, Community health promoters sell products such as WaterGuard, PUR, modified clay pots,

Garhwal Community Development and Welfare Society (India/1991)	Garhwal Community Development and Welfare Society collaborates with the state government of Uttarakhand (Tehri Garhwal district), and functions as district resource centre for accredited social health activists (ASHAs). ASHAs are selected by their communities at an open meeting in their village, with public representatives and qualified basic health workers present. ASHAs function as a link between the community and the government health system, and ensures the health of mothers and their children. They create awareness, motivate pregnant women to attend their antenatal checkups, and escort them to the health centre for comprehensive care (registration of pregnant mothers, four checkups, two tetanus vaccinations, iron and folic acid tablets, health teaching, etc.).	insecticide-treated bed nets, condoms, protein fortified flour, skin antiseptic, clean cook stoves, diapers, sanitary pads, soaps and detergents, and other products. GCDWS relies on donor funding and government grants to implement its various programs.

(Continued)

Table 15.A1 Continued

Programs	Levers Used by Programs		
	Staffing	Alliance Building	Financing
Primary care to integrated			
LifeNet International (Burundi and Uganda/2009)	LifeNet's staffing model comprises skilled clinical and management staff. LifeNet's medical education experts work closely with local nurse trainers, who then train partner staff on site once a month. In each church-run health centre, a staff of nurses will treat between 30 and 150 patients per day. LifeNet also invests in management staff and trains managerial staff at each of its partner health centres in financial management and accounting, pharmacy and human resource management, key data analysis, and planning and budgeting. With these skills, health centres avoid stock-outs, manage debt, and break even or operate at a profit, ensuring their sustainability.	LifeNet partners with community health centres to build their medical and administrative capacity and connect them with pharmaceuticals and equipment. Partnerships with faith-based organizations in Burundi and Uganda have enabled LifeNet's franchisees to build trust with the local communities in which they operate and deliver compassionate and quality care.	Filling a gap in local capital markets, LifeNet's growth financing loan program increases the scope of services health centres offer and the revenue they generate. Employing a proprietary underwriting system, LifeNet has disbursed mid-sized loans of US$5,000 to US$30,000 that have financed such projects as the construction of a maternity ward, expansion of a hospital, and implementation of an immunization program. Partners are eligible to apply for loans once they have achieved a score of 75% on LN's quality metric.

HealthStore Foundation formerly known as Child and Family Wellness Clinics (Kenya/2000)	The CFW model is a network of micropharmacies and clinics whose mission is to provide access to essential medicines to marginalized populations in Kenya. The network operates two types of outlets: basic drug shops owned and operated by community health workers, and clinics owned and operated by nurses who provide a more expanse set of essential medicines as well as basic primary care.	In 2001, Management Sciences for Health (MSH) and HealthStore formed an alliance under which MSH supplies technical advisory services to the HealthStore Foundation.	HealthStore operates and funds a network of 64 for-profit CFW clinics owned and operated by franchisees. Franchisees often subsidize their own patients who are unable to pay for services. HealthStore is establishing a donor-funded third-party payer pool to pay for the care that patients are unable to pay for themselves. Franchisees will be paid in full for all services and drugs delivered.
Kollyani Clinics (Bangladesh/2009)	Kollyani Clinics offer basic treatment for minor ailments, and maternal health services. The program expanded its scope of services to include immunization and family planning, which are provided by trained government health workers. To further expand its clinical offering, Kollyani Clinics linked its CHWs with a doctor or a registered health worker recognized by the government.		Kollyani Clinics rely on donor funding to sustain their operations.

(Continued)

Table 15.A1 Continued

Programs	Levers Used by Programs		
	Staffing	Alliance Building	Financing
Hope Foundation (Bangladesh/2009)	Hope Foundation uses different cadres of health care providers with a range of clinical skills including: Village Health Workers, midwives, nurses, and doctors. VHWs do extensive outreach in their communities to raise awareness about cleft palate and obstetric fistula repair. VHWs play a pivotal role in recruiting and referring patients to Hope Foundation's hospital and rural clinics.	Hope Foundation uses partnerships to obtain resources needed for expanding its scope of services. Partnerships have enabled the program to evolve over time from a narrow focus on primary care for women and children to include broader MNCH services and treatment for obstetric fistula, cleft palate, and burns. Hope Foundation's partners provide financial support and also capacity building support. The Fistula Foundation has trained Hope Foundation's surgeon to become certified in fistula repair. The foundation also has a partner that offers clinical training for burn victims. Hope Foundation's CHWs and staff are trained in new resuscitation for burn victims. Hope Foundation also has a partnership with BRAC University for its midwifery program.	Hope Foundation relies on donor funding and government grants to sustain its operations.

| PurpleSource Healthcare (Nigeria/2012) | PurpleSource Healthcare is a health care organization with a mission to create sustainable, scalable health care solutions for the mass market and focusing more specifically in maternal and child health. PurpleSource Healthcare aggregates providers into an integrated network. The clinics are staffed by medical officers and physicians, and registered nurses and auxiliary nurses trained by private hospitals, but who are not registered. | | PurpleSource Healthcare is a for-profit program that is self-funded. |
| Kheth'Impilo (South Africa/2009) | Kheth'Impilo's is staffed by doctors, nurse practitioners, and nurse practitioners that are supported by patient advocates. Kheth'Impilo's clinical program is supported by the Community Services Cluster, which provides adherence and psychosocial support interventions for patients through its patient advocate model. Ongoing treatment, counselling, and psychosocial support at the community level are provided with special attention paid to the very ill, pregnant, TB infected, children, and adolescents, as well as patients struggling with disclosure. | Kheth'Impilo works in close partnership with the South African Department of Health at a district level. | Kheth'Impilo relies primarily on donor funding to sustain it operations. The program also receives some government funding. |

(Continued)

Table 15.A1 Continued

Programs	Levers Used by Programs		
	Staffing	Alliance Building	Financing
	PAs are the link between the clinical services and the community, and enable Kheth'Impilo to identify challenges that may become barriers to treatment and refer patients for services to address these challenges. The Kheth'Impilo's patient advocates (PAs) are recruited from the areas in which they live, and provide a vital link between the community and clinic staff.		
Possible Health (Nepal/2005)	Possible Health's model comprises a hub-and-spoke health care unit built within the government's existing infrastructure. Its team delivers health care at a hospital, network of clinics, and via community health workers. The program has created a high-quality, low-cost health care system that integrates government hospitals, clinics, and community health workers. Community health workers constitute mobile teams	To provide health services to marginalized and hard to reach populations in Accham, Nepal, Possible Health partners with the Ministry of Health. By aligning with the government's priorities, Possible Health is able to secure in-kind resources and financial support. By expanding within the government system, Possible Health is able to expand its scope of services to include for example MNCH services or care for chronic diseases.	Possible Health has created a model called Durable Health Care, a health care system design that solves for the poorest patients. It is a public-private partnership that enables a non-profit health care company to be paid by the government to deliver health care within the government's infrastructure.

Village
Health Works
(Burundi/2006)

providing outreach, triage, treatment and follow-up services to a geographically dispersed population. All medical care is provided free of charge, with a focus on health equity and outreach to the poorest and most marginalized patients. They are also expanding the hospital to include surgical and mental health services.

VHW currently has one physician, four nurses, one lab technician and 60 community health workers.

VHW has forged a partnership with Partners in Health, which enables the program to refer patients with complex cases to Rwanda. They refer patients and often support them financially in the capital or get them to Rwanda. VHW also partners with UNICEF for capacity building support. UNICEF provides training to VHW's community health workers on a range of MNCH services.

It brings together the quality of the private sector, access of the public sector, and innovation enabled by philanthropy, and it ties core financing to performance.

Village Health Work relies primarily on philanthropic funds to sustain its operations. Philanthropic funding has enabled the program to expand its clinical capacity by building a Women's Health Pavilion. The Pavilion is a state-of-the-art teaching hospital designed to meet the specific health needs of women and children. The WHP will provide safe delivery of babies, safe emergency obstetrical care, vital neonatal care, and the capacity to develop comprehensive surgical services.

(Continued)

Table 15.A1 Concluded

Programs	Levers Used by Programs		
	Staffing	Alliance Building	Financing
Tello Mobile Health (Indonesia/2009)		As a mobile boat clinic, Tello Mobile's four-person medical team is sometimes unable to address certain medical cases. The medical team arranges transport for patients with complex cases to Tello Island to a government health facility or Catholic service centre. Patients requiring medicines and drugs are also referred to a government facility, as Tello Mobile's team does not supply medicines. Referrals are often made for patients requiring TB treatment or for pregnant women. In 2015, MAP International, the program's main funder, trained 162 health workers on how to perform tuberculosis skin tests.	To maintain and sustain operations, Tello Mobile depends on donor grants and funding.
Mwayi wa Moyo (on the border between primary care and MNCH) (Malawi/2011)	In Malawi, government-supported community health workers – called health surveillance assistants (HSAs) – deliver a range of MNCH interventions in	Carried out in under-resourced Blantyre District and in full partnership with the MOH, Mwayi wa Moyo can be viewed as a "learning lab" linked with	The Mwayi Wa Moyo program is funded by the Ministry of Health in Burundi, which has received funding from USAID.

several community packages, each developed vertically and supported by a different department within the Ministry of Health.	the USAID Mission's bilaterals for health systems strengthening and behaviour change. Mwayi wa Moyo partners with the MOH, funded by Save the Children, to streamline and integrate the current community packages into a single coherent package that fills the gaps in the continuum of care and delivers more interventions at better quality and less cost. Save the Children is working with the MOH to strengthen the integrated package to include PPFP.	The program is supported by USAID Support to Service Delivery Integration-Services (SSDI-Services) bilateral project.
World Health Partners (India and Kenya/2008)	WHP leverages resources from different types of partners to expand its scope of services. The program in Bihar secured funding from the Gates Foundation to provide TB treatment. Merck for Mothers has offered financial support to the program in India. In Kenya, WHP has developed a partnership with K-MET to enter into the health marketplace.	World Health Partner receives funding from donors (i.e., the Bill and Melinda Gates Foundation and Merck for Mothers) and governments. The program also generates some revenue through its franchise operations.

REFERENCES

Bhutta, Z.A., Ali, S., Cousens, S., Ali, T.M., Haider, B.A., Rizvi, A., Okong, P., Bhutta, S.Z., & Black, R.E. 2008. "Interventions to Address Maternal, Newborn, and Child Survival: What Difference Can Integrated Primary Healthcare Strategies Make?" *The Lancet* 372 (9642): 972–89. https://doi.org/10.1016/s0140 -6736(08)61407-5.

Bloom, P.N., & Chatterji, A.K. 2008. *Scaling Social Entrepeneurial Impact*. Fuqua School of Business.

Brousselle, A., Lamothe, L., Sylvain, C., Foro, A., & Perreault, M. 2010. "Integrating Services for Patients with Mental and Substance Use Disorders." *Health Care Management Review* 35(3): 212–23. https://doi.org/10.1097/HMR.0b013e3181d5b11c.

Bryce, J., Victora, C.G., Habicht, J.P., Vaughan, P., & Black, R.E. 2004. "The Multi-country Evaluation of the Integrated Management of Childhood Illness Strategy: Lessons for the Evaluation of Public Health Interventions." *American Journal of Public Health* 94(3): 406–15. https://doi.org/10.2105/ajph.94.3.406.

Christopher, J.B., Le May, A., Lewin, S., Ross, D.A. 2011. "Thirty Years after Alma-Ata: A Systematic Review of the Impact of Community Health Workers Delivering Curative Interventions against Malaria, Pneumonia, and Diarrhoea on Child Mortality and Morbidity in Sub-Saharan Africa." *Human Resources for Health* 9(27). https://doi.org/10.1186/1478-4491-9-27.

Dudley, L., & Garner, P. 2011. "Strategies for Integrating Primary Health Services in Low- and Middle-Income Countries at the Point of Delivery." *Cochrane Database Systematic Review* 1(7). https://doi.org/10.1002/14651858.cd003318.pub3.

Evans, J.M., & Ross Baker, G. 2012. "Shared Mental Models of Integrated Care: Aligning Multiple Stakeholder Perspectives." *Journal of Health Organization and Management* 26(6): 713–36. https://doi.org/10.1108/14777261211276989.

Garett, L. 2007. "The Challenge of Global Health." *Foreign Affairs* (January/February). https://www.foreignaffairs.com/articles/2007-01-01/challenge-global-health.

Gaziano, T.A., Abrahams-Gessel, S., Denman, C.A., Montano, C.M., Khanam, M., Puoane, T., Levitt, N.S. 2015. "An Assessment of Community Health Workers' Ability to Screen for Cardiovascular Disease Risk with a Simple, Non-invasive Risk Assessment Instrument in Bangladesh, Guatemala, Mexico, and South Africa: An Observational Study." *The Lancet Global Health* 3(9): e556–e63. https://doi .org/10.1016/s2214-109x(15)00143-6.

Gilmore, B., & McAuliffe, E. 2013. "Effectiveness of Community Health Workers Delivering Preventive Interventions for Maternal and Child Health in Low- and Middle-Income Countries: A Systematic Review." *BMC Public Health* 13(847). https://doi.org/10.1186/1471-2458-13-847.

Global Health Council. 2015. "Global Health Council." globalhealth.org.

Huselid, M.A., Jackson, S.E., & Schuler, R.S. 1997. "Technical and Strategic Human Resource Management Effectiveness as Determinants of Firm Performance." *Academy of Management Journal* 40(1): 171–88. https://doi.org/10.5465/257025.

Kodner, D. 2009. "All Together Now: A Conceptual Exploration of Integrated Care." *Healthcare Quarterly* 13: 6–15. https://doi.org/10.12927/hcq.2009.21091.

Kodner, D.L., & Spreeuwenberg, C. 2002. "Integrated Care: Meaning, Logic, Applications, and Implications – A Discussion Paper." *International Journal of Integrated Care* 2(4). https://doi.org/10.5334/ijic.67.

Provan, K.G. 1997. "Services Integration for Vulnerable Populations: Lessons from Community Mental Health." *Family & Community Health* 19(Supplement): 19–30. https://doi.org/10.1097/00003727-199701001-00002.

Shaw, S., Rosen, R. & Rumbold, B. 2011. *An Overview of Integrated Care in the NHS: What Is Integrated Care?* Nuffield Trust.

Shortell, S.M., Gillies, R.R., Anderson, D.A., Mitchell, J.B., & Morgan, K.L. 1993. "Creating Organized Delivery Systems: The Barriers and Facilitators." *Hospital & Health Services Administration* 38(4): 447–66.

Strandberg-Larsen, M. 2011. "Measuring Integrated Care." *Danish Medical Bulletin* 58(2): B4245.

Stuart, T.E., Hoang, H., & Hybels, R.C. 1999. "Interorganizational Endorsements and the Performance of Entrepreneurial Ventures." *Administrative Science Quarterly* 44: 315–49. https://doi.org/10.2307/2666998.

World Health Organization. 2005. *Handbook: Integrated Management of Childhood Illness.* WHO.

– 2008. *Integrated Health Services: What and Why?* WHO, Technical Brief No.1.

Conclusion

Private sector organizations, including both non-profit and for-profit actors, play an important but underappreciated role in LMIC health care. Indeed, private sector organizations are an essential source of innovation in both currently improving the lives of the poor and in refining novel approaches with the potential to improve health sustainably at scale. These innovations are wide ranging and include not just the proliferation of apps and digital tools but also new operating, marketing, and financing strategies. The innovations include microinsurance programs such as Pesinet (Mali), which creates incentives for patients to improve their health; SIMpill's South African innovation to send SMS reminders to patients; APOPO's Tanzanian approach to diagnose tuberculosis using giant pouched rats; and Lifebuoy Friendship Hospital's conversion of oil tankers into floating hospitals to treat patients in remote parts of Bangladesh. The potential for private sector engagement is so great that we see unprecedented interest and investment in innovative approaches to address the most pressing health issues the world faces.

The Private Sector in Health: A Diverse Set of Actors

The entrepreneurial creativity of private actors has led many of these organizations to focus on areas of greatest potential impact for the poor. From social enterprises such as Ross Clinics (India), Penda Health (Kenya), and salaUno (Mexico), to NGOs such as Population Services International (multinational), Aravind (India), and Building Resources Across Communities (BRAC) (Bangladesh), to public-private partnerships such as Karuna Trust (India), Public-Private Mix DOTS (Philippines), and the Tanzania National Voucher Scheme, these programs are engaging in innovative models to improve the health of the poor and reporting results on their progress.

Our research highlights this multidimensional aspect of for-profit and not-for-profit private sector health care in LMICs, which includes organizations of vastly different scale and scope. These organizations vary in their operating models and strategies to succeed in LMIC contexts where there is often a severe shortage of qualified staff, insufficient medical supplies, poor infrastructure, and a lack of sustainable financial support and investment.

In these contexts, small social enterprises operate quite differently compared to global diversified firms. The former may learn skills on the fly while the latter may bring skills from across its organization to bear on the challenges of the local environment. Smaller organizations tend to have focused missions on health care services, while more complex organizations such as multinational firms may be using health care services as a complement and/or marketing tool for other services, such as telecommunications or pharmaceuticals.

The for-profit versus non-profit distinction also generates differences. While for-profit organizations may be more motivated by profit than not-for-profit organizations, non-profits also need to be financially viable. One strategy non-profits are increasingly pursuing involves developing market-based revenue to support themselves financially.

In turn, not only are there a wide variety of innovative health organizations in the private sector, they are increasingly blurring the lines between categories, such that for-profit social enterprises are pursuing both financial and social goals while some non-profits are seeking sustainability by generating revenue. These hybrid forms are likely to become increasingly prevalent as organizations seek new ways to survive and scale while they serve the poor. Insights from the managerial literature on innovations in governance can further our understanding of these new forms (Capron & Mitchell 2012).

Strengths and Limitations of the Private Sector

The private sector, and the many varied organizations that encompass it, provides a key source of innovation in health care in resource-constrained contexts. However, despite its strengths, the private sector has many limitations. Private sector organizations must continually find sources of funding or revenue to support themselves, which can affect decisions surrounding the populations they are able to serve, the types of services they can offer, and where they can operate. Beyond identifying a need and addressing it, they need to develop financial models that allow them to engage in this work and sustain it over time, which may involve donor funding, revenue generation, and/or government contracts.

A consequence of these limits is that public sector organizations are able to tackle more multidimensional missions than the private sector. With access to more sustainable funding and a wide-reaching mandate for health care in a country, the public sector is able to focus on a wide variety of health areas, coordinate organizations and initiatives, and also develop policy to reinforce its efforts. At minimum, therefore, health care systems will contain a mix of public and private actors for the foreseeable future.

Strategizing for Effectiveness and Scale

We have found, however, that private sector health organizations are able to engage in a number of strategic activities to increase their impact and scale of their innovative models, including engaging in the use of strategic partnerships, breaking down geographic barriers and health silos, and the use of effective management skills.

For example, beyond simply operating in parallel, one approach to capitalize on the complementary strengths of the private and public sectors involves public-private partnerships. Such collaborations often entail alignment of objectives, coordination in service provision, and financial support between these two groups. Our research has found this to be a promising model not only in terms of improved performance but also in terms of potential for scale up. However, there are likely to be inherent limits to full incentive compatibility in such partnerships. Research grounded in theories of management can also help to further understand these opportunities (George, McGahan, & Prabhu 2012).

Some of these programs, such as Possible Health (Nepal), Tello Mobile Health (Indonesia), and Village Health Works (Burundi), are also having local systemic impact through breaking down traditional health care silos and integrating services such as primary care and maternal, newborn, and child health (MNCH) and connecting with others operating in the area. Further, some innovative health programs are able to work across geopolitical boundaries to serve populations in multiple countries. Programs such as Northwell, Microensure, and World Health Partners are having transnational impact through regional scaling (South-South interactions), while some models, such as Narayana Hrudayalaya and General Electric portable ultrasounds, are crossing South-North borders to create impact through reverse innovation (South-North interactions).

Effective management skills are also key for the success of these programs. This includes strong leadership skills that combine medical and management expertise, operational improvements and streamlining processes, using a variety of marketing techniques to connect with patients, and finding new financial models to support themselves and make their products and services more accessible to their clients. Of the ten programs we highlighted in chapter one, over the last seven years, we now find that almost all of them have grown, whether geographically, by numbers of patients reached, and/or by types of services offered. These exceptional programs tend to engage in multiple tactics to succeed, such as ensuring strategic alignment so all stakeholders benefit, pursuing multiple sources of financing, having a strong understanding of their target market, focusing on a specific health area, and innovating in the areas of marketing, operations and finance.

Opportunities to Build on the Efforts of the Private Sector

Given the proliferation of health innovation in LMICs, there are opportunities to leverage the activities of these private sector organizations that should be pursued. Once an innovative model has been tested, refined, and proved to work, efforts need to focus on increasing standardization to improve quality, efficiency, and ability to scale. Opportunities in this area include developing standard clinical protocols and operating procedures, standard platforms for registering medical devices, and standard credentialing of health care practitioners (especially new categories of providers) across borders. This can help to increase the spread and impact of effective models and further improve their performance.

These innovative health programs are pushing the boundaries of how we define and deliver health care, how health care organizations are structured, and how we measure and evaluate their performance. The T-HOPE team has endeavoured to explore and understand how these new health care models work, and our research has involved identifying metrics for assessing how well they perform, exploring evidence of impact in vertical and horizontal health areas, as well as examining factors shaping program scale up and integration of health programs in MNCH and primary care. We are part of a growing movement to support innovative health programs to develop, refine, and spread their models for the benefit of poor populations in LMICs through research, tools, connections, and training. This includes the collaborative Harnessing Non-State Actors for Better Health Care for the Poor (HANSHEP), the Bill and Melinda Gates Foundation, USAID, the Results for Development Institute, Innovations in Healthcare, the Global Impact Investing Network, NextBillion, the International Centre for Social Franchising, and many others. These groups are also engaged in spreading the skills and knowledge generated by innovative private sector and public-private health programs, including curating stories and examples of innovative private sector activities, accomplishments, and lessons learned, and sharing these learnings in an accessible way to help health care providers become more effective. While efforts are being made in this area, the need for learning, support, and collaboration is great, given the large number of unanswered questions. There are also further opportunities to engage in management, social science, and global health education that promotes a thoughtful, supportive mindset for students and practitioners to pursue the development of health innovation for poor populations and appropriately embrace the learnings in this field provided by the private sector.

Health innovations in resource-constrained contexts are emerging to address some of the worst health care dilemmas the world faces. Our research shows that the private health care sector in LMICs is a major contributor of these innovations, filling service gaps and offering impact across borders in ways that others, including geographically constrained national governments, often cannot. It is essential that we find ways to foster and learn from these innovative organizations for the benefit of all of us and, in particular, to reach those most in need.

REFERENCES

Capron, L., & Mitchell, W. 2012. *Build, Borrow, or Buy: Solving the Growth Dilemma.* Boston: Harvard Business Review Press.

George, G., McGahan, A.M., & Prabhu, J. 2012. "Innovation for Inclusive Growth: Towards a Theoretical Framework and a Research Agenda." *Journal of Management Studies* 49(4): 661–83. https://doi.org/10.1111/j.1467-6486.2012.01048.x.

Contributors

Kathryn Mossman, PhD

iD Research, 345 Adelaide Street West, Toronto, Ontario, M5V 1R5, Canada

kate.mossman@gmail.com

Dr Kathryn Mossman is an anthropologist and health systems researcher. She holds a PhD in Anthropology from McMaster University and was a postdoctoral fellow in Strategic Management at the Rotman School of Management at the University of Toronto. She has conducted research at a number of Toronto hospitals on the implementation and scale up of new health services, including digital tools, quality improvement initiatives, and telemedicine projects. She also managed the Toronto Health Organization Performance Evaluation (T-HOPE) team at the University of Toronto, an interdisciplinary group of global health innovation and performance researchers. She is currently a research consultant working in the areas of applied health, knowledge translation, insights and strategy, organizational effectiveness, and community engagement. Dr Mossman has published in a variety of publications, including *Harvard Business Review*, *Stanford Social Innovation Review*, *PLOS ONE*, *Health Management, Policy and Innovation*, and *Globalization and Health*.

Anita McGahan, MBA, PhD

Rotman School of Management, University of Toronto, 105 St George Street, Toronto, Ontario, M5S 3E6, Canada

anita.mcgahan@rotman.utoronto.ca

Anita McGahan is a professor of Strategic Management and George E. Connell Chair in Organizations and Society at Rotman (with a cross-appointment to the

Munk School of Global Affairs). Her research is focused on industry change, sustainable competitive advantage, and the establishment of new fields. An area of particular interest is in global health and the diffusion of knowledge across international boundaries.

Will Mitchell, PhD

Rotman School of Management, University of Toronto, 105 St George Street, Toronto, Ontario, M5S 3E6, Canada

william.mitchell@rotman.utoronto.ca

Will Mitchell is the Anthony S. Fell Chair in New Technologies and Commercialization at the Rotman School of Management, where he is a professor of Strategic Management and academic co-director of the Global Executive MBA for Healthcare and the Life Sciences. Will studies business dynamics in developed and emerging markets, investigating how businesses change as their competitive environments change and, in turn, how business changes contribute to ongoing corporate and social performance. Will teaches courses in business strategy, international business, and life sciences strategy. He serves as a board member of Neuland Laboratories, Ltd (Hyderabad).

Onil Bhattacharyya, PhD, MD

Women's College Hospital, 76 Grenville Street, Toronto, Ontario, M5S 1B1, Canada

Department of Family and Community Medicine, University of Toronto, 500 University Avenue, Toronto, Ontario, M5G 1V7, Canada

onil.bhattacharyya@wchospital.ca

Dr Onil Bhattacharyya is a family physician and the Frigon-Blau Chair in Family Medicine Research at Women's College Hospital. He is an associate professor in the Department of Family and Community Medicine and the Institute of Health Policy, Management and Evaluation at the University of Toronto. He was a 2015–16 Harkness Fellow in Health Care Policy and Practice, based at the Commonwealth Fund. He received his medical degree from University of Montreal, has a PhD in health services research from the University of Toronto, and was a Takemi Fellow at the Harvard School of Public Health.

He is one of the co-leads of the Toronto Health Organization Performance Evaluation group, which pairs management scholars and students with medical researchers and students to study innovative care delivery models. He is the clinical lead of the Primary and Integrated Care Innovation network for Ontario (Better Access to Care for Complex Needs), and co-chair of the National Leadership Council, both funded by the Canadian Institute for Health Research Strategy for Patient Oriented Research. His research focuses on innovative care delivery models, integrating methods from the software and design industries for service development with quality improvement, and implementation science approaches to evaluation.

Ameya Bopardikar, MD

Department of Anesthesia, University of Toronto, 123 Edward Street, Toronto, Ontario, M5G 1E2, Canada

ameya.bopardikar@mail.utoronto.ca

Jieun Cha, MD

Department of Surgery, University of British Columbia, 950 West 10th Avenue, Vancouver, British Columbia, Canada, V5Z

jieun.r.c.cha@gmail.com

Yu-Ling Cheng, PhD

Department of Chemical Engineering and Applied Chemistry, Faculty of Applied Science and Engineering, University of Toronto, 200 College Street, Toronto, Ontario, M5S 3E5, Canada

yuling.cheng@utoronto.ca

Abdallah Daar, FRCS

Dalla Lana School of Public Health and Department of Surgery, University of Toronto, 155 College Street, Toronto Ontario, M5T 1P8, Canada

a.daar@utoronto.ca

David Dunne, PhD

Gustavson School of Business, University of Victoria, Business and Economics Building Room 254, 3800 Finnerty Road., Victoria, British Columbia, V8P 5C2, Canada

dldunne@uvic.ca

Pavan Gill, BSc

Faculty of Medicine, University of Toronto, 1 King's College Circle #3172, Toronto, Ontario, M5S 1A8, Canada

pavan.gill@mail.utoronto.ca

John Ginther, MBA

Toronto Health Organization Performance Evaluation (T-HOPE), University of Toronto, 105 St George Street, Toronto, Ontario, M5S 3E6, Canada

john.ginther@gmail.com

Leigh Hayden, PhD

North York General Hospital, 4001 Leslie Street, Toronto, ON M2K 1E1, Canada

leigh.hayden@gmail.com

Sara Khor, MASc

University of Washington Surgical Outcomes Research Center, 1959 NE Pacific Street, Seattle, Washington, 98195, USA

sakhor@yahoo.com

David Leung, MD

Toronto Health Organization Performance Evaluation (T-HOPE), University of Toronto, 105 St George Street, Toronto, Ontario, M5S 3E6, Canada
    Peter Lougheed Centre and University of Calgary, 3500 26th Ave NE, Calgary, Alberta, T1Y 6J4, Canada

daviexleung@gmail.com

John A. MacDonald, MD

MIT Sloan School of Management, 30 Memorial Dr., Cambridge, Massachusetts, 02142, United States

johnangusmacdonald@gmail.com

Himanshu Parikh, MD, MSc

AstraZeneca Canada Inc., 1004 Middlegate Road, Mississauga, Ontario, L4Y 1M4, Canada

parikh.himanshu@gmail.com

Ilan Shahin, MD, MBA

Women's College Hospital, University of Toronto, 76 Grenville Street, Toronto, Ontario, M5S 1B1, Canada

ilan.shahin@gmail.com

Peter A. Singer, OC, MD, MPH, FRSC

Grand Challenges Canada at the Sandra Rotman Centre, MaRS Centre, South Tower, 101 College Street, Suite 406, Toronto, Ontario, M5G 1L7, Canada

Peter.singer@grandchallenges.ca

Raman Sohal, MBA, MA

Women's College Hospital, 76 Grenville Street, Toronto, Ontario, M5S 1B1, Canada
   Institute of Health Policy Management and Evaluation, University of Toronto, 155 College Street, 4th Floor, Toronto, Ontario, M5T 3M6, Canada

raman.sohal13@rotman.utoronto.ca

Dilip Soman, PhD

Rotman School of Management, University of Toronto, 105 St George Street, Toronto, Ontario, M5S 3E6, Canada

Dilip.Soman@Rotman.Utoronto.Ca

Jason Sukhram, MBA

Clinton Giustra Enterprise Partnership, 1271 Avenue of the Americas, New York, New York, 10020, United States

jason.sukhram@gmail.com or *jsukhram@clintonfoundation.org*

Christina Synowiec, MSc Public Health

Results for Development, 1514 17th Street NW, Washington, DC, 20036, United States

csynowiec@r4d.org

Andrea D. Taylor, MSW

Innovations in Healthcare, Duke University, 324 Blackwell Street, Suite 960, Durham, North Carolina, 27701, United States

andrea.d.taylor@duke.edu

Joseph Wong, PhD

Munk School of Global Affairs and Department of Political Science, University of Toronto, 1 Devonshire Place, Toronto, Ontario, M5S 3K7, Canada

joe.wong@utoronto.ca

Diane Wu, MD

Department of Family and Community Medicine, University of Toronto, 500 University Avenue, Toronto, Ontario, M5G 1V7, Canada

ddiane.wu@gmail.com

Max von Zedtwitz, PhD

Department of Strategic Management, Kaunas University of Technology, Gedimino 50 – 414, LT-44029 Kaunas, Lithuania

max@glorad.org

Stanley Zlotkin, MD

Department of Paediatrics, Dalla Lana School of Public Health and Department of Nutritional Sciences, University of Toronto, and Centre for Global Child Health and Research Institute, Hospital for Sick Children, 525 University Avenue, Suite 701, Toronto, Ontario, M5G2L3, Canada

stanley.zlotkin@sickkids.ca

Credits

Chapter 1: Innovative Health Service Delivery Models in Low- and Middle-Income Countries – What Can We Learn from the Private Sector?

Bhattacharyya, O., Khor, S., McGahan, A., Dunne, D., Daar, A.S., & Singer, P.A. (2010). "Innovative Health Service Delivery Models in Low and Middle Income Countries – What Can We Learn from the Private Sector?" *Health Research Policy and Systems* 8, 1–11.

Chapter 2: Global Health Innovation: Exploring Program Practices and Strategies

Bhattacharyya, O., McGahan, A., Mitchell, W., Mossman, K., Ginther, J., Sohal, R., Hayden, L., MacDonald, J.A., Parikh, H., Shahin, I. (2012). "Describing Practices of Innovative Health Care Programs in Low- and Middle-Income Countries." *Report Prepared for Results for Development (R4D)*.

Chapter 3: The Future of Health Care Access

MacDonald, J.A., Mitchell, W., McGahan, A., & the T-HOPE Team. (2013). "The Future of Health Care Access." *Stanford Social Innovation Review*, fall issue.

Chapter 5: Criteria to Assess Potential Reverse Innovations: Opportunities for Shared Learning between High- and Low-Income Countries

Bhattacharyya, O., Wu, D., Mossman, K., et al. (2017)." Criteria to Assess Potential Reverse Innovations: Opportunities for Shared Learning between High- and Low-Income Countries." *Global Health* 13. DOI:10.1186/s12992-016-0225-1.

Chapter 6: Assessing Health Program Performance in Low- and Middle-Income Countries: Building a Feasible, Credible, and Comprehensive Framework

Bhattacharyya, O., Mossman, K., Ginther, J., Hayden, L., Sohal, R., Cha, J., Bopardikar, A., MacDonald, J.A., Parikh, H., Shahin, I., McGahan, A., Mitchell, W. 2015. "Assessing Health Program Performance in Low- and Middle-Income Countries: Building a Feasible, Credible, and Comprehensive Framework." *Globalization and Health* 11. DOI: 10.1186/s12992-015-0137-5.

Chapter 7: Performance Measurement for Innovative Health Programs: Understanding Efficiency, Quality, and Scale

Bhattacharyya, O., McGahan, A., Mitchell, W., Mossman, K., Sohal, R., Ginther, J., Cha, J., Bopardikar, A., MacDonald, J.A., Hayden, L., Parikh, H., Shahin, I. 2012. "Performance Measurement for Innovative Health Programs: Understanding Efficiency, Quality, and Scale." *Report Prepared for Results for Development (R4D)*.

Chapter 8: Transnational Scale Up of Services in Global Health

Shahin, I., Sohal, R., Ginther, J., Hayden, L., MacDonald, J.A., Mossman, K., Parikh, H., McGahan, A., Mitchell, W., Bhattacharyya, O. 2014. "Trans-national Scale-Up of Services in Global Health." *PLoS ONE* 9, 1–8. DOI: 10.1371/journal.pone.0110465.

Chapter 9: Innovations in Tuberculosis Health Care: Exploring the Evidence on Emerging Practices in Low- and Middle-Income Countries

Bhattacharyya, O., McGahan, A., Mitchell, W., Mossman, K., Leung, D., Ginther, J., Sohal, R., Hayden, L., MacDonald, J.A., Parikh, H., Shahin, I., & the Results for Development Institute. 2014. "Innovations in Tuberculosis Care: Exploring the Evidence behind Emerging Practices in Low- and Middle-Income Countries." *Report Prepared for Results for Development (R4D)*.

Chapter 10: Innovations in Malaria Health Care: Exploring the Evidence on Emerging Practices in Low- and Middle-Income Countries

Bhattacharyya, O., McGahan, A., Mitchell, W., Mossman, K., Ginther, J., Sohal, R., Hayden, L., Leung, D., MacDonald, J.A., Parikh, H., Shahin, I., & the Results for Development Institute. 2014. "Innovations in Privately Delivered Malaria Healthcare: Exploring the Evidence behind Emerging Practices." *Report Prepared for Results for Development (R4D)*.

Chapter 12: Innovations in Global Mental Health Practice

Shahin, I., MacDonald, J.A., Ginther, J., Hayden L., Mossman, K., Parikh, H., Sohal, R., McGahan, A., Mitchell, W., & Bhattacharyya, B. 2017. "Innovations in Global Mental Health Practice." *Health Management Policy and Innovation 2.*

Chapter 13: Innovations in Privately Delivered Maternal, Newborn, and Child Health: Exploring the Evidence behind Emerging Practices

Bhattacharyya, O., McGahan, A., Mitchell, W., Mossman, K., Hayden, L., Ginther, J., Sohal, R., MacDonald, J.A., Parikh, H., Shahin, I., & the Results for Development Institute. 2013. "Innovations in Privately Delivered Maternal, Newborn, and Child Health: Exploring the Evidence behind Emerging Practices." *Report Prepared for Results for Development (R4D).*

Chapter 15: Integrating Primary Care and Maternal, Newborn, and Child Health in Low- and Middle-Income Countries

Sohal, R., Bhattacharyya, O., Parikh, H., Mossman, K., Hayden, L., McGahan, A., Mitchell, W. 2016. Integrating Primary Care and Maternal, Newborn, and Child Health in Low- and Middle-Income Countries. *Report Prepared for Results for Development (R4D).*